1/90

The Unknown O'Neill

Eugene O'Neill

The Unknown O'Neill

Unpublished or Unfamiliar
Writings of Eugene O'Neill

Edited with commentaries
by Travis Bogard

Yale University Press
New Haven and London

Published with the assistance of the
Frederick W. Hilles Publication Fund
of Yale University.

Designed by Sally Harris
and set in Electra type by
Brevis Press, Bethany, Connecticut.
Printed in the United States of America by
The Murray Printing Company
Westford, Massachusetts.

Library of Congress Cataloging-in-Publication Data

O'Neill, Eugene, 1888–1953.
    The unknown O'Neill: unpublished or
unfamiliar writings of Eugene O'Neill / edited
with commentaries by Travis Bogard.
    p.   cm.
    ISBN 0–300–03985–9 (alk. paper)
    I. Bogard, Travis.   II. Title.
PS3529.N5U5   1988
812'.52—dc19   87–24637
                        CIP

The paper in this book meets the guidelines for
permanence and durability of the Committee on
Production Guidelines for Book Longevity
of the Council on Library Resources.

10   9   8   7   6   5   4   3   2   1

Contents

Foreword

In nautical terms, the contents of this anthology might be described as the flotsam, jetsam, and lagan of the Eugene O'Neill canon. Attitudes, themes, and characters of much included here drifted through the dramatist's major creative work, surfacing often during his life to lend color, texture, and meaning to his writing. With O'Neill, as with any equally compulsive writer, what proved to be lacking in creative energy or tiresomely experimental was tossed over the side to sink and be forgotten. That which held promise was marked with a buoy of memory so that it could be recalled and salvaged when the time was right.

Here published for the first time are three full-length plays: *The Personal Equation*, which he wrote at Harvard in George Pierce Baker's 47 Workshop; the uncut, eight-act original version of *Marco Millions*, then titled "Marco's Millions," and a four-act melodrama based on his scenario *The Reckoning*, written, with his collaboration, by Agnes Boulton O'Neill under the pseudonym Elinor Rand. Other theatrical works appearing here for the first time in book form are his adaptation of Coleridge's "The Ancient Mariner" and the fourth act of *The Ole Davil*, the play that became "*Anna Christie*." Also gathered here are two short stories, "Tomorrow" and "S.O.S.," an unpublished love poem, and several critical and occasional pieces including the work diary recounting the composition of *Mourning Becomes Electra* and *The Last Will and Testament of Silverdene Emblem O'Neill*, written in memory of his Dalmatian, Blemie.

In conjunction with the standard editions of the major plays published by Random House and the Yale University Press and the several volumes of his minor writing,[1] this anthology makes generally available all of O'Neill's completed works of the imagination and his principal critical statements. Of these, "Tomorrow," the critical essays and tributes and *The Last Will and Testament of Silverdene Emblem O'Neill* appeared in periodicals near the time of their composition. *The Ancient Mariner* was published in the *Yale University Library*

---

1. Random House, New York: *The Plays of Eugene O'Neill*, 3 vols. (1951); *A Moon for the Misbegotten* (1952); *Chris Christophersen*, foreword by Leslie Eric Comens (1982); *Ten "Lost" Plays*, foreword by Bennett Cerf (1964). Yale University Press, New Haven: *A Touch of the Poet* (1957); *Long Day's Journey into Night* (1956); *Hughie* (1959); *More Stately Mansions* (1964). Ticknor and Fields, New Haven: *Poems (1912–1944)*, ed. Donald Gallup (1980); *The Calms of Capricorn*, ed. Donald Gallup, 2 vols. (1981). NCR Microcard Editions, Washington, D.C.: "*Children of the Sea*" *and Three Other Unpublished Plays by Eugene O'Neill*, ed. Jennifer McCabe Atkinson (1972).

Gazette in 1960. The remainder have been available only in typescript or manuscript. In editing the material that O'Neill can be assumed to have seen through the press, I have followed the published copy exactly. For writing that has never been edited, I have silently corrected obvious punctuation and spelling errors, being careful, however, to preserve spellings that appear to indicate dialect pronunciation and punctuation suggestive of dramatic rhythm.

Ingmar Bergman once wrote about a proposed revival of one of his early plays, *"Jack and the Actors* is dead, buried and not to be exhumed." It may be argued that much of what is here should be as rigorously entombed. Yet each is dedicated to the mastery of a difficult art, and each informs the reader of something about the author that could not otherwise be known. Each of the creative works of theatre and fiction represents a personal commitment of some cost as O'Neill tried to bring his life into conjunction with his artistry. When the artist is of O'Neill's ultimate stature, the steps taken toward the final achievement become of more than routine interest.

There is here no undiscovered masterwork, but much here foreshadows what was to come, as "Tomorrow," written in 1917, explores the ground on which *The Iceman Cometh* was to be created in the 1940s. In some of the writing, O'Neill is struggling to learn his craft: the scenario of "The Reckoning," for example, shows him in the process of forming a lifelong habit of detailing a play in a long narrative account, so complete that a decade later his wife could fill in the dialogue and produce a passable melodrama. In the poem to Jane Caldwell and the memorial for Blemie, glimpses of a gentle, private man can be caught. In the critical pieces, O'Neill attempts an uncharacteristic but interesting articulation of his theatrical principles. In all these fugitive works, the O'Neill voice sounds clear. Since that voice was ultimately of such power, whether it cracks in adolescent passion or sounds in the lowest murmur, it remains worth hearing.

Travis Bogard

Acknowledgments

"Tomorrow" is reprinted with the permission of the Theatre Collection of the Firestone Library at Princeton University; *The Personal Equation*, "*S.O.S.*," and *The Reckoning* are reprinted with the permission of the Harvard Theatre Collection of the Houghton Library at Harvard University. "To A Stolen Moment" is reprinted with the permission of Mrs. Rodney Washburn. Excerpts from the diary of Carlotta Monterey O'Neill are reprinted with the permission of Mr. Gerald Stram. All other material is reprinted with the permission of Yale University.

   In the preparation of this volume I have had the continual, invaluable assistance of Dr. Ralph Franklin, the director, and the staff of the Beinecke Rare Book and Manuscript Library and of Dr. Donald Gallup and Dr. David Schoonover, in turn curators of the American Literature Collection of that library. In the Library of Congress I have been well served by Dr. James Hutson, Chief of the Manuscript Division, and his associate Dr. David Wigdore, Dr. John Wayne of the Copyright Division, and Eveline Nave of the Photoduplication Service in tracking *The Guilty One*. Ruth Alvarez at the University of Maryland has aided me in obtaining a copy of *Marco's Millions*. "Tomorrow" was provided by Dr. Mary Ann Jensen, curator of the Firestone Library at Princeton University. Professor Judith Barlow has given me excellent counsel on the headnotes, and at the Yale University Press, Mr. Edward Tripp has proved the very model of a patient editor. Spending long hours before the word processor, Brian Meyers and Gregory Miller have typed the manuscript. They have been, as current jargon will have it, "user friendly."

Theatre

The Personal Equation

During the academic year 1914–15, O'Neill lived at 1108 Massachusetts Avenue, Cambridge, while he attended Harvard as a student in George Pierce Baker's course, English 47. The class that became known as the 47 Workshop was the first to teach playwriting in a major university. It was so salutary in its encouragement of ambitious young playwrights that it became a kind of mecca for all who were touched by a vision of a new, serious theatre in the United States. Not that Baker himself was a leader toward a new art of the theatre. Judged by his books on the subject, he was conservative even for his time. None of the excitement revealed by the New Theatre prophets, Sheldon Cheney and Kenneth Macgowan, is displayed in his selection of models for the aspirant; the dramatic carpentry of Arthur Wing Pinero remained his highest good. His students began by creating scenarios from assigned short stories[1] and progressed to one-act and ultimately to longer plays. In class, Baker read and criticized student work. Occasionally at the Radcliffe College Theatre he staged one or two of the better offerings, overseeing scenery and lighting with technical skills O'Neill found admirable.

Nothing of O'Neill's was so presented. The closest he came to the stage itself was to serve as assistant makeup technician, putting rouge on the men, not the "beautiful Radcliffe girls," as he wrote reassuringly to his New London sweetheart, Beatrice Ashe.

For Baker, he wrote three plays: a one-act war play, *The Sniper*; in collaboration with a classmate, Colin Ford, a tragedy in blank verse and seven acts entitled *Belshazzar*[2]; and the four-act tragedy *The Personal Equation*, which he first titled *The Second Engineer*. He worked on the tragedy during March and April 1915 and made a few references to it in his letters to Beatrice Ashe.

On March 12, 1915, while he was busy with the Radcliffe production, he confessed to being "in a frenzied state of mind about my 'Engineer' play—can't seem to fix in my mind what final form it will take. I know all the pangs of childbirth." On March 21, he noted that he and a friend were going to the Seaman's Institute in order "to get some dope for my play." His last mention of the play to Beatrice was on March 28: "Have been working on my 'Engineer' play, the first scenario of which you read, but the main theme has undergone such changes in my mind and wandered into such unforeseen ramifications and complications that it has me bewildered and a bit peeved. However, I hope it will all iron out in the writing."[3]

Presumably, he wrote the play during the remaining weeks of the semester. A

1. For an example of such a scenario, see below, "The Reckoning."
2. The play was destroyed. O'Neill referred ironically to it in a canceled passage in his short story "Tomorrow." See p. 315, n. 11.
3. The correspondence with Beatrice Ashe is in the Theatre Collection of the Houghton Library, Harvard University.

letter to Beatrice, dated July 25, 1916, and sent from Provincetown after he had left Harvard, makes no mention of it but refers to his writing a three-act comedy and, more importantly, to his directing rehearsals of his short sea play, *Bound East for Cardiff*, "which the Provincetown Players are to produce next Friday and Saturday in a delightfully quaint place—an old storehouse on the end of a long dock owned by Mary Heaton Vorse, the writer." *Bound East for Cardiff* was the play that had gained his admission to the 47 Workshop, despite the fact that Baker had made light of it, declaring it was not a play. Its production in 1916, two years after its composition, marked the beginning of O'Neill's career in the theatre with a significant return to his point of creative origin— to the sea and the fate of the men who sailed upon it. Shortly, shucking off Baker's tutelage, he would write three other plays about the crew of the S.S. *Glencairn*, the ship that provided the setting for *Bound East for Cardiff*. Nothing in "The Personal Equation" matches the poetic, yet realistic treatment of the sea, the crew, and the ship in the *Glencairn* plays, but the truest dramatic writing in the pupil work concerns the crew and the engine room of the ship.

The undated draft of "The Second Engineer" was typed in New London after the Harvard term ended. Only when the typing was finished did he cross out his somewhat factual working title and pencil in the new name, the more abstruse "The Personal Equation," a title which appears to suggest that personal readjustments can bring human beings into right relationships despite their antagonistic individual beliefs and biases.[4] At the play's end, the anarchist woman and the conservative father find a way to meet in harmony over the hospital bed of the man they both love. It is then that the equation of their relationship is reduced and balanced.

The play reflects the somewhat naive radicalism of the century's beginnings. O'Neill's education in such matters began while he was in preparatory school on visits to Benjamin R. Tucker's radical bookshop in New York. Instruction continued through his pre-Harvard days in New London. Later, in Greenwich Village, through his friendship with John Reed and Louise Bryant, he came to adopt the character of a Village radical, with perhaps an excess of youthful, melodramatic posturings. Agnes Boulton describes a midnight scene when O'Neill stood on a corner and hinted darkly at a plan to mount machine guns in one of the buildings and shoot down the reactionary police when they came to put down the revolution.[5] At one time he was interested in following Reed to the Villa war in Mexico. None of his ventures into radical social action amounted to much, nor if one judges by the political stances taken by Olga, Tom, and Hartmann in "The Personal Equation," did his political convictions run deep. His characters look like newspaper cartoons of the bomb-throwing anarchist and the sensual "Russian" woman-spy, and they speak in clichés appropriate to their skimpy characterization.

Louis Sheaffer and Virginia Floyd have pointed to autobiographical elements underlying the play.[6] In the components of the "equation," there is as Sheaffer notes a reminiscence of Beatrice Ashe, who in coloring resembled the black-eyed beauty of O'Neill's imagination. Sheaffer also draws a parallel between Thomas Perkins, the second engineer of the title, and James O'Neill, who was a second-rank actor shackled to the

4. The phrase derives from astronomy and refers to the allowance required for the difference in point of view toward a star from two widely separated sites on earth.
5. Agnes Boulton, *Part of a Long Story* (New York: Doubleday, 1958), pp. 46–47.
6. Louis Sheaffer, *O'Neill, Son and Playwright* (Boston: Little, Brown, 1968), pp. 307–08; Virginia Floyd, *Eugene O'Neill at Work* (New York: Frederick Ungar, 1981), pp. 260–63.

mechanics of the melodrama *Monte Cristo*, much as Perkins was the slave of the ship's engines. The contempt for his father expressed by Tom, his son, may be comparable, as Sheaffer suggests, to that which Eugene felt for his father's failure as an actor. O'Neill's interest in the second-rank position recurs in *Chris Christophersen*, the first version of *"Anna Christie*," where the hero, a second mate, must debate the virtues of staying safely out of the struggle as against attempting to rise in a shipboard hierarchy.

The play reveals a number of O'Neill's literary interests garnered from books he had read. Shaw's ideas about the woman as a breeder of a new race surfaces in the first act, and the ending of the play with Tom babbling insanely as the sun pours through the window appears to owe a debt to Ibsen's curtain scene in *Ghosts*.

Many seeds of later themes can be uncovered in the course of the action. Tom's mention of "the contrast between us grimy stokers and the first cabin people lolling in their deck chairs" points ahead to the second scene of *The Hairy Ape*. In act 4 there sounds a faint precursor of the conception of the "hopeless hope" with which *The Straw* concludes and which becomes the central theme of *The Iceman Cometh*. Old Perkins's love of his engines anticipates the anthropomorphic comforts of the machinery in *The Hairy Ape* and *Dynamo* and also, curiously, Ephraim's need for the comfort of the barn and the cows in *Desire Under the Elms*.[7] Perkins says,

> Sometimes when I touch them I seem to know they feel me. I seem to hear them speaking like a friend to me, times when I'm lonely and, well, sort of sick of things—and they've a comfort. . . . One gets to be friends with them—and even love them.
>
> [II, p. 29]

Yet, even though the shape of what will come can be faintly discerned, the play remains a banal, amateur work, whose chief significance in O'Neill's development perhaps lies in its return to sea themes, as if, stuffed with "technique" in Baker's classes, he was searching for some part of the truth that had earlier made *Bound East for Cardiff* a play of importance. O'Neill read two acts of the play to the Provincetown Players, but it remained unproduced.

The text exists in a single, unrevised, uncorrected copy in the Theatre Collection of the Houghton Library at Harvard University. I have silently corrected obvious errors (for example, "it's" for "its," "loose" for "lose") and altered punctuation as needed for clarity and minimal correctness. I have preserved spellings that appear to indicate dialect pronunciation.

---

7. In part 2, scene 2, Ephraim says he is going "whar it's restful—whar it's warm—down t' the barn. . . . I kin talk t' the cows. They know. They know the farm an' me. They'll give me peace."

The Personal Equation
~~The Second Engineer~~

CHARACTERS

Thomas Perkins, 2nd engineer of the S.S. *San Francisco*
Tom, his son
Henderson, 1st Engineer of the S.S. *Empress*
Olga Tarnoff ⎫
Hartmann   ⎪
Enwright   ⎬   Members of the International Workers Union*
Whitely   ⎭
Mrs. Allen
O'Rourke
Cocky   ⎫
Harris   ⎬   Stokers of the *San Francisco*
Schmidt   ⎭
Hogan
Murphy, an oiler
Jack, an engineer's apprentice
A Doctor
Miss Brown

ACT ONE

SCENE: *Main room of the headquarters of the International Workers Union in Hoboken—a large bare room with white-washed walls. In the rear, two windows looking out on a dingy back street. On the wall between the windows, a large framed engraving of a naked woman with a liberty cap on her head, leaning back against the two upright beams of a guillotine. In the left hand corner, a desk with chair. In the middle of left wall, a door opening into hall. In right*

*In the text the Union is called "The International Workers of the Earth."

corner, a small table with typewriter on it. In the middle of left wall, a door opening into hall. In the middle of right wall, another door. In the center of room, a long table with four or five straight-backed chairs placed around it. On the table, newspapers, periodicals, stacks of pamphlets, etc. Flooring of coarse, uncovered boards. Framed cartoons, mostly in color, from Jugend, Simplissimus, etc., are hung here and there on the walls.

It is evening and already dark. Two gas lights of the Welsbach type, fixed on the tarnished chandelier which hangs over the table, throw a cold white light about the room, revealing every detail of its bare ugliness.

OLGA stands at one end of the table reading a newspaper. She is very dark; strong, fine features; large spirited black eyes, slender, supple figure. ENWRIGHT sits on the chair nearest her. He is thin, round-shouldered, middle-aged, clean-shaven, wears glasses.

ENWRIGHT [Languidly] What have our dear friends, the Socialists, to say about us today? Are we luring their honest working man to his ruin; are we planting the insidious seeds of anarchy in the unsuspecting bosoms of their voters, or, or—what?

OLGA Bah, the same old stuff! What's the use of repeating it? [Her eyes flashing] Oh, these Socialists! How I loathe their eternal platitudes, their milk-and-water radicalism, their cut-and-dried sermons for humble voters! As if to vote were not also to acquiesce in the present order of things, to become a cog in the machine which grinds the voter himself to bits! Revolution by act of Congress! The dolts! [As ENWRIGHT smiles amusedly and glances at his watch] What time is it?

ENWRIGHT Nearly eight. Are you waiting for Tom, or Hartmann?

OLGA Both. Tom ought to be here now. Hartmann sent word he wanted to see us here tonight on something important.

ENWRIGHT Something to do with the talked-of strike of the dock-laborers, seamen and firemen, I expect. I hear there's a contemplated move in that direction.

OLGA Ah, so that's it. I couldn't imagine what it could be.

ENWRIGHT [After a pause] May I ask an impertinent question, Olga? Do you think Tom's zeal in our activities is inspired by deep inward conviction, or—I'll be plain—do you think it's merely an outcropping of his love for you?

OLGA [Indignantly] How can you imagine such a thing? You know Tom. You know how hard he has worked with us.

ENWRIGHT   It's just a feeling I have. Somehow he doesn't seem to fit in. He's a fine intelligent fellow and all that, but he isn't our type, now is he?

OLGA   He was interested in our movement and used to come to our meetings before I ever met him.

ENWRIGHT   Curiosity and a craving for adventure might account for that. He probably wanted to see a real bomb thrown.

OLGA   [*Angrily*] Oh! [*Then coldly*] You're wrong and you know it.

ENWRIGHT   Hm, am I? Well, I shouldn't have asked you. You love him. What do you know of the real man? Now, don't fly into a rage. Tom is my good friend, and no matter what he's inspired by, a valuable addition to our ranks. I must go and see if those pamphlets have come. [*He goes to door on right.* TOM *enters just as* ENWRIGHT *is closing door.* ENWRIGHT *shouts:* "Hello, Tom" *and shuts door behind him.* OLGA *runs to Tom and they embrace and kiss each other passionately.*]

Tom is a husky six-footer in his early twenties, large intelligent eyes, handsome in a rough, manly, strong-featured way. His manner is one of boyishly naive enthusiasm with a certain note of defiance creeping in as if he were fighting an inward embarrassment and was determined to brave it down.

OLGA   I thought you'd never get here and yet you're on time. [*They laugh and come over and sit down*—OLGA *in chair at end of the table,* TOM *on edge of the table beside her*]

TOM   Hartmann showed up yet?

OLGA   Not yet.

TOM   Wonder what he wants us for.

OLGA   It's something to do with a coming strike of dock-laborers and firemen, Enwright thinks.

TOM   Anything in the paper about it?

OLGA   Not much; they're trying to hush it up. [*She picks up a paper*] But there's quite an editorial here about you and me and other dangerous inciters to riot—you know—for our speeches in Union Square last Saturday. Listen to this. He's referring to what I said against war with Mexico. [*Reads*] "A crack-brained young female, Olga something-or-other, arose to howl invective against the government which protects her, against all sense of decency and national honor"—and so forth. Here again: "Over-strung lady anarchists of the Olga type are a constant and dangerous menace to society and should be confined in some asylum for the criminal-insane."

TOM [*Fiercely*] Damn him! [*Puts his arm protectingly around Olga*]

OLGA [*Resisting this protective attitude*] It seems I'm a dangerous anarchist inciting to murder because I call upon men not to shoot their brother men for a fetish of red, white and blue, a mockery called patriotism. [*She laughs angrily.*]

TOM The cowardly hound!

OLGA [*Throwing the paper on the floor scornfully*] I won't read what he said about you—something about your looking like a broken-down college boy whom a desire for cheap notoriety had led into the International Workers. [*Fiercely*] Liar!

TOM [*With a smile*] Well, I'm a college boy if that one year I wasted in college makes me one. [*Slowly*] I don't care what they say about me; but, damn him, he ought to have the manhood not to sling his muddy ink at a woman.

OLGA What an old-fashioned idea! Aren't we equals when we fight for liberty—regardless of sex?

TOM [*A bit sheepishly*] I know it's a mistaken notion—logically. I can feel that way about all the others—the other women who are working with us, I mean—but where you are concerned, I can't. It's different, somehow. [*Slowly*] You see—I love you, Olga.

OLGA [*Calmly*] And I love you, Tom; but what difference does that make? Are we not comrades fighting in the ranks—before everything? Don't you put that before our own miserable little egos?

TOM Before my own little miserable ego, yes; but not before yours. [*As* OLGA *looks at him reproachfully*] I can't help it. Our love comes first. [*Moodily*] That's why calumnies against you like the one in that paper drive me wild. I'd like to take that editor and twist his measly neck for him.

OLGA [*Frowning at his attitude of protection*] I'm used to such things, I'm strong enough to bear them. You ought to know that.

TOM I do, Olga. Good Lord, you're strong enough to bear anything. I'm not, that's the thing. I'm not strong enough to bear the insults against you, and by God, I never will be.

OLGA [*Rather impatiently*] Don't take them so seriously.

TOM I can't help it—especially the things they say against you—[*He hesitates*] on account of me.

OLGA On account of you? What do you mean?

TOM On account of—our relationship.

OLGA   You mean that stupid Philistines sneer at me because I'm living with you and we're not married?

TOM   Yes.

OLGA   [Indifferently] Very well; let them. They do not enter into my world. I expect their denunciations and I revel in them.

TOM   But don't you see I can't help blaming myself—

OLGA   [Impatiently] Blame yourself for what? Because when I knew I loved you I gave myself to you freely and openly? It seems to me the responsibility is mine. Don't be foolishly sentimental.

TOM   [Doggedly] Still, I wish you—[He hesitates—blurting it out] Marry me.

OLGA   [Frowning] We've argued this out before.

TOM   [Lamely] I thought you might have reconsidered.

OLGA   [Vehemently] I haven't done so, and I won't do so. I tell you I won't marry you or anyone. [Seeing the hurt look on Tom's face—contritely] You dear old Tom, you, don't you know I love you with all the love I have in me? Isn't that enough?

TOM   Yes, of course, but—

OLGA   Listen: Am I not all to you that a wife could be?

TOM   Yes.

OLGA   You don't believe in marriage as an institution, do you? You know that the voluntary union of two people is something which concerns them and them alone. You don't believe that the sanction of the law we hate or a religion we despise could make our relationship any holier, do you?

TOM   No.

OLGA   Then why speak of marriage?

TOM   [Doggedly] It's just this Olga. Though we know it is all wrong, we've got to face facts as they are. Marriage is a fact. I agree with you it ought to be abolished. But what are we to do? It won't be destroyed in our time in spite of all our efforts and we're living now, not in the future. We've got to make some concessions to society in order to be free to do our work. It's foolish to waste time butting one's head against a stone wall.

OLGA   [Getting up and walking up and down—vehemently] What are we beside the ideal we fight for? We cannot change conditions in our lives, perhaps, but we can make our lives a living protest against those conditions.

TOM   I don't want you to be a martyr—on my account.

OLGA   It's not on your account. I'm fighting for an ideal. You're only the man I love. Oh, can't you see? Some of us must be pioneers, some of us must prove by our lives that the dream we're striving for can be realized. [*Passionately*] We love each other. Our love is a fine love, freed from all the commonplaces of marriage. Why would you change it. There's no feeling of enforced servitude on my part. There can be no complacent sense of ownership on yours. [*With smiling irony*] Perhaps that's what you regret?

TOM   [*Indignantly*] Olga!

OLGA   Do you want a signed certificate proving I am yours—like a house and lot?

TOM   [*Hurt*] Don't, Olga. [*Impatiently*] You don't understand.

OLGA   I understand this: To compromise is to acknowledge defeat. [*More and more determinedly*] No, we'll live as we believe! And let all the self-righteous jackasses go to the devil!

TOM   You'll have to pay; I won't. It's the devilish unfairness which drives me wild. I want you to be happy, that's all.

OLGA   Then let me fight for my own soul with my own life. That's my happiness. And don't adopt that protective masculine attitude. I'm better able to bear my share of the burden than you are. It's in my blood—the exultation of the fight against tyranny. I was born with it. My father was exiled from his country for living and speaking what he thought; and I shall preserve his heritage in this country where I was born. It's harder for you, Tom, with years of conventional prudery behind you.

TOM   [*Shaking his head*] You haven't considered the most important reason for my proposal. [*Slowly*] Supposing we should have children? Would it be fair to them?

OLGA   [*Passionately*] We'll never have children. No, no, anything but that! I would go through anything, kill myself rather than have that happen!

TOM   Olga!

OLGA   No. To me the birth of a child is a horrible tragedy. To bring a helpless little one into a world of drudgery and unhappiness, to force upon it a mouldy crust of life—what heartlessness and needless cruelty! There are much too many of us here already. No; I will wait until life becomes a gift and not a punishment before I bestow it upon a child of mine. I will offer no children to Moloch as sacrifices. [TOM *stares at the floor but does not answer—a pause*] Make me a better world, O Husband-Man, and I'll be proud and not ashamed to bear children.

TOM [*Frowning*] I was only asking you to consider the possibility—

OLGA [*Fiercely*] There's no possibility! There never will be a possibility I tell you, I'd die first!

ENWRIGHT [*Hopelessly*] Let's drop the subject, then.

OLGA [*Coming over to kiss him*] I love you, Tom; and there's only one way to be true to you and to myself at the same time, and that's our present comradeship.

TOM [*Giving in—tenderly*] All right, as long as you are happy.

OLGA I am! I am! [ENWRIGHT *enters from door on right with a pile of pamphlets in under his arm*]

ENWRIGHT What are you, pray? [*Comes over to them*]

OLGA Happy.

ENWRIGHT Why not—with youth and love and [*With a smile*] inexperience. [*Sets pamphlets on table*] Hartmann hasn't come yet? He's late as usual.

TOM You think he wants to see us about the seamen and firemen's strike?

ENWRIGHT Yes, I imagine so—can't think what else it could be.

TOM They're talkjng of nothing else down at the office. [*With sudden recollection—laughing*] Oh, I'd forgotten to tell you the tragic news, Olga. I've lost my job.

OLGA [*Smiling*] Really?

TOM Yes, I'm bounced. No longer is your co-revolutionist assistant cashier of the Ocean Steamship Co. No longer is he a wage-slave.

OLGA When did all this happen?

TOM This evening. You know those pamphlets Hartmann gave me to distribute among the crew of the *San Francisco* when she arrived from Liverpool?

ENWRIGHT Yes.

TOM Well, in spite of the fact that my revered old man is, as I've told you, second engineer of the *San Francisco*, I managed to get rid of every single one of them without, as I thought, getting caught at it. I was wrong. Some coward must have reported me, for the manager called me into his office tonight at closing time—and fired me.

ENWRIGHT What did he have to say?

TOM Gave me a silly sermon for the good of my soul: told me of my evil ways and so forth. Said he hated to discharge the son of one of the company's oldest and most faithful employees—he might just as well have said servants—but my outrageous conduct made it necessary, as I must see for myself. Stirring up mutiny among the crew of the Company's largest and finest ship! Oh, he's a smooth party, that manager. Talked to me in a regular it-hurts-me-more-than-it-does-you way. Damn his nerve.

ENWRIGHT   Has your father heard the news yet?

TOM   [*Frowning*] Haven't seen him except for a moment at the office since the *San Francisco* docked. I promised I'd go up home for dinner tonight but I can't make it now. I suppose I'll have to go up later, and break the bad news to him then.

OLGA   What'll he say?

TOM   [*Shrugging his shoulders*] Go off into a nervous spasm of fear the Company will hold it against him for having such a son.

ENWRIGHT   Is he as bad as that?

TOM   Bad? No, nothing as alive as the word bad. Weak is a better term. You'd have to know him to understand what I mean.

OLGA   Tell me about him. I'm interested. We've been together for nearly half a year now and you've hardly ever mentioned him except to say that he was second-engineer on the *San Francisco*.

TOM   There's nothing much about him to tell except that. He's a common type, more's the pity. No backbone, no will power, no individuality, nothing. Just a poor servile creature living in constant fear of losing his job. You know the kind of man I mean. [*They nod*] He's been a second engineer on the boats of the Ocean Steamship company ever since I can remember. That fact gives you a glimpse into his character. He really knows marine engines from a to z—that's the strange part of it. Thirty years in the same little rut—and contented! Good God, think of it! They've never promoted him because he's never had the courage to demand it? They've taken him at his own valuation.

ENWRIGHT   But surely there must be some positive side to his character.

TOM   Oh, he's got a positive love for his engines, for his ship, and even for the rotten old Ocean Company itself. I remember he actually cried—real tears—when he was transferred from the old ship to the *San Francisco*—said he hated to leave the old engines he was used to. His life is bound up in just that one thing—marine engines. He'll talk to anyone who'll listen for hours on that subject. He knows nothing else. [*With a groan*] I think I was lulled to sleep in my cradle with a triple-expansion, twin-screw lullaby.

OLGA   [*With a smile*]
But how do you two ever get along together?

TOM   We don't. He's too afraid of me to have any affection for me. Cringes before me as abjectly as if I were his chief engineer. It's sickening but I guess it's just as well. I've none of that feeling for him we're supposed to have for our parents. How could I? He stands for everything I hate." [HARTMANN *enters from the door on left. He is an undersized man in his late forties, dressed in black, white shirt with soft collar, flowing black Windsor tie. His head is massive, too large for his body, with long black hair brushed straight back from his broad forehead. His large dark eyes peer near-sightedly from behind a pair of thick-rimmed spectacles. His voice is low and musical. He continually strokes his mustache and imperial with thin nervous hands*]

HARTMANN   Ah, you are already here. I am late, nicht war? Ach, such a talk we've been having. Phew! I could not make my exit. [*He comes over to the table and sits down, after patting Olga affectionately on the back*]

ENWRIGHT   Same old subject, I suppose—Colorado?

HARTMANN   Nein, nein, we did not Colorado mention, this evening. It was of something far more important we spoke; but have you not the evening papers read?

TOM   Haven't seen one.

OLGA   What is it, Hartmann?

HARTMANN   [*Shaking his head slowly*] It may be nothing or it may be much. I am wrong to have such fear, but there is in me a premonition, a dread unspeakable. I seem to see coming a disaster to us and to our hopes. [*As the others show signs of impatience*] War, I am speaking of—war which it is rumored, not without foundation, will soon break out.

TOM   Nothing new in that. They've been writing up war with Mexico for months.

HARTMANN   Nein, I mean not Mexico, or this country—yet. That, in truth, would be horrible enough, but this, that I mean, is more terrible a thousand times. It will all the nations involve [*Nodding his head*] Over there— in Europe. Too long have the jealous dogs growled over their bones. This time, I fear, they will fight. If they do—[*He makes a hopeless gesture*]—it will be the smash-up, le débâcle. And our cause will most of all suffer. The revolution will be fifty years put back.

OLGA   [*Jumping to her feet impulsively*] Then now is the time for us to show what we can do. We're strongly organized over there. The socialists—

surely their millions will fight shoulder to shoulder with us on this issue. We'll declare the general strike if they declare war. We'll defy them to make war when production ceases. Let every working man in those nations refuse to work, refuse to bear arms, and there will be no war. [*Enthusiastically*] Think of what it would mean—that strike! No electricity, no cars, no trains, no steamers, the factories dark and deserted, no newspapers, no wireless, nothing. The whole world of workers on a holiday. Think of how foolish those kings and emperors, those cabinets and parliaments would look when they found no one to fight for them, when they realized if they wanted war, they would have to fight themselves.

HARTMANN [*Shaking his head—with a sad smile*] The general strike is a solution possible in fifty years, perhaps. Now, no. All their lives the comrades shall proclaim it, fight for it—and gradually the workers will their stupid patriotism unlearn, will feel their power and take what is theirs. But now—how is it possible? They have not yet outgrown their silly awe when a stained rag on the end of a stick is waved over their heads. [*Solemnly*] And that is why I am afraid—that they are yet too ignorant, these workers; that at the first blare of a band, the first call to fatherland or motherland or some such sentimental phantom, they will all our teachings forget. Time, time is necessary for our ideas to grow into the hearts of men. Now they are in his brain only. The emotional crisis blots them out. We must the hearts of mankind touch—for it is what is in his heart he fights and dies for, and his brain is as nothing, that foolish animal. Yes, we must reach his heart, nicht war? And that time is not yet.

TOM [*After a pause—cheerfully*] Well, the war hasn't started yet, and I'll be willing to bet it'll be like this Mexican business of ours. Much talking, much writing, much patriotic gush—and that's all. They go through the same thing in Europe every few years, don't they?

HARTMANN [*Shaking his head—slowly*] But this time—[*Throwing off his depression*] Ach well, it is on the lap of the Gods. Yet I would not see millions of madmen butchering each other for [*With an expressive wave of his hand*] wheels in the head. [*A pause*] The soul of man is an uninhabited house haunted by the ghosts of old ideals. And man in those ghosts still believes! He so slowly unlearns, or understands, or loves what is true and beautiful, the stupid animal! [*With a sardonic laugh*] And he dreams he is God's masterpiece, wie, was? Ha-ha. And yet God is his masterpiece—that is truth. [*He chuckles to himself*]

ENWRIGHT [*Slowly*] Why not encourage war? It's the great purgative. It destroys the unenlightened. Let them fight until nothing but weaklings are left— and we others who refused to fight. Then we'll come into our own. We'll take what we want. Then we can start life anew with a new generation, a new art, a new ideal. Therefore vive la guerre!

HARTMANN [*Amused*] There is much in what you say—if we could those armies persuade to fight until annihilated. Unhappily there remains always so many still in uniform.

OLGA And the women remain. How would they be remodeled into your new world?

ENWRIGHT The civilized woman has long been living beyond her mental means. She will be only too glad to find a good excuse to throw aside her pretense of equality with man to return to polygamy. Her pose was interesting to her when it was new. Now it bores her. The constant strain of keeping up mental appearances, of having a soul,—

OLGA [*With a disdainful toss of her head*] When you once start, Enwright, you're impossible.

ENWRIGHT [*In same thoughtful tone—as if he had not heard her*] At the end of my supposititious war of manly extermination there will be ten or twenty womanly women for every unmanly man who has refused to die on the field of honor. Yet breeding must go on. The women, above all, will demand it. The new race must be created in order to enjoy the new freedom. What will be the result?

OLGA [*At first irritably—finally breaking into a laugh*] Hartmann, please tell him to shut up; or, at least, tell us the reason you wanted to see Tom and me, and let us make our escape. Enwright has found a pretty little strange idea. He's going to play with it, cuddle it, turn it over and over to see what's inside—and I refuse to waste an evening listening to him.

ENWRIGHT I'm serious, Olga. All that might very well happen. [*Taking hat from table*] You people want to talk, and so do I, so I better leave in search of an audience.

HARTMANN Ach no, Enwright, sit down. It is necessary also that you know what is to be done, and to have your opinion of our plan.

ENWRIGHT That's different; if I can be of any use—

TOM [*Looking at his watch*] Is it going to take long, Hartmann?

HARTMANN Nein, my boy, a few moments only. You must go? This is very important that you should at once know the facts and to a decision come.

TOM I promised to run up and see my father tonight. He sails in a day or so and I won't have another chance. [*Impatiently*] Damned bore! [*Sitting down at table*] Well, let him wait.

HARTMANN   Attention, then. [*All assume attitudes of tense expectation.* TOM *closes his hand over one of Olga's on the table but she releases it with a frown at his childishness.* HARTMANN *commences slowly*] You have rumors heard, no?, of a strike, a strike which would be truly international, among the seamen and firemen of all ocean steamships, and of all the dock laborers?

ENWRIGHT   I was saying I thought that was what you had in mind.

HARTMANN   What you do not know is that this strike is hanging fire; it hesitates. There is needed a push to start it on its way. It is for us of the International to strike a blow, to give courage to those wavering ones. This we have decided to do. [*They nod in assent*] You know the Ocean Steamship Company?

TOM   [*Smiling*] I have made its acquaintance.

HARTMANN   Ach, it is there you work, nicht war? For the moment I had forgotten.

TOM   [*With emphasis*] It is where I *worked*.

HARTMANN   [*Puzzled*] Was?

TOM   I was fired—for distributing pamphlets.

HARTMANN   So. So much the better. You are free to undertake—[*He raises his brows with a questioning look*] anything?

TOM   [*Steadily*] Anything! Anything you think would help.

HARTMANN   I need not to ask you, Olga.

OLGA   [*Quietly*] Anything. Go on.

HARTMANN   And now before I go further I must a question ask. [*To Tom*] Did you not tell me once that you had worked as a stoker, fireman, on an ocean steamer.

TOM   Yes, two summers ago. Did it for a stunt more than anything else. [*With an abashed smile*] I had no serious conception of anything in those days. I and a pal of mine made the round trip. [*Boyishly*] I tell you, though, it opened my eyes to conditions I had never dreamt of. It made me think—seeing the contrast between us grimy stokers and the first cabin people lolling in their deck-chairs.

OLGA   It was on one of the Ocean Company's boats you made the trip, wasn't it, Tom?

TOM   Yes.

HARTMANN   [*With an air of satisfaction*] Then, you know all the ropes, no? You would make no blunders which would attract attention should you ever again as fireman work?

TOM   I guess not, It was drilled into me hard enough.

HARTMANN   That is good, very good. I told them, the others, that you were the exact one for it.

TOM   I don't see what shipping as stoker—

HARTMANN   It is just that you must do if you would help us.

TOM   [*Begining to understand*] Ah.

OLGA   And I?

HARTMANN   A moment and you will clearly understand [*Slowly*] The unions on both sides of the ocean were all in favor of this strike. It was to be in bitterness waged to the end. There was to be no compromise. But now the unions are afraid, they seek to waste time doing nothing. The Steamship Companies fear this strike. They are endeavoring before its birth to crush it, to buy off the union leaders so no strike will be declared.

ENWRIGHT   Are you sure of this—that the union leaders are dickering with the Companies?

HARTMANN   Very sure. They have a traitor among them who is true to us. He has written us everything from Liverpool, where, it was intended, the strike should break out first.

ENWRIGHT   Do you mean Whitely?

HARTMANN   Yes, Whitely—the one strong soul among them over there. [*He takes a letter from his pocket and hands it to Olga*] Here is a letter to Whitely, Olga. You must to him present it the moment you reach Liverpool. [OLGA *nods*]

TOM   But—I don't see—

HARTMANN   It is time for us to strike, to prove the International no foolish dream. Let these rumors of a great war of nations but continue, and in a short time, these seamen and firemen and dock laborers will be in the streets like foolish school boys cheering for the flag which their oppression symbolizes. We must strike now, immediately, or not at all. We must from their lethargy awake these workers, these unions. We must put fear into the hearts of capitalism. [*Rising to his feet, his voice trembling with his earnestness*] We must at the heart of capital strike. There is necessary in this crisis a blow which, like the spark in a magazine of gunpowder, will the conflagration establish. A blow must be struck so powerful that on it will the eyes and minds of all be focussed. We must the attention of the world call to the International Workers of the Earth and to the issue of this strike.

TOM   [*His eyes growing bright*] But what is my part in this?

HARTMANN   Wait! Have patience! Soon you shall know. Our blow is at the heart of the Ship Trust to be directed, at the Company which controls the whole ship combine.

TOM   You mean the Ocean Company? [HARTMANN *nods*] Good enough!

HARTMANN   [*Solemnly*] There is something I must warn you of before you accept definitely this mission. It is very dangerous, very dangerous. The one who undertakes it risks death, imprisonment.

TOM   [*Steadily*] I understand. Go on.

HARTMANN   You accept?

TOM   Yes.

OLGA   [*Taking his hand with impulsive admiration*] Tom!

ENWRIGHT   Good boy!

HARTMANN   My boy, I am glad. Whatever happens, your soul will rejoice. It will know you are the good fight fighting, the fight of suffering humanity.

TOM   What is it I am to do?

HARTMANN   A steamer, the finest steamer of the Ocean Company, sails the day after tomorrow. [TOM *is struck with some thought and glances quickly at Olga*] You will ship—is it that you call it?—on her as a fireman. Here are your fireman's papers. [*Takes papers from pocket*] They are made out in the name of Tom Donovan. You will know, better than I, where you can find clothes suitable, and how to disguise yourself.

TOM   But where does Olga come in?

HARTMANN   She will as second class passenger on the same ship go. When Liverpool is reached she will the letter to Whitely present, and he will give her dynamite which she will give to you when you come on shore.

TOM   Dynamite?

HARTMANN   Whitely will instruct you how to use it, and when. Some time during the steamship's stop in Liverpool you will dynamite the engines— without loss of life—if possible.

TOM   [*Confused by the suddenness of all this*] But what good will that do—to dynamite the engines?

ENWRIGHT   [*Breaking in*] Just this. All the men will realize that it was one of their number who did it. There will be no attempt at concealment of that fact. It will give them confidence in their power; and it will hit the Ocean Company a hard blow. The Companies will make no compromise after that. Instead they will probably adopt harsh retaliatory measures. The strike will break out and it will be a fight to the finish.

OLGA [*Eagerly*] And this explosion will point to sabotage as the logical method of waging the war of labor—that force alone can be effective against force. For many years the workers have appealed to the humanity and fairness of capital, and they have always found it unfair and cruel. They have thought Capitalism impregnable behind its fortress of law, and they have been afraid. A few successful assaults of this kind and their eyes will be opened. They will realize their strength and they will unite and *demand*, not beg.

HARTMANN The words of Danton—"It is necessary to dare, and again to dare, and still again to dare."

TOM [*Resentfully*] It wasn't the daring I was thinking of, Hartmann. If I'm to risk my life I want to know it's going to do some good. [*Still more resentfully*] And I don't see why you have to drag Olga into all this.

OLGA [*Impatiently*] Tom! Please!

TOM Oh, I know it makes you sore to have me say that. I don't care. I don't think it's right to make a woman run risks—

OLGA But don't you see? I won't be running risks. They'll never suspect me.

ENWRIGHT That's the answer, Tom.

TOM Maybe it's safe enough—still—I feel—

OLGA Tom! You're not going to back out now?

TOM [*Fiercely*] Olga! [*Turning to Hartmann*] You haven't even told me the name of the steamer yet.

HARTMANN Ach, so it is. [*Reaches in pocket and peers at the card he takes out*] Hmmm—yes—here it is—the *San Francisco*. [*In a flash of understanding* ENWRIGHT *and* OLGA *look at each other than then at Tom*]

OLGA Good heavens.

ENWRIGHT The devil!

TOM [*With a grim smile*] By God, I thought so.

HARTMANN Thought what? I do not understand—[*Looks from one to the other*]

TOM My father is second engineer of the *San Francisco*.

HARTMANN [*Stunned*] Ach Gott! So? So? I remember—you said your father was engineer on a boat—but there are of boats so many, wie? was? How could I know?

TOM [*Slowly*] It makes no difference. [*With a meaning look at Olga*] I am not going to *back out*.

HARTMANN What! In spite of this you will—

TOM I said I would do it, Hartmann, and I'm going to.

HARTMANN But your father? He will recognize—

TOM I'll see that he doesn't, never fear; and I'll see that the thing happens when he's off watch and ashore.

HARTMANN [*Unconvinced—wringing his hands*] Ach, the miserable luck of it. It was all so fine, so certain.

TOM [*Picking up his hat*] If you knew what kind of man my father is you wouldn't worry. [*Contemptuously*] He isn't much of an obstacle. I'll take care of him. [*Moving toward door*] I'm going up to see him now. [*He laughs*]

HARTMANN [*Jumping to his feet in a flurry of angry fear*] Gott in Himmel, you will not tell him?

OLGA [*Indignantly*] Hartmann!

HARTMANN [*As he sees the expression on Tom's face—haltingly*] A thousand pardons.

TOM [*Coldly*] You needn't have asked that question, Hartmann. I'll see you here tomorrow morning about nine. Good-night. I won't be long, Olga. [*He goes out as*

THE CURTAIN FALLS

ACT TWO

SCENE: *Sitting-room of Thomas Perkins' small home in Jersey City—a small room crowded with cheap furniture. On the right, two windows with drawn shades and stiff white curtains. In the right corner, a sofa. In the middle of rear wall, a door leading into the hall. On the right of door, a bookcase half filled with a few books and stacks of magazines. In the left corner, a stand on which is a potted rubber plant. In the left wall, forward, a door. Ugly straight-backed chairs are pushed back against the walls which are papered in some dreary floral design.*

It is about nine o'clock on the same night. THOMAS PERKINS *and* HENDERSON *are discovered at the table playing cards.* PERKINS *is a nervous, self-conscious, awkward little man with a soft timid voice. He is half bald but an unkempt fringe of thin grey hair straggles about his ears. He wears spectacles, carpet slippers, ill-fitting shabby clothes.* HENDERSON *is a tall, lean Scotchman with grey hair and bristly mustache. He is dressed in the uniform of a ship's engineer.*

They are just finishing a hand at euchre. HENDERSON *is fiercely intent upon the game, a gleam of triumph in his eye.* PERKINS *pays but little attention to his cards but continually glances at the door in rear. His manner is worried, his expression troubled, and evidently his playing is ragged in the extreme for* HENDERSON *grunts with contemptuous satisfaction as he rakes in the tricks.*

HENDERSON   [*Whacking his last card down*] That does for ye, I tak' it, Perkins.

PERKINS   [*With a nervous start*] Eh? Oh yes, yes, of course. [*Hopefully*] That makes game, don't it, Henderson?

HENDERSON   {*Looking at his counters—grumblingly*] I ha' one more to go. [PERKINS *sighs, casts a quick glance at the door, takes up cards, and prepares to deal again*] Shuffle the cards, mon, shuffle the cards! [*A sudden thought strikes him*] It's no your deal, mon, it's no your deal! Gie them here to me!

PERKINS   [*Timidly apologetic*] I was forgetting. [*Hands cards to Henderson*]

HENDERSON   [*Shuffling the cards with a great clatter—sarcastically*] Forgettin'. Na doot ye'll be likewise forgettin' yon's the seventh game ye've lost and ye arre thrupence hapenny my debtor. [*He licks his thumb and commences to deal*]

PERKINS   Seven cents, that is. [*Commences to fumble in his pockets*]

HENDERSON   [*Irritably*] Dinna bother wi' it the noo. Canna ye take a joke? Play your hand! [PERKINS *snatches up his hand, and plays. Whenever* HENDERSON *looks at his hand,* PERKINS *glances with pitiful hopefulness at the door.* HENDERSON *takes a trick, ponders with knit brows, plays a card.* PERKINS *hears the flap of the card. He has been taking advantage of Henderson's preoccupation to glance surreptitiously at his watch. He hurriedly plays the first card his hand touches and starts to pull in the trick. Henderson's big hand grips his wrist.*]

HENDERSON   No, ye don't! [PERKINS *stares at him with amazement*] I little kenned I'd see the day I'd be gamblin' for gold wi' a card sharp.

PERKINS   A card sharp!

HENDERSON   D'ye ken the trumps?

PERKINS   Diamonds.

HENDERSON   An' this card I played? [*Holding it up accusingly before Perkins*]

PERKINS   Ten of diamonds.

HENDERSON   [*Solemnly, impressing him with the terrible outrage*] An' ye played the jock o' spades on it—*and took the trick!*

PERKINS   I was thinking it was right bower.

HENDERSON   [*Picking up Perkins' hand and looking at it*] An' ye had diamonds to follow suit wi' [*Shakes his head solemnly*] an' ye dinna do it. Mon alive, whur are your wits? [*Throws the cards disgustedly on the table*] We'll play na more the nicht. 'Tis na sport playin' wi' one so ha'-witted.

PERKINS   [*Gathering up the cards with a sigh of relief*] I'm sorry. I couldn't keep my mind on the game. I kept wondering if Tom—

HENDERSON   [*With a grunt*] Ay, Tam, Tam—always Tam!

PERKINS   [*Looking at his watch*] It's early yet, isn't it? He said he'd come. I do hope—[*With a sigh*] I told Mrs. Allen to keep supper warm for him. [*Apprehensively*] She'll be mad. I do hope he'll come. [*Hopefully*] Don't you think he will? [*He plays nervously with the cards on the table*]

HENDERSON   Ay, ay, he'll come—when he's good an' ready.

PERKINS   [*Goes to the window and peers out—returns with a sigh*] Will you have a little something to drink now?

HENDERSON   I'll sup a wee drop o' whiskey. [PERKINS *goes slowly out of the door on the left.* HENDERSON *fills and lights his pipe. The sound of a woman's shrill, irritated voice comes from left.* HENDERSON *smiles grimly and remarks to himself, half-aloud:* "Ay, he's catchin' it the noo." *A moment later* PERKINS *enters hastily from the left carrying a bottle of Scotch, a pitcher of water and two glasses. He places these on the table. The woman's voice still shrills on from the left*]

PERKINS   [*Agitated*] Mrs. Allen is very mad—about the dinner. She says she won't try to keep it any longer. It's burnt, she says. [*Worriedly*] And I know Tom will be hungry.

HENDERSON   [*Grunting*] Ay, you wi' your Tam an' your Mrs. Allen.

PERKINS   [*Fearfully*] Ssshh! Here she comes now. [*The flow of shrill talk grows quickly louder and* MRS. ALLEN *enters from left. She is a thin, angular, middle-aged woman with sharp features. Her voice is unpleasantly high and rasping*]

MRS. ALLEN   [*Taking a hat pin from her mouth and jabbing it into her hat*] And not another minute, not another second will I stay if you was to git down on your knees to me. I ain't one, and I never was one to balk at workin', and no one knows it better'n you, Thomas Perkins. Ain't I come in regular every day you was here for the past five years, and once a week when you was on ship, scrubbin' my hands off, and dustin', and lookin' after things? And I ain't never missed once—and all the time I got a husband and family of my own to tend to besides. And what d'you suppose my man'll think when I come back this late in the night? Liable to accuse me of skylarkin' with you, Thomas Perkins, that's what he is, with his temper, and you a widower.

PERKINS   [Faintly] No, no, Mrs. Allen, I'm sure he won't.

HENDERSON   [Gruffly]-Tush, tush, woman, is your mon daft?

MRS. ALLEN   [Turning furiously] Don't you tush me, Mr. Henderson! And don't you be slingin' slurs at Mister Allen. He's a better man than you are or ever will be for all your bein' a chief engineer. He ain't daft! No, nor he ain't a sot with a bottle of whiskey at his elbow all the day, neither. [HENDERSON nearly bursts with rage at this but makes no reply]

PERKINS   [Interposing] It was just this once, Mrs. Allen. I won't ask you to do it again. It was very, very nice of you indeed. You see I thought Tom would be hungry, and—

MRS. ALLEN   [With a snort] Tom! You're always thinkin' about him; and much he cares about you, never comin' to see you, and leavin' you here eatin' your heart out with lonesomeness night after night. Why isn't he here for dinner at seven o'clock like he said he would be, and him knowin' you was here all alone?

PERKINS   They kept him at the office, I'm sure; or something came up to prevent him, or— [Pitiably] It's early yet for a young man like him. Don't you think he'll come, Mrs. Allen?

MRS. ALLEN   Lawd knows! And if I was you I wouldn't bother whether he did or not. A pretty way he's treated you after you've sweated in a dirty engine room—

PERKINS   [Hastily resenting this slur] The engine room is not dirty, Mrs. Allen. It's as clean as—as—as your kitchen. Isn't it, Henderson? [HENDERSON grunts]

MRS. ALLEN   [Ignoring this correction] After you've sweated in a dirty engine room to send him through school—

PERKINS   [Feebly expostulating] Mrs. Allen!

MRS. ALLEN   Oh he can't pull the wool over my eyes like he does you. That's what you get for eddicating him so much. It's just what Mr. Allen tells me when I spoke about sending our Jim to high school. No, he says, none of those high-fangled schools for a son of mine. I wants 'em to be workers, not loafers, he says; and he was right.

PERKINS   No doubt, no doubt, Mrs. Allen.

MRS. ALLEN   [*Proudly*] And that same boy's a good plumber right now, and earns good wages, and has a wife and children, and never drinks 'cept on Saturday nights like his father told him.

PERKINS   Yes, of course, a fine boy.

MRS. ALLEN   And when I think of your Tom it jest makes my blood boil— the best part of a good dinner burnt up. How long is it since he's been here to so much as eat a bite with you, tell me that!

PERKINS   [*Vaguely*] Why—er—not so long ago—

MRS. ALLEN   It's more than three months, that's what it is! And three times during that time I've cooked dinners for him, and he ain't never come till the dinner was spoiled and I'd gone home.

HENDERSON   [*Drily*] I dinna blame the lad. [*He puffs furiously on his pipe.* MRS. ALLEN   *glares at him*]

MRS. ALLEN   And are you foolish enough to think, Thomas Perkins, that it's that job you got for him that keeps him from coming up here? Well you may think so, but t'ain't; [*Impressively*] Your Tom is skylarkin' around with some girl, that's what he is, and that's the reason he ain't got no time for his father.

PERKINS   [*Eagerly*] A girl?

MRS. ALLEN   Yes, young Dugan says he sees him every night pretty near, and always with the same girl.

PERKINS   [*Delighted*] Why that explains everything, doesn't it? You couldn't expect him to be coming up here in that case, Mrs. Allen. And he's never let on a word about it, the young rascal. [*With pitiful eagerness for more details*] She must be a nice girl, Mrs. Allen?

MRS. ALLEN   [*Grudgingly*] Well, young Dugan says he didn't notice nothin' wrong about her—but he's a man.

PERKINS   She must be a pretty girl, Mrs. Allen?

MRS. ALLEN   Young Dugan says she was pretty enough, but Lawd knows what people think is pretty nowadays.

PERKINS   And does young Dugan know who she is, Mrs. Allen?

MRS. ALLEN   No, he don't know nothin' 'bout her 'cept what I've told you, but he heard Tom call her Olga once.

PERKINS   [*Fascinated by the name*] Olga. Olga. A pretty name, isn't it, Mrs. Allen?

MRS. ALLEN   [*With a sniff*] Sounds furrin to me. [*With a sigh*] I'm glad you take it so easy, Thomas Perkins.

PERKINS   [*Smiling happily*] Thank you so much for telling, me, Mrs. Allen. I'm very glad. A young man like Tom ought to get married.

MRS. ALLEN   [*With a martyred air*] Course it ain't none of my business and I ain't got no right to be talkin' about it; but you've been kind to me, Thomas Perkins, and you've been a friend to me and Mr. Allen when we needed a friend bad, and you've always paid me well, and—[*She is on the verge of tears*]

PERKINS   [*Terrified by this demonstration*] It's nothing, nothing, nothing at all, nothing—

MRS. ALLEN   [*Swallowing her tears—indignantly*] And even if you do take it so easy, I say again that you been treated shameful—and I know Mr. Henderson will agree with me. [HENDERSON, *during the conversation between Perkins and the housekeeper, has been fidgeting in his chair as if on pins and needles. Several times it has seemed as if his irritation would compel him to speech but with mighty—and apparent efforts—he has controlled these impulses*]

HENDERSON   [*Jumping at this unexpected question, turns around and surveys Mrs. Allen icily for a second; then ejaculates forcibly*] I dinna agree wi' one word that ever came from your mouth, Mrs. Allen; and I would considerr it a kindness of ye not to address me. [MRS. ALLEN *is dumb with fury.* HENDERSON *turns his back to her and puffs on his pipe, then turns with a satisfied air to the bottle at his elbow and starts to pour out a drink*]

MRS. ALLEN   [*Seeing her chance—as* HENDERSON *lifts the bottle—in a loud stage whisper*] Keep you eye on that bottle is what I says, Thomas Perkins. He might git vilent. [HENDERSON *sets down the bottle on the table with a crash—but before his rage can find expression,* MRS. ALLEN *sweeps out the door in rear with a good-night to Perkins*]

PERKINS   [*Coming over to the table with a sigh of relief*] She's gone.

HENDERSON   Mon, mon, what a deeil of a woman! The Lord God pity puir Mr. Allen. [*Smiting his clenched fist on the table*] Was I her husband I'd drop poison in her tea, on ma conscience I would. [*Testily*] How can ye put up wi' her?

PERKINS   [*Sitting down*] It's just her way. She's a very good woman, really—very good-hearted—and works very, very hard. [HENDERSON *grunts*] You haven't taken your drink yet, Henderson.

HENDERSON   Ay, I ha' forgotten it. [*Takes a sip*] Yon woman's clatter addled my wits. [PERKINS *sips his glass of water. The two men are silent for a moment,* HENDERSON *engrossed by his Scotch and* PERKINS *staring mournfully before him*]

PERKINS [*With a sigh*] The *San Francisco* sails the day after tomorrow.

HENDERSON Ay, and the *Empress* as well.

PERKINS I was down on board this morning.

HENDERSON Canna ye keep off the bloody ship when ye've no call to be there. I never saw a mon sae fond of his job as ye are.

PERKINS [*Simply*] I was lonely.

HENDERSON [*Genuinely sympathetic*] Ye puir unfortunate body! And so ye go doon to your engines for companionship! Mon, but you're the queer person!

PERKINS [*His eyes lighting up*] I love those engines—all engines.

HENDERSON An' I hate the bloody things—most o' the time.

PERKINS No, you don't. You can't mean that.

HENDERSON Ay, I do. Twenty-five years I ha' been sweatin' in the bowels of a ship till my stomach's turned wi' the lot o' them. [*Very seriously*] An' I tell ye now, Perkins, I'm goin' to chuck the sea an' spend the remainderr of my days on shore.

PERKINS [*Horrified*] You're going to work on shore!

HENDERSON Ay; in the marine engine works at Liverpool.

PERKINS You don't mean—you won't sail on the *Empress* any more?

HENDERSON I ha' given in my notice. At the end of this trip, I'm through.

PERKINS [*Stunned by this news, sits blinking his eyes rapidly—clears his throat huskily—in a trembling voice*] I'm sorry—[*Quickly*] Of course, I'm glad for your sake, very glad—see you better yourself—you know that. What I meant was—sorry we won't—[*He falters*] Have any more nights together here—like this.

HENDERSON [*With feeling*] On that point, Perkins, ye are na more sorry than I am. [*Dryly but kindly*] 'Tis a wet walk from Liverpool to the States, Perkins. [*A pause*]

PERKINS [*Sadly*] Twenty years, isn't it, Henderson—We've known each other.

HENDERSON Ay, in the neighborhood o' that.

PERKINS You were fourth engineer on the same ship I was second on, the old *Roumania*, when we first met.

HENDERSON   Ay.

PERKINS   [*With a pitiful attempt at a smile*] And now you're a chief engineer and I'm still where I was—second.

HENDERSON   [*Forcibly*] An' ye ken more about a ship's engines than I everr had in my head. I canna understand it. [*Savagely*] They're a rotten lot—that Ocean Steamship Company—or ye'd ha' received promotion years agone.

PERKINS   [*Protestingly*] No, no, they're all right.

HENDERSON   Bosh! If ye'd threatened them to chuck your job—if ye had more push to ye—

PERKINS   Yes, that's it; of course you're right enough, maybe; but you see I never was born that way. [*Slowly*] It isn't in me. [*Brightening*] But I'm not complaining. I'm contented enough where I am. I don't think after all I'd be happy with the whole responsibility of the engines on my shoulders. I think maybe I wouldn't make a good first—and the Company knows that.

HENDERSON   [*Disgustedly*] The deeil damn the Company.

PERKINS   You see—I know—they all know—I've no strength, no force of character.

HENDERSON   [*Scornfully—knocking out his pipe*] Na force of characterr? I suppose ye'd na force of characterr the day the boiler burst on the *Roumania* an' ye went below in the scaldin' steam.

PERKINS   [*Embarrassed*] It was nothing. Someone had to. I was young them. [*Abruptly*] You haven't finished your drink.

HENDERSON   'Tis no use talkin' to you. Ye will na credit aught good o' yourself. I ha' neverr encounterred such a mon. [*He finishes his drink—starts to fill pipe*]

PERKINS   It's going to be lonely—when you're gone—

HENDERSON   Ye can live on the ship then and be near the dear engines all o' the time.

PERKINS   [*Seriously*] Yes, I'm thinking of that.

HENDERSON   [*Surprised*] Surely ye canna mean that.

PERKINS   Yes, I do. I have a reason now, after something I heard tonight.

HENDERSON   [*With sly sarcasm*] I dinna dream I'd ever be rivals in a body's affections wi' a quadruple expansion engine.

PERKINS   [*Not knowing whether Henderson is really offended or not*] No, no! [*Seeing the twinkle in Henderson's eye*] Oh, now you're joking. But I do love those engines. [*Enthusiastically*] Seems as if I could never get tired watching them. [*slyly*] I've got to know them so well, and sometimes I think—I know this sounds foolish to you—that they know me. [HENDERSON *grunts.*] Oh, I know it sounds foolish, doesn't it, but I can't help believing it. Sometimes when I touch them I seem to know they feel me. I seem to hear them speaking like a friend to me, times when I'm lonely and, well, sort of sick of things—and they're a comfort. [*Eagerly*] And in a storm, I know I can hear them groan with pain, and suffer, and I feel so sorry and try to do all I can to help them. [*Nervously*] I know you'll think all this is very silly and—childish, don't you.

HENDERSON   No, I canna say I ha' na felt somewhat o' the same at times, myself.

PERKINS   [*Pleased*] Then it's only natural, isn't it? You see I've been with them so much. One gets to be friends with them—and even [*Hesitating shyly*] love them, in a manner of speaking—[*Sadly*] People never have seemed to understand or like me, somehow—except you.

HENDERSON   The deeil damn them for a pack o' fools.

PERKINS   Oh, it isn't their fault. It's just that I don't know how to act with people. I'm stupid. I can't say the things I want to say. You—you know how I act. Why even Tom, I feel embarrassed even with him, he's been so much away. [*Looking anxiously at his watch*] I wonder what can be keeping him.

HENDERSON   [*Fiercely*] Ah, Tam, Tam! T'is a shame the mannerr you've spoilt that boy. And what thanks does he give ye? Were he mine I'd take a whip to him, big as he is.

PERKINS   [*With real anger*] Henderson! You mustn't talk that way about Tom. I can't permit it, even from you.

HENDERSON   Ah weel, dinna fly off the handle. I'll say naught more.

PERKINS   You don't understand, Henderson. Tom isn't like me. He takes after his mother. [*A pause*] You remember his mother, don't you?

HENDERSON   [*With an expression indicating his disapproval of that lady*] Ay.

PERKINS   She was just like Tom—large and forceful.

HENDERSON   [*Grimly*] Ay she was; an' neverr perrmitted ye to call your soul your ain.

PERKINS   Oh, not as bad as that, Henderson; but she never could understand why I didn't become president of the Steamship Company. [*Quaintly*] I was lonely—after she died. That's why I came to love the engines so. Of course I couldn't have Tom at home alone when he was only a little chap, and I was away most of the time. So he's been away ever since then till he grew up, and I haven't seen much of him. [*Sadly*] That's the whole trouble. He doesn't know me.

HENDERSON   'Tis time he did. [*Disgustedly*] Larkin' around wi' lasses!

PERKINS   I was very glad to hear that, Henderson. If he would only marry—

HENDERSON   There are many ways wi' lasses besides takin' them for wife.

PERKINS   That couldn't be so in this case. Tom isn't the kind to trifle or do anything wrong.

HENDERSON   An' why are ye so anxious to ha' him married?

PERKINS   Well you know I spoke of closing up this house and living on board—I couldn't stand it here alone when you can't come any more. But if Tom gets married I was thinking—You know I've just paid off the last of the mortgage, and I've always intended to give this house to Tom for a wedding present. That's what I've been saving for. I've been thinking that when Tom and his wife came to live here they might let me stay with them when I was in port, and—it would be like home again [*Shyly*] And maybe there'd be children and I'd be a grandfather, wouldn't I? [*He falls into a smiling reverie*]

HENDERSON   I had na thought Tam was earrnin' enough to take on a wife.

PERKINS   Oh, Tom has a very good position now.

HENDERSON   He has you to thank for it.

PERKINS   I only got him a start, that was all. Very good of the Company to have done me the favor, don't you think? [*Proudly*] Tom's been promoted twice since then. He's well liked in the office and—[*He stops abruptly as if struck by some alarming thought. An expression of dismay comes over his face*] I do hope nothing will happen, Henderson.

HENDERSON   [*Surprised by his change of tone*] Eh?

PERKINS   [*Greatly agitated*] I have so set my mind on having him rise in the Company—and what I heard today—Oh. I know it can't be true. There must be some mistake.

HENDERSON   [*Impatiently*] Speak your mind! What is it?

PERKINS   It's had me so upset, ever since. Listen. When I was passing by the manager's office this morning Mr. Griffin stopped me and said he wanted to warn me about Tom.

HENDERSON   [*As if this was no more than he expected*] Hmm!

PERKINS   I couldn't say a word I was so frightened. He said he wanted me to say a word to Tom about the company he was keeping. It seems one of Tom's best friends in the office was discharged a short time ago for being an Anarchist or a Socialist or a—I forget the other—it's three letters, I remember.

HENDERSON   The I.W.E.?

PERKINS   Yes, that's it. What does it mean?

HENDERSON   The International Workers of the Earth they call themselves.

PERKINS   What kind of people are they? What is it? A club? A secret society?

HENDERSON   They're a lot of scamps who will na work themselves an' canna endure the thought of anyone else worrkin'. They go around makin' speeches, an' gettin' men discontented wi' their jobs. 'Tis they who help start all the strikes. Ha' ye no heard about the seamen and firemen's strike they say is going to break out in a week or two?

PERKINS   Yes, the Chief spoke about it this morning.

HENDERSON   The same I.W.E. you were speakin' of is back of it all. They'll be askin' for a Turkish bath in the stokehold next. I would be verra sorry to hear Tam had any truck wi' such rogues.

PERKINS   [Hastily] Oh, I'm sure not. Mr. Griffin didn't say that. He only said Tom's friend was one of their members. [Brightening] Mr. Griffin said everyone in the office liked Tom, and it would be a pity if—But of course there must be some mistake. Don't you think so?

HENDERSON   I ha' na doot there is. Tam's no a scoundrel. [A knock at the door. Without waiting for anyone to come TOM pushes open the door and walks into the room]

TOM   [With careless indifference] Evening, father. Sorry I wasn't here for dinner but I couldn't make it. [To HENDERSON, curtly] Good evening.

HENDERSON   [Coldly] Good evening to ye.

PERKINS   [Pitiably self-conscious, nervous, and confused] Oh, it doesn't matter. I tried to have Mrs. Allen keep something warm for you but it was so late for her—poor woman—you know how she is.

TOM   [Irritably] Is that old pest still coming here?

PERKINS   Oh, she isn't so bad. I'm used to her, you see. [TOM smiles at him with amused contempt. PERKINS cringes before this smile]

HENDERSON   [Getting up and picking up his hat] I'll be gettin' doon to the ship, I'm thinkin'. [Goes to door]

PERKINS   [Beseechingly] Oh, don't go yet. It's so early. Surely you can stay a while—

HENDERSON   [*Firmly*] I ha' some letters to write before I turn in. [*Nodding*]

TOM   [*Carelessly*] Good night.

PERKINS   [*Going over and shaking* HENDERSON's *hand*] But you'll come up again tomorrow night, won't you? The last night, you know.

HENDERSON   Ay.

PERKINS   We'll have another hand at euchre, wouldn't you like to?

HENDERSON   Verra' weel. [*With a smile*] But dinna forget ye are already thrupence hapenny my debtor. [*He goes out.* TOM *sits down in his chair.* PERKINS *comes over and sits down in his old place.* TOM *looks steadily at his father but remains silent.* PERKINS *squirms. A pause*]

PERKINS   [*At last—desperately*] Henderson's going to give up his position on the *Empress* and work on shore—marine engine works at Liverpool.

TOM   Ah.

PERKINS   I'll miss him coming up here nights.

TOM   [*With a significant glance at the bottle*] He'll probably miss it too—in a way.

PERKINS   Oh no, Tom, you mustn't think that. He's my best friend in the world. It's going to be lonely without him.

TOM   [*Banteringly*] You'll have no one to talk engines with any longer, will you? Except on ship.

PERKINS   [*Innocently*] No.

TOM   But you'll still have the engines themselves—that's a comfort.

PERKINS   [*Seriously*] Yes, that's a comfort.

TOM   And you'll have the ship—the *San Francisco*.

PERKINS   Yes.

TOM   And the Ocean Steamship Company—L—T—D.

PERKINS   [*Feeling the mockery in Tom's voice for the first time—fidgeting miserably*] Now you're trying to have a joke on me, aren't you?

TOM   Not at all. I was only reminding you of the many sources of consolation for the loss of Henderson.

PERKINS   [*Desperately*] I wish you could get up oftener. [*As* TOM *frowns*] Oh, I know you're very busy. I mean just once in a while.

TOM   [*With a sigh*] I'll try and do so.

PERKINS   It's been such a long time since you've been here. [*Gulping*] It doesn't seem like home anymore, when you're not here.

TOM   Well, you didn't need me as long as Henderson was here. He understands all about engines—and I don't.

PERKINS   [*Humbly*] I'll promise not to talk about engines in future.

TOM   [*Perfunctorily*] Oh, I like to hear about them well enough, when you're not so technical I can't follow you.

PERKINS   It's the only thing I know about, you see—and like.

TOM   [*Who has been relenting, hardens*] Yes, I realize that.

PERKINS   [*Feeling he has said something offensive is in a pitiable quandary. A pause*] I'm thinking of giving up the house and living on board, after this.

TOM   [*Surprised*] Why, I thought you liked the house.

PERKINS   I do, but—it's lonely.

TOM   What do you intend to do? Sell it?

PERKINS   Oh no, no, I couldn't do that.

TOM   Rent it?

PERKINS   No, no—you see—er—you see—I was—[*He stutters with confusion before* TOM's *steady look*] I just paid off the last of the mortgage a month ago.

TOM   Ah.

PERKINS   [*With satisfaction*] It's all mine now.

TOM   [*Not interested*] That's fine.

PERKINS   I was thinking that you—

TOM   What?

PERKINS   Might want to live here.

TOM   And if I did? Why should you live on board ship in that case?

PERKINS   [*Confused*] Well, you see, I—er—

TOM   Do you think I'd live way out here alone?

PERKINS   No, no, not alone.

TOM   Not alone?

PERKINS   You see—I thought—maybe—[*With a feeble attempt at slyness*] Mrs. Allen has been telling me all about it.

TOM   [*Frowning*] About what? What bit of gossip has the old witch got hold of now?

PERKINS   About—about—the girl.

TOM   What girl?

PERKINS   She said—name—was Olga.

TOM   [*Wonderingly*] The old witch! How did she ever hear of that?

PERKINS   She said young Dugan—

TOM   So he's the one, eh? I remember we've met him a couple of times. [*With a sudden laugh*] So you're willing that Olga and I should come here to live?

PERKINS   [*Beaming*] Yes, yes, of course!

TOM   But you'll preserve your sense of propriety by staying on the ship. [*In half-angry amusement*] If that isn't just like you!

PERKINS   I—I—I don't know what you mean.

TOM   [*With real gratitude*] At that, it's darn nice of you, father, and I want you to know I appreciate it, and Olga would, too. I never suspected you of being so broadminded. Thank you just the same; but Olga and I will stay where we are for the present.

PERKINS   You live—at the same place?

TOM   [*Perplexed in his turn*] Certainly.

PERKINS   Together? I mean—with her?

TOM   Why yes.

PERKINS   [*Eagerly*] Then you're married already! And you never told me! [*Joyfully*] I'm so glad to hear it, so glad—[*He stops in confusion at the look on Tom's face*]

TOM   [*Slowly*] Olga and I are not married.

PERKINS   [*Bewildered*] Not married?

TOM   No.

PERKINS   And you're living together—as man and wife!

TOM   Yes; as comrades.

PERKINS   But you are going to be married—you're intending—

TOM   No. Look here, what did Mrs. Allen tell you?

PERKINS   That you were keeping company—with a girl—named Olga.

TOM   That all?

PERKINS   Yes.

TOM   And I thought[—] [*Thoughtfully*] Now I see what the use of the house was to be—a wedding present. [*Looking at his father keenly*] Now you know the truth of it.

PERKINS   [*All at sea*] You're joking, aren't you, Tom? You wouldn't do that. Live with a girl—and not married. It's—it's wicked.

TOM   That's a matter of opinion.

PERKINS   But I can't see—It's not right, Tom. What if they heard of this at the office?

TOM   Damn the office!

PERKINS   [*Shocked*] Don't say that, Tom. [*Miserably*] I never thought you'd go around with that kind of girl.

TOM   [*Sternly*] She's the girl I love, and I respect her as much as I would my own mother if she were alive. That's enough for you to know, father. We won't talk about it any more—unless you want me to leave.

PERKINS   [*Abjectly cringing*] No, no, please don't go. I won't speak of it. Don't go! [*Obsessed by the idea*] That's what Mr. Griffin warned me of.

TOM   Eh?

PERKINS   He said you'd be getting into trouble.

TOM   Then you knew—? When did Griffin speak to you?

PERKINS   This morning.

TOM   Ah. What did he say?

PERKINS   He said you were keeping bad company.

TOM   [*Enraged*] The imbecile! Who did he mean by bad company?

PERKINS   Some friend of yours in the office who was discharged for being a member of the I.W.—the I.W.—

TOM   The I.W.E.?

PERKINS   Yes, that's it.

TOM   [*Grimly*] Did he say that I belonged to the I.W.E. too?

PERKINS   Oh, no, nothing as serious, as bad as that.

TOM   Well I do.

PERKINS   —You—what?

TOM   I am a member of the I.W.E.

PERKINS   [*Trying to force a smile*] You're trying to make fun of me now, I know.

TOM   I mean it. I'm serious.

PERKINS   But aren't they—don't they start strikes—and throw bombs—and blow up places with dynamite?

TOM They use force when force is used against them, when they have to.

PERKINS But you wouldn't do anything like that—I mean dynamite.

TOM Yes, I would. [*Looking keenly at his father*] If they asked me to dynamite the engines of the *San Francisco* tomorrow, I'd do it.

PERKINS Dynamite my engines! [*With surprising firmness and decision*] I'd never permit that.

TOM [*With a contemptuous smile*] How would you stop it?

PERKINS I don't know, but I would, somehow. [*Seeing Tom's smile*] Or the Chief would.

TOM Ah, I thought you'd wait for the Chief's orders.

PERKINS Of course you're joking. Who would ever think of such a thing.

TOM [*Easily*] Yes, I was only joking.

PERKINS [*Excitedly*] Dynamite the engines of a ship! Why, it would be a crime. No one but Anarchists or criminals would do such a thing.

TOM Don't get excited about it. It would be a good lesson to the rotten old Ocean Steamship Company if someone did something of the sort.

PERKINS [*Flushing*] I don't like to hear you speak of the Company so disrespectfully.

TOM [*Throwing his hands in the air*] Disrespectfully! Why, good heavens, that thieving Line is owned by the biggest financial bandits in Wall Street or in the country, and you ought to know it.

PERKINS [*Rising from his chair—tensely*] I know nothing of the kind.

TOM Then it's time you did. The sooner you do, the sooner you'll get over your servile fidelity to the Line and everyone connected with it. Don't you know that the Ocean Company is the head of the ship combine, and that the ship combine was organized by the greatest gang of crooked capitalists in the world?

PERKINS [*Breathing hard*] I know nothing of the kind.

TOM Don't you know that the seamen and firemen on their ships, and on your own ship, the *San Francisco*, are shamefully underpaid and overworked? That the Company will not listen to their just demands, but grinds them down and gives them no chance? Oh, but what's the use of talking to you? I tell you right now the Ocean Steamship Company is rotten from top to bottom.

PERKINS [*Bristling with indignant rage*] It's a lie. [TOM *looks at him in amused astonishment*] It's a lie! [*Sputtering*] How dare you say such things?

About the Company I have worked for for thirty years and never had a complaint to make.

TOM   And who have promoted men over your head time after time! A lot you have to be grateful to them for! Why you ought to hate them as—as much as I do.

PERKINS   [Commencing to wilt before Tom's contempt] No, no Tom, you're very wrong. It's my own fault I haven't been promoted. I haven't the ability and they know it.

TOM   You haven't got the pull behind you, that's the answer. Ability? You know twice as much about marine engines as the fleet engineer. I've heard him say so myself.

PERKINS   [Beaming for a second] Did he really say that? He must have been only joking. [Then worriedly] You're wrong to run down the Company, indeed you are. It's all this I.W.—whatever-their-name-is foolishness you've got in your head. [Anxiously] You mustn't go around with them any more. You mustn't belong to them. Supposing the Company should hear of it!

TOM   They have heard of it.

PERKINS   What!

TOM   [Slowly—letting the words sink in] Yes. They fired me this afternoon for just that.

PERKINS   [Staring wildly at TOM—aghast]   They—discharged—you?

TOM   I was fired this afternoon. So you see your warning is too late.

PERKINS   You've lost your position! [He crumples up into his chair]

TOM   I meant to tell you before. [With airy indifference] It's of so little importance I'd forgotten it.

PERKINS   [Half-aloud] They've discharged you! My son discharged in disgrace! After the thirty years I've worked for them! What will they think of me?

TOM   [With angry contempt] What will they think of you? I knew that was how you'd take it—the damned old Company before everything else in the world! [Disgustedly] Hell! [Rises to his feet]

PERKINS   [Hastily] I didn't mean that, Tom, not in that way. You don't understand. I was only thinking they might discharge me too, because—because—

TOM   Because I was your son, eh?

PERKINS   No, no, Tom, not that! I mean they might think I was connected with this I.W.—

TOM [*Scornfully*] Don't worry. There's no danger of their getting rid of so faithful a *servant*! They'd have a hard time finding another like you.

PERKINS [*Pitifully*] I know you think it's weak of me—I can't help it—Don't look at me that way, Tom. I wouldn't lose my position on the *San Francisco* for anything in the world. I love the work—and the ship—and the engines—I'm just beginning to know them.

TOM Bah!

PERKINS If you've lost your position, Tom, you must need money. Let me give you some, won't you?

TOM No.

PERKINS Let me help you, won't you? Let me loan you some. You can pay it back sometime.

TOM I don't want any more of the *Company's* money.

PERKINS Listen! If I went to them—I've worked faithfully for thirty years. They've never had a complaint to make of me—if I went and asked them—

TOM [*Frowning*] What?

PERKINS And you were to promise them to give up this I.W. foolishness—you're only a boy, you know—and you promised not to live with that woman any more—I think—I think—they might—

TOM [*In hard tones*] Take me back?

PERKINS Yes, yes, I'm almost sure. I'll see Mr. Griffin the first thing in the morning and I'll—

TOM And *you* advise me to do this?

PERKINS [*Faltering*] I think—I think—

TOM You advise me to cringe like a yellow mongrel and lick the boot which has kicked me out?

PERKINS [*Half-insane with nervous fear of everything*] I don't know—I don't know—You must go back to your position, really you must—I've dreamed so much—You'll be president of the Company some day—I've failed—You must succeed—Please, Tom, please go back! I know they'll take you if you'll only—

TOM [*With cold rage*] By God, I'm through! I've had enough of all this. I've tried to think of you as my father, tried to feel like a son toward you, but it's time to give up the pretence. You're in one world and I'm in another. We'd better say goodbye now while we still have some kindly feelings for each other. When the best you can advise your son is to become a cur, it's time to quit. Goodbye!

PERKINS   No, no, no! Please! You mustn't go, Tom, you mustn't leave me this way! I can't say goodbye to you! [*But* TOM *has gone out shutting the door behind him.* PERKINS *stares at the closed door in dumb anguish for a moment—then stumbles to chair and leans forward on the table, his head hidden in his arms*]

PERKINS   [*Sobbing wildly*] Tom! Tom!

THE CURTAIN FALLS

ACT THREE   SCENE ONE

SCENE: A *section of the firemen's forecastle on the* S.S. SAN FRANCISCO *at dock in Liverpool—two weeks or so later. Bunks, ranged three deep with a space of two and a half to three feet between them, occupy the rear and left walls. Over the upper tier of bunks in rear, several open portholes. In front of the bunks, low wooden benches. In under the lower tier a glimpse can be had of seachests, suit cases, etc. jammed in indiscriminately. In the middle of right wall, a door. On either side of it, more tiers of bunks. A row of steel stanchions extends down the middle of the room. Everything is steel, painted white, except the board floor.*

It is night. As the curtain rises, the ship's bell is heard ringing four bells.

A number of stokers are seated on the benches or lying in their bunks, the majority smoking clay pipes. Most of them are either stripped to the waist or in their undershirts, for the smoke-laden air in the forecastle on this August night is stiflingly hot. TOM *is seated in their midst, smoking a cigarette, staring moodily before him.*

O'ROURKE   [*A giant of a red-headed Irishman—knocking out his pipe—savagely to Tom*] Let them do somethin' and be quick about ut, and not be maikin' bloody fools av the lot av us.

TOM   They will, O'Rourke. Give them a chance.

O'ROURKE   A chance, is ut? Wid us sailin' tomorry and the rist av the ships durin' the week, and a new lot comin' in. [TOM *gets up impatiently and strides up and down the forecastle.*]

HARRIS   [*A tall, wiry, grey-headed man with round shoulders*] I think the whole damned thing's off, s'what I think.

TOM   I tell you it isn't, Harris. I tell you—

COCKY   [*Squat, broad-shouldered, pasty-faced—interrupting scornfully*] Tell 'im! That's wot you been tellin' us arll the parst week 'ere. I ain't seen nothink 'appen yet, I 'avent. [*Still more scornfully*] International Workers of the bleedin' world! Bloody swankers I calls the lot uv them.

TOM   [*Contemptuously*] Shut up, Cocky. The heat's bad enough without having to listen to your drivel.

COCKY   [*With injured indignation*] Gawd blimey! Listen to 'im! Carnt a man say wot 'e thinks?

O'ROURKE   [*Savagely*] Close yer big mout', ye little scut, or I'll close ut for ye.

COCKY   [*Whiningly*] Aw naw!

HARRIS   Just the same, Cocky's right. [*To* TOM] Ain't you been sayin' all week even if the union's gone back on us, this I.W.E. would help us out and start the strike?

TOM   Yes; and I still say it.

HARRIS   Well, it looks 's if the union is afraid to start anything, don't it?

TOM   Yes, damn them. It looks that way.

HARRIS   [*Rising to a climax*] Then where's the I.W.E. comin' in, that's what we wants to know?

TOM   There's still time for that.

SCHMIDT   [*A giant of a shock-headed German—spitting disgustedly*] Time? Mit one more night in port only?

TOM   [*With decision*] It'll be done tonight.

HARRIS   It? What's it? That's what we wants to know, Donovan.

TOM   You'll know soon enough. [*Evasively*] I'm waiting for someone now.

O'ROURKE   Divil take all this sneakin' business! Who is ut you're waitin' for?

TOM   I don't know exactly or I'd have told you—Whitely, probably.

O'ROURKE   [*Encouraged*] Whitely's a man that'd stop at nothin'. I know that, none betther. Betune the two av ye ye should be able to think av somethin'; but for the love av the saints be quick. The rest av us'll folly ye to the divil, if need be. [*A murmur of assent from the others*] Only, be quick wid ut. Wid only wan night more in Liverpool, there's little toime to be speech-maikin', and I'm not for puttin' up wid this dog's life wan day longer. [*Chorus of assent*]

TOM   [*Resolutely*] Look here, men, I've promised you if the union leaders failed you—

HARRIS   Well, they have, ain't they?

TOM   We're not absolutely sure yet. They've been weakening. Tonight's meeting of the officers of the union will decide whether they intend standing to their guns or not.

HARRIS   'N if they don't?

TOM   [*Firmly*] I'll act—we'll act immediately.

O'ROURKE   That's the talkin'

COCKY   But 'ow are we to know—abaht this 'ere meetin'?

TOM   Whitely's there. He'll be down to tell us what happened. He ought to be here any minute now.

O'ROURKE   [*Savagely*] Thin let thim go back on us for the black scuts av traithors they arr, and be damned to thim. We're men enough widout the say-so av the unions to show a thing or two to the ship's officers and teach thim to be swillin' their guts wid wine and champagne at the Company's dinner on shore, and us dyin' wid the heat and thirst in this stinkin' rat's hole. [*A chorus of angry growls*]

HARRIS   The Company thinks they'll be no strike. That's why they're givin' this rotten dinner on shore to the ship's officers.

TOM   Well, we'll show them they haven't got us whipped, and never can have as long as we're men enough to demand our rights. We'll hit them a blow they'll never forget.

HARRIS   How're you goin' to do it, 's what I want to know?

TOM   When the time comes you'll know.

O'ROURKE   No betther toime than this night wid no officers on board the auld hooker but the mate and the second engineer. And meanin' no disrespect to Molly Perkins he's nat the wan to sthop us if we once get starthed.

TOM   [*Easily*] We'll get the second engineer out of the way easy enough. He'll be too stunned to do anything.

O'ROURKE   He's a civil-spoken bit av a man, is the second, and I'd not loike to see him hurted.

TOM   I'll warn him in time. He won't bother us.

SCHMIDT   Ha ha! If he gets funny, dot leedle man, I will—[*Makes a gesture with his great hands as if he were breaking a stick across his knee*]

TOM   [*Promptly*] No, you won't, Schmidt! Remember that! Every man in this fo'castle has got to promise, no matter what happens, he won't touch the second engineer, or—you can all shift for yourselves as far as I'm concerned, or the I.W.E. either.

THE STOKERS   Aye—a dacint little man—Wouldn't hurt a fly, he wouldn't—Who'd wanta mash him?—Shut up, Dutch! etc. [SCHMIDT *is sullenly silent before this criticism.*]

O'ROURKE [*Walking over to* SCHMIDT *and laying a hand on his shoulder— fiercely*] Ye'll not lay a hand on him, me bucko!

SCHMIDT [*Defiantly*] Iss it you would stop me, was?

O'ROURKE The same—Red O'Rourke. Ye've guessed ut, Dutchy.

SCHMIDT I am not Dutch. I am German.

O'ROURKE 'Tis all the same breed av swine, I'm thinkin'. Kape this in your thick skull: If ye lay a finger on the little second engineer, ye deal wid me.

SCHMIDT [*Jumping to his feet*] I am not fraid of you or no Irish, py damn!

TOM [*Jumping in between the two men*] Here! Here! Stop this nonsense. What chance have you against the Company if you don't fight shoulder to shoulder and stop scrapping among yourselves. Don't you know that's just what the Company would like to see you do, you fools, you! [SCHMIDT *sulkily sits down again*]

O'ROURKE [*Walking back to his place*] I'll see ye again, Dutchy.

TOM [*Addressing the crowd—earnestly*] If you men want to win the big fight you'll have to put aside your private scraps. Remember if you don't work together, you're licked before you start. I thought Olga Tarnoff had impressed that on your minds at the meeting on shore the other night.

COCKY I 'eard 'er but it fair drove me balmy—sick of 'er silly jossin', I wuz—like one of them blushin' Suffrygette meetings, it wuz. Blimey if any female can stand jawin' at me. Let 'er be 'ome a-nursin' of 'er babies, I says. Men is men and—

O'ROURKE [*Stretching out a long arm and placing a big hand over* COCKY's *mouth.*] Will ye be still, ye insect? Or must I choke ye. 'Tis too hot entoirely to listen to your squawkin'.

TOM Never mind the fool, Red. [O'ROURKE *releases Cocky, who is about to continue his outburst when the sound of maudlin singing is heard. As it grows nearer the words can be distinguished*]

THE VOICE "Whiskey is the life of man
　　　　　Whiskey! O Johnny!"

O'ROURKE 'Tis Hogan comin' back wid his skin full av ale. I wish I had half av ut. Where'd he get the dough, I wonder.

HOGAN [*Appearing in the doorway—a stout, broad-shouldered man*]
　　　　　"Oh whiskey killed my poor aunt Ann.

Whiskey for my Johnny!"

[*He stands reeling and blinking in the doorway, holding a newspaper in one hand. The others look at him with broad grins*]

O'ROURKE   [*Genially*] Won't ye come in, ye drunken baboon?

HOGAN   [*Singing*] "Beer, beer, glorious beer!
     Fill yourselves right up to here."
[*Waving his newspaper*] War! War! Bloody war wid the Dutchmen comin'. 'Tis truth I'm tellin' ye. 'Tis here in black and white.

SCHMIDT   [*Getting up quickly*] Gif me dot baper. [*Snatches it out of Hogan's hand, and, sitting down, commences laboriously to pick out the words*]

HOGAN   [*Dazedly*] Aisy, aisy, me son. Ye'll know all about it soon enough. [*He hiccoughs*] When the British navy gets after ye. The war is not yet, the paper says, but 'tis apt to come any day if things kape on the way they are. [*Angrily*] Give me back that paper, ye Dutch swine! [*Lays his hand roughly on Schmidt's shoulder*]

SCHMIDT   Oud! [*Jumps to his feet and throws Hogan aside.* HOGAN *goes down in a heap*]

O'ROURKE   [*Fiercely*] Hit a helpless man, wud ye? [*He hits* SCHMIDT. *They grapple.* TOM *and the others rush in and pull them apart*]

HARRIS   No fightin' in the fo'castle. Out on the for'ard square if you wants to settle it.

THE OTHERS   [*Delighted at the prospect of seeing a fight*] Come out and settle it! See who's the better man! Out on the for'ard square! etc.

O'ROURKE   Will ye see who's the better man, Dutchy, or are ye a coward?

SCHMIDT   [*Raging*] Come oud! I show you! I show you! [*All crowd out the doorway except* TOM *and* HOGAN]

HOGAN   [*Weaving drunkenly toward his bunk—sings*] "We are the boys of Wexford" [*Speaks*] 'Tis my fight but no matther. I'm too drunk, God help me. [*Climbing into his bunk—philosophically*] No matther! O'Rourke will bate him. [*He falls asleep and is soon snoring.* TOM *walks up and down impatiently. A moment later* OLGA *enters. She is dressed in a dirty sweater and dungaree jumper, patched dungaree trousers, rough shoes, and has a cap pulled down over her eyes, hiding her hair. Her face and hands are grimed with dirt*]

OLGA   Tom!

TOM   [*In surprise*] Olga! [*Takes her in his arms and kisses her—pulls the cap from over her face*]

OLGA   Don't!

TOM   There's no one here.

OLGA   Where are they all?

TOM   [*Disgustedly*] Out on the for'ard square fighting as usual. But how do you happen to be here?

OLGA   Whitely sent me to warn you.

TOM   When did you see him?

OLGA   Not half an hour ago. He had just left the meeting of the union officers.

TOM   What happened at the meeting?

OLGA   [*Contemptuously*] Just what we expected. They decided not to declare the strike at present. Whitely says they have been bought off by the Companies, every one of them. He himself was offered money by one of the Companies' agents if he would go away for a time and stop his agitating.

TOM   The scoundrels!

OLGA   Whitely was wild with rage. He pleaded with them but they wouldn't listen. Finally he told them what he thought of them and resigned his office. [*With a smile*] They're not liable to forget what he said, I'll bet.

TOM   But didn't they offer some excuse?

OLGA   Traitors are always full of excuses. They crawled behind patriotism, said it wouldn't be right. [*Contemptuously*] Right! To call a strike now when beloved Britannia might become involved in a great war.

TOM   What hypocrites!

OLGA   [*Indignantly*] Whitely told them that now, above all times, was the moment to strike in all branches of organized labor and thus paralyze the sinews of war. They couldn't see it that way; or rather, with the Companies' money in their pockets, they decided not to see it.

TOM   [*Shaking his head*] It looks as if all this war talk would result in something this time.

OLGA   Oh, how can they be such idiots!

TOM   I've been thinking of what Hartmann said—that such a war would put back the cause of true liberty fifty years.

OLGA   There's no doubt of that. [*With deep feeling*] Oh, it can't happen. Men can't be such fools—after all they've been taught, all we've preached to them, all the Socialists have done—

TOM   You forget they've been taught patriotism at home, in government schools along with their first reader. It's in their hearts, as Hartmann said. You can't make them forget it by reasoning.

OLGA   You're right. [*Impulsively*] Ah, I'll bring up our child with a soul freed from all adorations of Gods and governments if I have to live alone on a mountain top to do it.

TOM   Our child?

OLGA   [*Avoiding his look—betraying confusion—hurriedly*] Why do you pick me up like that? You know I was only stating a supposition. [*Hurriedly*] You haven't asked me how I sneaked on board.

TOM   No need to. The master-at-arms on the gangway is one of us. Even if he'd recognized you he wouldn't have stopped you.

OLGA   But isn't my disguise good?

TOM   [*With a grin*] You look exactly like—like an adorable woman with a dirty face.

OLGA   [*Disappointedly*] Oh. [*But this time she allows herself to be kissed*]

TOM   [*After a pause*] Now that the unions have backed down it's up to us.

OLGA   Yes.

TOM   Did Whitely say anything about the dynamite?

OLGA   That's what he asked me to tell you—that he had gone to Sims' shop to get it and would be down immediately. He wanted you to be prepared.

TOM   [*Frowning*] Tonight's the best time, if it must be done. All the officers are on shore at that dinner the Company is giving. The curse of it is that the only engineer left on the boat is the very one—

OLGA   Your father?

TOM   Yes.

OLGA   He hasn't found out that you're on the boat?

TOM   No.

OLGA   You think he'll make trouble?

TOM   Not trouble in the sense you means. But he's sure to be pottering around in the engine room petting his engines, and—I'll have to explain, threaten, get him out of danger somehow. [*Irritably*] I wish it could have been some time when he wasn't on duty. I could use force if it was anyone else.

OLGA   There won't be anyone else in the engine room?

TOM   All the men are with us.

OLGA   Do you know anything about dynamite?

TOM   Only what Whitely has told me.

OLGA   [*With growing agitation*] Isn't it liable to go off prematurely sometimes?

TOM   I suppose so; but there isn't much danger of that as long as one is careful, Whitely says.

OLGA   As long as one is careful. You *will* be careful, won't you, dear?

TOM   [*Struck by her tone*] Of course I will.

OLGA   [*After a pause—with growing embarrassment*] Whitely said that he—don't you think it might be better—more sure—if Whitely were to do it?

TOM   [*Looks keenly at her for a moment—She turns away—slowly*] So you still think I'm a quitter, do you?

OLGA   No, no, it isn't that.

TOM   You must or you wouldn't propose such a thing.

OLGA   [*Lamely*] I was only thinking the results would be more certain if a man who knew all about dynamite—

TOM   [*Shortly*] I know enough for the purpose.

OLGA   [*Impulsively*] I wish you'd let him do it. I don't know why but I've a premonition, a fear—

TOM   [*Going to her and putting his hands on her shoulders, and looking into her eyes*] Olga, what's the matter? Tell me.

OLGA   [*Avoiding his look*] Nothing at all.

TOM   Yes, there is. Ever since we arrived in Liverpool you've been different, changed from the old Olga. What is it? Tell me.

OLGA   Nothing. It's only your imagination.

TOM   No, it isn't. [*Tenderly*] You know I love you.

OLGA   Yes, yes, you must!

TOM   And you love me, don't you?

OLGA   Yes, I do, I do!

TOM   Then tell me.

OLGA   I can't. There's nothing to tell.

TOM   Olga! In New York you would have scorned me if I had shown the slightest sign of shirking; and now you are advising me to—

OLGA   Conditions have changed since then.

TOM   What conditions?

OLGA   Oh, everything is different now.

TOM   How?

OLGA   [*Haltingly*] It doesn't seem—I don't think—[*Desperately*] I don't think it's going to do any good, this dynamiting. I don't believe it will have the effect Hartmann expected.

TOM   [*Quietly*] Why?

OLGA   [*Wildly*] Don't ask me so many questions. It's just what I think.

TOM   I should say the present conditions of things demanded drastic action on our part more than ever. We have this coming war to fight against now. The strike must be started.

OLGA   [*Trying to collect herself*] Yes, perhaps you're right. Then all the more reason for your letting Whitely do the dynamiting. It can't fail, then.

TOM   You know that's impossible. Whitely is well known. He'll be suspected as it is. He must be able to furnish an iron-clad alibi. You see it's impossible, don't you?

OLGA   [*Dully*] Yes.

TOM   And you know you'd despise me for a quitter if I gave up at this point. It's my duty. I've got to do it. [*Resolutely*] You needn't worry about my lack of ability. I know exactly what to do. [*To reassure her*] They'll never find out who did it—unless some of the men squeal on me.

OLGA   [*Sitting down on one of the benches—sadly*] Ah—*unless*!

TOM   they're real men, all of them. They won't squeal.

OLGA   I wouldn't trust them.

TOM   Even if it is known that I'm the one, the men only know me as Tom Donovan; and Whitely has arranged a hiding place where even the devil himself couldn't find me.

OLGA   But you'd never be able to come out. They'd always be looking for you.

TOM   [*Coming over to her*] What you've been saying doesn't sound like you at all, Olga. There *is* something the matter. Please tell me—like a good comrade.

OLGA   I've overtaxed my strength, I think. I feel—run down. That's all.

TOM   [*Tenderly*] Poor little girl.

OLGA   [*Wildly—breaaking away from him*] Don't pity me. I don't want pity. I want to be someplace all alone—and think.

TOM   When we get back we'll both take a trip into the country. I know a place—a farm in the Jersey hills—nice people—be glad to have us. We'll go there.

OLGA   [*Slowly giving way to the dream*] That would be wonderful. I feel as if I could lie for days in the cool grass, looking up at the sky—and dreaming. [*Coming back to the present with a start*] But you may never—[*Her eyes widen with horror*]

TOM   [*Putting his arm around her*] Olga, you mustn't have such thoughts.

OLGA   [*Half-sobbing, her head on his shoulder*] Tom, please let Whitely do it.

TOM   Olga!

OLGA   If you knew—if I could tell you—why I ask this—[*Regaining control of herself, walks up and down fighting down her emotion. TOM looks at her wonderingly. Finally she speaks quite calmly*] You're right. You're the only one who can do it. I've been making a fool of myself.

TOM   [*Cheerfully*] I'm glad you see it that way again. I couldn't quit. I've promised the men—and you would despise me later.

[WHITELY   *enters quietly and stands for a moment in the doorway looking at them. He is a swarthy, dark-eyed, bull-necked, powerfully-built man of about 35. He wears a black mustache and is dressed in a dirty suit of dungarees*]

OLGA   [*Seeing him*] Here's Whitely now.

TOM   [*Shaking hands with him*] I've heard the bad news.

WHITELY   [*His eyes flashing*] The yellow cowards! They sold themselves like the slaves they are—and I told them so. The meeting nearly broke up in a riot. Where are all the men?

TOM   Watching a fight in the for'ard square. O'Rourke and Schmidt are at it. I stopped them once but—[*He shrugs his shoulders*]

WHITELY   [*Grimly*] The war has commenced already, eh?

TOM   It can't last much longer. They'll be back soon.

WHITELY   Before they come back I've more bad news for you.

TOM   What?

WHITELY   There'll be no dynamiting.

OLGA   [*In spite of herself—joyfully*] Ah!

TOM   You mean?

WHITELY   Sims, the man in whose shop the stuff is hidden, has been arrested.

TOM   On suspicion?

WHITELY   I don't know whether it has anything to do with this affair or not. I didn't go around to learn particulars. I was afraid they might nab me. I went home and put on these clothes and slipped down here to tell you.

TOM   Then it's all off—the whole thing?

WHITELY   That part of it, at least.

TOM   And I had promised the men—What can we do?

WHITELY   If there was only some way to prevent the *San Francisco* from sailing tomorrow! If we could only start a little strike of our own on board this ship and keep her here, I know the crowd from the other ships would join in. It only needs a spark and the strike will spread everywhere—unions or no unions. Haven't you some influence with the men?

TOM   I did have.

WHITELY   You *did* have?

TOM   I've been losing it lately. They've been waiting for me to do something, and they're beginning to think it was all talk.

WHITELY   Then now is your time to show them.

TOM   Yes; but how?

WHITELY   How? Can't you think of something, man? You know a ship better than I do.

TOM   I'm trying to think.

WHITELY   If we can throw the *San Francisco* off her schedule—delay the mails. That will hit the Company hard. They stake their reputation on this ship. Think of the encouragement it will give to the men.

TOM   I've a plan, but it means mutiny.

WHITELY   What of it? So much the better. It means a fight and that's what we're looking for. It means the consolidation of the men under the International Workers, and the destruction of their petty unions. If you can only get this thing going here, I'll guarantee to keep it going.

TOM   [*Resolutely*] I'll do my best.

WHITELY   [*Enthusiastically*] Good!

OLGA   [*Apprehensively*] What are you going to do, Tom?

TOM   If I can get them to follow me, I'll prevent the ship from sailing on time all right. When the men come in I leave it to you to tell them the way the union leaders have betrayed them. If that doesn't make them fighting mad, then they've lost their spirit and there's nothing to be done.

WHITELY   I'll rouse them—by telling the truth—just what happened.

TOM   They're coming now. [*Noise of voices from without*]

WHITELY   Hadn't Olga better go ashore?

TOM   [*Turning to her*] Yes, Olga, I think you—

OLGA   [*Vehemently*] Why should I? They've heard me speak. They all know I'm their friend.

TOM   [*Protestingly*] But—

OLGA   [*Firmly*] I insist upon staying. [TOM *shrugs his shoulders helplessly*]

WHITELY   Oh, there's no harm, I suppose. [*The crowd of excited stokers pour in the doorway. In their admiring midst is the conqueror* O'ROURKE, *stripped to the waist, his face bloody, one eye closed, his swollen lips parted in a triumphant grin. Schmidt is not among them*]

COCKY   Gawd blimey, wot a swipe!

HARRIS   That last punch knocked him cold. [*All the stockers lower their voices and cease their admiring oaths when they see Olga and recognize her. She nods calmly from one to the other of them*]

O'ROURKE   Give me me shirt, ye scuts. Am I fit appearin' to be in the presence av a lady—[*With a comical glance at Olga's pants*] Aven if she is a man. [*One of the crowd hands him his shirt, which he puts on*]

TOM   Where's Schmidt?

HARRIS   The other Dutchies are pourin' water on him.

O'ROURKE   [*Jovially*] Down wid the Dutch and success to the British army—the Irish part av ut I mane.

TOM   Men, Whitely has just come from the meeting of the officers of your union. He wants to tell you what happened there.

COCKY   [*In a loud aside to the man next to him*] Glad it ain't one of them blarsted Suffrygette speeches we've got to 'ear. [*With a withering glance at Olga*] Wearin' of men's clothes naw.

O'ROURKE   Spake up, Whitely. We know it's the truth you'll be tellin' us.

WHITELY   [*Stands on one of the benches. The men crowd around him*] You all know me. [*Chorus of assent*] You know I've always fought my damndest for you whenever I've had the chance. The Companies have had me pinched, and they've tried to buy me off only a few weeks ago; but they've never been able to shut my mouth, and I'm still here fighting them.

O'ROURKE   Divil a lie, ye arr. Three cheers for Whitely, boys!

TOM [*Hurriedly interposing*] Not now, not now, O'Rourke! We've got to be quiet if we want to do anything.

WHITELY Donovan's right. We can't let them suspect there's anything up.

O'ROURKE Right ye arr, and I'm an auld fool. [*Gleefully*] If there's throuble comin', 'tis Red O'Rourke'll be in the midst av ut. [*All the stokers show pleased expectation*]

WHITELY I've just come from the meeting and I want to say this about the officers of the union, of which I was one before I resigned tonight—They're traitors to you, every rotten one of them! [*An angry growl from the crowd*] They've decided to let the Companies go on oppressing you without your saying a word. They've decided not to strike! [*A chorus of angry exclamations from the stokers*]

HARRIS And what reason do they give, s'what I wants to know.

WHITELY It's not the reason they give that counts. They say it isn't the right time to strike but they're liars and they know it. They know this is the grandest opportunity to get their rights the workers on the ships have ever had. Never before have you had the same chance of waging a successful war against the thieving ship corporations.

COCKY 'Ear! 'Ear!

O'ROURKE True for ye, thieves they arr, iviry divil's wan av thim.

WHITELY The officers of your union knew they were lying when they gave that excuse for not striking. It wasn't the real reason. The real reason was that every rotten one of them had some of the Company's dirty money in his pocket. They had sold you to the Companies. The Companies had bought every cowardly one of them—and I told them so! [*He is interrupted by a clamor of rage from all sides*]

O'ROURKE The dirthy blackguards!

HARRIS How do you know all this, Whitely?

WHITELY How do I know it? Because a week ago, when I was still an officer of your union, one of the agents of the Companies came to me and offered me one hundred pounds—five hundred dollars—if I would betray you. And do you know what I told him? I told him to go to hell! [*Expressions of enthusiastic approval from all sides*]

O'ROURKE That's the talkin'.

WHITELY But the others didn't tell him that—not them. They took the money and sold themselves, and all of you into the bargain. That's why I resigned tonight as an officer of your union. I wouldn't lower myself by being associated with such a pack of yellow curs.

COCKY   Dahn with the bleedin' swine, says I!

O'ROURKE   Let me catch wan av thim face to face. [*He brandishes his fists*]

WHITELY   Are you going to stand for this treatment?

ALL   No, no!

WHITELY   Then listen to Tom Donovan. He's one of you, a stoker himself. He represents the International Workers, the only organization true to the interests of the workers. He'll tell you what to do; and if you're real men with guts you'll follow him. [*He gets down amid acclamations.* TOM *gets up in his place*]

TOM   [*In determined tones*] Are you willing to follow me?

O'ROURKE   To the divil and back, me boy.

ALL   Yes, yes.

TOM   Then we'll start the strike here and teach them a lesson. If we just went ashore on strike they'd get a crew of scabs tomorrow morning and sail on time. We want to make the Company pay for the way they've treated us. We want to keep the *San Francisco* from sailing tomorrow.

O'ROURKE   [*In his element now*] We'll sink the auld scow.

TOM   I had a plan by which I alone was going to put the engines on the bum, but, through no fault of mine, the plan fell through. Now I've got to have your help. Will you help me?

ALL   Yes! Yes!

TOM   Then we'll go to the stokehold and get the men there to join us. We'll pull out the fires. We'll get splice bars and shovels and everything else that's handy. We'll go to the engine room and smash everything we can. We may not be able to do any permanent damage, but, by God, we'll keep the *San Francisco* from sailing tomorrow! [*A chorus of delighted approval*]

WHITELY   And I'll go to the other ships and get their men to join you.

TOM   Come on then, those of you who are with me.

O'ROURKE   We're all av us wid you! [*They crowd toward the door, waiting for Tom to lead the way.* OLGA *steps to his side*]

TOM   Where are you going, Olga?

OLGA   With you.

TOM   [*Sternly*] You can't!

OLGA   I must! [*She throws her arms about his neck*]

TOM   [*Kisses her*] It's impossible. Take her ashore, will you, Whitely? [*To the grinning stokers who stand waiting for him*] Come on! [*He goes out. The men crowd after him.* OLGA *covers her face with her hands. A sob shakes her shoulders*]

ONE OF THE LAST STOKERS   [*As he is going out the door*] It's easy. There's no one on watch but old Molly Perkins.

WHITELY   [*Gently—after a pause*] We'd better go, Olga.

END OF SCENE ONE

ACT THREE   SCENE TWO

SCENE: *The engine room of the* SAN FRANCISCO *facing the engines.* PERKINS *is discovered in his working clothes, his face and hands smeared with grease. He stands back, surveying the engines lovingly, humming a tune with a satisfied air. He comes forward and rubs off a speck of dust with the sleeve of his coat; then stands back and watches the oiler, Murphy, who is busy above.*

PERKINS   That will do, I guess, Murphy.

MURPHY   Yes, sir. [*He comes down and stands beside* PERKINS]

PERKINS   Everything look right to you, Murphy.

MURPHY   Right as rain, sir.

PERKINS   [*Rubbing his hands with satisfaction*] That's good, that's very good indeed.

MURPHY   Yes, sir.

PERKINS   [*His eyes taking in every detail of his pets*] Beauties, aren't they?

MURPHY   Fine engines, sir.

PERKINS   And old Henderson of the *Empress* tried to tell me that his were better—just imagine! You've worked on the *Empress*, haven't you, Murphy?

MURPHY   Yes, sir.

PERKINS   Well—er—hm—do you think her engines are as good as these?

MURPHY   [*Diplomatically*] Not on your life, sir. A regular, rattlin' bunch o' junk they are, it's the truth.

PERKINS   [*Pleased*] Oh come, Murphy, that's exaggeration, now, isn't it? They're very good engines, I'm told; but not as good as these. Haven't we beaten the *Empress* nearly every time? Isn't that proof enough, eh, Murphy?

MURPHY   Proof enough, yes sir.

PERKINS   I wish I could make Henderson see it. He's so pig-headed. [*A slight pause*] You might as well go, Murphy.

MURPHY   [*Gladly*] Thank you, sir. [*Prepares to go up*]

PERKINS   [*Uncertainly*] Er—hm—there isn't any trouble among the men, is there?

MURPHY   [*Closing up*] I don't know, sir.

PERKINS   Er—surely—hm—surely you wouldn't think of striking, would you, Murphy—I mean you seem satisfied.

MURPHY   It all depends on what the union says, sir.

PERKINS   Hmm—yes, yes, of course, the union. You—er—you don't belong to the I.W.—?

MURPHY   The I.W., sir? No, sir.

PERKINS   You know something about them, don't you?

MURPHY   Yes, sir.

PERKINS   Well—er—do you think a young man—say 22—would come to any harm belonging to them?

MURPHY   Couldn't say, sir.

PERKINS   [*With a troubled sigh*] I hope not, indeed I hope not. They say there's some of them been making speeches in Liverpool.

MURPHY   [*Cautiously*] Don't know, sir.

PERKINS   All right, Murphy, you can go. I'll stay here for awhile.

MURPHY   Good night, sir. [*He climbs up*]

PERKINS   Good night. [*He walks up and down the engine room with a troubled air. A moment later the clattering sound of running steps is heard on the iron stairs and* JACK, *an engineer's apprentice, hurries down to where* PERKINS *is standing. He is a shock-headed, freckle-faced youth, wildly excited and breathless*]

JACK   [*Breathlessly*] Mr.—Mr. Perkins! [*He gasps*]

PERKINS   [*With nervous solicitude*] There, there, get your breath. What under the sun brings you down here?

JACK   They're coming!

PERKINS   Who are coming? What do you mean? Have you had the nightmare?

JACK   N—no. I wasn't asleep. I was listening.

PERKINS   Listening?

JACK   Outside the door of the fo'castle.

PERKINS   What fo'castle?

JACK   The firemen's fo'castle. I heard everything they said, him and her.

PERKINS   Him? What him?

JACK   The one they call Donovan.

PERKINS   Did you say her? Do you mean there was a woman in the fo'castle?

JACK   Yes, sir.

PERKINS   You must have been dreaming.

JACK   No, I wasn't, sir, honest I wasn't. I saw her plain as anything— even if she was dressed up in men's clothes.

PERKINS   Dressed in men's clothes! Are you sure?

JACK   Yes, sir; I am, sir.

PERKINS   Why didn't the the man-at-arms stop her from getting on board? [Unable to believe] You're sure you saw her, Jack?

JACK   Yes, sir; and I know who she is too. I heard her make a speech last Wednesday. She's that I.W. woman who's been talking about striking.

PERKINS   [Frightened] I.W. woman!

JACK   Her and that Tom Donovan were talking while the men was out fighting on the for'ard square. I heard them talking about dynamite—

PERKINS   [Terrified] Dynamite!

JACK   The Chief told me to listen whenever I got a chance; and I was outside where no one could see me. They were talking about dynamite.

PERKINS   Good heavens!

JACK   Then another fellow came in and they all talked low, but I heard them say dynamite again.

PERKINS   [As if the name fascinated him] Dynamite!

JACK   Then all the stokers came back and the last fellow made a speech to them about the unions and strikes and things and they all got crazy mad.

PERKINS   Strikes! Unions! What are they going to do? [Helplessly] I wish the chief was here.

JACK   Then this Donovan fellow makes a speech and tells them to smash the engines—

PERKINS   [Indignation showing beneath his terror] Smash the engines! No, he couldn't have urged them to do that.

JACK   Yes, he did, sir. I heard him plain as can be.

PERKINS   That Donovan fellow must be a rascal.

JACK   Then they all rushed outa the fo'castle to get splice-bars and shovels in the stokehold, like Donovan told 'em, to smash everything with.

PERKINS   Smash the engines! [*He walks up and down*] No, no that's impossible. They wouldn't do that. [*Growing more and more indignant*] Only scoundrels would do such a thing.

JACK   Then I ran down here fast as I could to tell you. [*More and more excited*] They'll be down here in a few minutes, sir. You better look out.

PERKINS   [*In an agony of perplexity*] What shall I do? I do wish the Chief was here.

JACK   Probably they'll bring the dynamite with them.

PERKINS   [*Aghast*] Do you think they really mean to blow up the engines?

JACK   They're crazy mad, sir. They'd do anything.

PERKINS   Dynamite these engines! [*Resolutely*] No, I'll never permit them to do that. I couldn't. [*Miserably*] I wish the chief was here.

JACK   You better give them a wide berth, sir. They're fighting mad. You better go up on deck, sir, before they come.

PERKINS   [*Paying no attention*] Blow up those engines! [*His anger rising*] The blackguards!

JACK   [*Glancing around apprehensively*] Better hurry, sir, or it'll be too late. They'll be here soon. Come up on deck, sir.

PERKINS   [*Goes toward the stairs irresolutely, then stops, then resolutely*] No, I'll stay here. They mustn't harm the engines. I must see to that.

JACK   But how, sir?

PERKINS   [*Helplessly*] I don't know, yet. [*Bursting into rage*] The scoundrels. The scoundrels! Why can't they go on strike and leave the engines alone? [*Suddenly goes to his uniform coat, which hangs on one side and takes a revolver from the pocket and holds it in his hand gingerly*] The Chief told me to carry this, in case of trouble. [*Holding it out to Jack*] Is it loaded? I can't tell. I've never touched one of the things before.

JACK   [*Takes the revolver and breaks it—then hands it back*] Yes, sir, it's all loaded.

PERKINS   I might scare them off with this.

JACK   [*Astonished*] You're not going to wait here till they come, sir?

PERKINS   Yes, of course. I can't let them touch the engines, you know, can I? [*Furiously*] The scoundrels!

JACK   [*His eyes wide with surprised admiration*] Gee, you've got some nerve, sir.

PERKINS   You better run up and tell the mate to go ashore and get the police—and tell him to send someone to the Chief and ask what I better do.

JACK   [*Reluctantly*] They're crazy, sir; and it's a hundred to one against you.

PERKINS   [*Sharply*] Hurry now and do what I told you. [JACK *runs up the stairs.* PERKINS *looks wildly around, terrified at finding himself alone—takes up his stand with his back to the engines, his knees trembling, his expression one of hopeless indecision. A moment later a crowd of the stokers enter the engine room. Many of them carry shovels, steel bars, etc.*]

PERKINS   [*Weakly—the revolver hidden behind his back*] What do you men want here?

COCKY   Blimey, if it ain't old Molly Perkins.

HARRIS   [*Derisively*] What do *you* want down here, s'what we wants to know.

COCKY   Better sling yer 'ook aht of 'ere, Molly.

PERKINS   [*Dazed with terror at the threatening attitude of the crowd*] What do you want here?

HARRIS   We wants to repair yer engines for yer, that's what. [*A burst of laughter from the crowd*]

THE MEN   Tell him the air's better on deck
Push him outa the road!
Let's get to work!

COCKY   Yes, the blarsted hofficers'll be 'ere in 'arf a mo.

A VOICE   [*Angrily*] Fetch him a crack!

OTHER VOICES   Outa the way, Molly!
Git up on deck!
We don't wanta hurt you, Molly!
Where's Tom Donovan? He said he'd fix him.
Hell! Let's do something!
Where's Tom?

THE ANGRY VOICE   Kick the little runt outa the way! [*The crowd move threateningly toward* PERKINS]

PERKINS [*Protesting weakly*] Wait a minute, men. I want to say something to you.

THE ANGRY VOICE   Shut up!

OTHER VOICES   Let him talk if he wants to!
        Hurry up, Molly!
        To hell with him!
        Let's do something!
        No bloody speeches!

HARRIS   If yer got somethin' to say be quick about it; but I tells yer it ain't no use. We got a purpose in comin' here and we ain't goin' to weaken. [*To the crowd*] Are we, boys? [*A negative growl from the crowd*]

COCKY   'Urry, Molly, yer not standin' for Parliament.

PERKINS   Does—does this mean—you're on strike?

COCKY   Righto yer bloody well are, guv'nor.

HARRIS   That's what it means, Molly Perkins.

O'ROURKE   [*Coming in from behind and pushing through the crowd*] Lave me pass, ye scuts!

HARRIS   Where's Tom?

O'ROURKE   Pershuadin' some av the white-livered wans in the stokehold to jine the party. I was for mashin' in their faces but he said no. [*He stands in front of* PERKINS] Well if it ain't me auld friend, Molly Perkins. The top av the evenin' to ye, Molly. T'was to see ye were not hurted by these rough bhoys here Tom sent me ahead av him.

PERKINS   [*Pleading*] You're not going to harm the engines, are you, O'Rourke? [*A roar of angry laughter from the crowd*]

O'ROURKE   [*Winking at them*] Indade not; how cud ye think ut? We've been commishuned by the Company to mend them a bit. T'was thought they needed fixin'. [*Laughter from crowd*] And now, me little man, ye'd best be goin' up on deck to take a bit av fresh air. We've work to do, and 'tis no fit place for the loikes av you. [*Taking a step toward* PERKINS] Will ye go up on deck wid your own legs, or shall I carry ye?

PERKINS   [*Producing the revolver from behind his back—in a frenzy of fear*] Don't you—don't you touch me! [*The crowd shrink back involuntarily*]

HARRIS   Look out, Red, it might go off.

O'ROURKE   Put down that pisthol! It makes me nervous. Your hand is tremblin' so ye might pull the thrigger unbeknownst. I'll not touch ye yet awhile. [PERKINS *lowers the revolver*]

COCKY 'Ere's a bloody mess!

O'ROURKE [*Scratching his head*] What I'm to do, I dunno. Were it not for what Tom Donovan made us promise I'd not be afraid av that squirt gun av his.

A VOICE Here's Tom, now. [*They make way for Tom, who hurries through the crowd and confronts his father. He carries an iron bar on his shoulder. PERKINS looks at him as if he could not believe his eyes. His arm falls to his side. He seems to crumple up, grow small and pitiful*]

PERKINS Tom!

TOM [*Quietly*] You'd better go up on deck.

PERKINS Tom! Tom! Tom! Oh, who could think—[*He chokes with his emotion. The crowd murmurs: "Molly knows him!" etc.*]

TOM [*With quiet contempt*] You'd better go up on deck where you'll be safe; and give me that revolver. [*He reaches out his hand for it. PERKINS seems about to hand it over when one of the stokers reaches out with an iron bar and smashes the face of one of the steam gauges. PERKINS starts as if coming out of a dream, stiffens, a look of resolution coming into his face. He backs away from TOM*]

PERKINS [*Pointing his revolver in the direction of the man who smashed the gauge—in a firm voice*] Here, stop that! I can't permit that!

TOM [*Surprised*] Will you go up on deck, now?

PERKINS [*Firmly*] No, not until you have promised me not to touch the engines. [*Breaking down for a second*] Tom, how could you? What have I done to you?

TOM [*Coldly*] We won't discuss personal matters. I'm a stranger to you. I'm Tom Donovan.

PERKINS [*Horrified*] You—Donovan—that scoundrel. Don't talk like that, Tom—to me—please don't talk like that to me! [*The hand holding the revolver drops to his side. He is crushed*]

TOM I've urged these men to revenge their wrongs at the Company's hands and we're going to do it.

PERKINS No, no, I won't permit it! Not the engines! [*A threatening murmur from the crowd*]

HARRIS You've done your best to help him, Donovan. If he want to act foolish then let him take the consequences, 's what I say.

A VOICE Smash his damn head in!

TOM [*Whirling around—fiercely*] Who said that? [*No one answers— threateningly*] If anyone touches the second engineer—

THE VOICE [*Sneeringly*] Who is he—your old man?

TOM He *is* my father; and I won't have him touched!

PERKINS [*Wildly*] Tom! Tom! [*Murmurs of astonishment from the crowd; "Molly's his father! His name ain't Donovan. Maybe he's stallin'." etc.*]

O'ROURKE Ain't ut the divil's own luck now—wid all the other engineers we cud bate to a jelly!

TOM [*Pleadingly*] Please go up on deck, father.

PERKINS Will you promise—

TOM No. For the last time will you go up on deck or must I have you carried there by force?

PERKINS [*Weakening for a second*] Don't, Tom! Don't talk to me like that! [*The crowd push forward, jeering.* PERKINS *flushes with anger—points his revolver at the crowd*] Don't come too near, do you hear me! [*The men stop, awed by the resolution in his tones*]

TOM [*With angry contempt*] What rot! What will you do if they do come nearer?

PERKINS [*Bravely*] I'll shoot the first man who touches the engines.

TOM [*Looks at his father for a moment with wonder—then laughs mockingly*] Oh, you will? [*He steps carelessly toward the engines, gripping the iron bar with both hands*]

PERKINS [*Frenziedly*] Tom! Don't [*Lowers the revolver*]

TOM [*Pausing for a moment—laughs*] I knew you were only bluffing.

PERKINS [*Lifting the revolver again and pointing it in Tom's direction— in dead tones as if he didn't know what he was saying*] I'll shoot the first one who touches the engines.

TOM [*Laughing contemptuously*] Well, shoot then! [*With his iron bar he smashes the face of a gauge. There is a tinkle of glass followed by the report of a revolver. The expression on Tom's face turns to one of bewildered amazement. His knees sag and he pitches forward on his face and lies still*]

PERKINS [*Dully*] Stand back, or I'll shoot! [*The crowd push away from him in horror, saying to each other: "He's killed him! Dead as hell! His own son!"*]

A VOICE [*Loud with fear*] Let's get outa this! [*A sort of panic seizes the men. They rush from the engine room fighting with each other to be the first out.* O'ROURKE *alone stands his ground*]

O'ROURKE [*Looking down at Tom's body in horror*] He's hit in the head! [*To* PERKINS *in hoarse voice*] Ye've murdered him, I'm tellin' you! [OLGA *comes running down the ladder*]

PERKINS [*The revolver slips from his nerveless grasp and clatters on the floor. He looks down at Tom with eyes full of a dull amazement; then turns to* O'ROURKE *with an air of stupid bewilderment*] But I pointed it over his head, O'Rourke, I pointed it—over his head!

THE CURTAIN FALLS

ACT FOUR

SCENE: *A private room in a hospital in Liverpool—three weeks or so later. A dazzlingly-white, sunshiny room with a large, open, white-curtained window in the middle of left wall. Near the window, a rocking chair with cushions and a wicker table. In the rear, a white iron bed placed so that its occupant faces the audience. To the right of bed, a door. On the left of bed, a small stand with glass shelves on which are medicine bottles, glasses, etc. Two straight-backed chairs stand against the right wall.*

TOM *is discovered sitting in the rocking chair, gazing out of the window with listless, half-closed eyes. His head is bandaged and his face is pale and thin. He wears a light colored bathrobe over his pajamas, and slippers.*

A NURSE *is just finishing making up the bed. She is a short, stout, fresh-looking woman in her late thirties.*

THE NURSE [*Coming over to* TOM] You must go back to bed now, Mr. Donovan. [TOM *looks at her blankly but does not answer or move. The* NURSE *gives an irritated sigh.*] Bed! Bed! [*She points to the bed.*] Can't you understand? [*She puts her hand in under his arm. He gets out of the chair, slowly, mechanically, like a man in a dream. She supports him over to the bed, takes off his bathrobe and slippers, and tucks him in. He lies quietly, staring up at the ceiling. The* DOCTOR *enters. He is an elderly man with grey mustache and beard*]

THE DOCTOR Well? Any change?

THE NURSE No, Doctor, not a word out of him.

THE DOCTOR [*Looking keenly at Tom*] He seems much better, physically.

THE NURSE He's getting stronger all the time. He slept well last night and ate a hearty breakfast.

THE DOCTOR   Good! Any temperature?

THE NURSE   No, Doctor. 98.6 the last time I took it.

THE DOCTOR   Perfectly normal, then. He'll be able to leave us soon. That trepanning saved his life. [*Shakes his head sadly*] But I'm afraid his reason is gone.

THE NURSE   You don't think he'll ever be right in the head again?

THE DOCTOR   I'm afraid not—like a little child for the rest of his life.

THE NURSE   How awful! It would have been better if—[*She makes a suggestive gesture*]

THE DOCTOR   [*Solemnly*] You cannot set yourself against the laws of God and men without being punished. This is his punishment.

THE NURSE   And theirs?

THE DOCTOR   Theirs?

THE NURSE   All those who cared anything about him—his family.

THE DOCTOR   He doesn't seem to have any relatives alive. It's a pity. He might have been different if he had had the influence of a home. As it is, there's no trace of who he is or where he came from. He's one of those strange human strays one sometimes runs across.

THE NURSE   Didn't some say the engineer who shot him—was his father?

THE DOCTOR   Just a sensational fairy tale. It was absolutely discredited by the Ocean Company and by Mr. Perkins himself. Why, they're no more alike than—than you and I are.

THE NURSE   But the Anarchist woman whom they arrested and let go for lack of evidence—Olga something-or-other—She evidently cares about him. I was talking to her yesterday downstairs. She's been around every day to try and see him.

THE DOCTOR   [*Shrugging his shoulder*] She may care—in the way such people do. She was probably his mistress.

THE NURSE   She told me they were engaged to be married.

THE DOCTOR   [*With a yawn*] Perhaps they were; but I thought their tribe went in for free love. [*Suddenly*] Now that you remind me of it, she's waiting downstairs—she and that rascal, Whitely. I told her I might let her see him. [*Indicating* TOM] She might as well know his state first as last. I think I'll try an experiment. The sight of her might bring him back to himself. One can never tell in such cases. Will you go down and ask them to come up?

THE NURSE   Yes, Doctor. [*Goes out*]

THE DOCTOR [*Goes over and stands beside bed.* TOM *is still motionless, staring at the ceiling. The* DOCTOR *speaks in sharp tones*] San Francisco! Engine room! Olga! Strike! [TOM *does not move but turns and stares at the* DOCTOR *blankly*]

THE DOCTOR [*Turning away*] He's gone, poor chap! [*He goes to the window and stands looking out*]

THE NURSE [*Entering*] This way, please. [OLGA *enters followed by Whitely. Her face is weary and drawn, with dark circles in under the eyes. The* DOCTOR *turns around and watches keenly the scene which follows*]

OLGA Tom! [*She goes quickly to bed and leans over and kisses him, hiding her face on his shoulder*] Ah, how good it is to see you looking so well and your old self again—[TOM *pushes her away. He is staring at her blankly. She looks at his expressionless face in horror for a moment*] Tom! Tom! Speak to me! [*Dead silence. She continues in tones of anguish*] Tom! Don't you know me? I love you, Tom! It's Olga! Olga!

TOM [*Slowly—childishly mimicking her voice*] Olga! Olga! [*He turns his eyes away from her and stares at the ceiling. She shrinks away from the bed, hiding her face in her hands*]

THE DOCTOR [*With satisfaction*] Ah, he spoke. [*Comes over to bed*]

THE NURSE First words I've ever heard him say.

THE DOCTOR [*Studying* TOM *keenly*] He spoke; but it was only the mimicking of a child. There was no recognition, no intelligence behind the words. I'm afraid—[*Turns from the bed with a hopeless gesture*]

OLGA [*Taking her hands away from her face—to the* DOCTOR] So—this was what you meant when you said his health would return but he would never be the same again!

THE DOCTOR Yes.

OLGA [*In agonized tones*] Ah, why didn't you tell me?

THE DOCTOR [*Coldly*] I hoped you would understand.

OLGA And will he always be—like this?

THE DOCTOR [*Evidently voicing an opinion he does not feel*] Oh no, not necessarily. With care and the proper surroundings he will learn to speak again.

OLGA *Learn* to speak again!

THE DOCTOR He may even recover a part of his reason and memory.

OLGA You are saying things you don't believe.

THE DOCTOR   [*Sharply*] Don't jump at such hasty conclusions, Miss—er—Miss Tarnoff. The best of us are never absolutely sure in cases like this.

OLGA   [*Pinning him down*] But *you* don't think he will ever recover.

THE DOCTOR   [*Stiffly*] I must decline to answer such questions except to the immediate members of the man's family, if he has any.

OLGA   [*Fiercely*] I love him and he—*loved* me!

THE DOCTOR   [*Moved in spite of himself*] I understand from Miss Brown that you and he were engaged to be married?

OLGA   [*With a momentary show of hesitation*] Yes.

THE DOCTOR   Ah then, it is just as well to tell you that there is little hope for his reason—*but*—there is always a hope!

OLGA   [*Despairingly*] Oh!

THE DOCTOR   [*Looking at his watch*] I must be on my rounds. Perhaps if we leave the two of you alone with him—he knew you both well—it might—. We who are strangers to him may constitute an unfavorable influence. You might try to rouse some emotion, some memory [*To* NURSE] Come, Miss Brown. [*They go out.* WHITELY *moves over to window and looks out*]

OLGA   [*Going to the bedside*] Tom! [*His eyes fix on her face but there is no expression in them*] Tom, don't you remember me? [*She tries to kiss him, but he draws away from her with a frightened whimper—heartbrokenly*] Tom, don't you remember the happy days together—in our flat? And Hartmann? And Enwright? Surely you remember them! And the engine room on the *San Francisco*, and your father, and how you were shot? [*His eyes turn away from her face and he stares at the ceiling*] Tom! [*Her voice breaking*] Say you know me! I love you, Tom. It's Olga who is speaking to you! Olga! Olga!

TOM   [*Mimicking her childishly*] Olga! Olga!

OLGA   [*Turning from the bed—in a dead voice*] It's no use.

WHITELY   Shall I try?

OLGA   It's no use. Look at his eyes. They look at you and they don't see you. Oh, it's horrible! [*She shudders*]

WHITELY   [*Standing at the foot of the bed—in loud, commanding tones*] Look here, Tom, you haven't forgotten me, have you? [*A look of terror comes over Tom's face. He whimpers softly and draws the clothes up as if he were going to hide his head under them*]

OLGA   Stop, Whitely. He doesn't recognize you and your loud voice frightens him. See! He is going to hide his head in under the clothes. [*Tenderly*]

Just like a child, a little child. [*She goes and puts her hand on Tom's forehead. He immediately grows quiet*]

WHITELY   And to think of his being that way all his life! Good God!

OLGA   Don't! I can't bear to think of it.

WHITELY   Was it true, what you told the doctor—that he and you were engaged?

OLGA   No; we were just comrades.

WHITELY   I see.

OLGA   I had to tell them something which would give me a claim on him in their eyes. [*Bitterly*] That I love him doesn't count.

WHITELY   Then when he is able to be taken away, you—?

OLGA   I shall take care of him.

WHITELY   Are you able to?—I mean, financially.

OLGA   I have a little in the bank, the remnant of what my father left me. It will be enough to keep us for a time—till I get work. And I am sure the comrades in New York will do all they can to help, when they know.

WHITELY   But his father?

OLGA   [*Fiercely*] His father has no claim on him now.

WHITELY   He may not think so.

OLGA   No, the coward will be only too glad to get rid of such a living reproach. [*Scornfully*] The Company has promoted him, made him a chief engineer, presented him with a gold watch for his heroism!

WHITELY   Strange the papers didn't say more about Tom being his son. The must have heard. All the men knew it.

OLGA   His father denied it himself, and, then, I suppose, the Company had it hushed up for the hero's sake.

WHITELY   Yes, that must be it.

OLGA   [*Scornfully*] And then the papers gushed on about his sorrow! How he had hired a special room in the hospital for his victim! They would be sentimentalizing about it yet if the war hadn't broken out and given their silly patriotism an opportunity to slop over into pages of words.

WHITELY   It's just as well the *San Francisco* episode is forgotten. What a rotten fizzle it all was!

OLGA   [*Slowly*] Yes, a rotten fizzle.

WHITELY   And the attempted strike! What a fiasco!

OLGA   And now all your brave strikers are waving flags and singing "God save the King!"

WHITELY   [*Frowning*] This isn't an ordinary war, Olga. You can't condemn it on England's part.

OLGA   [*Looking at him searchingly for a moment*] You, too!

WHITELY   [*Flushing*] What do you mean?

OLGA   I mean that you are one of those Hartmann spoke of when he said that the ideal of the new freedom had interested their brains, but had not touched their hearts.

WHITELY   You're unjust, Olga. No one has fought for the I.W.E. more than I have or has suffered more for it!

OLGA   [*With a little sad smile—looking over at the bed*] Suffered?

WHITELY   [*Shame-facedly*] I had forgotten.

OLGA   Here we are arguing about war and the I.W.E.—as if we were alone. [*She goes over to bed and puts her hand on Tom's forehead*] Poor Tom! Forgotten already!

WHITELY   I wonder if his father is still on the *San Francisco*. She docks this morning.

OLGA   I suppose so. The papers said he wasn't to receive his new position till some boat they're overhauling gets out of dry dock [*She comes away from bed*]

WHITELY   He'll be up here, then.

OLGA   [*Fiercely*] I hope he does come. They told him before he left that Tom was sure to get well. They wanted to get rid of him. He'll know now how true his aim was.

WHITELY   You think he'll let you take Tom? He has the right, you know.

OLGA   He must! He must! Do you think I would let him have Tom after he has done his best to murder him? Never!

WHITELY   You might not be able to prevent it.

OLGA   He can't refuse when he knows—when I tell him—[*She stops abruptly with a frightened glance at* WHITELY]

WHITELY   [*Curiously*] What?

OLGA   Why it must be so.

WHITELY   This means giving up all your I.W.E. work, doesn't it?

OLGA   I will still do all I can. Even if it did mean giving up everything else in the world I would do it gladly. [*Proudly*] For I love him! He went to death or worse for me, not the I.W.E. I see that now. He was only a great big boy and he followed blindly where I led him. [*Choking with her emotion*] That is what makes it so hard. I realize it was all through me—this—all my fault. I owe him a lifetime of reparation.

WHITELY   [*Looking at* TOM *compassionately*] It's well he has someone, poor old chap!

OLGA   I had a foreboding of misfortune to him that night in the fo'castle. I had my moment of womanly weakness when, ideals or no ideals, I wanted to save the man I loved. I thought you were going to bring the dynamite, and I implored him to step out, to quit, as he said, and let you destroy the engines.

WHITELY   I wanted him to let me do it.

OLGA   I knew that; and I was afraid the dynamite would explode prematurely, or something of the sort.

WHITELY   [*With a grim smile*] It was perfectly right for me to blow up, eh?

OLGA   I was only thinking of saving him; I didn't care how. But he wouldn't. He thought I would despise him if he failed in his mission.

WHITELY   And you would have—afterwards.

OLGA   You don't understand. I love him.

THE NURSE   [*Knocks and enters—looks from one to the other*] He hasn't recognized you?

OLGA   No.

THE NURSE   The engineer, Perkins, is coming up.

OLGA   [*Fiercely*] Ah!

WHITELY   Then I'll be going.

OLGA   And I'll stay.

WHITELY   I'll come back for you in, say, a quarter of an hour, Olga?

OLGA   Yes. [WHITELY *goes out*] Has the Doctor told him about Tom?

THE NURSE   Yes. He's all broken up, poor little man, but he insisted on seeing him. [*The* NURSE *indicates* TOM] He told the doctor that it was true what they were saying—that this really is his son.

OLGA   Ah. [PERKINS *enters accompanied by the* DOCTOR. PERKINS *is bowed down by grief. He is sobbing and holds a handkerchief to his eyes*]

THE DOCTOR   See if he knows you.

PERKINS [*At the foot of bed—faintly*] Tom [*Then louder*] Tom! [TOM *turns his eyes and looks at his father blankly, without recognition.* PERKINS *puts the handkerchief to his eyes and turns away*]

THE DOCTOR [*Shaking his head*] Not a gleam of recognition. [*Turning to* OLGA] You were unsuccessful?

OLGA Yes.

THE DOCTOR [*To* PERKINS] You know Miss—er—Miss Tarnoff, the fiancée of your son?

PERKINS [*Looking at* OLGA—*timidly*] Is this—Olga?

OLGA [*Coldly*] Yes.

PERKINS And you and Tom—were to be—married?

OLGA Yes. [*To the* DOCTOR] Would you mind leaving Mr. Perkins and myself alone for a few minutes? I have something to say to him. And we might [*Indicating the form in the bed*] try again together.

THE DOCTOR [*With a shrug of his shoulders at the uselessness of such efforts*] Certainly. [*He and the* NURSE *go out*]

PERKINS [*Nervously*] Something—to say—to me?

OLGA [*In hard tones*] So you finally acknowledged he is your son? I should think you would have kept on denying it, as you started out to do.

PERKINS It was for his sake—I denied it before. I was afraid—when he got well that it would hurt his chances—having people know what he had done.

OLGA And what you had done. [*A pause*] Well? Are you satisfied?

PERKINS Satisfied?

OLGA Satisfied with your work by which you earned promotion?

PERKINS [*Wildly*] Don't, Miss Olga, please! If you knew how I have suffered since they told me. They said before I went away that Tom would be all right—and I believed them, really I did, or I wouldn't have made the trip. And now—[*Raises handkerchief to his eyes*]

OLGA [*Cruelly*] Your aim was better than you thought.

PERKINS Aim? [*Brokenly*] I couldn't aim. I never had one of those things in my hand before, really I didn't; and I pointed it over his head. I never meant to fire. I meant to scare them—and then—it went off. [*Seeing the incredulous look on Olga's face*] Oh, how can you think such a thing—that I could mean to shoot—Tom? He was the only one in the world I loved, the only one left to me—

OLGA [*With cruel enjoyment of his anguish*] You have your engines.

PERKINS   Don't! I hate them, now. I have ever since. I will always hate them. It's all changed, now.

OLGA   When it's too late.

PERKINS   I pointed it over his head! I didn't mean to fire—I swear I didn't. [Sobbing] Oh, why can't someone believe me? Nobody does. They say yes but I feel they don't. Why don't you believe me?

OLGA   It doesn't matter much now whether you meant to fire or not. It's done—and it can't be undone!

PERKINS   But the doctor said, with good care—there was hope.

OLGA   He say that but he knows it isn't so. There is no hope. Tom will be like that, like a child, for the rest of his life.

PERKINS   [With an apprehensive glance at the bed] Sshh! He may hear you.

OLGA   [Slowly] You forget—he can hear nothing now.

PERKINS   No, no, it can't be true! [Going to bed—pitifully] Tom! Tom! [But Tom's eyes are now closed]

OLGA   [Going over to bed quickly] Sshh! He is asleep! [They both lower their voices for the moment and come over by the window]

OLGA   The doctor says he is getting stronger every day—physically. He will soon be able to leave.

PERKINS   Yes; he told me, too.

OLGA   [With a defiant look at Perkins] I shall take him out in the country some place where no one knows us—

PERKINS   [Angrily] You—you will take him!

OLGA   Yes.

PERKINS   Take him—away from me!

OLGA   Yes. You must realize that you have forfeited all right by—what you did.

PERKINS   No! No!

OLGA   And you will be on ship. How could you look after him?

PERKINS   I am leaving—the Company.

OLGA   You have not accepted the promotion?

PERKINS   No.

OLGA   What will you do?

PERKINS I don't know. I hate the engines. I can't work with them any more.

OLGA [*With a frightened expression*] Then you're going to live on shore?

PERKINS Yes; in the house I meant for him. I resolved on this during the last trip—when I found I hated the engines. They've promised me a position on shore.

OLGA And you mean to take him with you.

PERKINS Yes. I have Mrs. Allen—

OLGA He hated her.

PERKINS —to keep house for me, and she will help to take care of him.

OLGA And I?

PERKINS You? [*With a burst of angry grief*] I wish he had never seen you. You are to blame for everything. It was you who got him in with the dynamite people. It was you who drove him to lead those men on strike. It's all your fault, all your fault!

OLGA [*Defiantly*] I love him.

PERKINS And don't his own father love him?

OLGA You shot him!

PERKINS [*Wildly*] I pointed it over his head! It was only to scare them. Oh, why can't anyone believe me? He was all I had to live for. You are young and I am over sixty. He is all I have in the world. I won't let you take him!

OLGA You must! He loved me, and not you.

PERKINS [*Wildly*] It's a lie, a wicked lie! He did! He did! He was only a boy—and thoughtless—and you led him away from me—

OLGA [*Relentlessly*]If he could choose, he would come with me. You know it.

PERKINS It's a lie, a lie! You can't have him. They know I'm his father. They won't let you have him.

OLGA [*Realizing the truth of this—pleadingly*] I will forget all—I will forgive all you have done to make my life miserable if you will let me take him.

PERKINS [*Touched in spite of himself*] No, I can't. What would I have left to live for alone—with the memory of him. I couldn't stand it.

OLGA I implore you, if you love him. You know he loved me. He must have told you.

PERKINS [*In a whisper*] Yes. He told me—once.

OLGA   You know it would be his wish to be with me if he could speak.

PERKINS   You don't know what you're asking. You would rob me—of everything. I must bring him back to himself so he can forgive me. I must make up to him—for what I have done—as far as possible.

OLGA   I owe him reparation too, for my sin against him. You were right—when you said it was my fault—as well as yours.

PERKINS   Ah, you admit it!

OLGA   He did follow where I led, but, oh, I never thought—I didn't realize the danger to him till it was too late. I didn't realize he was doing it only for me. [Pleadingly] So you see I have my debt to pay back, my forgiveness to win. Let him come with me!

PERKINS   No! It's impossible. You have no money, have you?

OLGA   I will work!

PERKINS   And no home of your own?

OLGA   I will make one for him!

PERKINS   You see? It's impossible. How would he get proper care? Who would look after him?

OLGA   [Wildly—begging] Please, Mr. Perkins! You love him, you say; and you know he loved me. I cannot live without him. Would you kill me, too?

PERKINS   [Affected—raising the handkerchief to his eyes] It is too much for you to ask, Miss Olga. Haven't you any pity for me? No! He has met harm through being with you.

OLGA   [Furiously] You dare to say that to me! And you shot him! Shot your own son in cold blood! Murderer! Murderer!

PERKINS   [Faintly] No, no! Not that name! I can't bear it! [Sobbing] Won't you believe me? I pointed it over his head.

OLGA   And not content with killing him, you will kill his child!

PERKINS   [Stupidly] His child? What child?

OLGA   The child I will bear which is his, your son's. If you do not let me have Tom, I will kill it, I will never allow it to be born. I will kill my child as you have yours! [She leans against the table, nearly fainting]

PERKINS   [Trembling] Dear God! You are going to have a child?—Tom's child? Did he know this before—

OLGA   No—unless he guessed—that last night on the San Francisco—I tried to make him understand—why I had changed so—grown so weak and tender toward him—

PERKINS [As if he didn't yet understand] My Tom's child!

OLGA [Pleadingly] Yes! The child of our love. You will not take its father away from me, will you? You cannot be as bad, as hard-hearted as that.

PERKINS [After a pause—hesitatingly] Do you—hate me so very much?

OLGA I will hate you from the bottom of my soul if you take him away from me. But I will forgive you everything—I will even love you as his father if you will let me take care of him.

PERKINS [Slowly] I have hated you too, God forgive me, because I thought—you were to blame. [A slight pause] If I let you have him—will you bring him to my home—and live there—with me?

OLGA Live—in your home?

PERKINS No one will ever know you were not married. We will say you were married over here.

OLGA Your home! No, I couldn't, I couldn't.

PERKINS You have no place to take him, you know—and I have the home I meant for him—for his wedding present. It will be his home and his child's. He has a right to come there—and you—

OLGA Give me time—to think.

PERKINS You have no money and you will not be able to work—soon. Who will take care of you and Tom—and the child—then? Please let me do it. It is my right, isn't it? When Tom knows—when he is in his right mind again—he might forgive—

OLGA [With deep sorrow] He will never be himself again!

PERKINS [Obstinately] The doctor said there was still a hope—with good care. I will work on shore or on the ship—anything for him—and I won't bother you much if I am on ship. And Mrs. Allen will take care of you when—

OLGA Oh, this is good of you—but—

PERKINS Please consent—if you don't hate me—too much. You are his wife, really. I know he loved you, and would have married you—if—if it wasn't for what I did. [OLGA is silent—simply] It is settled, then. When he's strong enough we'll take him home together.

OLGA [Holding out her hand to Perkins] I am very grateful—and I know you love him—and I know you didn't mean—what happened.

PERKINS [*Taking her hand—humbly*] Thank you so for believing that. You're the only one. [*He gulps*]

OLGA We'll take good care of him together, you and I, and we'll fight for that one hope the doctor held out. Who knows? It may be a real hope, after all.

PERKINS And do you think—when he gets back his mind—and knows—he'll forgive me?

OLGA I'm sure he will forgive—both of us.

PERKINS I do hope and pray so, I do, indeed. [*As an afterthought*] And when he's all right again, you can be married, can't you? [OLGA *doesn't answer—* TOM *stirs in the bed and opens his eyes.*]

PERKINS Look! He's awake again. He's looking at us. [*They both go to the side of the bed*]

OLGA [*Tenderly*] Poor little child! [TOM *reaches up and takes one of her hands*] See! He's taken my hand. [TOM *holds his other hand out toward his father*] He wants to take yours. [PERKINS *puts his hand in Tom's. He and* OLGA *look at each other in wonder across the bed*]

PERKINS [*In stifled tones*] Tom! [*To* OLGA] Do you suppose—he understands?

OLGA Yes, I feel sure he does.

PERKINS Then—he has forgiven me.

OLGA He has forgiven us. [TOM *lets both of their hands go and turns his eyes again to the ceiling*]

PERKINS [*Dabbing at his eyes with his handkerchief*] I must go and tell the doctor what we have decided—if you'll excuse me. He wanted to know what arrangements I would make.

OLGA Yes, you'd better tell him.

PERKINS I'll be right back, right back. [*He goes to the door. In the doorway he nearly collides with* WHITELY, *who enters as* PERKINS *goes out*]

WHITELY [*In a state of great excitement—pointing to the newspaper in his hand*] See what they've done now!

OLGA Who?

WHITELY The Germans—dropped bombs on an orphan asylum and killed twenty children! [*Then exultantly*] But they've paid for it, the swine! The Russians have beaten them in a big battle in East Prussia.

OLGA [*Amazed*] And *you* are rejoicing over a *Russian* victory!

WHITELY [*Abashed*] Anything to beat *them*.

OLGA [*Scornfully*] You'll enlist next.

WHITELY [*Flushing angrily*] By God, if they keep on doing things like this—[*Slapping the newspaper*] I *will* enlist! And so will every other red-blooded man.

OLGA [*With quiet scorn*] Don't you know these stories are written just to make people like you enlist?

WHITELY [*Insisting*] But this is true—vouched for by a person who was in the town and saw it! [*A faint sound of music*] Ssshh! Listen! [*The strains of a far-off marching tune come through the open window. Whitely's face lights up*] Troops! Off for the front! [*He hums the tune, beating time with his foot*]

OLGA Poor sheep!

WHITELY You'd understand—if it was your country engaged.

OLGA Liberty—that is my country.

WHITELY Can't you see that these swine must be crushed, or—it's a case of eat or be eaten. The country must be defended.

OLGA Every soldier in each one of the nations at war was called to arms to defend his country.

WHITELY [*Lamely*] Our case is—well, it's right, you can't deny it.

OLGA And each one thinks that. [*A pause*] So, as far as you are concerned, the social revolution can take care of itself, now when it needs you most!

WHITELY It's no time for it now. What's the use? Who would listen to you? This is the upheaval of everything.

OLGA You might be true to our ideals. We have preached against war always.

WHITELY This is different, Olga. This is just a war, a war forced upon us.

OLGA And each one of them thinks the same, poor fools!

WHITELY [*Angrily*] How about most of the great Radical leaders? Socialist, Syndicalist, or Anarchist, here and in France and Russia? Haven't they all realized that this was no time to quibble over theories.

OLGA Theories!

WHITELY Kropotkin, the great Communist? Hasn't he come out and said it was the duty of every man, no matter what he believes, to crush German militarism? I tell you we've got to back up the government until this war is won; and they're all doing it—Socialists, Syndicalists and all of them.

OLGA   Then they are all blind fools—or traitors.

WHITELY   [Irritably] I can't talk to you. You won't see. [After a pause, brutally] I shouldn't think you'd care much about the social revolution—now!

OLGA   [Slowly] You mean—after it has ruined my life? [WHITELY nods, a bit ashamed of what he has said. OLGA's eyes flash] Oh, you fool! You blind fool! What am I? What is my small happiness worth in the light of so great a struggle? We fight, and at times like the present, it seems hopelessly. We fight and we go down before the might of Society; but the Revolution marches on over our bodies. It moves forward though we may not see it. We are the bridge. Our sacrifice is never in vain. It is enough for us to know we are doing our small part, and that our little lives and little deaths count after all. No, let the others wave flags and cheer and forswear their faith. [Proudly] I have suffered and will suffer more than any of them; and I am proud that I can still cry from the depths of my soul: It is well done! Long live the Revolution! [She stands proudly, erect, inspired, exalted. WHITELY is awed in spite of himself. And then—]

TOM   [With a low, chuckling laugh—mimicking OLGA] Long—live—the Revolution. [His vacant eyes turn from one to the other of them. A stupid smile plays about his loose lips. WHITELY turns away with a shudder. OLGA stares at the figure in the bed with fascinated horror—then covers her face with her hands as

THE CURTAIN FALLS

The Reckoning *and* The Guilty One

The scenario *The Reckoning* and the four-act play *The Guilty One* together comprise the strangest item in the O'Neill canon. The scenario, written by O'Neill at Provincetown in 1917, is a melodramatic exploration into the problems of a forced marriage that gives in to jingoistic exultation at the thought of the United States entering World War I. Because *The Reckoning* was written according to the mechanical precepts of George Pierce Baker at a time when O'Neill had already defined a highly individual style with *Before Breakfast, Ile,* and the plays of the *S.S. Glencairn* series, his interest in a contrived narrative based on trumped-up emotional reactions, theatrically "thrilling" confrontations, and motivations and actions that fall far outside the range of human probability is hard to understand, especially since just ahead lay *Beyond the Horizon,* the play that was to establish him in the professional theatre.

O'Neill in 1917 was showing some impatience with the one-act play form, and perhaps the scenario was written with an eye on more professional productions than the Village theatres offered. In outline at least, *The Reckoning* is cut from the same cloth as many routine Broadway melodramas from the "Showshop" O'Neill professed to despise. Aspects of its narrative bear some resemblance to the work of Edward Sheldon, the fair-haired boy of Baker's 47 Workshop who a few years earlier had leaped from Baker to Broadway and whose success was the envy of many aspiring playwrights. *The Reckoning's* tale of the rise to political prominence of an unlikely individual had precedence in Sheldon's *The High Road* and *The Nigger,* and the climax of the latter play, wherein a politician at a crisis in his career finds a personal dilemma clouding his decision, is paralleled in the scenario.

At best, *The Reckoning* is a feeble imitation of Sheldon's plays, but it has interest as an example of the mundane scene with which O'Neill occasionally concerned himself as he sought out his true concerns and style as a writer. By nature, O'Neill was a theatrical poet, but no poetry is to be found in *The Reckoning,* nor is there here any sign of the theme of "belonging" to some larger force of nature that would lead O'Neill to his theological dramas of the 1920s. Later, in the encased, domestic environment of *Strange Interlude,* the soliloquies would enable O'Neill to open the domestic world inward and provide it with poetic and philosophical resonance. *The Reckoning* attempts no such expansion. The characters are closed in a domestic vacuum. The only horizon open to them is the war, but the young radical, who two years earlier had written understandingly of the anarchist's antiwar position in *The Personal Equation,* takes a remarkably prowar stance at the end of the scenario. In all respects, *The Reckoning* is a play without vision.

What perhaps interested O'Neill at the outset—autobiographer that he was—was the situation of a man forced to marry a woman he did not love because he had made her pregnant. His own first marriage forced on him by the pregnancy of Kathleen Jenkins was one from which he fled as far as Honduras, ultimately to return and go through the requisite formality of being found in bed with a woman so that a divorce, based on adultery, could be arranged. O'Neill's divorce, however, had been completed in 1911, and although perhaps he felt some remembered bitterness at having to undergo so shabby an ordeal, the theatrical development of the opening situation of the scenario, involving seeming murder and marital blackmail, is at a far remove from any true autobiographical significance.[1] It was a work well forgotten.

The difficulty, and in the end the interest of The Reckoning is that it was not forgotten. In 1924, apparently at her husband's urging, Agnes Boulton O'Neill undertook to develop the scenario as a play she called The Guilty One and copyrighted under the pseudonym of Elinor Rand. At the time, O'Neill had recently finished All God's Chillun Got Wings and Desire Under the Elms and was at work on The Great God Brown, Marco Millions, and Strange Interlude. He was deeply involved with Kenneth Macgowan and Robert Edmond Jones in The Experimental Theatre, Inc., which was committed to staging exhibits of the so-called New Stagecraft at the Provincetown Playhouse and the Greenwich Village theatres. Everything pointed to an energetic forward movement, to idealistic theatrical innovation—to anything but the trivialities of The Reckoning.

The O'Neills had recently moved to Bermuda and Agnes was pregnant with Oona. She was restless and bored and sought diversion in various social activities. O'Neill, consumed with his writing and resentful of the interruptions from what he felt to be casual social intercourse, appears to have tried to bring Agnes into the quiet circle of his own creativity. At one time, she had sold stories to pulp magazines with minor success. Early in their marriage, O'Neill had borrowed ideas from her, for example her story "The Captain's Walk," from which he derived Where the Cross is Made. In his letters he often urged her to develop a creative life compatible with his own. Whatever his motivation, in Bermuda he brought The Reckoning out of his files and gave it to her to work over. They discussed it, and O'Neill read her development and revised some of the dialogue.[2] The presumption, however, is that most of the replotting and the dialogue is hers, not his.

The play, like the scenario, concerns a rough laborer who has made a strong-willed country girl pregnant, who refuses to marry her, but who is led by the girl to think he has killed her stepfather. By threatening to reveal his "guilt," she forces him into marriage and, throughout their life together, drives him with blackmail to succeed in his career—in the scenario as a distinguished senator with power to swing the vote in the Senate so as to assure America's entry into the war, in the play as an industrial millionaire. Both climax in the revelation of the truth and grope their ways to sentimental endings.

Although it is more elaborate, the action and characterization of the play are not essentially different from those of the scenario. Since by 1924 America's entrance into the war could no longer be used as a plot device, the last two acts of the scenario required complete revision. The first acts, however, held to the scenario's plan, smoothing and simplifying the exits and entrances but adding nothing new.

1. Both Louis Sheaffer and Virginia Floyd suggest autobiographical elements in the scenario. Cf. Sheaffer, Eugene O'Neill, Son and Artist, pp. 147–48, and Floyd, Eugene O'Neill at Work (New York: Frederick Ungar, 1981), pp. xxiii–xxv.
2. Cf. Floyd, Eugene O'Neill at Work, p. 85.

In the revision of acts 3 and 4, the political scene was supplanted by a view of life in a millionaire's home, and a considerable change was made in the character of the son, Jud, and the ingenue, Mildred. In the scenario, the son is an all-American patriot and the ingenue comes simpering from the stockpile of trite heroines. In the play, he is turned to a roistering playboy on the verge of becoming alcoholic. She is carrying his child but has hidden the fact from him and rejects him as a suitor because of his conduct. Her plan is to leave, have the child, and disappear from the family's life. The situation is evidently intended to parallel the opening scenes wherein Jud's mother, Cora, also pregnant, tries to force his father to marry her. Comment is made on the difference in women in 1900 and in 1924, but little is proved by Mildred's "noble" conduct.

As in the scenario, the play concentrates on the relationship between Cora, her husband, James, and Cora's stepfather, Stephen, the man James thinks he has killed. Cora convinces James that he has in fact murdered Stephen and that the police are seeking him. She uses his false guilt as a weapon to force him into marriage and to follow her dictates as to the course of his life thereafter, causing him to rise in the business world rather than to go freely where he chooses. Both treatments end with the curious ethical view that what Cora has done—lying, cheating, blackmailing her husband—is somewhat admirable, or at least to be understood and accepted. As Agnes O'Neill has it with her feminist bias, the guilty one is not the woman, but the man who, in the play's final speech, cries "No. Forgive me! I've been the guilty one! You've given me everything. . . ." It is a conclusion acceptable only in a theatre designed to elicit soft whimpers from a matinee audience.

The most interesting motif in the play is one that lies a little apart from the authors' central concerns and perhaps veers close to a problem O'Neill may have felt at the time. James is an unambitious man, one who drinks too much, works little, and prefers to be on the road as a kind of tramp rather than to settle down in a suburban house with a job and a family. Yet he has in him a talent for organizing and running a business. (In the scenario he is said to have some talent as an inventor.) With this ability, he could go far, but he rejects it in favor of a free life, without responsibility, without roots, without any sort of personal obligation. In the middle 1920s, O'Neill was caught in a dilemma that was somewhat similar. The freedom of his days at sea and in the dubious liberty he knew in the saloons and flophouses are not very different from the rough freedom James appears to value. O'Neill was drinking to excess, and the domestic world troubled him with its demands for attention. It may well have seemed to him that there was a conflict between the sickening nirvana of alcohol and the compulsion to succeed as an author. Writing won out and he avoided alcohol for most of the rest of his life, but as work progressed on *The Guilty One*, he may have shared the feeling of the male protagonist, who is trapped by marriage and the potential for success.

Whatever contribution O'Neill made to the finished script, *The Guilty One* remains Agnes's play, not only in its concluding decision that the woman has been innocent because she has not been loved, but in the concerns shown for the excessive drinking of the men and the domestic life of the elegant house (revealed in the inventory taken by Mildred in act 3: "One 15th century Spanish desk . . . Two Italian chairs . . . One Ming Vase . . .") The shift of the scene from New England to Agnes's home territory, New Jersey, suggests her control of the play, as do the extravagantly impossible emotional reactions, as when Mildred in the play's final scene "grows crimson" and eight words later "pales." If more evidence of Agnes's hand were needed, it can be found in the novelistic stage directions such as

She stares ahead of her, hopelessly alone for a moment among her ruins—The woman of power and will, who has hesitated at nothing to gain her way—which she thought would be the right way—at last is broken, vanquished. Her shoulders sag. She slowly opens her hands, as though to let life and love drop from them—and closes them with the same slow gesture of despair. (p. 142)

O'Neill's interest in the play was minimal. In an entry in his Work Diary for January 10, 1925, he notes his work on "A's 'Guilty One' today—read three acts—but no interest. Last 2 acts very bad—need reconstructing." They apparently were revised because on February 14 he indicates that he "went over last 2 rewritten acts of A's and my 'Guilty One' which she is rushing to get off to Brady."

"Brady" was the producer, William A. Brady, whose daughter Alice was to create the role of Lavinia in *Mourning Becomes Electra*. He was never one who stood for more than a conservative, fiscally secure and routine production, a trait that may have interested him in *The Guilty One*. A series of letters and telegrams from O'Neill's agent Richard Madden to Agnes, dated between March and May 1925, reveal that Brady optioned the play, asked for revisions and a new title, and was in Madden's words "all aquiver" to see the new script. The extent of the revisions, other than O'Neill's mention of the need he felt that acts three and four be reworked, cannot be determined. In the end, Brady did not like the revisions and delayed plans for production until the interest of all parties quivered and died.[3]

Yet something of the scenario remained drifting in O'Neill's mind. Later in his career, O'Neill turned away from the experimental poetic theatre that had characterized his work through the 1920s, plays that were concerned with questions of man's faith and the nature of God. Thereafter he studied men and women who were confined to lives passed in domestic cells that formed a narrow arena where endless battles were waged for dominance. There one individual sought to stave off destruction by destroying another and to avoid being possessed by possessing. The last play of his projected cycle, *A Tale of Possessors, Self-dispossessed*, was to be called *A Hair of the Dog*. It developed from a play O'Neill began shortly after completing *Days Without End* in 1934 entitled *The Life of Bessie Bowen*. In *The Reckoning* the character Cora of the play was named Bessie, and her stepfather was a blacksmith. The later Bessie Bowen came from a similar world, a bicycle shop. Like the earlier Bessie, Bessie Bowen was to rise from lower-class beginnings to a position of power as an automobile magnate. In her ascent, she would ruin the lives of the men around her, as the women of *More Stately Mansions* and *The Calms of Capricorn* would prove to be destroyers of their men. Bessie's husband was to be an inventor of genius who refused to enter her world of thrust and parry, much as Bessie's lover in the scenario tries to reject his forced rise in the world. In the cycle, the end of the struggle was suicide, murder, or madness. In *The Reckoning* and *The Guilty One*, the woman's power over her husband, although melodramatically monstrous, is not viewed as a destructive force, nor has it any symbolic dimension. The resolution of both treatments in a theatrically "happy" ending, based on forgiveness, reconciliation, and hope for the future, will find no place in the cycle. To that dark work, the scenario and the play provide only shadowy antecedents.

3. The correspondence is in the American Literature Collection at the Beinecke Library, Yale University. Madden also mentions another play by Agnes titled "Little Hope." It featured a live horse on stage.

The Reckoning

SCENE: The interior of a small blacksmith's shop in the village of Hillvale, Ohio. It is late afternoon of a holiday in the spring of the year 1890.

CHARACTERS OF ACT ONE

Stephen Donohue, "Big Steve," the blacksmith
Bessie Small, his step-daughter
Jack Gardner, his helper in the shop

Bessie Small is discovered. She shows by her uneasiness, her air of irritated expectancy, that she is waiting for someone. Presently Jack Gardner enters. He is flushed and excited, shows that he has been drinking. She complains of this— he is half an hour late—she had had to wait an hour for him the night before. He tries to laugh it off—kisses her. She softens for a moment—asks him with keen anxiety if he thinks Ed Harris recognized them the night before when he met them in the dark out by his barn. If he did he will surely tell Donohue and the latter will raise the devil. Jack replies boastfully that he doesn't care whether Harris recognized them or not. He isn't afraid of Big Steve or any other man. Bessie asks him imploringly if he still loves her. He laughs and answers carelessly that of course he does. He loves them all. Bessie grows angry. Accuses him of going around with other girls—particularly one Alice. He becomes ugly. Sure he likes Alice. Alice is pretty. She isn't bawling and bothering a fellow all the time. Yes he was with her last night. That was why he was late. What about it? Bessie becomes weak and pitiful. Implores him not to throw her down. Finally tells him that she is pregnant. He is angry and scornful. A fine lie. She's just saying that to hold him. Maybe she thinks he will marry her? Not him. He wants it understood once and for all that he isn't the marrying kind. She can't tie him down to a wife and brats. Even if she is pregnant, how does he know it's his fault? He's heard some queer stories about her affairs before she met him. Bessie hotly denies this—all lies of the village gossips. Jack becomes jovial again. He doesn't want to quarrel on a holiday. He doesn't care whether the stories are true or not. She had a right to her fun; only let her remember that he has a right to his fun too, and he's not in on any marriage game. Isn't he taking her to the dance that night? That ought to satisfy her. Now he's going to get a drink. She can wait here for him. He promises to be back in a moment. He goes out. Bessie breaks down and sobs.

A moment later Donohue enters. The boys are playing quoits in back of the saloon and he has come to get some horseshoes. He is in an ugly mood and is half drunk. Asks Bessie what she is doing there. Wasn't it Jack he saw leaving the place just a moment before? She's got to stop her damn nonsense with that lad. Not because he gives a damn for her but he married her mother and she's got to stop shaming him in the eyes of the village. Everyone is talking about her. Ed Harris told him a pretty story about seeing them out by his barn the night before. Is it true? Bessie grow defiant. Yes, it's true. Donohue tries to force her to tell whether Jack is really her lover or not. She won't tell. He says if he suspected any such thing he'd damn soon make Jack marry her or know the reason why. He'd have Jack run out of the town on a rail if he didn't. Bessie shows that this threat has caused a plan to form in her head. She sees a chance of making Jack marry her. She pretends to break down and confesses to her step-father that Jack is indeed her lover and that she is pregnant. Donohue is furious. Jack will have to make her his wife, that's all there is to it.

Jack enters. The extra drinks he has taken have had an appreciable effect. Donohue immediately confronts him with Bessie's confession—tells him he will have to marry her and at once. Jack laughs defiantly. So that's their game, is it? Well, he won't marry her and that's certain. He'll show them he can't be forced into anything like that. Donohue and he engage in a furious brawl. Finally Big Steve tries to hit him. They clinch. As they struggle Donohue grabs up a hammer and tries to crown Jack with it. Jack takes it away from him after a hard battle and in a fit of drunken anger hits Donohue on the head with it. Big Steve goes down and lies motionless. Bessie shrieks and throws herself beside the prostrate man. Jack stands looking down, sobered by what he has done, and scared out of his wits. Bessie tries to bring the old man around but he seems dead. They both think he is. Jack doesn't know which way to turn. Bessie tells him he must run away immediately. But how? Then he remembers. He will go down to the freight yards and hide until dark when the freight goes out. Then he will hop it and go where ever it goes. She tells him she will write to him to G[eneral] D[elivery], Chicago as soon as it is safe to do so. In the meantime she will try to cover up the crime by saying that the old man was drunk and fell striking his head on the anvil. As soon as she can she will come and meet him in Chicago—she will let him know in her letter about that. But she will have to write to an assumed name. Let him keep his own first name and add the one of the people on the hill—Cockran. She will write to Jack Cockran and come and tell him everything in Chi[cago] as soon as she can without incurring suspicion. Jack is very grateful to her, calls her a brick, kisses her, says he will never forget. She implores him to hurry and make his get-away. It's luck it's a holiday and there won't be anyone down at the yards at this time. He leaves.

After he has gone she bends down beside the old man again—feels of his head—finally gets some water and throws it on his face—Donohue groans and comes to. He gets unsteadily to his feet—is still in a fighting rage—where is that damn cub that hit him? He'll smash the daylights out of him. He pushes her aside and rushes out to try and settle his account with Jack as the curtain falls.

SCENE TWO

A small bedroom of a cheap lodging house in Chicago—evening of a day about a month later. Jack enters, followed by Bessie. He is carrying her bag. He looks pale and drawn as if he had been through a period of nerve-wracking anxiety. He no sooner closes the door and locks it behind them than he asks her in a tense whisper for news of the old man. She lies to him—tells him that the old man died without ever regaining consciousness. Jack is prostrated by the news—thinks himself a murderer—tells her that he cannot stand suffering the pangs he does from his guilty conscience—says hopelessly that he knows it is useless to try to flee from the law which is bound to get him in the end. He might just as well go and give himself up. Life, as he has been enduring it, is not worth living anyway. She hastens to reassure him and get this idea out of his head. Although he was under great suspicion at first, she had done much to allay this by her story of the old man's drunken fall against the anvil. They still suspect Jack and if he were to dare to come back to the town again he would undoubtedly be apprehended, but as long as he stays away she thinks that the whole thing will blow over in time. He must stick to his assumed name and go to some other town far away to settle down—some New England foundry town, prefer-ably, where he can easily get a job. Also he must change his way of life, give up drinking, etc. He replies that he has already done this—that he has sworn never to take a drink again—that he will try and make a model life a partial reparation for his crime. She tells him he is a fool to suffer from the pangs of conscience. The old man was about to hit him—it was all in self-defense. Of course, it would be hard to convince people of this. Donohue was old and he is young. But she is the only one who could tell the real story to convict him and she is not likely to do so unless—. Unless what, he asks. She means if he will do the fair thing by her, her lips will be sealed forever. She is pregnant. Is he going to marry her or not? She swears that he is the father of the child. He groans and tells her that he does not love her—never has. He loved Alice. This infuriates her and she says that it is up to him to choose. If he will not act right, she will tell all she knows, even if she has to implicate herself to do so. What does life mean to her but disgrace if he won't marry her? She wouldn't care what happened. Very evidently frightened by her threat, he tells her that he had intended asking her to marry him anyway without any threats. He is deeply grateful for all she has done for him. All he wanted was that she should understand beforehand that he does not love her and that, although they will live before the eyes of the world as man and wife, he is determined not to renew a connection with her which he will always feel to be a guilty one, and which he blames for all his misfortunes. Under these conditions he will marry her. Otherwise, she may go and have him arrested. Bessie accepts this proposition gladly. She puts her arms around his neck and says intensely: "But you will love me! I'll make you!" as

THE CURTAIN FALLS

CHARACTERS OF ACT TWO

John Cockran.
Elizabeth Cockran, his wife
Jack, their son, aged nine
Mathew Lathrop, a partner of Cockran's
Brigadier General Isaiah King, G. A. R.
Jim O'Brien, Democratic Boss of the District
Stephen Donohue
A maid at the Cockrans'

SCENE: The living room of John Cockran's home in a large manufacturing town in New England, ten years later. Cockran, Lathrop, King, and O'Brien are discovered. Lathrop, backed up by the other two, is vainly endeavoring to obtain Cockran's consent to run for Congress on the Democratic ticket in the coming election. He rehearses Cockran's virtues as a candidate and by so doing reveals the life and achievements of John during the past ten years. Starting as a common mill-hand he had rapidly risen to be a foreman, then superintendent of the mill, and finally when the growing business caused the Company to expand, he had been taken in as a partner in their tool manufacturing plant. Once a partner, he had insisted, against Lathrop's judgment, in making theirs a model mill, in taking a deep personal interest in the welfare of their employees, in raising their wages, recognizing their union, and in many different ways earning their respect and gratitude. He is a solid certainty with the labor vote of the district as a consequence. Also he represents the monied mill-owners class and will have their backing. Then again, his home life is a model. His wife is noted for her charitable works. Both he and she are deeply religious. In fact, Lathrop declares, it will be a walk-over for him if he will only run. The others are equally confident that a glorious political career is open for him if he will accept the opportunity. And they need him to represent the industry in Congress.

But Cockran seems obstinately opposed to their plan. He appears to be having a great inward struggle with himself, to want to accept but have [sic] a strong inward reason which prevents him. He tells them that he is unwilling to give up his quiet home life for the glare and ceaseless activity of politics. He says that he is content as he is. His life is wrapped up in the development of the mill. The others finally leave him in disappointment and disgust—all but O'Brien, who says he has seen many a good man change his mind at the last moment. He will wait for Cockran's final answer until that night. Let him think it over in the meantime, and get some sense in his head, and telephone to him later. Cockran promises he will but holds out no hope to them of his changing his mind. They go out.

Mrs. Cockran enters. Her attitude toward her husband is one of humbleness and timidity—his toward her one of cold hostility. She ventures to remark about the request of the men who have just left. She has inadvertently heard part of their conversation in the next room where she had been sewing. Her husband listens to her with a frown—tells her brusquely not to meddle in his affairs but to remember the agreement she made when she forced him to marry her—that their lives should remain separate and their interests never interfere with one another. She is crushed by his cold indifference but lingers pitifully, remarking vaguely that for the sake of their son he ought to accept this chance. Their interests must be identical where little Jack is concerned. He interrupts her sternly by saying that *he* will attend to their son's future; then dismisses the subject by telling her that he must go to the mill on business. He goes out.

Little Jack runs in. There is a scene between him and his mother in which her great love for her boy is shown—a love in which her whole life is now centered.

The maid enters. She tells Mrs. C. that an old man is at the back door to see her. He has a card to her from the Aid Society, who thought Mrs. C. might be able to get him a position or help him in some way. He seemed sort of half-witted the maid explains. She hands her mistress the card. Mrs. C. reads aloud: Stephen Donohue! She tries to conceal her terror and amazement from the maid. At first she says she will not see him but, noting the maid's surprise, resolves to brave it out, and tells her to show him in. Then she sends Jack away to play.

Alone, Mrs. C. shows the tremendous effort she is making to steel herself to face her step-father. Finally the maid shows him in. He has grown bowed and old in the intervening ten years. His hands shake, his eyes have a vague, frightened, half-witted expression. He stands blinking at Mrs. C., who faces him tensely. Gradually a puzzled look of recognition comes over his face. He murmurs uncertainly "Bess" and approaches her. She replies coldly in a trembling voice that he must be mistaken. The blank look comes over his face again. He stops short, mumbling apologies. She looks like a daughter he once had— a step-daughter, he says. Seizing her advantage, with a great show of relief at his uncertainty, she quickly asks him what he wants. He needs help, she understands. Just what is his case and what can she do for him? He tells her about his once being a good blacksmith; but he was hit on the head in a quarrel and his wits seem to have been addled ever since. His daughter ran away. He lost his shop—the drink. Since then he has wandered here and there over the country, sometimes a tramp, sometimes working at odd jobs, but always poor. He isn't any good for work any more. Since that scoundrel hit him, a weakness is on him. If he could only meet that fellow again he'd be satisfied. He'd kill him if it was the last thing he ever did, yes, even if he had to hang for it. He grows wild, takes out a knife and shows it to her, describes the horrible vengeance he will take if he ever sees her husband again.

This subject is evidently a mania with him. Mrs. C. shudders with fear and horror and tries to get done with him and get him out of the way as soon as possible. What does he want to do? What can he do, he asks, growing calm again, a poor, broken old man? If only he had the money for passage he'd realize a dream he'd always had to go back to Ireland again and end his days in peace. Mrs. C. jumps at this chance. It opens up a way for her to get rid of this living evidence of the lie on which she had built her life. Also it is a way for her to get this half-mad man away from seeing her husband. She is frightened by the danger the latter will be in with this man with his craze for murder in the same town with him, liable at any time to meet and recognize him. She immediately offers to get the old man his passage to Ireland—tells him his ticket will be left for him at The Aid Society—Boston to Queenstown. The ticket will be there the next day. He can leave on the first steamer. She gives him a little money and promises to send him more to the boat. Donohue is overcome and tearful with gratitude. She tells him he must not return to her house in the meantime. She is going away. As he leaves, his sense of recognition comes back to him again. He bellows furiously: "Bess" and lifts his hand in a rage as if to strike her. But immediately he is all apologies again as he sees her shrinking away from him in terror. She will excuse a poor, half-crazy old man, he hopes; and may the good God bless her for her charity to him! He goes out.

Left alone, Mrs. C. breaks down and sobs with grief from the strain she has been under. Her little son runs in—asks her what is the matter. She evades answering him—finally asks him if he wouldn't like to see his father a great man in the United States. "President?" he asks. "Yes, perhaps even that," she answers and, as Jack shows his delight over such an idea, the light of a great resolution comes over her face.

Cockran returns. He has forgotten some important papers. Mrs. C. asks if she can talk to him alone for a moment. He frowns, but grudgingly consents. Jack is sent away. She then pleads with Cockran to accept the nomination which has been offered to him. He owes it to himself, to his son, she asserts.

Cockran is bitterly scornful. Of course, he would like to accept for his own sake as well as his son's. He feels he could accomplish a lot of good if elected. He has tried to make his life one of retribution for his crime, a life of service to others, and he knows that this would give him new opportunities for doing good. But she knows as well as he does that he cannot accept, and why. With the light of publicity focused on him someone would be sure to find out what he was—a murderer. And then—Jack's life would be ruined as well as his own.

Mrs. C. argues with him. It is all right. She is certain he will never be recognized. It was all so long ago. But he refuses to be convinced. He is palpably afraid. Several times during their talk she seems on the point of confessing her lie, of setting him free—but the thought of what will happen to her own life if she does so, each time prevents her. He is so cold and hostile. He hates her and would cast her off. She would lose him and little Jack—everything. She cannot do it. And yet, in the face of his obstinate refusals, she is determined to force him to go out and achieve every success. She feels she must partly make up for her lie by compelling him to live his life, even in spite of himself.

He grows angry and says there is nothing more to be said. He will not accept. Then she adopts another tack. She pretends to grow furious at his refusal. She deliberately threatens him. If he will not do as she asks, she will leave him and take her son with her. She knows well his love for their boy, his plans for his son's future. She will take him away and never let him see his father again. Jack is young. She will make him forget he ever had a father. And he, Cockran, will not dare to oppose her. If he does she will tell the truth about him. She will say that she has been afraid to confess it all these years on account of his threats of vengeance against her if she does.

He is crushed by her vindictiveness. He is convinced she means what she says. His idea of her has never changed since she forced him to marry her. He believes her to be absolutely unscrupulous and cruel. He sees but one way out— to shield his son as much as he can from this disgrace—to brave it out and take his chance of being recognized. He promises her to accept as she demands of him—for Jack's sake. But he will never speak to her again except when people are by—for form's sake. In future she is dead to him—a fiend of a woman who has ruined his life and whom he hates from the bottom of his soul. But he will only give in to her on one condition—that she will agree that their son's future will be left entirely to him. She must give up all claim on his life. Cockran says with horror that he is afraid of the influence of such a wicked woman on his son's life. The boy is old enough to be sent away from school. He must be sent there, away from her, as soon as possible.

Her point gained, she consents dully to all his demands

as

THE CURTAIN FALLS

CHARACTERS OF ACT THREE

Senator John Cockran
Elizabeth Cockran, his wife
Jack, their son
Mrs. Lathrop, wife of Cockran's partner
Harriet Lathrop, her daughter, fiancée of Jack's
Brigadier-General Isaiah King, G. A. R., father of Mrs. Lathrop
Albert Simms, secretary of Cockran's
Servants, etc.

SCENE: Library of Cockran's house in Washington D.C. in early April of 1917—morning. Simms is discovered working over some papers at a table. General King enters. He and Simms talk about the imminence of a declaration of war with Germany. Of course, King is rabidly pro-war and condemns in unmeasured terms the small body of senators who are trying to hold up the declaration in the Senate. Simms says that it won't matter. When Cockran makes his big speech as administration leader in favor of the war, all the opposition will wither away. King is enthusiastic about Cockran's patriotism and about the man himself. He speaks about how popular Cockran is with all classes, his wonderful success as a prop of the party, first during his years as Congressman, and afterward when he was elected by popular vote to the Senate, etc.

King has an appointment with the Senator, who is upstairs resting before going to the Senate to make his big speech. He and Simms go out together.

Jack and Harriet—(she and her mother are guests at the Cockran's)—enter. Jack is looking for Simms. He wants to find out the time when his father is due to speak because he and Harriet intend to go there to hear him. They sit down to wait. There is a love scene between them. Then Jack broaches the subject of the war which now seems certain. He does so doubtfully as if afraid Harriet would not care for what he tells her. He intends to enlist—in the aviation service, if he can, as soon as he hears that war is declared. Does she mind very much? He sees it as a duty he owes to the country and to himself. Harriet is overcome but controls her feelings and tells him bravely that he would not be the man she loves if he did not do as he intends. In a crisis like the present one she, whose ancestors fought in the Revolution, whose grandfather was a general in the Civil War, feels she would be small and mean to let her personal feelings interfere with what his duty to his country dictates. No, she will prove to him she will stand by him in whatever he does by going to the recruiting office with him herself. Finally, carried away by their growing enthusiasm they agree, since the war is a certainty, that they will go down together that very day instead of going to the Senate to hear his father speak as they had intended.

She asks him what his parents will think when they find out. Jack knows that his father will be proud; but of what his mother will think he is not so sure. He has never heard her express any opinion about the coming war. He even doubts if she knows or cares about it. Her life as long as he can remember has been strangely separated from any interests of his father's. She has appeared to take no interest in the affairs of the outside world, to be completely wrapped up in the business of running the household. After all, in spite of the great love he has for her, he really knows very little about his mother. He was sent away to school when he was so young. In summer he went to camps where his father came to see him but his mother never. Then after that there was college, and when he did come home for vacations, the house was always crowded with guests, and his father was continually encouraging him to make trips abroad, etc., to go out and see the world. No, when he comes to think of it, he really knows very little of his mother. But he does not doubt that she will bear up bravely when he convinces her that he is only doing his duty as he sees it.

Harriet is not so sure. She has sensed the tremendous love his mother has for Jack. She feels that she is very jealous of his being engaged to be married, that she even has a feeling of hatred for her, Harriet. Jack laughs at this. That would be too impossible.

Mrs. Lathrop enters. After a short conversation Jack and Harriet go to the billiard room to pass the time while they are waiting for the Senator.

A moment later Mrs. Cockran enters. She has aged greatly, her hair is now white. Her manner is furtive and timid. She seems to be always attempting to shrink into a corner, to avoid being seen or talked to. When she sees Mrs. Lathrop she appears about to run away but Mrs. L. notices her and makes her sit down. Mrs. L. is evidently inspired by great curiosity rather than by any liking for Mrs. Cockran. She commences to talk about the war—how horrible it will be if the U.S. becomes embroiled. She knows from her father's tales of his experiences in the Civil War how terrible it is. People have no idea, etc. There will have to be a draft, she has heard. All the young men will be taken whether they want to go or not. At this, Mrs. Cockran displays her first sign of concern. She has replied to everything said before mechanically, dully. She cares nothing about the war—has paid no attention to any of the talk about it— has accepted it as a mere alien affair connected with her husband's politics with which she is forbidden to meddle. But this news about a draft! All the young men, she asks Mrs. L.? Surely that would never happen. Mrs. L. replies that it looks as if war would be declared and, if so, her father says that a draft will be inevitable. But Jack, Mrs. Cockran inquires anxiously—surely a Senator's son would not be drafted. Mrs. L. laughs. They would take Jack first of all— he is so perfect physically. But of course Jack will volunteer and not wait to be drafted.

It is as if a bombshell had shattered the dull resignation of Mrs. Cockran's life. She is stunned as the real meaning of this war that she has ignored is brought home to her. They will take her Jack, the only reason she has for living! Suddenly she remembers what she had at the time read mechanically in the papers—the battles, the frightful losses, the pictures of the wounded, the cannon. Her Jack will be taken from her, forced into this slaughter, killed, perhaps! But no, that cannot happen. His father is powerful, a Senator. He will not allow such a thing to happen when he knows that his own son's life is in danger. They always do as he says. He will not permit war to be declared.

Mrs. Lathrop is astonished at this naive ignorance. Doesn't Mrs. Cockran know that her husband is one of the administration leaders? Why it is the speech he is going to make that day which is relied upon to smash the opposition to the war in the Senate. Mrs. Cockran cannot believe this. She gets up and says bewilderedly as she goes out: "I must see John about it. I must see John."

A moment later Cockran, Simms and King enter. Mrs. Lathrop goes out and leaves them. Cockran sends Simms to attend to something for him. King goes with the secretary. He is left alone. Mrs. Cockran enters. She wears an air of resolution, of desperate determination. Her husband ignores her, will not at first speak to her at all. But she is insistent. At length he asks her to sit down. He will listen to what she has to say but she must be brief. He has to go to the Senate in a short time.

Mrs. Cockran speaks of the war. They will take Jack. He will be killed. Does he know that? Then he must do his best to prevent it. He must get them not to declare war. Cockran is amazed. He tries to get her to mind her own business but she will not be put off. Then he tries to explain but she will listen to no explanations. He has to admit that Jack would have to go to war anyway in case he should not volunteer. But it is God's will. He tries to make her see the patriot's viewpoint but she cannot and will not. What are nations and national honor to her? Her world—her Jack—would be killed!

Finally Cockran explodes into exasperated anger. He refuses to discuss the matter further. He rises to go, but this is the signal for a wild burst of hysterical fury from his wife. She becomes strong, dominant. He will save Jack for her, and the other thousand of Jacks for their mothers, or she will ruin him. Let him dare not to do his best to prevent war and she will smash him utterly. She will tell the world what he really is—a murderer hiding behind a mask of success and respectability. She will reveal the secret she has kept so long. Jack shall know and hate his father for a cowardly criminal. Then she and Jack will go far away where they are not known and leave him to his punishment.

Face to face with this threat from a woman he still believes to be unscrupulous and cruel, and who very evidently means what she says, Cockran crumbles. He pleads with her abjectly. Let her ask anything else in the world and he will do it for her. But she wants nothing else from him. His hate for her, his years of obliviousness to her existence, his constant attempt to estrange Jack from her, have taught her to hate, too. She cares nothing for his fate as long as Jack is preserved to her. He tries to argue that any attempt he might make to stem the tide of war would be useless and would only serve to bring the contempt of the country on him. But she does not believe this. She has an exaggerated idea of his power, his influence. He has always got what he wanted. He can get this too if he tries hard enough. At all odds, he must fight to save his son or he would be guilty of a double murder—the deaths of her step-father and her son would both be on his conscience. She demands that he make the attempt or—he knows what will happen. She will tell Jack about his crime— Jack first of all!

Cockran, broken and crushed, at length promises he will do his best. He will change his speech into one against the war. It will mean political ruin for him, but anything rather than have his son know him for an escaped murderer.

Jack and Harriet enter—ask him if it is not time he made a start for the Senate. Cockran implores them not to come to the Senate to hear him. They notice his agitated manner and show concern; but they tell him with an air of great secrecy that they have decided not to go to hear him. They have something very important to do elsewhere. They go out with him, leaving Mrs. C. alone as

THE CURTAIN FALLS

CHARACTERS OF ACT FOUR

Senator John Cockran
Elizabeth Cockran, his wife
Jack, their son

SCENE: Same as Act Three—night of the same day. Mrs. Cockran is discovered sitting alone. She is evidently worked up to a nervous pitch bordering on hysteria by worry over the probable consequences of what she has done. Jack enters. He immediately tells her with great enthusiasm that war has been declared. Mrs. Cockran gives a cry of terror. Jack is too worked up to notice her agitation and he goes on to tell how sorry he is not to have heard his father speak in the Senate. But he had other, more important things to attend to. He and Harriet had gone together while he put in his application for enlistment in the aviation service. He tells her with boyish spirit about all this as if he expected her to be proud of him for his promptness in responding to the call of his country.

To his utter amazement, his mother, when the full realization of what he has done penetrates to her benumbed brain, becomes nearly mad with grief. She realizes that by her lies, her threats, she has forced her husband to do something which means ruin to his career and, since Jack has enlisted and war has been declared, this sacrifice is all for nothing. She grows hysterical—pleads with her son to run away, to do anything to save himself before it is too late. He will be killed. She is sure of it.

Jack starts to rebuke her sternly but, seeing her distracted state of mind, he begins to talk to her quietly, soothingly, as if she were a child. When she [has] grown calm he explains to her bit by bit why he felt that it would be dishonor for him not to do as he had done. He tells her of the high ideals he has of love of country, the true patriotism free from cant and windy phrases which actuated him. He feels his country to be his mother just as she is his mother. He can no more stand by and see his country suffer insult and humiliation than he could watch her, his mother, insulted and remain only a spectator. And this is a glorious cause he will be fighting for, one well worth giving one's life to. This is more than a mere fight between countries. It is a war for democracy, for the freedom of the world and every man ought to feel a personal concern in its success. Doesn't she understand? He had to do what he did—or be ashamed to ever look at himself in the mirror again.

Mrs. Cockran listens to him in silence, deeply moved, beginning to understand a little. The true nobility of self-sacrifice which she sees exemplified in her son awakens all that is good in her own character. She resolves to relieve her own conscience and make a clean breast of the big lie on which her life has been founded. But in the beginning of the confession when she tells Jack of the fight between his father and her step-father, she makes no mention of the big reason why she forced Cockran to marry her—because he, Jack, was to be born to her.

Jack listens to the story with a rapidly growing horror. As she goes on he begins to think he understands why she has been so silent and queer all these years. He thinks he understands why his father has so obviously tried to keep them apart. He begins to get the same idea his father has always had—that she is a wicked woman, hard and cruel, who has caused his father untold misery by her inexcusable deceit.

When she tells about the threat she made to force his father into politics, the bargain by which she gave up all claims to any part of the moulding of his—Jack's—life, her son shrinks away from her in disgust, revolted. How could his mother be so low? He cannot understand it. She does not tell him it was for his sake and his father's; she makes no excuses for herself; she endures his reproaches in a dead calm. She feels her life is over now. Nothing matters any more. But she has not told him the crowning sin of all—the scene of that morning when she had compelled his father to go out and ruin his career and play the coward before the world by the power of the same lying threat. If she tells this it will mean that her son, too, will cast her out of his life, but she feels she must hold back nothing from him. But he refuses to listen any more. Good God, hasn't he heard enough already! He cannot believe what he has heard. It is too fiendish! Why she must be mad to have done such things, to have lived the life she has!

As she is trying to get him to hear the finish of her story, Cockran enters. He seems older, as if he had been through a great struggle with himself, but there is something virile, of a defiant strength in his attitude. He comes slowly over to his wife and tells her with emphasis that he has made the speech in favor of the war and that war has been declared. To his surprise she merely answers: "I am glad" and starts to walk out of the room. But Jack, excited and wrought-up over what he has just heard, takes her by the arm and stops her. Now that the three of them are together he wants to reach some understanding. He asks her to sit down. She does so, dully and hopelessly. Then her son turns to his father and tells him all that he has just heard from his mother. Is it the truth?

When Cockran hears of the trick played upon him all his life he is dumbfounded. He rises to his feet and walks toward his wife threateningly as if he were going to strike her. He is speechless with rage. Jack restrains him, gets him to sit down again, and goes on with his story. Gradually as Cockran listens he grows calmer. He notices that his son makes no mention of the reason why he was forced to marry Mrs. Cockran. When his son finishes he asks him about this. Did his mother tell him anything about that? Mrs. Cockran breaks in hysterically. No, no, Jack must never know that! She constantly interrupts her husband when he tries to bring in the subject.

But Cockran has been pondering over the past while listening to his son, and has reflected that a large part of the blame for her action rests upon his own shoulders. After all, he was a dog in those days, and what she did she certainly did for love of him and her unborn child. So he insists on revealing the whole truth to Jack. He tells him that he, too, has a confession of guilt to make to his son—and he tells him the reason for her action in the past—to give him, Jack, a name. He confesses that he would never have married her, that he would have cast her aside and forgotten her if fear of the threat she made had not brought him to his senses. He also confesses that, looking back on it now, he finds himself guilty of having done his best to stifle her life and make her miserable, to separate her from Jack—and yet he owes it to that same threat that he is now one of the country's big men instead of being, through fear, merely a stick-in-the-mud small town manufacturer. It is the fear of the threat which has been responsible for all his successful climb from the time he had been a common mill-hand—that, and the urge of his uneasy conscience demanding that he make reparation by his own life for the crime he had committed. Without these things he would never have had energy enough to develop his latent powers, he would have lived and died in his little sordid rut.

Jack listens to all this with his face in his hands, prostrated. His father finishes by saying that he, Jack, is the judge of them both; but he reminds him to be charitable in his judgment of his parents, to remember that life was not as simple and easy a matter for them as they have made it for him by devoting their lives to his welfare.

Jack breaks down and sobs. How can they think that he would dare to judge them? He loves them, and whatever they have done, they have done it for him. His feeling for them is the same as his feeling for his country: "My country! May she always be right—but right or wrong, my country! There is only one thing that he cannot forgive and that is their continued estrangement. The house divided must stop. If he is to forgive, then they must forgive—each other.

Mrs. Cockran is weeping softly, her head bowed. Cockran looks over at her appealingly, deeply moved. Harriet's voice is heard from the hallway calling Jack. He calls back and rushes out. Mrs. Cockran murmurs brokenly: "He told me he'd enlisted, John." Cockran stretches his hand across the table to her and she takes it in hers. Cockran speaks softly and consolingly to her: "He'll come back to us, Mother—when it's all over. I know in my soul he will. The good God owes us that"

as

THE CURTAIN FALLS.

The Guilty One   BY ELINOR RAND

CHARACTERS

Martin Dunn
Cora Lynch, his step-daughter
James Smith
Judson, their son
Mildred Lord, private secretary
Mr. Walters, factory manager
O'Brian, private detective
Tudor, a maid
A Landlady
Two Police Officers

SCENES

ACT 1   Year 1900   SCENE 1 *A machine shop. Union, Ohio*
                     SCENE 2 *A room in a cheap rooming house. Chicago*
ACT 2   Year 1905   *The living-dining room of a small house in Paterson, N.J.*
ACT 3   Year 1924   *Drawing room in the home of James Smith*
ACT 4   *The same. Two o'clock the next morning*

ACT ONE

SCENE ONE: *The interior of a machine shop in Union, Ohio. There is a door in the rear. It is about eight o'clock in the evening. The place is dimly lit by a lantern, which is placed so that it cannot be seen from outside.* CORA LYNCH *sits motionless on a bench beside the lantern, which shines up into her face. Her face is set and her eyes bitter. After a moment the door in the rear opens and* JAMES SMITH *enters. When she hears his footsteps* CORA *makes a convulsive movement, but does not turn. He stands a moment in the dimness and then comes to Cora. He is dressed like a mechanic and is about 24 years old. Good-looking, his eyes wander, and he seems slightly uneasy.*

JAMES   I thought first you wasn't here. [*Pauses*] You haven't been waitin', have you?

CORA   [*With bitterness*] Only about an hour.

JAMES   Say, is it that late? [*Lights a cigarette*] We got into an argument over to Connelly's—

CORA   You don't mind telling me you spend all your spare time in bar-rooms, do you?

JAMES   Well, who's going to object? You? [*Pauses—more gently*] That's one reason I fell for you. You never pulled the preaching stuff.

CORA   [*Still bitterly*] I knew you wouldn't stand for it.

JAMES   [*Boastingly*] You was right. No woman's going to tell Jim Smith where he gets off—or no man neither. [*He suddenly sits down beside her*] Aw, come on, Corrie, don't get sore. If I'm over to Connelly's, you know I'm not with some dame, don't you? [*She does not reply. He breaks out*] An' what else is there to do in this burg? Everybody's in bed by nine o'clock, except th' gang over to Connelly's—an' they're only a bunch of small-town sports? I'm sick of it! Frisco, Denver, Chicago—them are the places. That's where I belong! I been to all of them. And say kid—[*He puts his arm across her shoulder*] I wouldn't have stayed in this one-horse town a week if it hadn't been for *you*!

CORA   [*Leans over and holds him fiercely, her head on his chest—in agony*] Jim!

JAMES   [*Holding her loosely*] Hey, what's the matter? You strangle a feller! [*She relaxes and lies on him, a lifeless weight. He sits her up beside him, one arm around her. In the other he still holds the lighted cigarette*] Aw, come on, Corrie, be a sport! You didn't think I was going to spend the rest of my life in Union, Ohio, did you?

CORA   Nobody wants you to, Jim.

JAMES   [*Uneasily*] I should hope not! I keep right on going—that's me! When a fellow's a mechanic he's got work anywhere in the world. Any place you say—South America, Panama . . . Africa . . . all of them places. He can see life! And if a feller feels like laying off, and having a good time, why he can. [*Brightens*] Say, you haven't no idea of what swell times you run into.

CORA   Yes—women! [*She laughs*]

JAMES   Aw—women! Say, women don't cut the ice in a man's life they like to think! Naw, I mean times without women—men's times. [*Pauses*] I ain't saying there hasn't been women—plenty of them, too. But—[*He makes a contemptuous noise in his throat, and taking a bottle from his pocket, drinks. CORA pulls away from him and gets up, her eyes blazing*] Aw, what are you acting like that for? I wasn't talking about *you*.

CORA   You said—[*She stands silent. He gets up and faces her*]

JAMES   Look here—you know what sort of a fellow I was when you first started going with me, didn't you?

CORA   Yes.

JAMES   You knew that I wasn't planning to do no settling down?

CORA   Yes.

JAMES   [*Comes closer*] I come right out from the first, that first night, and told you—didn't I? [CORA *is silent*] And that if it wasn't going to be my way, I wasn't goin' to bother—[*She remains silent. He goes up*] Sure. I was square. I told you that I'd be leaving in the fall—that I wasn't no marrying kind. [*He waits*]

CORA   [*Timidly*] Yes, but—

JAMES   [*More gently*] Well, then, what are you pulling this stuff for? [*Impulsively*] I'll write to you, Corrie. [*He sits down, and as she still remains standing in her tense attitude he adds: again*] I never tried t' fool you! did I?

CORA   I ain't saying you—tried to fool me. But—[*She stammers pitifully*] All you said afterwards—about—lovin' me. Don't you remember? You said— [*Breaks down*]

JAMES   Say! Didn't you want me t' say those things? That's all in the game. You wouldn't have liked it if I hadn't . . . if I'd just—

CORA   You loved me then. You couldn't a' been fooling.

JAMES   No—I guess I wasn't. I do like you better 'n any girl—for years. I been true to you all summer—it's th' first time that's happened!

CORA   [*Despairingly*] It all sounds different now from th' way it was. . . . You make it sound as if I didn't care—was just bad. But the first time I seen you, when I walked in here that day and you was standing over by the window in an old shirt without no sleeves—something happened to me. . . . I couldn't hardly bear to come near you, it got me so upset. Then you began talkin' to me. And we went for walks . . . and you began saying you was crazy about me—and then, like you said—you said—[*She breaks*] if I wouldn't give in to you—

JAMES   Sure. I'm glad you own up I never faked nothin'.

CORA   I—knew you meant it. I knew you wouldn't bother—if I didn't. I knew there was other girls—would. And then they'd have you—not me.

JAMES   They wasn't as nice as you. I wanted—you.

CORA   Do you remember that first night, when we went for a walk, and you stood at th' gate—arguing? I guess after you left you thought I was mad at you. . . .

JAMES I did—until the next day when you come down to th' shop and said—you'd go walking—again.

CORA [As though not hearing him] I was awake most of that night—thinkin' and thinkin' about things. It seemed like I went back over all my life, since I was a little girl. I guess you know what it's like not to have any parents—if yours died when you was a kid, too. But I guess you don't know what it means to have a step-father like the one I've got. It done something to me, havin' him act the way he has. And I couldn't get away. There wasn't anybody to go to. I got so no matter what he did to me, I always felt I had the better of him. He used to whip me, nights when he'd come home from the shop, and I'd hold my breath and think—you can't hurt me. It made me feel—strong about myself. And I used to think as soon as I was big enough, I'd do something wonderful. It made me feel as if I was different from the people here—as if I'd never live their kind of life, dyin' here in this awful place without ever havin' been alive.

JAMES You'd oughta gone to State Normal and been a teacher.

CORA I thought of all this, that night, and then of how every year'd gone by. Christmas wasn't over before it'd seem to be Christmas again . . . [Pause] and nothing ever happened. First thing I was eighteen, and then, first thing, I was twenty-six. [She sighs] And then it come back to me, that night, how when I was little I'd always think that something was going to happen to me in th' year 1900. I used to say I wish it was 1900, so's I could see what'd happen. . . .

JAMES So that's why you was willin' to be my girl, eh—because it was 1900?

CORA Don't joke at me! I'm just sayin' I—that it wasn't no easy thing. It seemed then as if everything else had gone by, and hadn't meant nothing, but I knew that this would, I'd have had something from you. I was willin' to let it be like that—to let you go, when you got tired. I thought that I'd be strong enough—[She is unable to speak]

JAMES [Uneasily] Well—as you said, you're two years older'n me. You ought to be able to do as you like. [Pauses] I'll write to you—want me to? [He gets up] Say, I better be getting back to the house, Corrie. I meant t' tell you—th' old lady, Mis' Smith, she wants her room this week—she's got some relations comin'. So I thought I'd beat it to Chicago tomorrow. [Evasively] You knew I was leaving this week anyhow.

CORA [With a dry throat] Listen—you can't go now. I got to talk to you. [She puts out her hands as if to stop him]

JAMES We talked enough. I don't want to hear nothing more about it,

Corrie. If you've got good sense you'll be like you was at first—no preaching. [*Glibly*] Maybe there's a chance of my coming back if you act like a pal.

CORA   You wouldn't let me tell you last night, either. You went off—

JAMES   Sure I went off, because your father's hired man come up and seen us behind the barn. D'you think I want to get shot at? He's liable to tell the old man. An' the old man's liable to be looking for us tonight, and see the light in here—

CORA   You can't see the light from the road.

JAMES   Well, I gotta beat it, anyway, Corrie. And we better end this now. There isn't no use dragging things along.

CORA   You've *got* to listen. Something's happened that—makes things different.

JAMES   [*Sullenly*] What? Aw, I don't want to hear!

CORA   I'm caught—that's what it is.

JAMES   You're crazy, Corrie—I don't believe it—You're lying. I might a' known you'd pull something like this!

CORA   [*In a low voice*] D'you think I'd lie about that? [*Proudly*] I'd a let you go, if—this hadn't happened. But—you've to to let me go with you now. I *can't* stay.

JAMES   [*Stubbornly*] I don't see how it—aw, it's a mistake!

CORA   No. I'm sure. [*Wildly*] That's why I've been actin' like this. We've got to do something.

JAMES   Well—that ain't so hard. There's doctors. I'll give you the money for that! [*He takes his bottle out, without looking at her*] And right now I'm goin' to take the biggest drink that was ever swallowed!

CORA   [*With great bitterness*] Yes—that's right! That's the whole trouble with you. Whenever anything happens that would help you make something of yourself, you go an'—drink. Because you've got that crazy idea about wandering everywhere. You told me yourself you done that, deliberate—like that time in St. Paul, when you discovered that new idea for a fan-belt.—And then went off, when you found they was goin' to make something of it, an' of you. An' you said th' same sort of thing's happened before. That's what I've felt about you all the time—that you could make anything out of yourself if you wanted to. An' that's—that's what I want you to let me help you do. I've got a little money—some my mother had.—We could start—You got to have somebody that'll care, Jim. Let me go with you—and then—we can talk it all over—[*She is trembling with nervous excitement*]

JAMES [*Sneeringly, the drink has evidently gone to his head*] So you want to help me make a man of myself, do you? That's kind of you! [*He goes to center and pulls on light*] Hey! This is better! What're we sitting in the dark for?

CORA Jim—don't do that! Some one'll see the light.

JAMES What do I care if they do! D'you think I'm afraid of your old man? No. T'hell with him! I'm leaving this bloody town, and I'd as soon give him a beatin' as not before I go.

CORA Jim! Don't act this way!

JAMES What way? I'll send you th' money to go to a doctor. There's plenty will do it.

CORA Jim! [*Throws herself on him hysterically*] Jim! Don't go off and leave me. Please—please! I'll do anything—I won't preach—

JAMES I'm going I tell you—[*He starts toward door.* CORA *stands motionless. The door opens and* MARTIN DUNN *comes in. He is a huge thick-set man, red-faced and mean-looking, and has evidently been drinking*]

MARTIN [*Closing door behind him*] What in hell is this? [*Bellowing to Cora*] So *this* is what you been up to, huh? I was told you two was seen sneakin' behind th' barn last night—[*Threateningly*] What are you doin' here in my shop the two of you. [CORA *gets to her feet*]

JAMES We don't need you around—whatever we're doing. [*Threateningly*]

MARTIN It's come to me—the game you and her's been playing all summer. Her name's gotten to be dirt—for the whole town. [*Turns to her*] Don't you never come into my house again, d'you hear me? [*To* JAMES] And you beat it—out of the town by morning, or I'll get you run out! [*He is in a terrible rage*]

JAMES You will, huh? Well, I'm leaving of my own free will, on the first train. I'm sick of the lot of you—[*He goes toward door*]

CORA [*Hysterically*] Jim! Jim! [*Blindly*] Don't go! You can't leave now— after what's happened to me! You can't go—

MARTIN [*Picks up an iron bar and rushes to door—blocking James, bellowingly*] What's this, huh? What's yer hurry? [*His back against the door, to Cora*] What do'you mean, what's happened to you? If there's a reason for him having to stay—do'you have t' get married, is that the answer? Going to have a kid, huh, is that it? I might have guessed it. You're no better'n a common street-bustler [*sic*]. [CORA *is silent, twisting her hands*] And he was going off to leave you on my hands? [*Shakes bar at* JAMES.—*To* CORA] You dirty, tart, you, is this the way you pay me back, after me feedin' you for years ever since your mother died! You'd like to make a laughing stock out of me in th' town, would you, where they've never had chance to hoot at me before! Well, he'll marry you, by God, I'll see to that!—and the two of you'll leave town in a hurry if you know what's good for you! [*To* JAMES] So you thought you'd sneak off, huh? Well you won't! You'll marry her like I says, d'you hear?

JAMES   Aw-w! Forget it! [*Drunkenly*] Wait and see if you make me marry her—just wait! [*Moves a step toward the door*] Get out of my way now!

CORA   [*Screaming*] Jim—

MARTIN   [*Holds the bar wickedly*] Come on! [JAMES *makes a rush at him, grabbing the bar, but* MARTIN *wrenches it away, and hits* JAMES *with it, knocking him across floor—then rushes on him in apoplectic fury to hit him again. But* JAMES *blindly picks up a lead pipe, and as the old man reaches him, hits him first on head.* MARTIN *stumbles, falls, and with a terrible groan, lies still. The blood comes from his head and mouth as* JAMES, *dazed, stands over him*]

JAMES   [*Slowly*] Hell!

CORA   [*Gives a prolonged sigh*] Oh-h. I knew something would happen. I knew it!

JAMES   [*In horror*] L-look at his face. [*Bends over*] Hey—Mr. Dunn! What's th' matter? [*Picks up his hand. It falls back lifeless*] He's—hardly breathin'. [*Listens, his face white*] He—ain't breathin'. I must a'—hit too hard! [*He gets up and stares helplessly at Cora, gone to pieces and shaking in a nervous reaction*]

CORA   Wait—[*She gets some water and puts it on the old man's head. Nothing happens.* JAMES *shakes his head, as though trying to throw off some ugly nightmare*]

JAMES   I've got to get out of here—[*Looks around as though trapped*]

CORA   He seems—dead. [*She looks at his still form a moment longer as though waiting*]

JAMES   I gotta—travel then. I got to get as far away as I can . . . while there's time. [*Sinks on seat—moans*] But what chance have I got? If I beat it, they'll know then for sure.

CORA   [*Tensely, standing before him*] I tell you what you do. You go on—get away. And I'll run out—and say I seen a light in here, and come in and found him drunk—and I tried to get him home—and he fell—and hit his head—[*Fiercely*] And you—you get on a train! [*She goes on desperately*] If you could only sneak on th' 10:12 tonight, at th' crossing, so nobody'd see you!

JAMES [*Slowly*] That's easy enough—[*Then dully*] But, what good'll it do. They'll get me anyhow.

CORA [*Recovering, and putting her hand on his shoulder—with intense devotion*] No—no! Don't lose your nerve now! You got to move quick! You got to buck up! And I'll try to make 'em believe he fell—Where's your ticket to?

JAMES Chicago.

CORA I'll write you as—as—James Brown—general delivery—and tell you what happens. [*Picks up his cap*] You better go. It's near ten now. You got to—go! [*She goes with him toward door*]

JAMES [*Dully*] I guess—it's my on'y chance. [*To her—almost pleadingly*] Say, you write me—so I'll know.

CORA [*Fiercely*] Yes, an' don't worry! I'll save you! [*She pulls his head down and kisses him*]

JAMES [*Jerking his head away*] You got me in this! Leave go! [*He goes out.* CORA *then after a moment, returns and sits on bench. There is absolute silence. She sits motionless. Suddenly she turns toward body as if she had heard something and her face takes on an incredulous frightened expression. After a few seconds of this she goes over and bending down by her father listens for his breath. Her face changes. She puts hand on his heart*]

CORA Pa! [*She feverishly gets water and bathes his face*] Pa! [*Suddenly a low groan comes form the old man*] Pa—you ain't dead?

MARTIN [*Feebly raising his arm and pushing her hand aside, in a weak voice*] Where is he?

CORA Pa—you ain't hurt, bad?

MARTIN It'd take more'n him! [*Succeeds in sitting up*] Where's that murderin' coward? [*He glares about him, then sinks back with a groan*] Get some cold water, can't you? My head's crackin'!

CORA [*Excitedly*] Wait a minute, can't you? I got to run after Jim. He thinks he killed you. I got to tell him—[*She gets to the door—stops—is struck by a sudden thought—struggles with herself—her face hardens—she mutters*] No. I'll wait. . . . I'll wait and see. . . .

MARTIN [*Exasperatedly*] Gimme some cold water, damn you! My head's bustin'.

CORA All right. [*She goes to sink as the scene changes*]

CURTAIN

SCENE TWO: *A week later. A small, cheap, furnished room in Chicago. It is about six in the evening. The dingy shades are drawn and the room is lit by gas.*

JAMES SMITH sits on the bed. He looks very much gone to pieces—thin, and with desperate eyes. There is a loud knock on the door. JIM shows abnormal dismay, goes to door, and with shoulders against it, and hand on knob, makes attempt to speak easily.

JIM   Who—is it? [*Door pushes in slightly. He pushes it back*] Who is it?

LANDLADY   [*Sulkily, from outside*] A woman wants to see you.

JIM   [*Opening door*] A woman? [*With quick suspicion*] What sort of woman? What does she look like?

LANDLADY   [*Disagreeably*] Say, what's th' matter with you, anyhow? You act as though th' cops was after you!

JIM   Me? [*He tries to laugh*]

LANDLADY   Yes, you! Didn't you tell me you was expecting a young lady today, or tomorrow?

JIM   Yes—sure, I suppose it's her. [*A pause, during which LANDLADY looks suspiciously round the room*] Kinda pretty—with dark hair?

LANDLADY   [*Harshly*] How'd I know? She's in black, with a veil over her face.

JIM   In—black? [*After a moment—dully*] Let her come up.

LANDLADY   Why didn't you say so at first? [*Exits, slamming door*]

JIM   [*Walks to window, looks out, turns back*] Hell! I guess it's all up with you, kid. [*Sits down on bed. Footsteps are heard and Landlady's voice—"That's the room."—Then a gentle knock. JIM springs to door, and opens it cautiously, with relief*]

JIM   Oh—hello! Come in!

CORA   [*CORA enters with bag, which she puts on floor. She is dressed in black, and the black veil is now pushed back, showing her face. She is pale, quiet, and with a certain dignity*] I—couldn't let you know the train—[*She stands looking at him: he watches her with a sort of desperate concentration on her words, with a corresponding ignoring of her as a person. She suddenly trembles and grows weak, as though going to faint. It is obviously her emotion at seeing him, which she is trying to control*] Jim!

JIM   [*Holding her*] Hey—don't cave in! [*She sits on bed, her eyes closed, trembling with a nervous spasm, but holding herself with tense control, while he*] *gets a glass of water from the wash pitcher and gives it to her]* Here! *[Watching her while she drinks—in a low voice, with intense interrogation]* The old man's dead then? Well—*[Draws a deep breath]* I knew that all along! *[She meets his eyes without flinching]* Didn't he—never come to—for a minute even?

CORA   *[Firmly]* No.

JIM   *[With relief]* I was afraid he would—and tell them it was me—*[Looks suspiciously at Cora]* What's the matter? What do you look so funny for? Do you mean—they're after me?

CORA   No. I'm just—so tired.

JIM   *[Relentlessly]* Well, tell me! They believed what you said—that he fell and hit his head?

CORA   Y-yes. They knew he'd been drinking.

JIM   *[Straightening up]* I've been afraid to go on the street—afraid at the sight of a cop! Every time th' doorbell rung here, I thought it was someone after me. I've set up here—*[He shakes his head, as though throwing something off]* I wouldn't go through it again—for all there was in the world! *[After a few seconds he looks again at* CORA, *who has said nothing. She is sitting there, waiting, and very near tears.* JIM *becomes suddenly conscious of her share in things. He moves toward her awkwardly, and puts his hand on her shoulder]* You've been fine, Corrie. *[Kisses her]* You've—sure got me out of this!

CORA   *[Bursting into tears, and throwing her arms violently about his neck]* Jim! Jim! I've—been through hell—too!

JIM   There—don't cry. *[He pats her. He comes near a breakdown himself, and for a moment the two people are in a real embrace]* It's been awful—awful! *[Whispers]* Knowing you'd killed someone!

CORA   *[Hysterically]* No, no, Jim! *[Then fiercely, seizing him]* Do you love me?

JIM   *[Kisses her, but without the conviction of the moment before. His mind is on the murder again]* D'you think there's any idea—among *any* of them—that I done it?

CORA   *[Hurt—bitterly]* Can't you think of me—one minute? You never even—kissed me, when I come in.

JIM   *[Gets up, stands with hands in pockets, impatiently]* Didn't I just show you—how thankful I was—You've been—fine. And I sure appreciate it. *[His eyes wander guiltily.* CORA *stares at him. There is an awkward silence]*

CORA   What am I goin' to do—tonight?

JIM   *[With forced consternation]* Sure—I'm a nice one, forgetting all about that! You better get a room at some little hotel. [*Her gaze makes him uncomfortable*] After you left your baggage—we could go an' get some supper—[*Hesitates, frowns*]

CORA   Isn't there a room—here?

JIM   [*Hastily*] She's full up. [*Lies*] She told me this was her last room. [*Pauses*] I was just goin' to say—about supper—[*Pauses*]

CORA   What?

JIM   Well—I don't know now if we ought to be seen together.

CORA   Oh—[*Her whole body seems to sag*]

JIM   [*Abruptly, changing the subject, with evident anxiety*] Didn't anybody out to Union—have any suspicion?

CORA   [*After a pause*] There was no proof. No one seen what happened—but me. An' I—lied. [*Pulls herself together; more determinedly, looking at* JIM] I said that night I'd save you. Some of them talked about you at first—about going after you.

JIM   [*Excitedly*] They did, eh? [*Pauses, thinking*]

CORA   They'd have suspected sure—[*Significantly*] if they'd known I was going to have—

JIM   [*Awkwardly*] That sure complicates things, Corrie. [*Embarrassed*] Well, we'll get that fixed—somehow. [*Abruptly*] And then—I'd better make a quick getaway—particularly if they was suspicious. [*Moves nervously about room*] It might get into their heads again—[*Looks from window as if he saw someone. Turns abruptly back to Cora*] I tell you Corrie, I'd stay here until everything was all right again with you—but it would be bad for both of us. Like as not they'd find you was here, and if I was around—see how it'd look? They'd arrest me sure—and then everything would come out about you and me. It would be pretty bad for you to have to go back to Union with them all wise—to that—

CORA   [*Dully*] I'm not goin' back to Union.

JIM   [*Amiably*] That's how you feel now. Well, I don't blame you. But after it's all over, you can go back an' nobody'll ever know th' difference. [CORA *gives him a peculiar look*] It—ain't good to break off with everybody in your home town. [*Rather sentimentally*] See where it led me. [*Hastily*] D' you know what I'm goin' to do, Corrie? I'm goin' to give you every cent I've got, except my fare—for wherever I blow to? See? And you can stay at a good place here—I'll find a doctor.

CORA   How about—me 'n you?

JIM [Weakly] Say, we talked that all over once. And it can't be done now, sure. You wouldn't want to be tied up to a man—who—who had murder hanging over his head. . . . [He pauses—then very kindly] You get straightened out—that's easy—an' forget me. I gotta blow—an' right away.

CORA You ain't got—murder hanging over your head. Nobody's after you.

JIM [Impatiently] But they might get suspicious—an' rake it all up.

CORA [Slowly] Not as long as I—don't say nothing.

JIM [After a perturbed pause] Well—I guess you won't, Corrie.

CORA [Takes off her hat and puts it on the bed—speaks in a low, monotonous voice] It seems to me things is different, now, Jim. It seems to me things is different from that night when you and me talked down to th' shop. You could 'a walked out, and left me then, and I'd just 'a stayed and gone on and had th' baby, I suppose, like other girls has had to. . . . There wasn't one thing I could do. There wasn't not one way I could make you do what was right. You could always say, well it's what happens—an' the way things is, there isn't any answer for a girl to make to that . . . [Suddenly her voice changes—it grows louder, and shakes with emotion] But now things is different! [With great emotion] If you go off now—roamin'—with the memory of—that in your mind—never staying any one place—drinking—what'll happen to you? [Pause] You and me could—

JIM [Wearily] Aw—don't pull that stuff! You mean if I live the sort of life you think best—instead of the sort of life I think best—

CORA It's because I know what you could do with yourself—

JIM There you go!—pretendin' it's for my good you want to marry me!

CORA You can't believe I mean what I say—about you? Well—I do. If it wasn't that I knew—that you could do anything you wanted—if you got started—with someone to help you, I'd—never do this. [Her voice suddenly drops] I couldn't do it—just for my sake.

JIM [In an exasperated voice] Now, don't start the argument all over again. I've said, that as things is, it's more'n ever impossible.

CORA You said—a little while back—that I've saved you—

JIM Say—somebody might be listenin'.

CORA Well—have I?

JIM [Grudgingly] I—suppose you have. But if it hadn't been for you—I'd never been there that night.

CORA If it hadn't been for me!

JIM Aw—let's stop talking about it now—

CORA We can't. It's all got to be said and decided here tonight. [*She makes a gesture*] I've thought about it, over an' over, in the last three days. It seems to me—there's one way that's the right way—and that's what we got to do. [*With almost hysterical fervor*] It seems to me that everything has happened—just to bring us together. An' I feel that it's in my hands to make you— to make you—do somethin'—instead of—[*Pauses*] We ought to forget all th' past—everythin'—and start over. Go somewhere, where nobody's ever seen us. You could get somewhere—in no time! You could be foreman—study—[*She seems possessed with a dream of power*] I seen it when I come into Chicago tonight—all the things that men can do—th' building, th' lights, th' machinery, all th' people pouring in and out, that can work for you. It's all lyin' around— waiting for a man to use! [*She suddenly begins to cry*] All you have in the world—everything anybody's ever had—[*She is sobbing*]

JIM [*Perplexed*] Say, Corrie—you're crazy, ain't you! [*Pauses*] You're right about my havin' to go somewhere—where I ain't known—but all this other stuff—say, can't you see I gotta keep goin' more than ever now—

CORA I want you to marry me, Jim. I—can't go back.

JIM I can't, Corrie. That's flat. I gotta get away. You—ain't no baby. [*He gets up*] Say—let's think about some hotel where you c'n go tonight. We c'n—talk some more—tomorrow.

CORA Wait a moment—Jim.

JIM What for?

CORA There's more—I got to tell you.

JIM [*Abruptly*] More?

CORA Yes! [*A pause*] Have you ever thought—that whether you're safe or not—is up to me? If I went back—an' told what happened—would you have much chance?

JIM —What're you talking about, Corrie—? [*He is perturbed, but tries to hide it*]

CORA Well—I done somethin' for you. [*Pause*] What are you goin' to do for me? I'm in a bad way, too—about as bad as a girl can be.

JIM I'm willin' to do anythin' sensible.

CORA Willin'—to get married? To go East—and start over? Look—[*She opens her bag*] Here's—that money I told you about. We could start—easy.

JIM   I'm glad you've got the money. You're all right now, sure. [*Goes to window, looks out*]

CORA   Will you—do that?

JIM   Aw, you don't realize nothin'. [*Opens his suitcase*] I ought to be beatin' it now.

CORA   You ain't goin'! [*He looks at her*] If you do—in fifteen minutes— the police'll be after you—for murder.

JIM   [*Slowly*] So that's—your game!

CORA   You'll be glad afterwards—I done it.

JIM   You mean—if I don't marry you—don't go and be what you want— you'll—

CORA   I've got to, Jim [*Desperately*] I've got to—for all of us.

JIM   [*In a rage*] Well, you won't do it to me!

CORA   [*Stubbornly*] I've—got to—

JIM   I'll kill you! [*He moves about the room as though it were a cage. Then he comes back and looks into her face. She is standing silently, all her will-power and determination showing in her eyes. It makes her look older—hard— almost powerful*] You—you do mean it—damn you! [*As though appalled*] You devil! You would do it—send me to prison! [*He sinks on the bed, and falls in a sort of trance, and in that moment it seems that he visibly weakens, while she grows stronger. At last he lifts his head—there is a look of hatred and despair on his face*] All right. You've got me. I gotta do what you say. I'll marry you—but remember this—now—I'll never touch you! We'll be married—you c'n force me into that—but you can't force me into love! [*He says this furiously*]

CORA   [*Suddenly crying out—with pathos*] Jim! [*Moves toward him*]

JIM   [*Pushing her violently away*] No! I hate you! Keep away! [*As the curtain falls*]

CURTAIN

ACT TWO

TIME: *The Fall of 1905.*
SCENE: *The living-dining room of a small house in Paterson, N.J. Center left, dining table with white cloth, partly set. Back wall, a window with lace curtains, a stand with rubber plant, a coatrack, on which hang two or three coats, a chair and a door opening on the porch and street. Right wall sofa, an oak book case, and a door with portieres, going upstairs. Left wall, rear, a sideboard of oak,*

with a lace cover, on which stand some fancy colored china dishes, front, a door opening into kitchen,—with the sink just beyond so that the water can be heard when it is turned on in the sink. The place small, but clean and well kept. JUDSON, a boy of five, is lying on his stomach on the sofa, looking at a book. CORA comes in from the kitchen door carrying a tray of dishes, which she arranges on a table. She is now a little over thirty. She looks older. Lines have come into her face—a certain hardness. One feels that every movement she makes has a purpose. Her voice is no longer pretty—it has grown determined and decisive. The only time it goes back to its softness is in certain moments with the boy. She wears a shirtwaist and skirt, plain and neat, and an apron. Her hands, noticeably pretty before, are now horny and red from overwork.

CORA   [*Putting tray on table*] It's getting too dark for you to read, dear. [BOY *pays no attention. She turns on the light*] You must take good care of your eyes, Judson. You'll need them when you grow up.

JUDSON   [*Looking up*] When are you going to let me go to school, mother?

CORA   [*Setting table*] You're only four now, Jud. In a couple of years—when you're ready—I'll be able to send you to a good school—

JUD   But I wanta play with the other kids!

CORA   Why, you do, Judson, quite enough! [*She is decisive, puts out dishes rapidly*] Are you hungry?

JUD   No—not very. [*Door rear opens, and* JIM *enters. He wears a workman's jacket, an overall suit, a cap, and carries a dinner pail, which he puts on a chair. His face is greyer, and the fullness of youth has gone; but he is still goodlooking—and much younger than Cora. His eyes are always lowered, or evasive in this scene. His manner is withdrawn, unsympathetic, even slightly aggressive. He does not particularly notice* CORA *or* JUD. *They greet each other indifferently*]

CORA   [*To* JUD, *who has ignored his father's entrance*] Why don't you speak to your daddy? It's the first time you've seen him today.

JUD   [*Mechanically, looking at his book*] I did.

CORA   Don't tell mother stories. [*To* JIM, *who is taking off his coat*] Ain't you home a little earlier tonight?

JIM   [*Sarcastically*] Always too early or too late! Say—it's bad enough having to punch the time-clock at the factory!

CORA   [*Evenly*] No need to be disagreeable, Jim. I wasn't saying nothing. [JIM, *without any answer, goes through door left, and there is the sound of water running as he washes up. To* JUD] Why don't you act nicer to your father when he comes in? You *know* you're still in bed when he goes mornings.

JUD [*Sitting up*] Ma—can I—have a banana?

CORA No—you're going to have your supper in a few minutes. [JIM *appears at door, drying his hands on towel. His hair is tousled and face pink*] We've got liver and bacon for supper tonight, Jim. Hungry?

JIM I forgot to ask you this morning—have my collars come back from the laundry?

CORA It's only Thursday. You get them Friday. [JIM *turns back to comb his hair. To* JUD] Come, set up dear!

JUD I want to go get my rabbit. [*Exits stairs, right*]

JIM [*Appears at the door again, hair combed. Crosses, takes his suit coat from rack, puts it on*] I think I'll run up town and get them collars. [*Rather self-consciously*] I haven't got a clean one left.

CORA [*Stops, surprised*] What? Why, it'll take you half an hour! [*Provoked*] Your supper's all ready—I was just going to fry—

JIM Well, I'll be right back. I'll catch a car. [*Slips out before she can say anything.* CORA *stands taken aback. Then she goes angrily to foot of stairs*]

CORA Judson! Come right down and have your supper! I'm not going to wait for your father.

JUD'S VOICE I'm looking for my bunny! [CORA *goes to window and pulls down the shade, and is turning back to the kitchen when there is a tap on front door center. Hesitates. Tap again. Assuming a conventional face,* CORA *goes to door, opens it*] Yes? [*She starts, then stands as if stricken. A man's mumbling voice is heard. She pushes door partially shut, in a reflex movement of fear*]

CORA What are you—doing here? [*The door is pushed open in her face.* MARTIN *comes in, and quickly closes the door behind him*]

MARTIN Oh, it's all right! I seen him board a car. [*He is bloated, dissipated, with a short beard, untidy and unclean. His manner changes in the following scene from a bullying to a whining tone alternately*]

CORA [*Her face hard and frightened*] What do you mean—comin' here?

MARTIN [*Sinks in chair by door*] I seen him leave, I tell you! [*Coughs loudly*] I seen him come in, too! I've been hanging around.

CORA He's coming right back. You've got to go. [*In a low, quick voice*] I thought you was in New York. What did you come out here for?

MARTIN I come out here to see how my dear daughter was gettin' on!

Hello Sonny! [JUDSDON *appears at foot of stairs holding toy rabbit.* CORA *goes over and pushes him back, closing door*]

CORA   Stay upstairs until mother calls you, dear. Play with Bunny. [JUD-SON *goes reluctantly. As she turns back,* MARTIN *regards her bellicosely*]

MARTIN   You know well enough what I come for. [*Threateningly*] Money!

CORA   I've been sending you all I could—for nearly two years.

MARTIN   [*Spits on floor*] Sure! . . . Buying me off! Paying me to keep my mouth shut . . . about him and you was drove out of town because of your dirty goings-on. [*Sneering*] Y' don't want your respectable friends here to know you *had* t' get married, eh? You know your old father's likely t' get drunk and spill all the beans, eh, if he's allowed around? So you buy me off. [*Grows furious*] And I don't believe that's all of it, either! I s'pose you're ashamed of me, now you're puttin' on airs! You don't want them to know you got a tramp in the family, now you've turned respectable, huh?

CORA   Stop—

MARTIN   I won't stop! It was his blow on th' head put me on th' bum. I was no good after that—[*Trembling suddenly, he touches his head*] And a nice greeting you gave me when I came beggin' to your back door, not knowing who you were!

CORA   [*Shortly*] I gave you fifty dollars.

MARTIN   Yes—to keep away so's not to let your fine husband know I ever left home—

CORA   Listen! He'll be back—[*Almost pleadingly*] Go out now! Come tomorrow!

MARTIN   [*Angrily*] And what if he does come? Why shouldn't he see me? What's the idea you've got—that he'll jump on me and commit murder?

CORA   [*Suddenly becomes hard, fierce*] Never mind! I told you then, didn't I, that if he ever knew you were around or heard of you—[*Struggling for control*] You couldn't get another cent—! I promised you—if you'd keep quiet—and away—and that I'd send you money—somehow—all I could. I have—More than enough—for that two years. You've stayed drunk—in the backroom of some saloon—and I've paid for everything. I've worked. I've took shirts from the factory; I've sewed some nights till it was getting light. I've washed—when I couldn't do anything else. And now—after that—you come out here—just the thing I said not to!

MARTIN   [*Sourly*] I come here because you said not t' write—for fear he'd see the letter. I was careful, wasn't I? And I've growed this—[*He rubs his hand over his beard*]

CORA   What do you want?

MARTIN   Change enough to get out. I'm sick of th' city. It's gettin' winter, and I want t' be where it's warm. [*Hesitates*] I'm askin' you to stake me the fare to th' Coast. [*Then sneers*] That'd be better for you, too. You needn't be afraid your fine husband'll be offended by the sight of me then!

CORA   [*Desperately*] I can't! Not now. We've just—I'll give you fifty dollars.

MARTIN   [*Blandly*] Borry it then. Fifty dollars wouldn't get me no farther than—

CORA   No—I can't—we—

MARTIN   [*Angrily*] Very well then, me fine lady, I'll go and get drunk in the nearest saloon and by mornin' the whole town'll know you for what you are—a slut that had to be married—and him a fellow that run away after nearly murderin' a poor old man. There's a charge on him yet for assault! And I'll tell them how you added a fancy name to his, Mr. Judson Jim Smith, because plain Jim Smith wasn't fine enough for a gent like him that wants to rise in the world.

CORA   [*Suddenly a curious change comes over her—she becomes like steel, vibrant, masterful. It is as though, seeing the whole structure of her life tottering, she suddenly calls on some reserve force, some tremendous will—built up probably by her idée fixe which seems to have the power of conquering any obstacle*] You'll do nothing like that! I'd have you locked up! You won't dare! You won't, because you know you'll lose the easy living you've got now and you'll have to work. [*He shrinks a little*] You're a coward at heart—like you always were. Go now. I'll send you that—as soon as I can—

MARTIN   [*Recovering a little*] I'll wait in town over night—you c'n send it to Hollys—

CORA   [*In tense calm*] Go now. He'll be back—[*She urges him to door*]

MARTIN   [*Mockingly*] He'll—He'll—! [*Suddenly there are footsteps on the porch. They are both paralyzed. She makes a movement as if to hide him. There is a knock. Her face floods with relief*]

CORA   It's somebody else—

MARTIN   [*Threateningly*] Remember—by noon tomorrow—[CORA *opens the door. A man's voice saying, "Good evening, Mrs. Smith"*]

CORA   [*In great confusion*] Why—good evening, Mr. Walters! [*She holds the door open, and as* WALTERS *enters,* MARTIN *slips obsequiously out.* WALTERS *is a pleasant, middle-aged man, well dressed and efficient. He is manager of the factory where Jim works]*

WALTERS   [*Genially*] Good evening, Mrs. Smith. How are you? I thought I'd drop in and see you and your husband for a few moments.

CORA   [*Still confused*] Won't—won't you sit down? [*It is evident from her manner that this visit is very unusual*]

WALTERS   Thanks—yes. [*Sits*] Nice little place you've got, Mrs. Smith. I understand that you own it, too. [*Genially*] That's the idea! It's a pity we haven't more people like you in this town. Most of 'em complain that they can't manage on what they get—

CORA   He's a foreman—

WALTERS   [*As though perplexed*] Yes! [*Shakes his head*] I dropped in to talk to you about that. Is he here, Mrs. Smith?

CORA   He's gone uptown. He'll be back soon.

WALTERS   [*Confidentially*] Well, perhaps it's just as well that he's *not* here Mrs. Smith! I can talk to you. [*Flatteringly*] As a wife, perhaps your influence—[*Shakes his head*] I don't understand him, I'll admit.

CORA   Is—anything wrong? [*She speaks and* JUDSON *comes in. He goes slowly toward the table, clutching his rabbit, and staring at* WALTERS. CORA *lifts him up absently and seats him at table. It is evident that she is bewildered by Walter's talk.* JUDSON *eats his bread and milk]* Is—anything wrong, Mr. Walters?

WALTERS   Why no, Mrs. Smith. I meant his refusing the new position.

CORA   Refusing—the new position?

WALTERS   [*Surprised*] He didn't tell you?

CORA   [*As though defeated*] No—nothing.

WALTERS   Good Lord! Well, what's the matter with him, Mrs. Smith? [*Suspiciously*] Do you suppose it's—socialism?

CORA   [*Feverishly*] No—no! What—position was it?

WALTERS   Superintendent of the factory here, Mrs. Smith. You can realize what that means. [*Impressively*] What it opens up to you—to the kiddy there!

CORA   [*Slowly*] Yes.

WALTERS   Garland, the old superintendent, is leaving next week. He's going with the Eastern. He wanted Smith to step right in. He refused. Said he couldn't take the responsibility. Well—that's foolish! We wouldn't ask him if he wasn't the man we wanted. [*Pauses*] In fact, we've had an eye on him for some time.

CORA   [*Slowly*] He could get anywhere—I always thought—

WALTERS   [*Brightening*] He could, Mrs. Smith. He's got the real qualifications. [*Pauses*] He's got a funny, glum streak, too [*Shakes his head*] I can't understand his refusing, and not telling you—

CORA   [*Her hands closing and unclosing nervously*] It's—some mistake. He'll take it, Mr. Walters—he'll—have to take it! [*Violently*] Why—it's—it's what we've been working for—the first step up—!

WALTERS   [*Rises*] I'm glad I stopped in, Mrs. Smith. And—[*Laughs*] glad he wasn't here! Now that you know how things stand, you can probably bring him around. [*Flatteringly*] *I'm* inclined to think that his wife has had a lot to do with the good luck of the Smith family! [*Suddenly*] You're ambitious—aren't you?

CORA   [*In a low voice*] For him—yes.

WALTERS   Well—buck him up!

CORA   [*Firmly*] I know he'll change his mind, Mr. Walters.

WALTERS   Good! Fine! Well, I must run along. My wife will be waiting dinner—[*Shakes hands with her*] Of course [*Hesitates*] I don't suppose there's a chance—that he's been offered a position with the Eastern?

CORA   [*Positively*] Oh no—I'm sure not.

WALTERS   [*Relieved*] Well—that's good, then! But it just seemed possible—when they told me that he'd drawn his money tonight, and said that he wouldn't report in this morning—in fact, that was what made me stop in. [*Heartily, as though ashamed of his suspicion*] Well, that's all right! Let him have a couple of days off! Work is slack now. Goodby, Mrs. Smith. Cheer up! He'll come round to our way of thinking. [*Bows, goes out. CORA stands in a queer daze*]

CORA   Jud—did Daddy say anything to you—about staying home tomorrow?

JUD   [*Shakes his head*] N-num . . .

CORA   [*Moves about room in panic*] Eat your supper, dear. [*Pauses, crosses to stairs*] I'm going up to Daddy's room for a moment. [*Exits. JUD eats slowly, his rabbit perched beside his plate. He offers it food. CORA returns, pale, tense. Hesitates. Then goes to Jim's work-coat and goes through pockets. Takes out an envelope—opens it—finds a railroad ticket. Stares at it a moment. Bitterly*]

Here's a ticket to California in your father's pocket, Jud! It's good—you're not old enough to know what that means—

JUD   Is Daddy—going—chu—chu?

CORA   No—I don't think he's going, Jud. [*She puts ticket in her apron pocket and grimly goes ahead setting the table. Her mouth is a tight line. She keeps listening. Finally steps are heard.* JIM *enters, with laundry.* CORA *pretends not to notice him; she stands with her back to him, sorting forks in the sideboard drawer.* JIM *hesitates a moment, as though to disarm her suspicions, then goes to work-coat, looks through pockets, all of them. His face shows concern, which he tries to conceal. He takes cigarette and lights it. Turning slowly*] What's the matter, Jim? You—look funny.

JIM   [*Frowning*] Funny?—you're crazy! [*Unconsciously he is going through the pockets of the coat that he wears. He is not sure where he has mislaid ticket. With an air of ease*] Supper ready?

CORA   [*Turns back to drawer*] Yes. [JIM *picks up laundry bundle and exits upstairs, his face a mixture of bravado and dismay.* CORA *turns, stands tensely, waiting for him to come back. In a moment he does so. His face is dark and angry, but he attempts to control himself*]

JIM   Where did you put my brown suit?

CORA   [*Dully*] Isn't it at the tailors?

JIM   What do you mean? Why it was—it was—right there!

CORA   How d'you know? You never go to th' closet unless it's Sunday and you're going to wear it.

JIM   [*Furiously*] It was on the bed! You've done something with it!

CORA   [*In the same dull, lifeless voice*] What was it doin' on the bed? And what was you getting your laundry for—this time o' week?

JIM   [*Hesitates*] What for? [*Stares at her*] When I've had my supper, I'm goin' down town, see? [*Works himself up*] Haven't I a right to, eh? what do you mean, taking my clothes? Where are they? You put them back! God! If I ain't got the right to have a little fun in the evening—without you stealin' my clothes—to keep me home! [*He makes a theatrical gesture*]

CORA   You never got dressed to go out evenings, before.

JIM   [*Sullenly*] How many evenings have I been out—in five years? [*Bitterly*] A dog's life!

CORA   Jim! [*It is a hurt cry.* JIM *gives her a look of deep dislike then goes to kitchen door and stands staring into kitchen. His face shows desperation. Turns back*]

JIM   [*More pleasantly*] Where is that suit, Cora? I told you—I've got to go uptown this evening.

CORA   Jim—that ain't all.

JIM   [*Nervously, hardenedly*] What d'you mean? [*Prepares to defend himself*]

CORA   Mr. Walters was here tonight—after you'd gone.

JIM   He was—eh? [*Angrily*] What'd he come here for? T' see you? Has it got out that *you're* boss—that—

CORA   Listen! [*Lifts her hand*] Everybody knows that in a case like this a man's wife would use her influence. . . . But that wasn't it. He came here to see you—to try an' persuade *you*—[*Bitterly*] Why didn't you tell me about this?

JIM   [*Ignoring her question*] Aw—I bet you had to butt in—[*Moves uneasily*]

CORA   [*Quietly*] Jim—you've forgotten—this thing—this chance—it's what we've been workin' for—for five years—we've planned—

JIM   You mean—*you've* planned—

CORA   [*Suddenly goes to him, and puts her arms about his neck. Her face is working, her eyes full of tears*] Jim! You've worked for it, too! You've been fine—too! D'you think that they'd have offered you th' job—if you hadn't worked—if you hadn't stood out as th' best man there? Why—you was foreman after two years! [*She tries to kiss him, but he turns his head sharply*]

JIM   Sure I've worked. I've done a good job there—because it's the only interest I've had in this hell of a life! [*Wildly*] A man's got to do something well, t' take his mind off his troubles!

CORA   [*Her voice trembles*] This—[*Makes gestures about room, including* JUD] doesn't mean nothing to you, then?

JIM   [*Sullenly*] How could it? [*Again fiercely*] How could it!

CORA   [*Pauses*] Juddie dear—you're through now—will you run upstairs and undress yourself? [*Leads him across to stairs*] Mother'll be up pretty soon, and tuck you in! [JUD *kisses her and goes upstairs.* CORA *returns and begins piling up his empty dishes. Her face is hard and stern.* JIM *watches her, as though waiting for her to speak. Her silence exasperates him*]

JIM   [*After a moment*] Did you think—that *you* was givin' me anything?

CORA   I think I have, Jim.

JIM   Sure—a nice little house with a rubberplant by the door, three meals a day—[*With disgust*] Ba!

CORA I've given you security, Jim—an' a home—an' comfort—an' a chance to—Why, remember what you was, Jim? And you'd be that, still—goin' from town to town—drinking—

JIM Now you're starting! [*Clenches his hands, but listens, as though, almost, she hypnotizes him*]

CORA I can't see how you feel about it, Jim. We own this house—we've bought those lots with th' building loan—they all like you at th' factory—an' now this chance comes. It—it's five thousand a year, Jim. You could have a car—an' everything, Jim. We could rent this house, and get another—in town. You—you could dress different. You know you care about nice things t' wear. You wouldn't be a workman no more. Don't you see that? An' Jud—th' baby—

JIM A bigger house an' a car don't mean nothin' to me. More work's more responsibility—no! I hate it all, I tell you! [*Sits down heavily in chair by table*]

CORA [*Flaming*] It doesn't just mean that, Jim! Not to me. I've told you about it before—that night. I don't want to just live in a bigger house, neither. If I thought that you would just be superintendent all your life, I wouldn't care. But—it's th' wedge. Don't you see? You c'n do anything. This is the proof. You c'n get power—an' money. It's here lyin' all around. We could have everything then—and everything for *him*—travel, and jewels, and beautiful things—servants to do everything, so as you don't *have* to work—and then, when you'd drive out, in your car,—people'll stare—that's him! [*She pauses, lit with the brilliance of her dream*]

JIM [*Laughs scornfully, then in a low voice—bringing it out with an effort*] Sure!—point me out!—a man wanted for murder!

CORA [*Coming out of her dream. Dazed, frightened by his words as though she had for a moment forgotten the power of what it is that she holds over him*] Oh—no! They've forgotten! That's forgotten—[*She trembles violently*] You—must forget—too!

JIM [*Bitterly*] Me? When th' reason I'm here is because of that? When every step I take—if I don't go *your* way—you hold it over my head? [*Laughs bitterly*] Say—what's th' use of talking? An' anyhow—all this stuff about limousines an' traveling, an' servants don't appeal to me. I don't want no dressed up froggie opening the door for me. That's why I wouldn't take th' job. [*Pauses; she is looking at him accusingly; he adds lamely*] I'd rather keep on livin' like this, Cora.

CORA You lie. [*Fixes him with her eyes*]

JIM Eh? [*Stares at her*]

CORA   You lie. Just as you did when you said that you was going uptown tonight. You didn't take the job—because you was running away. Tonight. That's where you was going. [*Laughs hysterically*] A ticket to California.

JIM   [*Dazed for a second, leaps to his feet*] You're crazy! [*Then he sees by her cold, smiling face that he is trapped*] You—devil! [*Goes to her, twists her arm*] Give me that ticket! [*She stands calmly, without wincing, staring into his eyes*] Where is it? You took it out of my pocket—an' I thought I'd lost it— [*Fiercely*] Give it to me!

CORA   [*Calmly*] Yes. You can have it. [*Takes it, gives it to him, still smiling fixedly*] Go on. Leave. I wonder how far you'll get—after I've let them know. Chicago, maybe. That's near Union, too. [JIM *watches her during this like a man on the point of insanity*] And deserting your wife and child too, It will—go hard with you. Yes, go—if you want that. [*Her eyes glitter. She looks ugly, old, powerful, viperish*]

JIM   You—lie. There's this house—th' building lots—I'm taking nothing.

CORA   You won't need anything—in jail.

JIM   [*With furious desperation*] Well—I'll take the chance! [*He looks about the room as though in search of something—looks at ticket in his hand— picks up his hat, and violently opens door—then with hand on the knob, he hesitates—turns back, his face is drawn, grey*] Corrie, for God's sake—don't do this! Let me go. Let me get away. It's hell. It's hell for us—for th' kid. It'd be much better for me t' disappear. They'd never get me, if you said nothing. You've got th' house and th' lots. You'd be well off. You could get a divorce an' marry again. You're young. You'd be happy. An' all this nightmare'd be over! [*She stands like a statue, her hands clenched, her burning eyes on him. He comes back, shakes her arm*] Let me go, Corrie! This thing of trying to be all that—with prison hangin' over my head—it's driving me crazy! I want t' be a tramp—anything! I want t' *forget*! [*He pleads*] It—can't make so much difference to you, Corrie. Your trouble's over. You were right making me stay before. But now—you're fixed fine. An' you know th' life we've had together. It's hell on you, too. [*Wilily repeats*] You could marry again—

CORA   [*Slowly turns, looks him full in the face*] No! Marry again? [*Laughs*] No. But—go. I ain't holding you. Only if you do—I'll have to tell th' whole story. [*Fiercely, loudly*] We've come this far, we've got to go further! I've worked—you've worked—we've got Jud—[*Pauses*] If you go now, I'll never forgive you.

JIM   [*For a long moment he stares at her; then his face grows as hard as hers. He laughs sneeringly. Takes off cap and throws it on chair*] That's your answer then? [*He puts ticket on table, walks to window, pulls up shade, looks out, pulls it down, comes back*] It's war now—from now on! I'll make you suffer for this! [*He shakes fist at her*] You're strong—but I'm strong too. You have something to hold over me. Well, all right, lets see what I can do to you! It's war—from now on! [*He has raised his voice in a frenzy during this speech; finished, he sinks in a trembling, crushed heap on the sofa.* JUD, *who has heard the noise, comes in from the stairs*]

CORA Jud!

JUD [*Goes quickly over to his father, tugs at his arm*] Daddy—Ma said you was going away—on a chu-chu—[*Announces, pleased*] I'm goin' wif you—too!

CORA [*Quickly goes over and pulls him away from* JIM] Jud—go up to bed—

JIM [*Suddenly lifts his head and puts his arm around* JUD, *holding him; looks at* CORA, *who has grown pale*] You want to go with me—do you? Well—maybe—some day, Juddie—some day. . . . [*They stare at one another with hatred, as the curtain falls*]

CURTAIN

ACT THREE

TIME: 1924
SCENE: A *large room, perhaps the drawing room, in the home of J. J. Smith, President of the Paterson Tin-Plate Products, at Paterson, N.J.*

It is obviously a millionaire's home—and obviously done by an interior decorator. There are tall French windows opening at back, a black marble mantel right, a door right and left. The furniture looks almost too good to be genuine—but it is.

Before a fine Spanish desk, right, MILDRED LORD is sitting with a pad and pencil. She has been taking an inventory of the things in the room. She is the Smiths' private secretary—not more than nineteen—very pretty—very well-bred. Her dress is dark and plain, but against it her vivid beauty flares up all the more brilliantly.

MILDRED [*Referring to another list—To herself*] One 15th Century Spanish desk—Zice and May, 1921. Value, $1,500. [*Writes, looks over at chair*] Two Italian chairs—[*Door left opens and* MAID (TUDOR) *enters with flowers. She is about forty, garrulous, in correct uniform. She puts flowers on central table.*

MILDRED *turning*] Oh—aren't they lovely! [*She goes over and touches them lightly*]

TUDOR   The gard'ner's been workin' on 'em all winter, Miss Lord—he says they're a real rare kind. [*She also looks at the flowers admiringly*]

MILDRED   [*Sighs*] Yes—they're lovely. [*Then, brightly*] By the way, Tudor—that Russian mosaic box—[*She shows the size with her hands*] Usen't it to stand on the table there? I'm taking an inventory—and I want to be sure.

TUDOR   Yes'm. But Mr. Jud, I think he took it over to the billiard room.

MILDRED   [*Rather coldly*] I see.

TUDOR   [*Dusting—with curiosity*] Whatever are you taking an inventory for, Miss Lord? [*Alarmed*] They isn't going to be a *sale*, is there?

MILDRED   [*Smiling*] No, hardly, Tudor. It's just one of the things I promised Mrs. Smith I'd get done before I left. [*Lightly*] You know I'm going Tuesday!

TUDOR   [*Pauses; sighs*] I know it, Miss Lord. And I want to tell you—for one, I'm sorry! I don't know how they're going to get along without you. Why, the three years you've been here—I don't see how they can let you go!

MILDRED   They *do* want me to stay, Tudor. But—I need a change. [*Writes in book*] One walnut—

TUDOR   [*Resumes dusting*] Well, it's more than just a secretary you've been, Miss Lord. You've done a lot. I've been here five years, and I know! It's a queer house, Miss—not like other people's houses—and I'll say that you've done something to make it more human. [*Pauses*] And as for Mr. Judson—why for a while there you had more influence—[*Sighs*] although it seems now that he's gone back—worse than ever. [*Shakes her head*] It's a great pity, Miss Lord.

MILDRED   Never mind, please, Tudor. That isn't our business.

TUDOR   [*Emphatically*] Well—I do wish you could have seen the dining room this morning! Even broken bottles—[MILDRED *has moved away to other end of the room.* JUDSON *enters.* TUDOR, *flustered, dusts rapidly.* JUDSON *is a very handsome fair boy, rather like his father. He is dressed remarkably well—with all the necessary negligence. He lounges, or stands with his hands in his pockets. His face shows little sign of dissipation—he is still too young—but it is revealed in his manner and in his voice. He has really great sweetness and charm—but it is obviously being rapidly ruined*]

JUD   [*Kiddingly*] What's that, Tudor, eh?

TUDOR   Nothing, Mr. Judson. [*Exits, still flustered*]

JUD   [*Seats himself*] What was old Tudor grumbling about? Didn't I hear something about bottles—*broken* bottles—or was it broken blossoms? [*Smiles with boyish pleasure at his smartness*]

MILDRED   [*Who has her back toward him, coldly*] I'm sure I don't know. I wasn't listening.

JUD   [*Easily*] She's been here too long. They all get fresh—after a few years. [MILDRED *is severely silent*] Mind if I smoke? [*Lights a cigarette*] I suppose she was fussing about the dining room being a bit upset this morning. Well, it's none of her business. *I* think that we were pretty darn quiet. Had all th' doors closed. You didn't hear anything, did you?

MILDRED   One Ming Vase—

JUD   [*With the monotonous talkativeness of the morning after*] We woke th' old man up all right. It must have been nearly five. [*Yawns*] Say—he's a good sport, though, Milly, d'you know it? Never said a thing—just asked me if I'd been having a good time. [*Laughs*] I guess he could see *that* all right!

MILDRED   [*Her back still toward him—sarcastically*] No doubt. [*Makes entry in book*]

JUD   It seems to me sometimes that he's—just anxious for me to—step out. As they would say in the latest manner—he's got a joy complex which he transfers to his son.

MILDRED   [*Loftily*] Your ventures into the idiom of psychoanalysis are inaccurate—to say the least!

JUD   Now Milly—don't be a high-brow! [*Affectionately*] You're much nicer when you're low-brow, old dear!

MILDRED   I'm busy—really! Would you mind—[*Her voice trembles, but she says determinedly, and rather loudly*] One pair of Russian candlesticks—

JUD   Say—what is this? Another of mother's damned inventories? [*Pauses—vehemently*] Honestly, Milly, it seems as though she even wants to keep tabs on the furniture—know just what everything costs—where everything is—just as she has with everybody in the house. Tagged and labelled. [*Sourly*] And what good does it all do her? I never saw a more miserable person than mother.

MILDRED   Please don't talk about your mother to me, Jud. She—she simply asked me to go over this inventory for her, before I left.

JUD   Listen, Milly—Turn around, won't you? [*She does not; very tenderly*] You're not really going, of course? Are you?

MILDRED   [*Faces him, she assumes a rather hard, light manner, beneath which is tenseness*] Certainly I am. Why not? There's no reason for my staying.

JUD   [*Evading her eyes*] There's no reason for your going, either.

MILDRED   [*Winces slightly*] I—I want a change. [*Hardens again*] Besides—I've been here three years now—ever since my father died. I—want to see something more of life.

JUD   [*Gloomily*] You are certainly the only life in *this* house.

MILDRED   Except what you bring in—late at night. [*A pause*]

JUD   Don't go, Milly. [*Goes to her, puts his arm about her*] Won't you— kiss me?

MILDRED   [*Matter-of-factly allowing him to embrace her, but not returning it, coldly*] Why should I? We don't love one another. [*He drops his hands, puts them in his pockets, turns away*] We agreed to that. If you were going away, I shouldn't ask you to stay. Why should you ask *me*?

JUD   [*Grumpily*] It's so damn foolish—your leaving. You'll never get a position like this again. You'll be up against all sorts of people. [*Pauses*] Here, you're really a member of the family.

MILDRED   [*With meaning—and a high color*] Decidedly!

JUD   Good Lord, Mildred!

MILDRED   [*In a business-like tone*] Beside, I've saved my salary. I have a nice nest-egg put away. I won't get another situation at once.

JUD   And such foolishness—not letting anyone know where you are going!

MILDRED   I prefer to do that. [*Forcing herself into a mock gaiety*] Now Jud, don't let's be so serious about it all! We're young. We've got the world before us—[*Turns away—her face suddenly twisting—controls herself*] I'll write you some day—really!

JUD   Oh, well—[*Disconsolately whistling through his teeth*] I suppose you know what you want. [*Goes to window, looks out*] Somctimes those damn parties do get to be a bore. [*A pause*] Well, I suppose—a hair of the dog that bit you— [*As he speaks, JIM enters. He is now J. J. Smith, president of the biggest tin-plate company in the East. His shoulders sag slightly, and he has grown decidedly larger around the waist. His hair is white. He is still handsome. He is also well dressed, and has become a man of the world, with the manner of one used to authority. But when he is not speaking—in repose—his face shows lines of care— a worn, harrassed look*]

SMITH   Well— up so early, after last night! [*Smiles*]

JUD   I was just going to get a drink, Dad—you know—a hair of the dog that bit you! I feel nervous.

SMITH   Well, I guess it won't hurt you. [*To* MILDRED] Miss Lord, Mrs. Smith wants to see you for a moment, please.

MILDRED   Oh, certainly! [*Puts tablet down, exits right*]

SMITH   [*Pats* JUD'*s shoulder*] Well, boy!

JUD   [*Suddenly*] Say, Dad—now that we're alone—there's a couple of things I want to ask you—

SMITH   Money?

JUD   [*Laughs*] Well, that's the least important! But as you happened to mention it—

SMITH   I've kept you pretty well supplied, eh, Jud? [*Harshly*] But you enjoy it. That's more than can be said of any other member of the family.

JUD   [*Impulsively*] Say Dad, I've thought of that, too. Why don't you go in for something—a yacht—or racing—or, gee, even the country club! It'd be great for you, Dad!

SMITH   Me? Golf? [*Laughs harshly*]

JUD   Sure. It'd get you out of yourself. You'd get to have some friends then. You'd have an interest in life. As it is—as it's been ever since *I* can remember—it's been nothing but business—or home here alone. Up in your room by yourself. [*Awkwardly*] And it isn't as if you and mother were—well, you know what I mean—pals. [*An embarrassed pause*] And Dad, I notice it's been getting worse lately—for you. You're home so darned much—

SMITH   [*Musingly*] Yes, for the last few years business has been too easy. I don't have to work now—or organize—or plan. It goes by itself. There's nothing left—but to watch the wheels go round.

JUD   And the money come in! [*Laughs*]

SMITH   [*Suddenly, gripping* JUD'*s shoulder*] I want *you* to enjoy it, Jud!— in *your* way! I want you to be free—to keep away from all the cursed, grinding monotony of this damned life! Power! Position! Money! Look at it! [*With a violent gesture*] See what it means to me!

JUD   [*Soberly*] You and mother sure do lead the worst known lives, Dad. No friends—no amusements—nothing! And you could have everything.

SMITH   [*Slowly*] No. *She* doesn't enjoy it much, either. [*After a long pause, suddenly*] Doesn't all this—what you see of—your mother and me—this home—turn you against marriage?

JUD   [*Reflectively*] It does, Dad.

SMITH   [*Pacing across room and back*] Don't let 'em get you, boy. Don't let life get you. Live yourself. Be what you are. [*Pauses, passionately*] I've lived twenty-two years of hell, Jud. Because—of a mistake. Life was mine, then!— When I was your age. [*In a lower voice*] I should have gone on—my own way— the way I wanted—

JUD   What was it, Dad?

SMITH   Something happened. Never mind that.

JUD   [*Slowly*] Dad—you spoke about my turning against marriage. Do you mean—perhaps—you shouldn't have married?

SMITH   Well—[*Assents, without words*]

JUD   [*Gaily*] Well, remember if you were still a jolly old bach, there wouldn't be any young Jud Smith to spend your money!

SMITH   [*Stands perfectly still—as though struck*] Y—yes.

JUD   [*In a half-ashamed voice*] And I *do* know, Dad, mother is pretty difficult to get along with. Why—I—the way she's been after me, ever since I can remember! You and she—it's always seemed that you've wanted me to do just the opposite!

SMITH   [*Almost as though he has not heard this last*] Jud—remember— you're the only human being—I care about.

JUD   [*Very much embarrassed*] Righto, Dad! Ditto! And—or—say, how about the golf, eh? Is it a go?

SMITH   [*Coming to himself*] I'm afraid not. [*Shakes his head*] I'll watch you enjoy yourself. [*Dryly*] I notice *you*—don't golf!

JUD   [*Delighted*] All right! Come along with me then, we'll stage a real party!

SMITH   Too late. [*Changing the subject*] Wasn't there something you wanted to speak to me about—[*Smiles*] beside money?

JUD   [*Startled—very embarrassed*] Oh, yes Dad—sure. [*Fidgets*] It's— about Mildred.

SMITH   [*Sharply*] Yes.

JUD   She's leaving, you know—some damn crazy idea.

SMITH   She told me she wanted a change.

JUD   Well—I don't know. You—want her to stay, don't you?

SMITH   I'd be glad to have her stay. But—[*Sharply*] after all, it's her business. Why are you so interested?

JUD   [*Lights another cigarette*] You see, Dad—it's rather hard to explain— [*Pauses*]

SMITH   I don't think you need to explain, Jud. I've seen what was going on. I said nothing. That was your business—and hers. But now, if she wants to go, I think it's the best thing. She—[Hesitates—then sharply, looking at JUD with anxiety] You're not in love with her?

JUD   [Awkwardly] Oh, no, Dad! I don't know what that means. There are too many girls—

SMITH   [Relieved] Yes. I shouldn't have worried. Aren't you—isn't there that—Follies girl—?

JUD   Yes. But she—I mean Mildred—she's really different. And I hate to see her go because—I—[Embarrassed] I feel it's my fault. Do you see? I ought to get her to stay. Perhaps I—took advantage—and it's all my fault—what's happened—

SMITH   [Tensely] You don't mean she's going because she's—in trouble?

JUD   [Ashamedly] Good Lord, no, Dad! It's not as bad as that. Just— I know she is leaving because of me—and she's so alone. I feel—sort of guilty. If she stays here, now—where she has a good home and everything—

SMITH   She's probably going because she can't stand seeing you off all the time with others when she'd like to have you to herself! Well, she's sensible. [Grimly] I've no doubt she's tried all her tricks—and failed! [Almost to himself] It's a wonder—she didn't try that last one. [Suddenly] Really, Jud, I think it's for the best that she goes. [Pauses] It's just the women who are different—who are dangerous.

JUD   I—I just thought that if—[He is seeking for words when MILDRED comes back]

MILDRED   Oh, excuse me—you were talking. I was just going to finish up the inventory—[Turns to go]

JUD   [Hurriedly—flushed] I think I'll go and get that long-delayed drink! [Exits. SMITH stands at the French windows, looking out. MILDRED goes on quietly with her work of inventory]

SMITH   [Turning suddenly] Miss Lord:

MILDRED   [Turns to him pleasantly] Yes, Mr. Smith?

SMITH   [Brutally] My son was just asking me to urge you not to leave us. [Pause] He seems to feel you will have a hard time—getting another position as good as this. [Meaningly]

MILDRED   [Flares] Thank you for telling me. I assure you that what your son says has absolutely no influence with me!

SMITH   No?

MILDRED   No. I am sorry to have to leave you, but I can't change my plans because of your son's sudden whim! [*Gives a hard laugh*]

SMITH   [*Provoked and angry with her defiance*] Look here— you aren't going to deny that you've had a love affair with him?

MILDRED   And may I ask, Mr. Smith, why, just because you employ me, you feel that you have a right to enquire into my personal affairs? But frankly— yes, I've had a love affair with your son. What about it? Has it done him any harm? [*Laughs*] It could hardly be called an entanglement! Some of his other affairs might—but not this!

SMITH   [*Grimly*] I've taught him to avoid entanglements!

MILDRED   [*Her face pale*] I dare say. You've given him license for a great deal, Mr. Smith. However—I don't see that this is your business at all. [*Turns away*]

SMITH   [*Rather taken aback*] You're—a hard one.

MILDRED   [*Pleasantly*] A young woman has to be hard—now-a-days.

SMITH   [*Abruptly*] You love him. You'd probably like to marry him. This—is all pretense—[*Makes gesture*]

MILDRED   [*Turns back—laughs*] You're very old-fashioned, Mr. Smith! [*Suddenly she lights up with passion and determination: goes closer to him*] I'll tell you the truth, Mr. Smith! You force me to it—though you won't like it. [*Forcibly*] Do you really think that *any* woman—with self-respect—or, even any woman simply looking forward to a decent, comfortable life—would marry your son? Do you? Think! [*She pauses;* SMITH *is absolutely taken aback*] Don't you realize—what he's becoming? Can't you look five years into the future and see—what he'll be then? Why—you can see the change working in his face now, day by day. He drinks all the time. He was sent home after his second year in college—in disgrace. He has no work—no ideas—nothing but *this* idea of the most dissipated life possible! And that he's gotten from you. That's the tragedy of it. He's not like this, really. He'd be like other boys—go through it, and go on to something else. But you corrupt him. You give him absolute leeway. You deride any attempt anyone—even his mother—makes to get him straightened out. And when he himself shows some sign of pulling out of all this—you do or say something which pushes him back! Look at the difference in him now, and last year. Just one year! [*She controls herself—in a calmer voice*] No, Mr. Smith. I can't see any girl—except one of his own sort—wanting to marry your son. Perhaps you've noticed that even the flappers—and they're gay enough—leave him strictly alone. I'm sorry you forced me into saying this.

But—your insinuations—are too silly. [*She picks up pad*] Jud's a nice boy—but I can't stay—not even for him.

SMITH [*In a grey, toneless voice*] You women are all alike. You think that because a man is free—enjoying himself in his own way—not slaving for the things that *you* think are good—power, money, position—that he's ruined. [*Passionately*] It's a woman's idea! It's a woman's world—all of it! [*Fiercely*] Why should a man be forced—to accomplish?

MILDRED You've accomplished, Mr. Smith.

SMITH What good has it done me? No. Let him have his fun!

MILDRED You talk to me like a man who'd stopped growing up—at twenty-two, Mr. Smith. You don't mind my saying your ideas are very adolescent.

SMITH [*Coldly*] It's just as well that you're going, Miss Lord. By the way—will you finish filing those letters? The new secretary is coming Monday.

MILDRED Certainly, Mr. Smith. [*Picks up pad.* SMITH *exits.* MILDRED *goes over and stands before plaque*] One—Spanish Madonna—[*Her voice trembles; she sinks down across the back of the chair, her face buried, her body shaking with grief. Silently, slowly,* CORA *appears at French windows, center, and opening them, steps in. She stands there silently, looking at* MILDRED. CORA *is now nearly fifty. Her face is ravaged and seared with unhappiness. Her figure sags, and she moves slowly, as though very tired. Her eyes have an expression almost painfully intense and burning. She is dressed in dark colors, without style, almost untidily. Her mass of grey hair is carelessly put up. Her bony hands, covered with large diamonds, twist and turn ceaselessly*]

CORA [*Finally moving into the room*] What is the matter?

MILDRED [*Stumbling up*] Oh—nothing, Mrs. Smith! [*Controls herself somewhat*] It's—just my going away, I suppose.

CORA [*Slowly*] You're not the crying kind. [*Looks into her face*] There's something wrong. What is it?

MILDRED No, Mrs. Smith. [*Softly*] Please forget that you saw me like this. I'm just a little tired out.

CORA Is that why you're going—because you're tired out? [*She looks at her keenly*]

MILDRED [*Uneasily*] Partly, I suppose. [*She picks up pad uneasily*]

CORA I want you to stay. [MILDRED *turns away*] I want you to stay, Mildred.

MILDRED I—I can't. I'm awfully sorry.

CORA Do you remember after your father the Judge died—and they found that he'd been ruined—

MILDRED And you paid for my secretarial course and gave me a position here, with you. Oh, yes, Mrs. Smith—I haven't forgotten—but—[*Turns away*]

CORA It seems as if you *had* forgotten—you're leaving now. I *ask* you to stay.

MILDRED [*Turns back as though cornered. Desperately*] It's impossible. *Please* don't ask me. [*Emotionally*] I'd do anything you'd ask me—that I could. You—you've been awfully good to me, Mrs. Smith.

CORA Then—stay! [MILDRED *says nothing*] What is the reason? [*Twists her hands*] I think I know. It's because you—love Jud. You think you should get away. That's why you're goin'.

MILDRED [*Paling*] Mrs. Smith, I—

CORA I—But that's why—I want you to stay. You must—help me. Stay—and help me.

MILDRED I don't understand you, Mrs. Smith.

CORA Did you hear, last night? Down there—drinking—till five. Do you know who they were? I know. I went down and listened to them. It was terrible. And the girls—they were—[*She shudders*] You can't imagine. [*Pauses*] And all th' time—this goes on. If it isn't here, it's somewhere else. [*Suddenly she pauses, and then seems to gather herself together*] It's got to be stopped somehow—before it's too late—[*Intensely*] I was awake all night—thinking and thinking what to do.

MILDRED No one can do anything. As for your idea about me—well, what good would that do—if it were true?

CORA I've always been able to work things out. But not this. He—hasn't any use for me. It's all his father. And—[*Slowly*] He's all I love—all I love—[*Her head droops—a pause—then going on with her train of thought*] Last night—I began to think about you—and your going. And I thought how much you'd done—toward keeping him here. You're young and pretty. He likes that. He likes to be with you. I've noticed it. He's always asking where you are. Yes, I noticed. And I came to know that that was why you was going. That you'd—fallen in love with him.

MILDRED [*Smiling*] Perhaps—Mrs. Smith! But if I have, shouldn't I be sorry for myself?

CORA You stay. You can do something with him. You can—help save him. Be nice. Keep him here. [*Goes over and puts her hand pleadingly on*

MILDRED's *arm*] Don't you see? You'll stay now, won't you? It's only through you that I can save him—from his father.

MILDRED   If I could—but I can't, Mrs. Smith. I must go Tuesday.

CORA   But you was crying when I came in—[*Slowly, as though feeling her way*] There's—some reason. And not letting us know where it is you're going to—[*Suspiciously—with dawning light*] There's some other reason—[*Suddenly her face hardens*] You—is it—*that* reason?

MILDRED   [*Defiantly*] What reason?

CORA   You've got to get away—because something is going to happen to you—?

MILDRED   [*Flushes deeply, hesitates, as though unable to decide what to say: finally, desperately*] Yes. That's why, Mrs. Smith. You know now. I'm glad—because you won't think now I'm ungrateful. That was why I couldn't let you know where I was going—

CORA   And he—Jud's letting you go?

MILDRED   [*Hastily*] He—he doesn't know, Mrs. Smith. You must promise me—you *must* promise—not to tell him. You see, he—he doesn't care—not really—I couldn't let him think—[*She is in a panic*]

CORA   [*Determinedly*] He'll have to marry you now. He's got to know.

MILDRED   [*Proudly*] No, Mrs. Smith. Listen. If it comes to that—if you do tell him—and he should offer to marry me—I'd refuse. I really mean it. I couldn't marry him knowing he doesn't love me. And I *won't* marry him—to reform him. [*She is quiet, and absolutely convincing. Smiles wanly*] You don't understand, I suppose—that I'd rather have freedom—than be miserably married to—Jud's dissipation!

CORA   [*In a sort of trance*] Maybe it's the hand of God. Maybe this will save him.

MILDRED   [*With a movement of weary impatience*] Do you mind my saying something, Mrs. Smith? I think that your idea about me—or about marriage—helping Jud—is wrong. To force him into marriage with someone, when he didn't care, would be the worst thing in the world for him. And I'll tell you why. It's because I know that he *is* capable of love. He thinks now that he's not. He never has loved—but he will. And then—he'll be ruined—or saved. [*Sadly*] That will depend on the girl.

CORA   [*Bitterly*] It'll be—some chorus girl.

MILDRED   I think he's seen too much of them. It'll be someone pure—fine. [*She breaks*] We should save him for that.

CORA   But meantime—[*She makes a desperate gesture*] Mildred: I want to talk to him. Will you send him in to me?

MILDRED   You must promise me first—not to let him know.

CORA   I promise. [*She sinks into chair.* MILDRED *silently assents, and goes.* CORA *stares about the room—picks up inventory list, looks at it, drops it on the floor with listless fingers. Her head bows. The door opens.* JUD *comes in. His manner is very different with his mother. He is constrained, almost formal—with just a suspicion that he has some dread of her*]

JUD   [*Politely*] Good night, Mother, how are you?

CORA   [*Lifelessly*] Not well this morning, Judson. After last night—

JUD   I'll have my parties away from home after this. [*Frowns*] I don't see why we ever came back here. It was foolish.

CORA   [*Quickly*] No. I'd rather have you bring your friends here. I told you that—[*Twists her ringed hands*]

JUD   [*Formally*] Well, I'm sorry to have bothered you. [*As if wishing to go*] Er—did you want to see me about anything in particular, Mother?

CORA   [*Hesitates*] Yes. [*A pause.* JUD *waits impatiently. She seems undecided. Suddenly, and with incongruous awkwardness she gets up and goes over to* JUD. *He appears terribly embarrassed and surprised. She puts her arms about him. It is a rather terrible moment—his resistance and her pitiful appeal. One feels that he dislikes her for this affection—though he tries to hide it*]

CORA   Jud—I—Do you care for me, dear?

JUD   [*Petulantly*] Of course, Mother.

CORA   You were my little boy once. Now—

JUD   [*Very embarrassed; fools with paper-knife on table*] I—I—

CORA   [*Stung by his unresponsiveness, turns away a moment; controls herself*] Judson—I want—[*Pauses*]

JUD   Yes, Mother? [*Coldly*] I suppose it's about last night and so on. I promise you it won't happen again.

CORA   No. Not that. [*Pauses*] You're twenty-four. Don't you think at all— of settling down?

JUD   [*Laughs*] Not yet, Mother. The thought has never occurred to me!

CORA   [*Hesitantly*] You'll—marry some day.

JUD   [*Perplexed*] Me? Not for a long time.

CORA   [*With difficulty*] I think—it would be the best thing for you, Jud.

JUD   Well, you see—that's a matter of opinion. Dad thinks it would be the worst thing.

CORA   [*Eagerly*] Has he been talking to you about it?

JUD   This very morning.

CORA   This morning? How—why was he speaking of it?

JUD   Well—indifferently. I believe it came up because I asked him to urge Mildred to stay.

CORA   What has that to do with it?

JUD   It just led to a conversation about the fairer sex!

CORA   [*Carefully*] Was he—speaking about Mildred?

JUD   [*Frowning*] Certainly not, Mother. By the way—I hope that you're trying to persuade her not to go?

CORA   [*With meaning*] I certainly am.

JUD   [*Uncomfortably*] Perhaps you can—[TUDOR *enters with card*]

TUDOR   This gentleman's been waitin'. He says he's got to catch the next train back to New York and it's very important.

CORA   [*Takes card—turns pale*] Important? All right. [*She is visibly trying to control her agitation*]

JUD   What's the matter, Mother? Something wrong?

CORA   No—just business.

JUD   [*Looks at her keenly*] I'll blow then. [*Exits*]

CORA   Tell him to come here at once. [TUDOR *exits.* CORA *paces up and down the floor until* O'BRIAN *enters. He is a man of forty—obvious detective type—moves and speaks cautiously*]

O'BRIAN   Good day, Mrs. Smith. How are you?

CORA   Very well, Mr. O'Brian. What's the trouble? You—had to come out?

O'BRIAN   Yes, Mrs. Smith. The old man—since he's out of jail he's been raising the dickens all over the place. There's no keeping him down. We give him the allowance and he drinks that up—and then he's after more—and we give him what we think right according to your instructions. But it seems he's got a crazy streak. An' now—

CORA   Yes?

O'BRIAN   That's why I came out, Mrs. Smith. He's slipped away from us—and from all that we could find out, he's headed here. [*Shakes his head*]

CORA [*Bitterly*] It's a pity they didn't lock him in for life when he broke into that place!

O'BRIAN Mrs. Smith, I tell you the truth—I think that livin' like this—gettin' money from you—not seein' any of the family—has affected his mind. We're agreed on that at th' office. It seems now that he swears he doesn't want your money—that all he wants is to bring you down, you might say, by announcing to th' world that he's th' father-in-law of th' Smith Tin-Plate millions! He seems to bear a grudge against you all, for you wanting to keep him out of sight.

CORA Then, if he came here—you don't think it would be for money—it would be to—to—

O'BRIAN Sure—to announce himself to th' family!

CORA [*Moves near to him*] That can't happen! Not now! You must find him! You must keep him away—somehow! [*Grimly*] Use any method. [*Angrily*] I've paid you enough money all these years.

O'BRIAN [*Nettled*] We're a detective agency, Mrs. Smith, not a kidnappin' crew! All we can do is keep you informed about his doings, and pay him his allowance, and even that's goin' out of our line! [*He shakes his head*]

CORA Yes, I'm not complaining. But—isn't there some way—that he could be—kept away. For—just another month. [*She looks at him desperately*]

O'BRIAN We'll do our best. But—he's got this mania—and I doubt if money'd hold him off now.

CORA You, personally, Mr. O'Brian—if you would manage—I'd give you a thousand dollars. It's so important just *now*. [O'BRIAN *shakes his head, but his eyes gleam*]

O'BRIAN If I can locate him, I'll do it somehow. I'll find a way, Mrs. Smith! [*As he finishes speaking* SMITH *enters.* O'BRIAN *bows awkwardly,* SMITH *curtly*]

CORA Very well, then—you do that? I won't keep you any longer—if you want to catch that train—

O'BRIAN Thank you, Mrs. Smith. Good-day! [*Exits*]

SMITH Who is that man? [*He faces* CORA *in a curt, abrupt manner. She stares at him sullenly*]

CORA He's with the brokerage firm—in New York.

SMITH [*Sneers*] Your investments, eh? Well—you've done well!

CORA So—have you. [*They stand and look at one another, like two an-*

imals desiring to destroy. In that moment of silence one can feel their entire past rise up between them] Well?

SMITH   Well? [*Angrily*] What do you mean, *well*? Isn't it possible for us to see each other without it meaning that one demands something—from the other?

CORA   You haven't spoken to me—or looked at me—half a dozen times in the last six years, except when it's been absolutely necessary. I ask you, what is it now?

SMITH   Or except the times that you have ordered me to take your advice! [*Bitterly*]

CORA   [*Somberly*] It's been good advice. When you've set your mind on a thing—it comes natural to know what to do—

SMITH   [*Sarcastically*] Glad it gives you pleasure to think so. You don't seem to get any other pleasure out of—what you wanted.

CORA   [*Stubbornly*] Before the war, when I got you to buy up the old Wheeler interests, and you didn't want to—

SMITH   I suppose you know the war was coming, eh?

CORA   [*Stubbornly*] We made a million—

SMITH   [*Impatiently*] What's all this talk? What are you trying to dig up?

CORA   Nothing. I wanted to speak to you about something else.

SMITH   Yes. And I want to talk to you. You were right. That's why I came here. [*Pauses*] About—Jud.

CORA   About—Jud? [*She watches him cautiously, her fingers twisting*]

SMITH   Well indirectly. Perhaps I'd better say—about Mildred Lord.

CORA   [*Almost inaudibly*] Yes—

SMITH   Jud wants her to stay. He asked me to persuade her. He said he would ask you. Did he?

CORA   Yes.

SMITH   [*With sarcasm, briefly*] This is probably one subject on which we will both agree. I want her to go. You will probably be glad also. You must have—seen. The sooner she's out of the place the better.

CORA   You know, then?

SMITH   I'm not blind!

CORA   And you—want to turn her out?

SMITH   It's not turning her out! Damn! She wants to go. She's probably sick of the whole thing, too. [*Brutally*] Women are more modern in that respect than they were in *your* day!

CORA Men haven't changed. [*Bitterly—looks at him with scorn*] So you come to me—to see that she goes! Counting on *me* wanting her to go! Me! [*She gives a queer laugh*] D'you think I've forgotten—that I'd turn against another woman—unfortunate like I was! That I'd ask my son to commit that wrong—? To forget his duty—as you tried to forget yours?

SMITH You talk like a crazy woman! If that's his duty, then he should marry—several.

CORA [*Suddenly enraged*] Yes! You want his child cast out—illegitimate—unknown—as you would have had *him* grow up if it hadn't been for me!

SMITH [*Steps back*] His *child*! [*Laughs loudly*] Ah-ha! Now I see it! The whole thing! I thought she was a pretty clever girl! Well—[*He draws a long breath of determination*] We'll see! We'll see if this will get her anywhere!

CORA That's why he must marry her.

SMITH [*Turning on her with blind determination*] That's why he won't marry her! I'd rather have him out and pick up someone out of the gutter— and marry *her*! Do you think I'll let him be forced into the hell I was forced into? No! A trap, that's what it is. A damnable trap—that women use! [*Pauses; looks at her smiling maliciously, seems confident in his power*] In this one respect I have power! [CORA *raises her hand as though she wished to strike him*] He won't go against my wishes! For years I've talked to him. I've trained him *my* way. He won't marry her! This girl—he doesn't care about her. He wanted her to stay, simply because he was sorry for her. He knows nothing about this.

CORA I know. And when he does, he'll want to marry her.

SMITH If he *should* want to, I'd prevent it!

CORA [*Like steel*] No.

SMITH [*Turning on her, vibrant*] Yes! This one thing—I will not give it to you. I won't see his life spoiled—no matter what.

CORA It's you who are spoiling his life. I've always tried—

SMITH [*Interrupting*] You say that!—you, who sent him off to boarding school at seven—!

CORA I wanted him to be away from the unhappiness at home. It was you who ruined him—sending him money—visiting him—teaching him to hate me, when he was home on his vacations, because I had to take a stand against the badness in which you encouraged him—little by little destroying his love for me—ah—[*She is trembling*]

SMITH   And I want him to be kept out of more unhappiness—and see that he is!

CORA   [*Moves across the room—her face shows desperate struggle, comes back*] Do you think he'd care for you as much—if he knew the truth about you?

SMITH   What—truth? [*There is a silence.* CORA *seems to dominate. She fixes her burning eyes on her husband, and under their gaze, although he struggles against it, he seems to weaken and lose power. He looks away*]

CORA   The truth about the man he admires so—the fine man—the great man—his father—And the truth about his mother—whom he thinks so stupid—whom he thinks—oh, I know—is a drawback—to the wonderful father! Yes, that's what you've let him grow up to believe! And I could never deny it—without telling the whole truth. How you wanted to leave me—how you had to be forced by me, step by step—

SMITH   [*Breaks out violently, it seems that her words have brought him back his strength*] Yes—tell him that! Tell him what I've been crushed under all these years. Tell him—what all this is built on! Then—[*He makes a sweeping gesture*] the whole thing may smash—but out of the smash he'll be free!

CORA   [*Almost frightened, then pulls herself together for her last effort*] There's no need for me to speak to him of that. [*Pauses*] But he must marry Mildred. [*Slowly*] He will—if *you* ask him to. You know that. He'll do anything for you.

SMITH   No. I'm strong now. I see—what may happen. Never mind. I'm strong now!

CORA   Then I'll—let him know everything. You'll lose his love—his respect—his friendship. You'll have nothing then. I mean it! [*Wildly*] This is the last time I'll use the power over you—but you force me to use it! I've got to save him from you! [SMITH *has sunk in the chair behind the table, his head bent on his hands so he cannot see her.* CORA *leans over him and slightly shakes his shoulders*] And you must—you must! [*Her voice rises determinedly*]

SMITH   [*Without moving, his voice muffled but strong*] No! No! No! [*The curtain goes down on this picture*]

CURTAIN

TIME: *A quarter after two in the morning, the next day. The same room—but only one dim light is burning.*

SCENE: *Door left opens cautiously.* JUD *enters, carrying a tray with bottles and two glasses. He moves with the exaggerated care of the intoxicated. Puts tray down on table, after looking about to be sure that room is empty. Hesitates. Then takes the bronze paper-knife, and one or two small articles of value and hides them under the pillows on sofa. Smooths pillows over them carefully. Then goes back to door, left, speaking to someone outside: Turns on the switch for light.*

JUD   It's all right!—Come on in—th' coast's clear! [*Waits a moment, a good-natured grin on his face. An old tramp, dirty, heavy with fat and with malicious eyes comes in, equally cautious—but not intoxicated. It is* MARTIN. *He is shaved and cleaned up somewhat. He stands there stupidly, looking about.* JUD *pulls him in*] I better close th' door. [*Closes door*] Now we're all safe! [*Goes to tray, pours two drinks*] This is better'n th' dinin' room. They c'n hear every-thin' from th' dinin' room. [*Drinks*] Well—wh' do you think of it? Disappointed?

MARTIN   [*In a hoarse voice*] [*Cautiously*] It's—all right. [*Watches* JUD]

JUD   [*Laughs*] You're not very en'thus'astic! [*Suddenly*] Say—honest! Was that why you were hangin' round th' gate? Just wondering what a rich guy's house was like—inside?

MARTIN   Sure—didn't I tell you?

JUD   When I first saw you I thought you had designs on our silverware! [*Slaps him on shoulder*] But you're a good old guy! You're no second story man. Like t' see *you* climb through a window! [MARTIN *is standing in sort of a stupor—covetously eyeing everything in the room.* JUD *points to food*] Here—you said you were hungry. Go to! An' have a drink. [*Pours himself another. Sits down—to himself*] They objected last night—but tonight, th' blind—th' maimed—th' hungry—[*Suspiciously, turning to* MARTIN] Say—you're—hungry, aren't you?

MARTIN   [*As though remembering his role*] Sure. [*Drinks some of his whis-key*] It's fine booze y'got—for these days!

JUD   Sure—Say—eat something! [MARTIN *eats*] W'd you like me to' give you a suit of clothes?

MARTIN   [*Growls*] They'd hardly fit me.

JUD   I'll swipe a suit of the old man's. He won't care.

MARTIN   No, I suppose he won't miss it, with so many. [*Cautiously*] He's a very rich man, I'm told.

JUD   The richest in Melville County—an' the finest!

MARTIN [*With a faint sneer*] You think he's a fine man, eh? [*Hurriedly*] Well, that's right—honor yer father—! And your mother—what's she like?

JUD She's all right—

MARTIN A fine lady, all covered with diamonds, ridin' around in a li-mysene. Sure!

JUD [*Pours another drink*] Hey—I get you now! You're one of th' far-famed I.W.W. Right in the dooryard, too! [*Drunkenly*] Well I don' know as I blame you! 'ts a hard life—[*Shakes his head. Fumblingly pulls out roll of bills—takes one off and hands it to* MARTIN] Here—that'll help you. [*Other bills fall to the floor. He picks them up and puts them back in pocket.* MARTIN *watches him covetously, putting bill he has received in his trousers.* JUD *suddenly stands perfectly still—listening*] I thought I heard footsteps. [*Goes to door, listens—comes back*] Jus' my nerves, I suppose. Had a lil' party las' night—woke 'em all up—Don' want to wake 'em up tonight!

MARTIN How is it you're not having a party tonight—a fine young fellow like you?

JUD [*Sits on sofa—oddly silent; stares at floor*] Tonight? Jus'—gettin' drunk. Wan' to forget something. [*A long pause, during which* JUD *stares at floor*] Dad's right. Responsibility? . . . . No. . . . Not for me. [*He gets up suddenly and pours himself an immense drink, which he takes in one swallow*] Here you—have another! An' then—you better be blowin', old guy! [*Goes back to sofa*] I wanted to find out how th' other half lives. But nev' mind—tonight. [*Fumbles in pockets; brings out two more bills*] Here—take these; [MARTIN *takes them*] I'll take you to th' door. [JUD *does not move however after these words, but sits with bent head.* MARTIN *seats himself in chair nearby, says nothing.* JUD *sighs. Lies back on couch. There is silence.* JUD *begins to breathe heavily*]

MARTIN [*After a moment—in a low voice*] How about lettin' me out? [*Waits; no reply; goes over, touches* JUD *lightly*] Hey! [JUD *groans, turns over. He is sound asleep.* MARTIN's *expression changes. He becomes alert, crafty. Looks about room—shakes his fist—sneers. He examines several things in the room. Pretends disgust, but is really awed. Suddenly it is obvious that a new thought comes into his mind. He goes to* JUD, *speaks gently to him again—no response—he then proceeds to pick his pockets. Gets the money. Hesitates over beautiful watch, then can't resist and takes that too. Starts toward door, and then pauses, turning back to the sleeping boy*] I'll be back tomorrow, me fine boy! But I'll come up the front steps and make a noise that'll be heard all over the town. None of your fine airs then! [*He sees matchbox on table, and is pocketing it as a last thought, when the door slightly opens, and* CORA *enters. She stands dazed and staring. She is dressed, but wears a house jacket of the old-fashioned type*]

CORA [*Not seeing* JUD] You—what—

MARTIN What are you staring at? [*Aggressively*] I got a right to be here!

CORA [*Looks about room, sees* JUD *on sofa; her face fills with anguish and despair; glides toward sofa*] What have you done?

MARTIN [*Sneers*] He's drunk—only drunk! [CORA *straightens—gives him a searching glance*] No, you can't blame it on me. He was drunk when he brought me into this house. [*In a low, malicious voice, going closer to her*] Blood 'll tell! Blood 'll tell!

CORA [*In a low, frightened voice—standing with boy behind her*] You go now. Please—go now!

MARTIN [*Ignoring this*] It doesn't seem to have helped much—keepin' th' old man out of th' way, eh? [*Laughs*]

CORA Won't you go. Tomorrow—I'll see you—and do what you want. [*Pauses*] Only—go now.

MARTIN Don't you worry about tomorrow; I'll come right to th' front steps tomorrow and tell them who I am! I'll make a show you won't forget for a while. It's a treat I've promised myself. [*Bitterly*] It'll pay you back for these years you've been hidin' me away!

CORA Sh-h-h! You'll wake him!

MARTIN [*Contemptuously*] Nothing short of a cannon'd wake *him*!

CORA [*In quick, tense voice*] If you'll leave town—I'll give you anything— anything [*Holds out hands covered with diamonds*] If I haven't all you want— I'll sell these—

MARTIN [*Covetously*] Give me one! [*She slips off ring and gives it to him*] The fine lady—all decked out in her jools!

CORA Will you—do that?

MARTIN Sure, I'll do it—[*Puts ring in pocket*] If you'll let me have one thing that I want—that's t' be recognized before th' world as a member of this family!

CORA [*Cornered*] For just a month then—after that—come back. [*Tensely*] I—promise.

MARTIN [*Maliciously*] No, I'll not wait a month. I'm coming tomorrow— if I don't decide to stay tonight! [*Suspiciously*] What is all this great fuss to keep me out of the way? There's something more than I thought at first, I'll be bound. There's some sort of dirty work here! [*Peers at her*] What is it? [JUD *moves and groans*]

CORA   Sh-h-h! He'll wake up! [*In anguish*] Go—go! I'll talk to you to-morrow—[*She pushes him slightly toward door*]

MARTIN   [*Stiffening*] What are ye doin'? Pushin' me out of th' house? Just for that I'll stay all night! [*Sits down determinedly*] There's something back of this—and I'll find out what it is!

CORA   [*Trying to control her temper*] You can't stay. You have no right to stay—like this.

MARTIN   [*Rising—in a furious temper*] I can't stay, eh? Well, who's goin' to put me out? Him? I could break him in two with one fist! Or your bum of a husband, perhaps! Th' drunken bum of a loafer that never held on to a job all his life until you took him by th' ears and held his nose to the grindstone! You run away after him and got him to marry you somehow, and by th' same method, I guess, y' got him t' work—for he'd never done it himself! But you—ah. [*He spits on floor*] I've known you since you was a kid and you was always after your own way—an' t' hell with th' world! But you won't have your way with me, me fine lady. Not now.

CORA   [*Furious—white*] Go—you—go—

MARTIN   Go, eh? I'm told to go by a slut that was th' talk of th' town—that had to force a feller to marry her—[CORA *goes close to him—as though to push him from the room; she does not see that behind her* JUD *is coming to*] Why you bum—I'll show you—[MARTIN *in a frightful rage grasps her by the throat and begins to choke her. His eyes are popping out of his head with fury.* JUD *makes one dazed leap, picks up poker, and hits the old man with all his force on the head.* MARTIN *loosens his hold slowly, turns dazed look on* JUD, *and sinks to floor—dead.* CORA *totters back, almost falling—gives low, protesting scream—but it is too late*]

JUD   [*Dazed*] Mother! My God—he'd have killed you! [*Bends over body with white face—completely absorbed*] God—I've done for him! [CORA *moans*] I—I—had to, Mother. [*With excitement*] See? [*Watch and chain have fallen from* MARTIN's *pocket.* JUD *picks it up—also money—with sober, frightened face*] He must have—gone through me, all right. God, I never thought—[*self-accusing*] He'd have killed you, Mother, if I hadn't waked up. [CORA *sits up in chair, covering her eyes;* JUD *touches her gently*] It was self-defense, Mother. [*Suddenly*] I better telephone the police right away.

CORA   [*Sharply*] No!

JUD   We'll have to—he can't stay here all night.

CORA [*Feverishly*] Yes—if they could come right away—and take him. [*With agitation*] We'd better do it now—before anyone hears—[JUD *goes to telephone. Asks for police station*] If they'd come right away—and take him. [*She walks distractedly about the room.* MILDRED *enters—listens to* JUD]

JUD This is the home of J. J. Smith—Judson Smith speaking. I've killed a man, officer—a tramp—he was attacking my mother—yes—yes, he had some loot on him—will you—all right—yes, five minutes [*Hangs up. Turns to* CORA *with real tenderness*] There, Mother—it will be over soon [*Pats her on shoulder, soberly*] I believe I better go now and call Dad.

CORA [*With anguish*] No—don't do that, Jud. It's better—it would up-set—wait until after they've—taken him—[*She shudders*]

JUD [*Surprised*] Why no—I think—[*They both turn as* JIM SMITH *enters. He wears a dressing gown and slippers. His hair is rumpled, giving him a more boyish look. He is amazed.* MARTIN *during this scene lies with his back to* SMITH *so that his face cannot be seen*]

SMITH What—in God's name—has happened?

JUD [*Soberly*] I guess I've killed a man, Dad.

SMITH Killed a—man! [*He stares at his son, as though he had received a physical blow—then laughs—wildly*] You—killed a man! [*Looks at* CORA—*then puts his arm up over his face and groans*]

SMITH [*Goes to him. Tries to remove his arm*] Dad! He was choking Mother. He'd robbed me. See! [*Points to watch and money on table*] Dad! Don't mind! [*During this scene,* CORA *stands like a ghost, silent, immovable, in the background. Only her burning eyes, following every movement, betray her anguish*] Dad! [*But* SMITH, *looking old and broken, mutters something under his breath and moves to where he can see the dead man's face. Looks at him. Slowly, over* SMITH's *face, comes the amazement and terror of recognition mixed with incredulity. In a trance he goes nearer* JUD, *watches him with growing amazement—*CORA *is steeling herself against the blow which she knows now will inevitably fall. At last* SMITH *lifts his eyes to* CORA—*stares at her for a long moment*]

SMITH [*With terror and hatred*] It's him! [CORA *cringes back, with a cry—*SMITH *drops to his knees before the old man—looks into his face—sees a scar, touches him.* JUD *watches in amazement*]

JUD [*Cries*] Dad—what's the matter?

SMITH [*Struggles to his feet—chokingly*] You—you lied then! [*In white fury he raises his clenched fist over* CORA] You—you—! [*She shrinks back*] God—all these years! [*He drops his arm, with dazed expression*] These—years. . . .

JUD   [*Going to him*] Hey! Dad!—what's the matter? [*Takes his arm*]

SMITH   [*To* JUD] The matter? [*Laughs wildly*] Nothing's the matter—now. No! But something has been the matter—for twenty-four years. [*He points to body*] Do you remember—just this morning—I said—there had been something—all these years?

JUD   Yes, Dad.

SMITH   [*Points to* CORA] This man is her step-father!

JUD   God!

SMITH   Twenty-four years ago—I knocked him down—just as you did now. I thought—that I'd killed him. I left, thinking that—then *she* came—to where I was hiding. She told me he was dead. She told me they suspected me. [*His voice raised*] She lied! She lied! [*His voice shakes*] For twenty-four years she has let me think—that I was a murderer—that I was guilty. Prison—was always before me—I've been haunted—day and night—

JUD   No, Dad, No! [*Looks at* CORA *with incredulity*]

SMITH   Yes! That's why—I've had no friends—no pleasure. [*He shakes* JUD *by the arm*] She's made me into a weakling—a coward.

JUD   [*Dazed*] But why? I don't understand. [*He looks at* CORA]

SMITH   That's the worst part of it. She's—used it over me. She's threatened—terrorized—

JUD   Dad!

SMITH   She's threatened to expose—to give me up to the police—

CORA   [*Suddenly breaks out of her trance*] Jud! You don't understand! Please! [*Puts out her hand to him.* JUD *turns away from her with an aversion he cannot conceal.* CORA *shrinks back as though he had struck her*]

JUD   No—please—[*Puts his arm about his father*] What you've done to Dad—is unforgivable. [*Loud bell is heard—front door*] There—it must be the police—I'll go. [*Starts for door*]

SMITH   [*Laughs hollowly*] No! I'll go! It will be the first time—in twenty-four years—that I'll be able to face a policeman—without shrinking! [*Exits*]

JUD   My God! [*He stands with his head bent—then gives his mother a look of horror—turns away from her and walks across room; pauses beside the body and looks down at it, somberly*] I've grown up tonight. I never dreamed a woman could do such things.

CORA   [*With anguish and appeal*] Judson! [*But he deliberately turns away from her, without a word. After a second* SMITH *returns with two police officers*]

FIRST POLICEMAN [*Bows to* CORA] This is bad business, Ma'am. [*Shakes his head. Goes over to body To* JUD] You say he had hold of your mother, sir?

JUD [*After a pause*] Yes—he was choking her.

SECOND POLICEMAN He's a bad customer, sir, you c'n see that! [*Examines body*] An' look here! [*Holds up ring*] He got this, ma'am! Is it yours? [CORA *silently takes it*]

SMITH [*In a hard voice*] You better get him out of here, officer, as soon as you can. [*Points to money and watch on table*] It's a clear case of robbery and assault. [*Policemen nod; he adds*] My son and I will come down, first thing in the morning—

FIRST POLICEMAN Your word's as good as your bond, sir! [*Starts to pick up body*] We'll take him right out to the ambulance, now, sir.

SMITH Yes. [*He holds door open as policemen, after touching their caps to* CORA, *pick up the body and take it off.* SMITH *and* JUD *go with them.* CORA *is left alone with* MILDRED]

MILDRED Mrs. Smith—[*Hesitates—starts to go*] I'll—go—

CORA No—please stay. [*But she says this as though not realizing that* MILDRED *is there. She stares ahead of her, hopelessly alone for a moment among her ruins—the woman of power and will, who has hesitated at nothing to gain her way—which she thought to be the right way—at last is broken, vanquished. Her shoulders sag. She slowly opens her hands, as though to let life and love drop from them—and closes them with the same slow gesture of despair. The slam of a door is heard. Then* SMITH *comes back, followed by* JUD, *who sits down in a chair by door, his head bent in his hands.* SMITH, *after entering abruptly, walks across room—turns back to* CORA, *who appears not to see him*]

SMITH [*In a harsh voice*] I came back here—it's impossible to spend another night in this house—without an agreement—now—at once. [*Sharply*] Do you hear?

CORA [*Dully*] Yes.

SMITH Judson and I—leave tomorrow. We'll stay away—until you go. Or . . . [*He smiles in an ugly, mocking way*] if you insist in staying on—if you want to have your own way once more—inform my attorney. I will arrange to turn this house over to you. [*A pause*] My son and I'll manage somewhere else very well.

CORA [*In a hollow voice*] Judson! [*He raises his head and looks at her*] You—won't stay if I do?

JUD [*Briefly*] I couldn't stay here—after what's happened.

CORA   [In a voice of anguished appeal. To SMITH] You know I was justified—

JUD   [Springs to his feet. Faces his mother, his eyes blazing] There's no possible justification—for having done this—to a man like Dad. [His voice shakes] It's horrible!

CORA   [Turns her dumb, anguished eyes to her husband] Won't you see—

SMITH   [Turns away from her] Yes—twenty-four years of torture!

CORA   [Sinks back in chair. In apathy; it is though she had lost all strength; all power of resistance] Yes. I thought I could do something—make something—of it all. [Turns to SMITH, almost piteously. She has gone back somewhere to her girlhood diction] When it happened—I remember talking—that very night—about thinkin' I could do somethin' great. [SMITH and JUD are compelled by the power of her words. MILDRED, who stands away, listens mechanically. Suddenly CORA pulls herself together as though facing reality. Puts up her hand] I'm through now. It's no use. [She rises] You needn't go—because I'm going, first thing in the morning. [Suddenly she seems swept with a new thought] I'll go with Mildred. [To MILDRED] We'll go together. [Pauses] Perhaps—

SMITH   [In a hard abrupt voice] A good idea. You'll have your share— your money—of course—

CORA   [To MILDRED] May I—come with you?

MILDRED   Mrs. Smith—yes. But first—[She steps forward out of the obscurity in which she has stood during previous scene. They look at her in some amazement—her voice is so assured, so dominant] Do you mind—if I ask one or two questions?

SMITH   I don't see—[He frowns]

MILDRED   I've seen—what's happened tonight. I—couldn't very well help it. It's a dreadful thing. [She pauses. They all watch her] But perhaps I, being an outsider, can see—understand—a lot that is hidden—

SMITH   [Interrupting her] Miss Lord, I can't see . . .

MILDRED   You think I've no business doing this? Well—I suppose I haven't—but—I am fond of Mrs. Smith . . . [Her voice softens] She's been very wonderful to me. For three years I've lived here—with her. And I've seen— how she has suffered, all the time—in her love for Jud and yes—[To SMITH] for you! I've felt sorry for her—terribly sorry. And I think now that she's being misjudged! [Suddenly she turns to JUD] Listen! Haven't you wondered why—for what reason—your mother did this? Have you asked her that? [SMITH puts his hand on the boy's shoulder as though to stop him]

JUD [Hotly] It's just that, that makes it so awful. There can't be any reason! Why *should* she—except for power—

MILDRED [Softly] But why did she want that power, in the first place? [Suddenly, to SMITH] *You* tell him why! [She makes this a dramatic accusation. SMITH turns away, beginning to show fear and confusion. She continues insistently] You refuse to answer because you're afraid—[Then to JUD, who is watching her with bewilderment] Ask your father why your mother first used that threat!

JUD [Bewilderedly] Dad! For heaven's sake! This is frightful!

CORA [Suddenly, to MILDRED] Don't—it's better not to. [She seems still in her daze]

MILDRED [To CORA] No! I won't see you condemned unjustly! [To all] I happened to be outside when he—the old man—said many things. He spoke a great deal of the past. [To CORA] He wasn't even sure what *you* had done— but [To SMITH] he knew what you had done—and been! [To CORA] Did you ever use this power except for good?

CORA [In low voice] I thought not.

MILDRED [To SMITH] Tell your son the truth! Tell him!

CORA No. [Anguished] Don't—there's no use!

JUD [Bewilderedly] Dad—what is it? [SMITH is obstinately silent]

MILDRED Then I'll tell! [To JUD] That threat was first used, in desperation to force your father to give *you* a name!

JUD [Stares stupidly at her—then weakly] No—

MILDRED [Relentlessly] Then after that, she used it to keep him straight, to keep him away from what was ruining him, to make a man of him! [To CORA] Isn't this true?

CORA [Brokenly] I thought I saw happiness for the three of us—that way. I wanted to save him—give him power—life—

SMITH [Suddenly gets to his feet—throws out his arms with defiant gesture] Well, what of it? It's true—true! I was nothing—but I was free! She said I could do great things. But I didn't want to do great things! I didn't want to settle down—to marry! She forced me! Step by step! [Vehemently] All this fortune is hers—yes, by right! She kept me here— [Suddenly he breaks a little and turns to JUD] You'll understand me. I've taught you—you will want—to be free, too. [Pauses, as though exhausted]

JUD [Slowly] I can remember years ago—something about a ticket to California. I wanted to go too. But you stayed. [In sudden confusion] You were leaving us—mother and me, then? [SMITH *avoids his eyes*] I used to wonder what had happened then. Now—I see. [*He turns to his father, in anguish*] Then everything I thought about you—is wrong—[*Abruptly—after a pause*] You let me think that mother was holding you back! And all the time it was she who was making you do things! [*He stares at the two of them*] She was helping you!

SMITH   [*Bitterly*] Her idea of help!

JUD   Then everything you've done—wouldn't have happened—except for mother?

SMITH   No. I suppose not.

JUD   I—why ever since I was a little kid I've admired you for having done all that! [*His voice quavers*] God, I don't know—what to think! Mother! Forgive me—if you can. I've been unjust to you—cruel—I've always thought you— please forgive me—I can't say it now—I'm busted up! I've got to get away for a time and think! [*Laughs, crazily. Turns toward door.* CORA *murmurs brokenly:* "Jud." *If ever a boy of that age is near tears,* JUD *is—tears of desperation. They watch him with consternation—although* MILDRED's *is concealed. Suddenly, at the door,* JUD *does a surprising thing. He turns back blindly and abruptly and almost brutally takes* MILDRED *by the arm. His face is a picture of mortification and resolve!* MILDRED *draws back, growing crimson*]

JUD   You—you come with me! You've got to!

MILDRED   [*Pales*] Are you crazy?

JUD   No! [*Stubbornly—almost in tears*] I—you've got to stick with me! [*In anguish—as though they were alone*] Milly!

MILDRED   [*Dazed*] You mean now—you need me?

JUD   [*Humbly*] Yes. I do need you. I love you! I see now what a fool I've been. I've been fighting against needing you, fighting against myself! [*His voice breaks*] Please—don't you see? I didn't know I loved you. I didn't know it was love—until—[*Passionately*] Milly—come. We'll be married—and go away somewhere for a time—

MILDRED   [*Stands wordless—but a sudden, inner illumination comes over her face. Her hand reaches out and touches his.* JUD *turns to his parents*] Mother—Dad—we've got to do this! [*But* SMITH *and* CORA *are silent—They both seem completely broken*] But—they? [*There is compassion in her voice*] What will they do? [*To* CORA] Won't you come with us?

CORA   [*Dully*] No. I'm going alone. [*She is like a person in a trance, like one who has suddenly been cut off from the world*]

SMITH   [*In a determined voice*] No. I'll go. [*Bitterly*] I should be the one to go. Everything here is yours. My success—that's yours. Even Jud—I've no claim on him. He's yours. If you hadn't used that threat—I'd never have known him. [*Brokenly*] I've wronged you all these years. Now—when it's too late—I'll go. It's the only recompense I can give—to leave you free of me. [*They all stare at him—amazed at this new, humble spirit. Suddenly* CORA *moves across the room and faces him. Her face is wet with tears. It seems as though she wants to reach out and touch him—but dares not*]

CORA   Jim! Don't say that! It's *you* who've done everything. [*Suddenly her face twists*] And if you've suffered all these years, Jim, can't you see how I've suffered? [*Faintly*] All the time—I've loved you—just as I did back there in Union. I've lain awake nights longing for you and knowing that you hated me! [*Her voice breaks*] and knowing that if I told you the truth—and set you free—that you'd *go*—and I'd never see you again! [*She pleads passionately*] Jim—stay! Forgive me! [*She kneels at his feet, weeping*]

SMITH   [*Dazed*] No. Forgive me! I've been the guilty one! You've given me everything, Corrie. [*He passes his hand across his eyes, then, reaching down, he pulls* CORA *to her feet*] Shall we—let them go, then? [*Slowly*] and try to work it out—together? [*As* CORA *smiles brokenly through her tears,*

THE CURTAIN FALLS

The Ole Davil, Act IV

In March 1920, hard upon the success of his first professionally produced play, *Beyond the Horizon*, O'Neill's second try for Broadway, *Chris Christophersen*, closed out of town. To leave the freedom and protection that the undemanding amateurism of the Provincetown Players had provided him was an important step in his career. *Beyond the Horizon* had triumphed after a hesitant premier in a series of special matinees and had won a Pulitzer Prize. Not only was it O'Neill's first success in the professional theatre, but it brought onto Broadway many of the new concepts of theatrical art that were exciting the smaller theatres. It had given the new movement in theatre an auspicious start. The quality of its successor was crucial.

Chris was a picaresque adventure story on which O'Neill tried to load more philosophic and ethical weight than was possible. Deeply influenced in its theme by Joseph Conrad, the play concentrated on the ethical dilemma of the second mate of a freighter and the resolution of his relationship with Chris, a Swedish barge captain, and his daughter, Anna, a somewhat aloof, thoroughly respectable typist from London.

When *Chris* failed, O'Neill set to work on a complete revision, simplifying the story, changing the characterizations of the daughter and her lover, and bringing the three central characters onto the same focal plane. In so doing he wrote a play that was to become a lasting popular favorite around the world. Yet *"Anna Christie,"* as the play was finally titled, was not one in which he took particular pride. Something about it was too easy, too cheerful. At the time of its composition, O'Neill was ambitious for the highest drama, which meant a work close to the tragic in story and theme, but the new play simply refused to cooperate.

The revision was formed from the same materials as he had used in a number of successful, somber one-act plays, notably those concerned with the crew of a tramp freighter, the *S.S. Glencairn: Bound East for Cardiff, The Moon of the Caribbees, In the Zone*, and *The Long Voyage Home*. In these short works, he had written in a style of poetic Naturalism of sailors who were part of the sea, belonging to it as a child is bonded to its mother or a man to his god. To leave the sea was an apostasy that the sea punished. However, if one remained content in the destiny the sea's silent will determined for its children, one could find the contentment of belonging to a god-like, protective power.

In revising *Chris*, O'Neill saw his barge captain as an apostate who had fled from the sea and was now living as the captain of a coal barge, sailing self-protectively in shallow waters close to shore—neither a landsman nor one who was where he belonged on the deep sea. His antipathy to the sea he had once known was shown in his concern that his daughter have no contact with the sea. He has sent her far inland, to be brought up on a farm. Chris's hatred of the sea formed the thematic center of the revision. Now the sea, in Chris's view and in the view the play set out to assert thematically, was a devil without mercy, dooming men and women to what O'Neill conceived of as their "ironic fate." By the logic of O'Neill's Naturalism, the sea was required to punish both Chris and Anna for their desertion.

The dark emphasis created the problem that led to the dilemma of the endings of the two revisions of *Chris*, *The Ole Davil* and "*Anna Christie*." As the new story developed, the question was raised: Was the sea in fact malevolent as Chris claimed it to be, or did it care for those who were its children and who accepted its will as the crew of the *Glencairn* had done? Anna, forced to live far from the sea, has become a prostitute. Returning to the sea, she feels herself to have come "home" and to be purged of guilt and shame. The sea welcomes her back and in the night on her father's barge brings her a lover, the survivor of a shipwreck, an Irish stoker named Mat Burke, literally casting him at her feet. She recognizes the truth of his brag that he possesses a strength equal to the power of the sea itself. It follows that in bringing her Mat, the sea has given of itself to Anna.

On land, their relationship turns awry. Chris's antipathy to the sea extends violently to the thought of his daughter marrying a sailor. Anna's story must be told so that Mat, who at first cannot tolerate the thought of her past, can come to accept her essential decency. In the end, the land's truths being told and purged, the relationships come to right adjustment, and the sea's way wins, with an added ironic twist: Chris determines to return to deep water and unintentionally signs on the same ship as has Mat. Faced with this, the two men are reconciled in a form of friendship. Inevitably, the story brings the three protagonists together in a relationship that promises harmony and the untroubled future of all lovers in romantic comedy.

Romantic comedy, however, was not the kind of play with which an aspiring artist of the theatre felt at ease. As the European and American Naturalists had done, O'Neill wished to show men and women as the doomed playthings of an implacable life force. Tragedy or nothing was the cry. O'Neill therefore attempted to show that Chris's antagonism toward the sea was a perception of the true nature of the hostile trickster, and that in sailing on the same ship the two men would be brought to their deaths. In Chris's gloomy foreboding of tragedy-to-come, O'Neill attempted to point to a dark irony in the apparent happiness with which the play concludes.

The irony, however, does not run deep into the thematic center of the play but remains as an element of Chris's character. Its shallowness led to the problem O'Neill found with his conclusion. If the sea is a "davil," why has it welcomed Anna home? Why was Mat rescued from the shipwreck to come to Anna's feet? Why has Chris been brought back to the main deep where he belongs? Throughout the action, Chris asserts that the sea plays tricks, but the action denies the truth of his prophecies and reduces his hostility to a personal idiosyncracy without general truth.

O'Neill's story did not permit him to avoid an ending that insisted on being theatrically "happy." In this, perhaps, he wrote more truly than he was willing to admit. It is also possible that he was influenced by the skill of his director, the eminent, experienced Arthur Hopkins, who well knew how to shape a pleasing play for the professional stage.

The Ole Davil and "*Anna Christie*" are substantially the same play. No doubt Hopkins's hand is to be seen in the neat trimming that the final version received. The elimination of the scene that begins act 4 between Anna and the Donkeyman may well be the work of a producer wondering why he must hire an extra actor to deliver three pages of unnecessary exposition. Some changes, however, such as the elimination of Anna's agreement to become a Catholic, are clearly authorial, and as O'Neill approaches the play's last moments, the difference in tone between the two endings reveals the author's uncertainty as to how to handle a love story that is at odds with Chris's insistence that what has happened is one of the sea's "dirty tricks."

The Ole Davil ends in laughter. Anna and Mat rejoice in their reunion and delight in the prospect of children to come. In the final moments, Mat makes the play's thematic point:

> MAT. The sea means good to us only. . . . She'll be welcoming you [Chris] back like a long-lost child, I'm thinking.

Together, the lovers laugh down Chris's fatal predictions, reducing the tragic view to an old man's mumble.

"Anna Christie" ends on a darker note. Chris is allowed the last words, which suggest that the sea may destroy them all, and that its fog will penetrate and blight their lives:

> CHRIS. [*Looking out into the night—lost in his somber preoccupation—shakes his head and mutters*] Fog, fog, fog, all bloody time. You can't see vhere you vas going, no. Only dat ole davil, sea—she knows! [*The two stare at him. From the harbor comes the muffled wail of steamers' whistles*]

Reviewers of the Hopkins production speak of *"Anna Christie"* as ending in laughter, which suggests that the play was first produced with the ending of *The Ole Davil*, the more somber ending being a revision made before the play's publication. Whatever occurred, O'Neill appeared to be particularly disturbed by the romantic joy appropriate to the traditional theatrical moment when boy gets girl. He called the ending a "Henry Arthur Jones compromise" and defended the loftiness of his intentions in a long article for the *New York Times*.[1] Writing to George Jean Nathan, he described the ending as "merely the comma at the end of a gaudy introductory clause with the body of the sentence yet unwritten." And he added, "In fact I once thought of calling the play *Comma*."[2] His suspicion of the play as coming perilously close to what he called the "Broadway Showshop" remained, even when the play brought him his second Pulitzer Prize. He refused to include it in an early anthology of his work.

His attempt to render the ending tragic has not availed. The play remains a popular favorite, and, although the final version of the play is slimmer and somewhat more poetic, the ending of "The Ole Davil" shows matters as they essentially are, undisguised by editorial revision or darksome second thoughts.

1. December 18, 1921.
2. Quoted in *The Theatre of George Jean Nathan*, ed. Isaac Goldberg (New York, 1926), p. 154.

The Ole Davil, Act IV

SCENE: *The scene is the same as Act Three, about nine o'clock of a foggy night two days later.*

The whistles of steamers in the harbor can be heard. The cabin is in complete darkness. Then the door in the rear from the deck is opened and ANNA's *figure can be dimly made out, outlined in the doorway. She carries a suitcase in her hand. She feels her way forward to the table, sets down the bag and lights a small lamp. She wears a hat; is dressed up as in Act 1. Her face is pale, looks terribly tired and worn, as if the two days just past had been ones of suffering and sleepless nights. She sinks down into the rocking chair with a weary sigh and stares before her despondently, her chin in her hands. There is a sharp knock on the door in rear.* ANNA *jumps to her feet with a startled exclamation and looks toward the door with an expression of mingled hope and fear.*

ANNA   [*Faintly*] Come in. [*Then summoning her courage: more resolutely*] Come in. [*The door is opened and the* DONKEYMAN *appears. He is a tall, lanky, grey-haired man with a thin, weather-beaten face, small gray eyes, bushy grey moustache. He is dressed in oil-stained dungarees: is smoking a briar pipe*]

DONKEYMAN   [*Respectfully*] Can I come in for a second, ma'am?

ANNA   [*Disappointed when she sees who it is*] Why, sure, come in, Mr. Donk.

DONKEYMAN   [*Shutting the door behind him: turning to her with a grin*] I'll bet you think that's my name, ma'am?—Mr. Donk? [*He chuckles*]

ANNA   [*Indifferently*] Sure. Ain't it? I've heard 'em all call you that.

DONKEYMAN   [*Chuckling*] It's short for Donkeyman. That's my job—running the donkey engine on this tub. Now you know. No, my right name's Smith—just plain Smith.

ANNA   [*Indifferently*] Oh—that so?

DONKEYMAN   [*Looking around the cabin inquisitively*] The Old Man ain't showed up yet?

ANNA   No—not 'less he come while I was ashore and beat it again.

DONKEYMAN   [*Shaking his head*] No, I been on the lookout for him. [*Curiously*] I seen you going ashore with your bag about sundown, ma'am. I thought maybe you was leavin' us, too.

ANNA [*Evasively*] No. I was just taking some things to get cleaned.

DONKEYMAN [*Sympathetically*] You must feel lonesome the last two days—bein' here all 'lone. No need to git scared, tho'. There's always one of us on the barge somewhere.

ANNA I ain't scared.

DONKEYMAN And anything we can do for you, you only got to tell us.

ANNA Thanks. [*With a sigh*] But there ain't nothing.

DONKEYMAN [*Scratching his head*] It's darn serious, d'you know it, ma'am,—the Old Man staying ashore so long. Where d'you s'pose he's keeping himself?

ANNA [*Bitterly*] I don't know. He's on a drunk, that's all.

DONKEYMAN [*A bit shocked by her frankness for a second: then with a grin*] Yes, I guessed that was it. Well, all of us goes on a bust at times. [*Then seriously*] But he'd ought to show up. He's liable to lose his job if he don't. I've been doing my best to cover him up and keep things going as if he was on board—but I know they got their suspicions, and if he ain't here tomorrow— I'd hate to see him fired. I've worked under him now for two years and he's the best ever I struck. [ANNA *smiles scornfully*] You ain't got no idea where I'd find him, have you, ma'am?

ANNA No.

DONKEYMAN Well, I think I'll go ashore and take a look in some of the places I know and see if he's there. [*He turns to go*]

ANNA [*With a sudden harsh laugh*] Be sure and look in all the houses.

DONKEYMAN What houses, ma'am?

ANNA Oh, nothing. All the gin mills, I meant.

DONKEYMAN Yes, of course. Well, I hope I find him. Goodnight, ma'am.

ANNA Goodnight. [*The* DONKEYMAN *goes out. Suddenly there is the sound of talking, his voice and Chris's from the deck outside.* ANNA *gets to her feet, her face growing hard and hostile*]

DONKEYMAN [*Putting his head in the doorway: reassuringly*] Speak of the devil—. Here he is, ma'am. I just run into him coming aboard. [*In a sharp whisper, hand to his mouth*] He's all sobered up, tho'. [*He disappears. A moment later* CHRIS *appears in the doorway. He is in a very bleary, bedraggled condition, suffering from the after effects of his drunk. A tin pail full of foaming beer is in his hand. He comes forward, his eyes avoiding Anna's*]

ANNA [*Looking him over with contempt*] So you come back at last, did you? You're a fine looking sight! [*Then jeeringly*] I thought you'd beaten it for good on account of the disgrace I'd brought on you.

CHRIS [*Wincing faintly*] Don't say dat, Anna, please! [*He sits in a chair by the table, setting down the can of beer, holding his head in his hands*]

ANNA [*In the same tone*] It must be awful hard on a respectable Old Man like you to find out all at once he's got a no-good bum like me for a daughter. [CHRIS *allows a miserable sigh to escape him, but makes no other reply.* ANNA *looks at him with a certain sympathy*] What's the trouble? Feeling sick?

CHRIS [*Dully*] Inside my head I feel sick.

ANNA Well, what d'you expect after being soused for two days? [*Resentfully*] It serves you right and I'm glad of it! A fine thing—you leaving me alone on this barge all that time!

CHRIS [*Humbly*] Ay'm sorry, Anna.

ANNA [*Scornfully*] Sorry!

CHRIS But Ay'm not sick inside head vay you mean. Ay'm sick from tank too much about you, about me.

ANNA And how about me? D'you suppose I ain't been thinking too? Gawd, I ain't slept a wink or eaten a thing!

CHRIS Ay'm sorry, Anna. [*He sees her bag and gives a start*] You pack your bag, Anna? You vas going—?

ANNA [*Forcibly*] Yes, I was going right back to what you think!

CHRIS Anna!

ANNA I went ashore to get a train for New York. I'd been waiting and waiting till I was sick of it. Then I changed my mind and decided not to go today. So I come back to wait some more. But I'm going first thing tomorrow, so it'll be all the same in the end.

CHRIS [*Raising his hand: pleadingly*] No, you never do dat, Anna!

ANNA [*With a sneer*] Why not, I'd like to know?

CHRIS You don't never gat to do—dat vay—no more, Ay tal you, Ay fix dat up all right.

ANNA [*Suspiciously*] Fix what up?

CHRIS [*Not seeming to have heard her question: sadly*] You vas vaiting, you say? You vasn't vaiting for me, Ay bet.

ANNA [*Callously*] You'd win. No, I wasn't waiting for you. Why should I?

CHRIS   For dat Irish fallar?

ANNA   [Defiantly] Yes—if you want to know. [Then with a forlorn laugh] I thought maybe he'd come back to say goodbye before he shipped away. Swell chance! If he did come back it'd only be 'cause he was drunk and wanted to beat me up or kill me, I suppose. But even if he did I'd rather have him come— that way—than not show up at all. I wouldn't care what he did.

CHRIS   Ay guess it's true you vas in love with him all right.

ANNA   You guess!

CHRIS   Ay know. [Turning to her earnestly] And Ay'm sorry for you like hell he don't come, Anna!

ANNA   [Softened] Seems to me you've changed your tune a lot.

CHRIS   Ay've been tanking and Ay guess it vas all my fault—all bad tangs dat happen to you. Ay vas bad fader by you. [Pleadingly] You try for not hate me, Anna. Ay'm crazy ole fool, dat's all. Ay mean good.

ANNA   Who said I hated you?

CHRIS   Ay'm sorry for everytang Ay do wrong for you, Anna. Ay vant for you be happy all rest of your life for make up. It make you happy marry dat Irish fallar, Ay vant it, too,—even if he is on sea.

ANNA   [Dully] Well, there ain't no chance of that no more. There never was, I guess. But I'm glad you think different about it, anyway.

CHRIS   [Supplicatingly] And you tank—maybe—you forgive me some-time for wrong Ay do to you?

ANNA   [With a wan smile] I'll forgive you right now.

CHRIS   [Seizing her hand and kissing it: brokenly] Anna lilla! Anna lilla!

ANNA   [Touched, but a bit embarrassed] Don't bawl about it. There ain't nothing to forgive, anyway. It ain't your fault and it ain't mine and it ain't his neither. We're all poor nuts, and things happen, and we yust get mixed in wrong, that's all. What's the difference, anyway? The whole world's a joke.

CHRIS   [Eagerly] You say right tang, Anna, py golly! It ain't nobody's fault! [Shaking his fist] It's dat ole davil, sea!

ANNA   [With an exasperated laugh] Gee, won't you ever can that stuff? Lay off the sea for a while. What's the good of picking on it all the time? [CHRIS relapses into injured silence. After a pause Anna continues curiously] You said a minute ago you'd fixed something up—about me. What was it?

CHRIS   [After a hesitating pause] Ay'm shipping avay on sea again, Anna.

ANNA   [Astounded] You're—what!

CHRIS Ay sign on tonight on steamer sail tomorrow morning. Day gat all crew but bo'sun signed on dis morning. Fallar tal me in saloon and Ay go down to ship see first mate. Ay gat my ole yob—bo'sun. [ANNA *stares at him. He goes on, a bitter smile, coming over her face*] You see, Anna, Ay tank dat's best tang for you. Ay'm ole fallar. It ain't no good for keep young gal like you by me. You hate me soon dat vay. Ay only bring you bad luck, Ay tank. Ay make you moder's life sorry. Ay don't vant make yours dat vay, but it looks like Ay do yust same. Dat ole davil, sea, she makes me Yonah man ain't no good for nobody. And Ay tank now it ain't no use fight with sea. She beat me sure dis time. No man dat live going to beat her, py yingo!

ANNA [*With a laugh of helpless bitterness*] So that's how you've fixed me, is it?

CHRIS Yes, Ay tank if dat ole davil gat me back she leave you alone den.

ANNA [*Bitterly*] But for Gawd's sake, don't you see you're doing the same thing you've always done all over again—running away? Don't you see? [*But she sees the look of obsessed stubbornness on his face and gives it up helplessly*] But what's the use of talking to you? You ain't right, that's what. I'll never blame you for nothing no more. You ain't all there. But how could you figure out that was fixing me?

CHRIS Dat ain't all. Ay'm going gat dem fallars in steamship office to pay you all money is coming to me every month vhile Ay'm away.

ANNA [*With a hard laugh*] Thanks. But I guess I won't be hard up for no small change.

CHRIS [*Hurt: humbly*] It ain't much, Ay know, but it's plenty for keep you so you never gat go back—

ANNA [*Shortly*] Shut up about it now, will you? We'll talk about it some other time, see?

CHRIS [*After a pause: ingratiatingly*] You like Ay go ashore look for dat Irish faller, Anna,—tal him you vait?

ANNA [*Angrily*] Not much! think I want to drag him back?

CHRIS [*After a pause: uncomfortably*] By golly, dat booze I drink don't go vell dis time. Give me fever. Ay feel hot like hell. [*He takes off his coat and puts it on the table*]

ANNA Here, I'll hang it up for you. [*She takes the coat*] What you got in the pocket, for Pete's sake—a ton of lead? [*She reaches in and pulls out a revolver: looks from it to him in amazement*] A gun? What did you get that for? You ain't turning gun man in your old age, are you?

CHRIS   [*Sheepishly*] Ay forgat. Ain't nutting. Ain't loaded, anyway.

ANNA [*Breaking it open to make sure, then closing it again: looking at him suspiciously*] That ain't telling me why you got it?

CHRIS   [*Sheepishly*] Ay'm ole fool. Ay gat it vhen Ay go ashore first. Ay tank den it's all fault of dat Irish fallar—what happens and—

ANNA   And you bought this to go after and get him, did you? [*With a shudder*] Say, you're crazier than I thought. I never dreamt you'd go that far.

CHRIS   [*Quickly*] Ay don't—Ay gat better sense right avay. Ay don't never buy bullets even. It ain't his fault, Ay know. Killing him don't do no good. It's ole davil, sea, Ay'd like to kill—if Ay could.

ANNA   [*Still suspicious of him*] Well, I'll take care of this for a while— loaded or not. [*She put it in drawer of table and closes the drawer*]

CHRIS   [*Placatingly*] Throw it overboard if you vant, Ay don't care. [*Then after a pause*] Py golly, Ay tank Ay go lie down. Ay'm dead for sleep. Ay feel sick. [*He gets up*] You don't vant to go to bed, Anna?

ANNA   Me? No. Think I can sleep? You go in and lie down. I'll look at this for a while. [*She takes a magazine from the table*]

CHRIS   [*Hesitating by her chair*] Ay gat turn out early in morning for get aboard.

ANNA   [*Dully*] I suppose. I was forgetting you was leaving. Where's this ship going to?

CHRIS   Cape Town. Dat's in South Africa. She's British steamer called *Londonderry*.

ANNA   I expect that's a long trip, ain't it? South Africa sounds like it.

CHRIS   [*Dismally*] Yes, it's long. [*He stands hesitating: finally blurts out*] Anna—you forgive me sure?

ANNA   [*Wearily*] Sure I do. You ain't to blame. You're just—what you are—like me.

CHRIS   [*Pleadingly*] Den—you lat me kiss you again once? Maybe it's last time.

ANNA   [*Raising her face: forcing a smile*] Sure. No hard feelings.

CHRIS   [*Kisses her: brokenly*] Anna lilla!

ANNA   Goodbye.

CHRIS   Goodbye. Ay— [*He fights for words to express himself, but finds none: miserably, with a sob*] Ay can't say it! Goodnight, Anna.

ANNA   Goodnight. [*He picks up the can of beer and goes slowly into room* on left, his shoulders bowed, his head sunk forward dejectedly. He closes the door after him. ANNA turns over the pages of the magazine, trying desperately to banish her thoughts by looking at the pictures. This fails to distract her, and flinging the magazine back on the table she springs to her feet and walks about the cabin distractedly, clenching and unclenching her hands. She speaks aloud to herself in a tense, trembling voice] Gawd, I can't stand this much longer! I'll go crazy. I'll jump overboard. Why'd I come back here? What am I waiting for anyway? Like a damn fool! [She laughs helplessly, then checks herself abruptly as she hears the sound of heavy footsteps on the deck outside. She appears to recognize these and her face lights up with joy. She gasps:— Mat! A strong terror seems suddenly to seize her. She rushes to the table, takes the revolver out of the drawer and crouches down in the corner left, behind the cupboard]

[A moment later the door is flung open and MAT BURKE appears in the doorway. He is in bad shape: his clothes torn and muddy, covered with sawdust as if he had been groveling or sleeping on barroom floors. There is a red bruise on his forehead over one of his eyes, another over one cheekbone; his knuckles are skinned and raw—plain evidences of the fighting as he has been through on his "bat." His eyes are bloodshot and heavy lidded, his face has a bloated look. But beyond these appearances—the results of heavy drinking—there is an expression in his eyes of wild mental turmoil, of impotent animal rage baffled by its own abject misery]

BURKE [Peers blinkingly about the cabin: hoarsely] Let you not be hiding from me, whoever's here, tho' 'tis well you know if I'd the guts of a man in me at all I'd have a right to come back and murder you. [With a great sigh] But I've no guts left, and 'tis a poor weak scut you've made of me entirely, God help me! [He stops to listen. Hearing no sound he closes the door behind him and comes forward to the table. He throws himself into the rocking chair: despondently] There's no one here, I'm thinking, and 'tis a great fool I am to be coming. [With a sort of dumb, uncomprehending anguish] Yerra, Mat Burke, 'tis a great jackass you've become and what's come into you at all, at all? [Then with sudden hope] But here's the lamp burning and someone must have lit it. [Despondent again] 'Tis himself done it, likely, the old ape, and him ashore now after a drink. [Mournfully] She's gone out of this long ago, I'm telling you, and you'll never see her face again. [ANNA stands up, hesitating, struggling between joy and fear. Burke's eyes fall on Anna's bag. He leans over to examine it] What's this? [Joyfully] It's hers! She's not gone! But where is she? Ashore? [Darkly] What would she be doing ashore on this rotten night? [His face suddenly convulsed with grief and rage] 'Tis that, is it? Oh, God's curse on her! [Raging] I'll wait till she comes and choke her dirty life out with my two hands! [ANNA *starts, her face growing hard. She steps into the room, the revolver in her right hand by her side]*

ANNA *[In a hard, cold tone]* What you are doing here?

BURKE *[Wheeling about with a terrified gasp]* Glory be to God! *[They remain motionless and silent for a moment, holding each other's eyes]*

ANNA *[In the same hard voice]* Well, can't you talk? I asked you what you was doing here?

BURKE *[Trying to fall into an easy, careless tone]* You've a year's growth scared out of me, coming at me so sudden and me thinking I was alone.

ANNA You've got your nerve butting in here without knocking or nothing. What d'you want?

BURKE *[Airily]* Oh, nothing much. I was wanting to have a last word with you, that's all. *[He moves a step toward her]*

ANNA *[Sharply: raising the revolver]* Careful now! Don't try getting too close. I heard what you said you'd do to me. I'm wise to your game.

BURKE *[Noticing the revolver for the first time]* Is it murdering me you'd be now, God forgive you? *[With a contemptuous laugh]* Or is it thinking I'd be frightened by that old tin whistle in the hand of a girl? *[He walks straight for her, grinning]*

ANNA *[Wildly]* Look out, I tell you!

BURKE *[Who has come so close that the revolver is almost touching his chest]* Let you shoot, then! You haven't the guts, I'm thinking. *[Then with sudden wild grief]* Let you shoot, I'm saying, and be done with it. Let you end me with a shot and I'll be thanking you, for it's a rotten dog's life I've lived the past two days since I've known what you are, till after wishing I was dead itself or never born at all!

ANNA *[Overcome: letting the revolver drop to the floor as if her fingers had no strength to hold it: with an hysterical laugh]* No—it ain't loaded, anyway. *[Wildly]* What d'you want coming here? Why don't you beat it? Go on! *[She passes him and sinks down in the rocking chair]*

BURKE *[Following her: mournfully]* 'Tis right you'd be asking why did I come. *[Then angrily]* 'Tis because 'tis a great weak fool of the world I am, and me tormented with the wickedness you'd told me of yourself, and drinking oceans of booze that'd make me forget. Forget? Divil a word I'd forget, and your face grinning always in front of me eyes awake or asleep till I do be thinking a madhouse is the proper place for me.

ANNA *[Glancing at his hands and face: scornfully]* You look like you ought to be put away some place. You're a nice mess! Wonder you wasn't pulled in. You been scrapping, too, ain't you?

BURKE   I have—with every scut would take off his coat to me! [*Fiercely*] And each time I'd be hitting one a clout in the mug it wasn't his face I'd be seeing at all, but yours, and me wanting to drive you a blow would knock you out of this world where I wouldn't be seeing or thinking more of you.

ANNA   [*Her lips trembling pitifully*] Thanks!

BURKE   [*Walking up and down: distractedly*] That's right, make game of me! Oh, I'm shamed to my face and a great coward surely, to be coming back to speak with you at all. You've a right to laugh at me.

ANNA   I ain't laughing at you, Mat.

BURKE   [*Unheeding*] You to be what you are, and me to be Mat Burke, and me to be drove back to look at you again! 'Tis black shame is on me.

ANNA   [*Resentfully*] Then get out! No one's holding you!

BURKE   [*Bewilderedly*] And me to listen to that talk from a woman like you and be frightened to close her mouth with a slap! Oh, God help me, I'm a yellow coward for all men to spit at! [*Then furiously*] But I'll not be getting out of this till I've had me word. [*Raising his fist threateningly*] And let you look out how you'd drive me! [*Letting his fist fall helplessly*] Don't be angry now! I'm raving like a real lunatic, I'm thinking, and the sorrow you put on me has my brains drownded in grief. [*Suddenly bending down to her and grasping her arms: intensely*] Tell me it's a lie, I'm saying! That's what I'm after coming to hear you say.

ANNA   [*Dully*] A lie? What?

BURKE   [*With passionate entreaty*] All the badness you told me two days back. Sure it must be a lie! How could a fine girl the like of you—? How could I be losing my love to you if you was that? Say it's a lie, Anna! You was only making game of me, wasn't you? You was only trying to see would I lose all thought of you easy and believe the worst. It's so you'd not believe me the like of that that I'm back here to you now. Tell me 'twas a lie, Anna, and I'll be saying prayers of thanks on my two knees to the Almighty God!

ANNA   [*Terribly shaken: faintly*] I can't, Mat. I wish to God it wasn't true, but it is. [*As he turns away: imploringly*] Oh, Mat, won't you see that no matter what I was I ain't that any more? Can't you see I've changed? Why listen! I packed up my bag this afternoon and went ashore. I'd been waiting here all alone for two days—waiting—thinking maybe you'd come back—thinking maybe you'd think over all I'd said—and maybe—. Oh. I was afraid you'd only come back to beat me up or kill me—and yet I hoped you'd come. Oh, I don't know what I was hoping! But I was afraid to even go out of the cabin for a second, honest—afraid you might come and not find me here and think—. Then I gave up hope when you didn't show up and I went ashore with my bag and went to the railroad station. I was going to New York. I was going back—to the same old life.

BURKE   [*Hoarsely*] God's curse on you!

ANNA   Listen, Mat! You hadn't come and I'd gave up hope. But—in the station—I couldn't go. I'd bought my ticket and everything—see—here it is. [*She takes the ticket from her dress and tries to hold it before his eyes*] Look! But I got to thinking about you—and I couldn't take the train. I couldn't! So I come back here—to wait some more. Oh, Mat, don't you see I've changed? Can't you forgive what's dead and gone—and forget it?

BURKE   [*Turning on her: overcome by rage again*] Forget, is it? Haven't I tried drinking oceans of booze that'd make me forget and they only made it worse? I'll not forget till my dying day, I'm telling you, and me tormented with thoughts of all the dirty scuts you'd been kissing these years. [*In a frenzy*] Oh, I'm wishing I had wan of them forninst me this minute and I'd beat him with my fists till he'd be a bloody corpse! I'm wishing the whole lot of them will roast in hell till the Judgment Day—and yourself along with them, for you're as bad as they are, God's curse on your soul!

ANNA   [*Shuddering*] Mat! [*Then after a pause: in a voice of dead, stony calm*] Well, you've had your say. Now you better beat it.

BURKE   [*Starts slowly for the door: hesitates, then after a pause*] And what'll you be doing?

ANNA   What difference does it make to you?

BURKE   I'm asking you!

ANNA   [*In the same tone*] My bag's packed and I got my ticket. I'll go to New York tomorrow.

BURKE   [*Helplessly*] You mean—you'll be doing the same again?

ANNA   [*Stonily*] Yes.

BURKE   [*In anguish*] You'll not!

ANNA   I will too. What else is there for me to do? And who gives a damn what I do? Not me, at any rate.

BURKE   You're after telling me you'd changed. That was a great lie, surely.

ANNA   It ain't no lie, either. But what's the use of changing? It's a rotten game and I might as well be as rotten as the rest.

BURKE   [*In anguish*] Don't torment me with that talk! 'Tis a she-divil you are, sent to drive me mad entirely.

ANNA   [*Her voice breaking*] Oh, for Gawd's sake, Mat, leave me alone! Go away! All you do is bawl me out when you see I'm down! Don't you see I'm licked? Why d'you want to keep on kicking me? Is that what a real man— with guts to him—does to a woman?

BURKE   [*Indignantly*] And don't you deserve the worst I'd say. God forgive you?

ANNA   All right, maybe I do. But you've said it. Don't rub it in! Why ain't you done what you said you was going to do? Why ain't you got that yob on some ship was going to take you to the other side of the earth where you'd never see me again?

BURKE   I have, so.

ANNA   What? Then you're going—honest?

BURKE   I signed on this today, drunk as I was—and she's sailing tomorrow morning.

ANNA   [*Alarm creeping into her voice*] So you're really going?

BURKE   I am, surely. I've to be on board of her at six sharp.

ANNA   And where is the ship going to?

BURKE   Cape Town.

ANNA   [*The memory of having heard that name a little while before coming to her: with a start, confusedly*] Cape Town? Where's that? Far away?

BURKE   'Tis at the tip end of Africa. That's far for you.

ANNA   [*Forcing a laugh*] You're keeping your word all right, ain't you? [*After a slight pause: curiously*] What sort of ship is it?

BURKE   A British tramp, the like of the one I was on got wrecked.

ANNA   [*Trying to conceal a feeling of fright*] Supposing she gets wrecked, too?

BURKE   [*Bitterly*] Then I'm hoping all hands will be drowned and myself the first.

ANNA   [*Frightenedly*] Oh! [*Then with great curiosity again*] What's the boat's name?

BURKE   *The Londonderry.*

ANNA   [It suddenly comes to her that this is the same ship her father is sailing on] The Londonderry! It's the same—Oh, this is too much! [With wild, ironical laughter] Ha, ha, ha!

BURKE   What's too much? What's up with you now?

ANNA   Ha, ha, ha! It's funny, funny! I'll die laughing!

BURKE   [Irritated] Laughing at what?

ANNA   It's a secret. You'll know soon enough. It's funny. [Controlling herself: after a pause] Say, you mustn't talk that way about getting drownded. [Cynically] You'll get over that. You won't even remember you ever saw me by the time you get there!

BURKE   That's a lie and you know it!

ANNA   What kind of a place is this Cape Town? Must be an awful dump, ain't it?

BURKE   It is not. 'Tis a fine big city the like of this.

ANNA   And plenty of dames there, I suppose?

BURKE   To the divil with them! That I may never see another woman to my dying hour!

ANNA   That's what you say now, but I'll bet by the time you get there you'll have forgot all about me and start in talking the same old bull you did to me the first one you meet.

BURKE   [Offended] I'll not, then! God mend you, is it making me out to be the like of yourself, you are, and you taking up with this one and that all the years of your life?

ANNA   [Angrily assertive] Yes, that's yust what I do mean. You been doing the same thing all your life, picking up a new girl in every port. How're you any better than I am?

BURKE   [Thoroughly exasperated] Is it no shame you have at all? I'm a fool to be wasting talk on you and you hardened in badness. I'll go out of this and lave you alone forever. [He starts for the door, then stops to turn on her furiously:—] And I suppose 'tis the same lies you told them all before that you told to me?

ANNA   [Distractedly] Oh, for Gawd's sake! Go, can't you, if you're going to keep on nagging me? I can't stand it.

BURKE   You was telling them you loved each one of them like you told me!

ANNA   [Indignantly] That's a lie! I never did!

BURKE   [*Miserably*] You'd be saying that, anyway.

ANNA   [*Forcibly*] I never did, I tell you! I never told 'em nothing!

BURKE   But if you didn't itself, you must have felt love for some in the lot of them, I'm thinking, and you meeting all kinds of men, and those would know well how to trick a girl the like of you.

ANNA   [*With growing intensity*] Are you trying to accuse me—of being in love—really in love—with *them*!

BURKE   I'm thinking you were, surely.

ANNA   [*Springing to her feet: furiously, as if this were the last insult, advancing on him threateningly*] You mutt, you! I've stood enough from you— but don't you dare fling that in my face! Don't you dare, d'you hear, or—[*With scornful bitterness*] Love 'em! Oh, my Gawd! You damn thick-head! Love 'em! [*Savagely*] I hated 'em, I tell you! Hated 'em, hated 'em, hated 'em! If they'd all drop dead I'd die laughing! The very sight of 'em made me sick! I hated 'em all and I still do and always will! And may Gawd strike me dead this minute and my mother, too, if she was alive, if I ain't telling you the honest truth!

BURKE   [*Immensely pleased by her vehemence: a light beginning to break over his face, but still uncertain, torn between doubt and the desire to believe: helplessly*] If I could only be believing you now!

ANNA   What? Don't you believe it—after all I've yust said?

BURKE   [*Miserably*] I don't know, God help me.

ANNA   [*Distractedly*] Oh, what's the use? What's the use of me talking? What's the use of anything? [*Pleadingly*] Oh, Mat, you mustn't think that for a second! You mustn't! Think all the other bad about me you want to and I won't kick, 'cause you've a right to. But don't think that! [*On the point of tears*] I couldn't bear it! It'd be yust too much to know you was going away where I'd never see you again—thinking that about me.

BURKE   [*After an inward struggle: tensely forcing out the words with difficulty*] If I was believing—that you'd never had love for any other man in the world but me—I could be forgetting the rest, maybe.

ANNA   [*With a cry of joy*] Mat!

BURKE   [*Slowly*] If 'tis truth you're after telling, that your love for me— is the first time of your life—I'd have a right, maybe, to believe you'd changed— and that I'd changed you myself till the thing you'd been all your life wouldn't be you any more at all.

ANNA   [*Hanging on his words: breathlessly*] Oh, Mat! That's what I been trying to tell you all along!

BURKE   [*Simply*] For I've a power of strength in me to lead men the way I want, and women, too—maybe; and I'm thinking I'd change you to a new woman entirely so I'd never know, or you either, what kind of woman you'd been in the past, at all.

ANNA   Yes, you could, Mat! I know you could!

BURKE   And I'm thinking 'twasn't your fault, maybe, but having that old ape for a father that left you to grow up alone, made you what you was. And if I could be believing 'tis only me you—[*Breaking out: with bewildered anger*] But how can I put trust in your word—and you lying to all men all your life till you've had great training in it, and you'd find it easy to be making game of a simple man the like of me.

ANNA   [*Distractedly*] You got to believe it, Mat! What can I do? I'll do anything, anything you want to prove I'm not lying!

BURKE   [*Suddenly seems to have a solution. He feels in the pocket of his coat and grasps something in his left-hand pocket: solemnly*] Would you be willing to swear an oath—now—a terrible, fearful oath would send your soul to the divils in hell if you was lying?

ANNA   [*Eagerly*] Sure. I'll swear, Mat—on anything.

BURKE   [*Takes a small, cheap crucifix from his left pocket and holds it for her to see*] Will ye swear on this?

ANNA   [*Reaching out for it*] Yes. Sure I will. Give it to me.

BURKE   [*Holding it away*] 'Tis a cross was given me by my mother, God rest her soul! [*He makes the sign of the cross mechanically*] I was a lad only, and she told me to kape it by me if I'd be waking or sleeping and never lose it and it'd bring me luck. She died soon after. But I'm after keeping it safe with me from that day to this, and I'm telling you there's a great power in it, and 'tis great bad luck it's saved me from and me roaming the seas, and I having it tied round my neck when my last ship sunk, and it bringing me sound to land when the others went to their death. [*Very earnestly*] And I'm warning you now, if you'd swear an oath on this, 'tis my old woman herself will be looking down from Hivin above and praying Almighty God and the Saints to put a great curse on you if she'd hear you swearing a lie.

ANNA   [*Awed by his manner: superstitiously*] I wouldn't have the nerve—honest!—if it was a lie. But it's the truth and I ain't scared to swear. Give it to me.

BURKE   [*Handing it to her: almost frightenedly as if he feared for her safety*] Be careful what you swear, I'm saying.

ANNA   [Holding the cross gingerly] Well—what do you want me to swear? You say it.

BURKE   Swear I'm the only man in the world iver you felt love for.

ANNA   [Looking into his eyes steadily] I swear it.

BURKE   And that you'll be forgetting from this day all the badness you've done and never do the like of it again.

ANNA   [Forcibly] I swear it! I swear it by God!

BURKE   And may the blackest curse of God strike you if you're lying. Say it now!

ANNA   And may the blackest curse of God strike me if I'm lying!

BURKE   [With a stupendous sigh] Oh, glory be to God, I'm after believing you now! [He takes the cross from her hand, his face beaming with joy: is about to put it in his pocket]

ANNA   Wait a minute. [Gravely] I want you to swear something.

BURKE   [Grinning] What is it? Anything you plaze.

ANNA   Swear you'll forget, too.—that you'll never remind me of what's past and gone—that you'll forget the whole business once and for all.

BURKE   [Joyfully] I swear it by all the Saints! Sure, 'tis forgetting I'm wanting, and divil a thought or word will I ivir waste on it again! So I'll swear a thousand times if you like. [He kisses the crucifix] There now! Does that suit you? [He puts his arm about her waist and is about to kiss her when he stops, transfixed by some terrible doubt]

ANNA   [Alarmed] What's the matter with you?

BURKE   [With sudden fierce questioning] Is it Catholic ye are?

ANNA   [Confused] I don't know. No. Why?

BURKE   [Wailing] Oh, God help us both! What divil's trickery is in it, to be swearing an oath on a Catholic cross and you wan of the others. [Passionately] Oh, I'd a right to stay away from you—but I couldn't, God forgive me! I was loving you in spite of it all and wanting to wed with you no matter what you are. I'd go mad if I'd not have you! I'd be killing the world—[Mournfully] And now when 'tis all settled and done and you've swore the oath, 'tis good for nothing at all.

ANNA   [Distractedly] Oh, Mat, I don't know what you mean! Don't you believe me? Didn't you hear me swear? What more d'you want?

BURKE   If it isn't a Catholic you are—

ANNA   What's the difference? I don't know what I am. I ain't nothing.

BURKE [A *ray of hope penetrating his despair*] If you're a heathen itself 'tis better than being one of them is the enemies of God.

ANNA [*Eagerly*] Well, can't I learn to be a Catholic, then? I'll become a Catholic, if you want. I'll be anything you want me to!

BURKE [*With sudden wild exultation*] Will you now? 'Tis a darling woman you are, and I'm bursting with joy this minute! A Catholic, is it? Then you'll be changed into a new woman, surely, and divil a bit of the old will be left at all. Hurroo! You're a swate angel from Hiven, God bless you! [*He seizes her in his arms and kisses her with frantic joy*]

ANNA [*Remonstrating: tender*] O-ow, Mat! You don't know how strong you are! You hurt! [*The door on the left is pushed open and* CHRIS *appears in the doorway. He stands blinking at them. At first, the old expression of hate comes into his eyes instinctively. He seems about to spring at* BURKE. *Then he relaxes, a look of resignation and relief comes over his face*]

CHRIS [*With an embarrassed cough*] Anna! [*They break away from each other with startled exclamations and stand staring at him*]

BURKE [*Explosively*] God stiffen it! [*He takes a step toward* CHRIS, *threateningly*]

CHRIS [*His face lighting up with a sudden happy thought: excitedly*] Vait! You vait! [*He rushes back into the bedroom*]

BURKE [*Bewilderedly*] What's up with him? [*Then savagely*] If 'tis more trouble he's planning to make between us I'll put a head on him he'll not forget!

ANNA [*Putting a restraining hand on his arm*] I don't think he means no trouble, Mat.

CHRIS [*Appears with the tin can of beer in his hand: grinning*] Ve gat have drink on dis, py golly! You get glasses, Anna.

ANNA [*Happily*] That's the way to talk! [*With a laugh*] And say, it's about time for you and Mat to kiss and make up. You're going to be shipmates on this African trip, d'you know it?

BURKE [*Astounded*] Shipmates—on the *Londonderry*? Has himself——?

CHRIS [*Equally astounded*] Ay vas bo'sun on her.

BURKE The divil! [*Then angrily*] You'd be going back to sea and leaving Anna all alone, would you?

ANNA [*Quickly*] It's all right, Mat. He's doing the right thing. That's where he belongs and I want him to go. [*With a laugh as she gets the glasses*] And as for being left alone, that runs in the family and I'm used to it. [*Pouring out Burke's glass*] If you're away a lot of the time, Mat, I'll 'preciate you all the

THE OLE DAVIL, ACT FOUR ◊ 165

more when you do come home. [*Pouring out Chris's glass*] That goes for you, too, father.

CHRIS   [*Uncertainly*] Ay don't know, Anna. You tank it's better Ay go?

ANNA   Sure I do. We'll all get along better that way. I'll get a little house somewheres and [*With a smile*]—if you both give me *all* your money I'll make a regular place for you to come back to, wait'n see. And now you two drink up and be friends.

BURKE   [*Happily*] Sure! [*Clicking his glass against Chris's*] Here's luck to you! [*He drinks*]

CHRIS   [*Subdued: his face melancholy*] Skoll! [*He drinks*]

BURKE   [*To Anna, with a wink*] You'll not be lonesome long, I'm thinking. I'll see to that, with the help of God! 'Tis himself here will be having a grandchild to ride on his foot within a year, I'm telling you!

ANNA   [*Turning away*] Quite the kidding now. [*She picks up her bag and takes it into room on left*]

CHRIS   [*Who has been staring at his beer absent-mindedly: moodily, with a sort of somber premonition*] It's funny—you and me shipping on same boat dat vay. It's queer. It ain't right. Ay don't know—it's dat funny vay ole davil, sea, do her vorst dirty tricks, yes. It's so!

BURKE   [*With a hearty laugh of scorn*] Yerra! Don't be talking! The sea means good to us only, and let you lave her alone. She'll be welcoming you back like a long-lost child, I'm thinking.

CHRIS   [*Shaking his head: implacably*] Dirty ole davil!

BURKE   [*Shouting to* ANNA] Will you listen to the old bucko, Anna? He's after putting up his fists to fight the sea again.

ANNA   [*Coming out: laughing*] Oh, for Gawd's sake!

THE CURTAIN FALLS

The Ancient Mariner

Although O'Neill wrote *The Rime of the Ancient Mariner* because of an emergency in the production schedule of the Experimental Theatre at the Provincetown Playhouse, it represented a kind of drama for which he had long expressed admiration. In 1920, for example, he had briefly considered a new adaptation of his father's melodrama, *Monte Cristo*, and had written to George Tyler, his producer, that such an undertaking would require "a new system of staging of extreme simplicity and flexibility which, combined with the art of lighting, will permit of many scenes and instantaneous changes, a combination of the scope of the movies with all that is best of the spoken drama."[1]

By 1923, when he made his adaptation of Coleridge's poem, he had already written two dramas such as he described, *The Emperor Jones* and *The Hairy Ape*, and in his program note to Strindberg's *The Spook Sonata*, he had implicitly dedicated the Experimental Theatre of which he was a director to the fluid staging modes of the Expressionist theatre.[2]

The adaptation was an easy matter. He had had it in mind as a possibility for some time—perhaps from his early days as a writer when he wrote the one-act plays *Thirst* and *Fog* under the spell of the poem. In an undated letter written during the summer of 1923 to his co-producer Kenneth Macgowan, he mentions "'The Ancient Mariner' adaptation [which] might be worked as a novel form of recitative, pantomime, Express.[ionistic] set drama."[3] Presumably prepared during the latter months of 1923, it opened the third bill of the Experimental Theatre season on April 6, 1924, sharing the evening with Stark Young's translation of Molière's *Georges Dandin*. The play originally scheduled for the date had been O'Neill's *All God's Chillun Got Wings*, but the production was not ready and the somewhat hasty substitution had to be made.[4]

The staging of *The Ancient Mariner* at the playhouse was made stylistically possible by virtue of the plaster dome that the theatre's first impresario, George Cram Cook, had built for *The Emperor Jones*. Against the concave half-dome at the back of the stage, light played freely and actors were to be seen in partial or total silhouette. As the players had found when they produced the earlier play, heavy scenic pieces were not only

1. Eugene O'Neill to George Tyler, December 9, 1920. The correspondence is in the Firestone Library, Princeton University.
2. See below, "Strindberg and Our Theatre."
3. *"The Theatre We Worked For..." The Letters of Eugene O'Neill to Kenneth Macgowan*, ed. Jackson R. Bryer with introductory essays by Travis Bogard (New Haven and London: Yale University Press, 1982), p. 36. O'Neill also suggested an adaptation of a Norse saga, featuring Eric the Red.
4. A condition that lasted through the season's fourth bill in May, when a revival of *The Emperor Jones* was offered. *All God's Chillun Got Wings* was finally staged as the fifth bill at the end of May.

unnecessary, but a hindrance. Light and shadow, actors in chiaroscuro were sufficient. No doubt under theatrical circumstances that were then unique in New York City, O'Neill and his co-producer, the designer Robert Edmund Jones, felt that for *The Ancient Mariner* they could fully achieve the "Express. set drama" O'Neill had first described to Macgowan. An example of the new theatrical art was in the making.

The masks for the chorus, designed by the director, James Light, were O'Neill's first significant use of a device for which he was ultimately to demonstrate a perhaps inordinate fondness. A year earlier, in *The Hairy Ape*, masks had served to dehumanize the mannequin-like denizens of the Fifth Avenue scenes. Their use was suggested by Blanche Hays, the Provincetown costumer, and O'Neill was excited by their effectiveness. He was later to feel that from the opening of the fourth scene, Yank, the titular "ape," should enter a masked world.[5] Masks were to play a large role, not only in his stagecraft but in his understanding of the complexities of human nature as *All God's Chillun Got Wings* (1924), *The Great God Brown* (1926), *Lazarus Laughed* (1928), and drafts of *Mourning Becomes Electra* (1931) were to demonstrate.[6]

For all its aspiration to high theatrical art, *The Ancient Mariner* was not received with enthusiasm. The newspaper critics shrugged it off, saying that the play diminished the imaginative scope of Coleridge's poem. George Jean Nathan's review suggests something of the quality of what was on the stage: "While an actor with a voice full of cramps and a face full of whiskers, thus depicting the Ancient Mariner, stood at stage right and declaimed, the electrician periodically turned on and off a green light which illuminated the center of the stage and revealed a group of sailors engaged in retailing a pantomimic accompaniment."[7] He reminded the Players and his friend O'Neill that a theatre is nothing "if it fails to realize that the play is ever and alone the thing." The play closed on April 26 and has not been professionally revived.

O'Neill's script was written in the margin and interleaving of a copy of the poem.[8] The present edition prints stage directions taken from the poem or its marginalia in boldface type. O'Neill's additions are in italic type. The text was first published in the *Yale University Library Gazette*, 35 (1960), in an edition by Donald Gallup.

---

5. See below, p. 408, "Memoranda on Masks, Second Thoughts."
6. The presence of a chorus created less excitement in the minds of O'Neill and Jones than the masks. Nevertheless in a few years, O'Neill would develop the chorus together with the masks in forming *Lazarus Laughed*. Both chorus and the conception of mask-like faces would reappear in *Mourning Becomes Electra*.
7. *American Mercury*, June 1924.
8. *The Rime of the Ancient Mariner and Cristabel* (New York and London: G. P. Putnam's Sons, Knickerbocker Press, n.d.)

The Ancient Mariner
(A Dramatic Arrangement of Coleridge's Poem)

PART ONE

Night—A background of sky and sea. On the right, a screen indicates a house. A door with three steps leading up. A lighted ship's lantern over door. A large window with a semi-transparent white shade. Music from within—Tchaikovsky, "Doll's Funeral March," to which guests are dancing. Their shadows come and go on the window like shadowgraphs.

The Mariner stands at foot of steps. His long hair and beard are white, his great hollow eyes burn with fervor. His hands are stretched up to the sky, his face is rapt, his lips move in prayer. He is like a prophet out of the Bible with the body and dress of a sailor.

The three Wedding Guests enter arm in arm. They are all dressed identically in their festive, proper best. All are comparatively young. Two of them have mask-like faces of smug, complacent dullness; they walk like marionettes. The third, with the same type of face, is nevertheless naturally alive—a human being.

They stop before the Mariner, who is blocking their way. They make motions for him to step aside; they pluck at his sleeve. His arms fall, his eyes come back to earth. He stares into the first two faces, waves them aside. They enter the house.

A blast of music. The Mariner fixes his eyes on those of the third Guest—then reaches out his hands and grabs him by the shoulders.

> **It is an ancient Mariner,**
> **And he stoppeth one of three.**

WEDDING GUEST By thy long gray beard and glittering eye,
Now wherefore stopp'st thou me?
The Bridegroom's doors are open'd wide,
And I am next of kin;
The guests are met, the feast is set:
May'st hear the merry din.

> **He holds him with his skinny hand,**
MARINER There was a ship, **quoth he.**

The Chorus—six old sailors wearing the masks of drowned men—bring in the ship from left. Two carry sections to indicate the bow—two, the bulwarks of sides—one the mast on which is a white sail—and one, the tiller. All these are placed in position thus

```
        ---- ----  \
            o  o    \      ¦¦¦ o
 ----    o  o              o
   o         o  o   /
        ---- ----   /
```

WEDDING GUEST   Hold off! unhand me, gray-beard loon!

Eftsoons his hand dropt he.

He holds him with his glittering eye—
The wedding-guest stood still,
And listens like a three years' child:
The Mariner hath his will.

The wedding-guest sat on a stone:
He cannot choose but hear;
And thus spake on that ancient man,
The bright-eyed Mariner.

The Chorus hums a sailor chanty in time to his words. (The "Doll's Funeral" continues to be heard from the house.) The Chorus sway to the roll of the ship. They haul cheerfully on the ropes—rhythmically—the one near mast up and down, the other four in a line sideways. The man at the tiller sways with it as he steers.

MARINER   The ship was cheer'd, the harbour clear'd,
Merrily did we drop
Below the kirk, below the hill,
Below the light-house top.
The sun came up upon the left,
Out of the sea came he!
And he shone bright, and on the right
Went down into the sea.

Higher and higher every day,
Till over the mast at noon—

The Wedding-Guest here beat his breast,
For he heard the loud bassoon.

The bride hath paced into the hall,
Red as a rose is she;
Nodding their heads before her goes
The merry minstrelsy.

The Bride and Groom appear for a moment in the doorway. They smile but like two happy dolls, then kiss as dolls might. The Wedding Guest beats breast and supplicates them to rescue him, but they do not seem to see him. They dance for a second—then go back shutting door. The Wedding Guest beats breast in despair. The Mariner ascends to the top step. The House fades and disappears.

> **The Wedding-Guest he beat his breast,**
> **Yet he cannot choose but hear;**
> **And thus spake on that ancient man,**
> **The bright-eyed Mariner.**

MARINER
> And now the storm-blast came, and he
> Was tyrannous and strong:
> He struck with his o'ertaking wings,
> And chased us south along.

The Chorus keen high like the wind; they stagger about; the mast sways.

> With sloping masts and dipping prow,
> As who pursued with yell and blow
> Still treads the shadow of his foe,
> And forward bends his head,
> The ship drove fast, loud roar'd the blast,
> And southward aye we fled.

> And now there came both mist and snow,
> And it grew wondrous cold:
> And ice, mast-high, came floating by,
> As green as emerald.

The Chorus grow stiff and frozen. Their voices are a dead wail. A greenish white screen is revealed behind the Mariner.

MARINER
> And through the drifts the snowy clifts
> Did send a dismal sheen:
> Nor shapes of men nor beasts we ken—
> The ice was all between.

> The ice was here, the ice was there,
> The ice was all around:
> It crack'd and growl'd, and roar'd and howl'd,
> Like noises in a swound!

Instruments (?)

At length did cross an Albatross:
Thorough the fog it came;
As if it had been a Christian soul,
We hailed it in God's name.

The Albatross appears above the mast. It is like a large Dove of the Holy Ghost.
A mystic halo surrounds it with light. The sailors fall on their knees. Sunlight
floods down seeming to come from the Albatross. The ice disappears. The sailors
take bread from their pockets and offer it to the albatross. The bread is in wafers
like Communion wafers.

MARINER   It ate the food it ne'er had eat,
And round and round it flew.
The ice did split with a thunder-fit;
The helmsman steer'd us through

The sailors sing a hymn to a sort of chanty rhythm, pulling on the ropes, swaying
slowly, happy.

MARINER   And a good south wind sprung up behind;
The Albatross did follow,
And every day, for food or play,
Came to the mariners' hollo!

In mist or cloud, on mast or shroud,
It perch'd for vespers nine;
While all the night, through fog-smoke white,
Glimmer'd the white moon-shine.

A pause. The Mariner's face assumes an expression of haunted horror. The Wed-
ding Guest is terrified and shrinks away.

WEDDING GUEST   God save thee, ancient Mariner!
From the fiends, that plague thee thus!—
Why look'st thou so?—

MARINER   With my cross-bow
I shot the Albatross.

The Mariner makes the motion of shooting. The Albatross disappears. The Mar-
iner sinks to his knees, bowing his head. The Chorus, after one staccato scream
of horror, fall on their faces.

PART TWO

Fog hiding the sun.

The Chorus chant mournfully, swaying. The corpse of the Albatross is laid out on a bier by the mast, a mystic light proceeding from it.

CHORUS   The sun now rose upon the right:
          Out of the sea came he,
          Still hid in mist, and on the left
          Went down into the sea.

          And the good south wind still blew behind,
          But no sweet bird did follow,
          Nor any day, for food or play,
          Came to the mariners' hollo!

MARINER   And I had done a hellish thing,
          And it would work 'em woe:
          For all averr'd, I had kill'd the bird
          That made the breeze to blow.
          Ah wretch! said they, the bird to slay,
          That made the breeze to blow!

The Chorus point at him accusingly.

CHORUS (*chant*)   Ah cursed wretch, the bird to slay
                    That made the breeze to blow!

The Mariner shrinks and stumbles down the steps stretching out his arms to them, imploring forgiveness.

MARINER   Nor dim nor red, like God's own head,
          The glorious sun uprist:
          Then all averr'd, I had kill'd the bird
          That brought the fog and mist.
          'T was right, said they, such birds to slay,
          That bring the fog and mist.

The Fog clears.

But when the fog cleared off, they justify the same, and thus make themselves accomplices in the crime.

The Sun rises. The Chorus point to this and chant:

CHORUS   'Twas right, say we, such birds to slay,
          That bring the fog and mist

The light disappears from the Albatross.

The fair breeze continues.

MARINER	The fair breeze blew, the white foam flew,
	The furrow stream'd off free;
CHORUS	We were the first that ever burst
	Into that silent sea.

The ship hath been suddenly becalmed.

MARINER	Down dropt the breeze, the sails dropt down,
	'T was sad as sad could be;
CHORUS	And we did speak only to break
	The silence of the sea!
MARINER	All in a hot and copper sky,
	The bloody Sun, at noon,
	Right up above the mast did stand,
	No bigger than the Moon.

The copper sun rises and blazes down from above the masthead. The Chorus chant—they stare accusingly and point skinny hands at Mariner. His face is tortured by guilt. He approaches the ship with gestures of despair. The Wedding Guest follows him step by step imitating each gesture as if hypnotized.

CHORUS	Day after day, day after day,
	We stuck, nor breath nor motion;
	As idle as a painted ship
	Upon a painted ocean.
	Water, water, every where,
	And all the boards did shrink;
	Water, water, every where,
	Nor any drop to drink.
MARINER	The very deep did rot: O Christ!
	That ever this should be!
	Yea, slimy things did crawl with legs
	Upon the slimy sea.
CHORUS	About, about, in reel and rout
	The death-fires danced at night;

The death fires dance on sky and sea.

	The water, like a witch's oils,
	Burnt green and blue and white.

A spirit had followed them.

| MARINER | And some in dreams assured were |
| | Of the spirit that plagued us so: |

The spirit rises beside the ship—a figure all in white planes like a snow crystal. The Chorus wail with fear. They kneel, praying to the Albatross. The Mariner enters the ship and kneels with them. The Wedding Guest kneels outside.

CHORUS	Nine fathom deep he had follow'd us
	From the Land of Mist and Snow.
MARINER	Ah! well a-day! what evil looks
	Had I from old and young!

They all stare at him.

The shipmates in sore distress would fain throw the whole guilt on the ancient Mariner; in sign whereof they hang the dead sea-bird round his neck.

> Instead of the Cross, the Albatross
> About my neck was hung.

The Spirit points accusingly at the Albatross, then to the Mariner—then makes a gesture of command. The Chorus rise as one and hang the Albatross about his neck. Its wings are at right angles making a white cross. They pull the Mariner to his feet and push him to the extreme bow—then retreat from him as if he were a leper, chanting:

| CHORUS | Instead of the Cross, the Albatross |
| | About his neck was hung. |

PART THREE

Blinding sunshine—terrific heat—the Chorus are lying, huddled together, on deck. The Mariner stands in the bow.

MARINER	There pass'd a weary time. Each throat
	Was parch'd, and glazed each eye.
CHORUS	A weary time! a weary time!
	How glazed each weary eye!
MARINER	When looking westward, I beheld
	A something in the sky.

The Ancient Mariner beholdeth a sign in the element afar off.

The Chorus totter to their feet.

CHORUS   With throats unslaked, with black lips baked,
          We could not laugh nor wail;
          Through utter drought all dumb we stood!

. . . and at a dear ransom he freeth his speech from the bonds of thirst.

MARINER   I bit my arm, I suck'd the blood,
          And cried, A sail! a sail!

          **With throats unslaked, with black lips baked,
          Agape they heard me call:**

They drag themselves to the bulwark and look over.

          Gramercy! they for joy did grin,
          And all at once their breath drew in,
          As they were drinking all.

**And horror follows. For can it be a ship that comes onward without wind or
tide?**

MARINER   See! see! (**I cried**) she tacks no more!
          Hither to work us weal;
          Without a breeze, without a tide,
          She steadies with upright keel!

          Alas! (**thought I, and my heart beat loud**)
          How fast she nears and nears!
          Are those *her* sails that glance in the Sun,
          Like restless gossameres?

**And its ribs are seen as bars on the face of the setting Sun. The spectre-woman
and her death-mate, and no other on board the skeleton-ship.**

MARINER   Are those *her* ribs through which the Sun
          Did peer, as through a grate?
          And is that Woman all her crew?
          Is that a Death? and are there two?
          Is Death that woman's mate?

*The ship appears from left. Its hull is hidden by the other hull. Death holds up
the mast with its transparent sail and black pennant while with the other hand
he shakes dice with the Woman.*

MARINER   His bones were black with many a crack,
All black and bare, I ween
Jet-black and bare, save where with rust
Of mouldy damps and charnel crust
They were patch'd with purple and green.

Death a black skeleton—the mask of a black skull on a robe of verdigris and rust.

MARINER   Her lips were red, her looks were free,
Her locks were yellow as gold:
Her skin was as white as leprosy,
The Night-Mare Life-in-Death was she,
Who thicks man's blood with cold.

Her face like a white skull—(make-up not mask)—vampirish and terrible in a robe of pale red like blood diluted with water.

**The naked hulk alongside came,
And the twain were casting dice;**

Woman— The game is done! I've won, I've won!

Quoth she, and whistles thrice.

She whistles—She and Death disappear as darkness rushes down.

**The Sun's rim dips; the stars rush out:
At one stride comes the dark;
With far-heard whisper, o'er the sea,
Off shot the spectre-bark.**

CHORUS   We listen'd and look'd sideways up!

MARINER   Fear at my heart, as at a cup,
My life-blood seem'd to sip!

CHORUS   The stars were dim, and thick the night,

MARINER   The steersman's face by his lamp gleam'd white;
From the sails the dew did drip—
Till clomb above the eastern bar
The horned Moon, with one bright star
Within the nether tip.

The Moon rises. It reveals the chorus huddled together on the deck. Each one is pointing accusingly at the Mariner.

MARINER   One after one, by the star-dogg'd Moon,
Too quick for groan or sigh,
Each turn'd his face with ghastly pang,
And cursed me with his eye.

One by one they sink back dead, forming a heap of bodies which the moon floods with a ghastly light.

MARINER   Their souls did from their bodies fly,—
They fled to bliss or woe
And every soul, it pass'd me by,
Like the whizz of my cross-bow!

The light of the six souls shoots up the sky.

PART FOUR

The Mariner stands at the prow staring hypnotically at the Wedding Guest who is on his knees, his voice trembling with fright.

WEDDING GUEST   I fear thee, ancient Mariner!
I fear thy skinny hand!
And thou art long, and lank, and brown,
As is the ribb'd sea-sand.
I fear thee and thy glittering eye,
And thy skinny hand, so brown.—

MARINER   Fear not, fear not, thou wedding-guest!
This body dropt not down.

Alone, alone, all all alone,
Alone on a wide wide sea!
And never a saint took pity on
My soul in agony.

He paces the deck appealing to Heaven in his agony.

The many men, so beautiful!
And they all dead did lie;
And a thousand thousand slimy things
Lived on; and so did I.

He turns from the horror of the dead to look over the side. He is disgusted with the life he sees there as with his own.

MARINER   I look'd upon the rotting sea,
               And drew my eyes away;
               I look'd upon the rotting deck,
               And there the dead men lay.

               I look'd to Heaven, and tried to pray;
               But or ever a prayer had gusht,
               A wicked whisper came, and made
               My heart as dry as dust.

He tries to pray. His prayer turns to a curse in the delirium of his brain caused by the heat.

MARINER   I closed my lids, and kept them close,
               And the balls like pulses beat;
               For the sky and the sea, and the sea and the sky
               Lay like a load on my weary eye,
               And the dead were at my feet.

He reels about half-mad, in terror of the dead.

               An orphan's curse would drag to Hell
               A spirit from on high;
               But oh! more horrible than that
               Is the curse in a dead man's eye!
               Seven days, seven nights, I saw that curse,
               And yet I could not die.

In pantomime. He pleads with God for death to end his torture. The Moon rises. Exhausted he lies over the bulwark and stares at the Moon.

MARINER   The moving Moon went up the sky,
               And no where did abide:
               Softly she was going up,
               And a star or two beside—

He turns with a groan of pain over on his stomach and stares at the water.

               Beyond the shadow of the ship,
               I watch'd the water-snakes:
               They moved in tracks of shining white,
               And when they rear'd, the elfish light
               Fell off in hoary flakes.

He is suddenly exalted and weeps. He rises and makes the motion with his hands of blessing them.

O happy living things! no tongue
Their beauty might declare:
A spring of love gush'd from my heart,
And I bless'd them unaware!
Sure my kind saint took pity on me,
And I bless'd them unaware.

*He kneels on the bulwark. He lifts his arms up to Heaven and prays. The
Albatross drops into the sea.*

The self-same moment I could pray;
And from my neck so free
The Albatross fell off and sank
Like lead into the sea.

PART FIVE

*The sails of the ship are now like the wings of the Albatross—faintly luminous.
The Mariner is asleep on the prow. The Wedding Guest's eyes are closed too. His
head nods. The Mariner awakes, the Wedding Guest at the same second. The
Mariner kneels to pray his thanks.*

MARINER   Oh sleep! it is a gentle thing,
Beloved from pole to pole!
To Mary Queen the praise be given!
She sent the gentle sleep from Heaven,
That slid into my soul.

His appearance is more like a spirit's, his body is worn to nothing.

I moved, and could not feel my limbs:
I was so light—almost
I thought that I had died in sleep,
And was a blessed ghost.

*The sound of wind from the distance, a black cloud comes up from the horizon.
The sails quiver and flap strangely, like wings of an Albatross.*

And soon I heard a roaring wind:
It did not come anear;
But with its sound it shook the sails,
That were so thin and sere.

Wind—lightning—dancing stars.

The upper air burst into life!
And a hundred fire-flags sheen,
To and fro they were hurried about!
And to and fro, and in and out,
The wan stars danced between.

The loud wind never reach'd the ship,
Yet now the ship moved on!
Beneath the lightning and the moon
The dead men gave a groan.

A strange beautiful light comes down the sky and settles on the men's bodies.
They groan and stir with life. They get up. Their masks are changed. They now
have those of holy spirits with haloes about their heads.

MARINER   They groan'd, they stirr'd, they all uprose,
               Nor spake, nor moved their eyes;
               It had been strange even in a dream
               To have seen those dead men rise.

They go about their duties. The Mariner helps them.

The helmsman steer'd, the ship moved on;
Yet never a breeze up-blew;
The mariners all 'gan work the ropes,
Where they were wont to do;
They raised their limbs like lifeless tools—
We were a ghastly crew.

He and his nephew's body pull on a rope.

The body of my brother's son
Stood by me, knee to knee:
The body and I pull'd at one rope,
But he said nought to me.

The Wedding Guest is overcome by horror. He tries to escape, to run away but
cannot.

WEDDING GUEST I fear thee, ancient Mariner!

MARINER   Be calm, thou Wedding-Guest!
               'T was not those souls that fled in pain,
               Which to their corses came again,
               But a troop of spirits blest:

The dawn comes. They group about the mast and sing. The sun rises and floods them with light.

> For when it dawn'd—they dropp'd their arms,
> And cluster'd round the mast;

Music.

> Sweet sounds rose slowly through their mouths,
> And from their bodies pass'd.

> Around, around, flew each sweet sound,
> Then darted to the Sun;
> Slowly the sounds came back again,
> Now mixed, now one by one.

> Sometimes a-dropping from the sky
> I heard the sky-lark sing;
> Sometimes all little birds that are,
> How they seem'd to fill the sea and air
> With their sweet jargoning!

> And now 't was like all instruments,
> Now like a lonely flute;
> And now it is an angel's song,
> That makes the heavens be mute.

The music finally seems to proceed from the sails—the wings.

> It ceased; yet still the sails made on
> A pleasant noise till noon,
> A noise like of a hidden brook
> In the leafy month of June,
> That to the sleeping woods all night
> Singeth a quiet tune.

> Till noon we quietly sailed on,
> Yet never a breeze did breathe:
> Slowly and smoothly went the ship,
> Moved onward from beneath.

From under the ship the White Spirit again rises. He holds the body of the Albatross in one hand. He addresses the spirits, seeming to demand more vengeance on the Mariner. They shake their heads. He is in a rage at this, curses the Mariner again and disappears beneath the ship. The Mariner sees him just as he goes with horror.

Under the keel nine fathom deep,
From the land of mist and snow,
The spirit slid: and it was he
That made the ship to go.

But in a minute she 'gan stir,
With a short uneasy motion—

The ship rolls and pitches. The Mariner is terrified.

Backwards and forwards half her length
With a short uneasy motion.

The mast sways back and forth—the spirits steady it.

Then like a pawing horse let go,
She made a sudden bound:
It flung the blood into my head,
And I fell down in a swound.

He falls down unconscious. The Wedding Guest likewise. With closed eyes.

How long in that same fit I lay,
I have not to declare;
But ere my living life return'd,
I heard, and in my soul discern'd
Two voices in the air.

*It is night and moonlight. The Chorus is grouped about the unconscious Mariner.
One of the Spirits speaks.*

SPIRIT   Is it he? **quoth one,** Is this the man?
By him who died on cross,
With his cruel bow he laid full low
The harmless Albatross.

The spirit who bideth by himself
In the land of mist and snow,
He loved the bird that loved the man
Who shot him with his bow.

**The other was a softer voice,
As soft as honey-dew:**

OTHER SPIRIT   I say, "The man hath penance done,
And penance more will do."

PART SIX

The Mariner is discovered lying insensible—the Wedding Guest likewise. He wakes.

MARINER
I woke, and we were sailing on
As in a gentle weather:
'Twas night, calm night, the Moon was high;
The dead men stood together.

The masks of the chorus are the old ones of dead men. They stare down at him and point.

All stood together on the deck,
For a charnel dungeon fitter:
All fix'd on me their stony eyes,
That in the Moon did glitter.

He tries to tear his eyes from theirs, to appeal to heaven for aid but cannot.

The pang, the curse, with which they died,
Had never pass'd away:
I could not draw my eyes from theirs,
Nor turn them up to pray.

With a violent effort the curse is removed. He looks away out to sea. The chorus move far away from him to the darkness of the stern.

And now this spell was snapt: once more
I view'd the ocean green,
And look'd far forth, yet little saw
Of what had else been seen—

A land breeze from his home—for him alone—greets him. It is strangely formless, it fills him with a frightened joy, he breathes it in like a rare perfume.

But soon there breathed a wind on me
Nor sound nor motion made:
Its path was not upon the sea,
In ripple or in shade.

It raised my hair, it fann'd my cheek
Like a meadow-gale of spring—
It mingled strangely with my fears,
Yet it felt like a welcoming.

Swiftly, swiftly flew the ship,
Yet she sail'd softly too:
Sweetly, sweetly blew the breeze—
On me alone it blew.

A hill appears with a light-house, its light shining on a white church.

Oh! dream of joy! is this indeed
The light-house top I see?
Is this the hill? Is this the kirk?
Is this mine own countree?

The Mariner cannot believe his eyes—imagines he may be dreaming.

We drifted o'er the harbor-bar,
And I with sobs did pray—
O let me be awake, my God!
Or let me sleep alway.

The harbor-bay was clear as glass,
So smoothly it was strewn!
And on the bay the moonlight lay,
And the shadow of the moon.

The rock shone bright, the kirk no less,
That stands above the rock:
The moonlight steep'd in silentness,
The steady weathercock.

The angelic spirits leave the dead bodies, and appear in their own forms of light.

I turn'd my eyes upon the deck—
Oh, Christ! what saw I there!

The Chorus has come back. They now have again the masks of angels, white robes, haloes. A dazzling light surrounds them, seeming to proceed from them.

Each corse lay flat, lifeless and flat,
And, by the holy rood!
A man all light, a seraph-man,
On every corse there stood.

The Chorus of spirits signal to the land, waving their arms and swaying their bodies in unison.

This seraph-band, each waved his hand:
It was a heavenly sight!
They stood as signals to the land,
Each one a lovely light:

This seraph-band, each waved his hand,
No voice did they impart—
No voice; but oh! the silence sank
Like music on my heart.

The sound of oars.

But soon I heard the dash of oars,
I heard the Pilot's cheer;

PILOT   Ship ahoy

MARINER   My head was turn'd perforce away,
And I saw a boat appear.

The Mariner turns his head—the spirits disappear in the darkness as all light except the moonlight goes.

The Pilot, and the Pilot's boy,
I heard them coming fast:

PILOT'S BOY   Ahoy

PILOT   Stroke up!

MARINER   Dear Lord in Heaven! it was a joy!

The Mariner rejoices and breaks down.

The Hermit is singing a hymn.

I saw a third—I heard his voice:
It is the Hermit good!
He singeth loud his godly hymns
That he makes in the wood.
He'll shrieve my soul, he'll wash away
The Albatross's blood.

PART SEVEN

MARINER   This Hermit good lives in that wood
Which slopes down to the sea.

The Hermit sings.

How loudly his sweet voice he rears!
He loves to talk with marineres
That come from a far countree.

The skiff-boat near'd: I heard them talk,

PILOT Why, this is strange, I trow!
Where are those lights so many and fair,
That signal made but now?

HERMIT Strange, by my faith! **the Hermit said—**
And they answered not our cheer!
The planks look warp'd! and see those sails
How thin they are and sere!

PILOT Dear Lord! it hath a fiendish look—

(The pilot made reply)

I am fear'd—

HERMIT   Push on, push on!

Said the Hermit cheerily.

Sound of oars nearer.

MARINER The boat came closer to the ship,
But I nor spake nor stirr'd;
The boat came close beneath the ship,
And straight a sound was heard.

Under the water it rumbled on,
Still louder and more dread:
It reach'd the ship, it split the bay;
The ship went down like lead.

The ship suddenly sinketh. *A roar—darkness. For a moment the Mariner is
seen floating on water like a corpse. When the moonlight returns the Mariner is
with the three in the pilot's dory.*

Like one that hath been seven days drown'd
My body lay afloat;
But swift as dreams, myself I found
Within the Pilot's boat.

The Pilot faints.

**I moved my lips—the Pilot shriek'd
And fell down in a fit;**

The Hermit prays.

> **The holy Hermit raised his eyes**
> **And pray'd where he did sit.**

The Mariner takes the oars. The Pilot's boy goes crazy.

> **I took the oars: the Pilot's boy,**
> **Who now doth crazy go,**
> **Laugh'd loud and long, and all the while**
> **His eyes went to and fro.**

PILOT'S BOY   Ha! ha! Ha! Ha! **quoth he,** full plain I see
         The Devil knows how to row.

They get out of the boat. The Pilot and Pilot's Boy run away, shrieking. The Hermit trembles.

MARINER   And now, all in my own countree,
         I stood on the firm land!
         The Hermit stepp'd forth from the boat,
         And scarcely he could stand.

The Mariner falls on his knees before him.

MARINER   O shrieve me, shrieve me, holy man!
         The Hermit cross'd his brow.

HERMIT   Say quick, **quoth he** I bid thee say—
         What manner of man art thou?

MARINER   Forthwith this frame of mine was wrench'd
         With a woful agony,
         Which forced me to begin my tale;

With a screech of agony he begins his Tale—"There was a ship." Darkness for a moment. Then the Mariner still on his knees receives the absolution of the Hermit who goes away. The Mariner and Wedding Guest are now in same position by steps as when he started his Tale. The House gradually appears behind them.

> And then it left me free.
>
> Since then, at an uncertain hour,
> That agony returns:
> And till my ghastly tale is told,
> This heart within me burns.
>
> I pass, like night, from land to land;

I have strange power of speech;
The moment that his face I see,
I know the man that must hear me:
To him my tale I teach.

Noise again of music—"Doll's Funeral March."

What loud uproar bursts from that door!
The wedding-guests are there:

Sounds of girls singing.

But in the garden-bower the bride
And bride-maids singing are;

Bell from the kirk.

And hark the little vesper bell,
Which biddeth me to prayer!

O Wedding-Guest! this soul hath been
Alone on a wide wide sea:
So lonely 't was, that God himself
Scarce seemed there to be.

O sweeter than the marriage-feast,
'T is sweeter far to me,
To walk together to the kirk
With a goodly company!—

To walk together to the kirk,
And all together pray,
While each to his great Father bends,
Old men, and babes, and loving friends,
And youths and maidens gay!

Farewell, farewell! but this I tell
To thee, thou Wedding-Guest!
He prayeth well who loveth well
Both man and bird and beast.

He turns to audience as a prophet proclaiming truth.

He prayeth best, who loveth best
All things both great and small;
For the dear God who loveth us,
He made and loveth all.

He bows humbly, prays for a moment, blesses the Wedding Guest and the au-
dience, crosses himself and walks slowly off the left. The Wedding Guest stares
after him dazedly like one awakening from a dream, then he bolts into the house
as if running from the devil. A blare of music and a chorused shout of welcome
as he opens the door. He shuts and locks it. His shadow appears on the blind
dancing with the bride. Music.

CURTAIN

Marco's Millions

Marco Millions, produced in January 1928, had been in O'Neill's mind for at least a decade. As early as 1917, he told a friend that he would someday write a play about Marco Polo,[1] and the following year, as he began work on *Beyond the Horizon*, he spoke of writing a play in "a multitude of scenes . . . the life story of a true Royal Tramp at his sordid but satisfying, and therefore mysterious pursuit of a drab rainbow."[2] Many critics have felt that the story of Marco is at least in part the story of Andrew Mayo, brother of the dreamer protagonist of *Beyond the Horizon*, who found in his voyages overseas nothing but soul-less commercial ventures.

Whatever personal sources the play had, *Marco Millions* owes much to Sinclair Lewis's *Babbitt*, which was published in 1922, the year before O'Neill began work on his own satire on the American businessman. Lewis's image of the mindless materialist was indelible and influential, but O'Neill had explored the ground in 1914 in the unproduced *Bread and Butter*, wherein an artist is corrupted by the materialistic Philistines, who cause him to prostitute his art and, in a melodramatic finale, drive him to suicide. The pathetic, soul-less American businessman was almost a cliché at the time Lewis wrote, and he would remain a standard feature of American drama at least until Odets wrote *Golden Boy*. Marco's character was nothing new. What was new then, and what even today remains comically appealing, is the juxtaposition of the quasi-stock figure with the glamour of ancient China. In the irony the setting provided there was a novel, comic potential, and O'Neill wrote his lavish story with much amusement and enthusiasm.

He began the scenario in the summer of 1923 and wrote to Kenneth Macgowan "'M. Polo' is proving grand pleasure. I have tentative plans drawn—floor plans—for all of it about. Am reading & taking millions of notes, etc. A lot of what the actual writing must be is now clear—and a lot isn't but will, God willing! I'll soon start a lengthy scenario of the whole to find out just how & where I stand—then get after the writing, I hope. There's a lot of reading still to be done. I feel satisfied with the development—elated, even! The child will be either a surpassing satiric Beauty—or a most Godawful monster. Beauty, I fondly opine. Satiric or not remains to be seen—but Beauty must be the word!"[3]

In June of the following summer, as he began the dialogue, the child had matured, and he had come to dote on it. He wrote Macgowan that he was "working hard as hell

---

1. Cf. Arthur Gelb and Barbara Gelb, *O'Neill* (New York, 1960), p. 352.
2. "A Letter from Eugene O'Neill," *New York Times*, January 22, 1928.
3. *"The Theatre We Worked For . . ." The Letters of Eugene O'Neill to Kenneth Macgowan*, ed. Jackson R. Bryer with introductory essays by Travis Bogard (New Haven: Yale University Press, 1982), p. 37.

on Marco. It's going to be humorous as the devil if the way it makes me guffaw as I write it is any criterion—and not bitter humor either although it's all satirical. I actually grow to love my American pillars of society, Polo Brothers & Son. It's going to be very long in first draft I imagine, but I'm letting the sky be the limit and putting every fancy in. I imagine its pretty nearly ½ done now but it's hard to estimate. One thing is sure, it's going quicker & is much more full of fun than I had conceived at first."[4]

He finished the draft in October, but it would be a long four years before the play found a producer. It was written at a time when he was in the first flush of his mature career, but his progress on the script was not unimpeded. Several plays interrupted its writing: *All God's Chillun Got Wings, Desire Under the Elms,* and *The Great God Brown* were in various stages of composition. It was in this period that he, Robert Edmond Jones, and Kenneth Macgown, assuming control of the Provincetown Playhouse, established their Experimental Theatre, where O'Neill was forced to undertake some of the responsibilities of a theatrical producer. Then too, the years, despite their creativity, were not easy ones for his personal life. He was struggling to overcome his alcoholism; there were increasing problems with his marriage to Agnes; and he was distressed by the difficulty he had in getting his plays produced with anything like the speed with which he created them.

In the busy, often troubled times, as his eagerness and amusement suggest, writing the Polo story was a pleasure. It was his first comedy except for an unproduced satire written in 1916, entitled *Now I Ask You,* and its amusements gave him a sense of release from the Freudian tragedies and from the personal difficulties that occupied the rest of his days. There was for him a freedom in its writing that he was not to achieve again until 1932 when he wrote his last comedy, *Ah, Wilderness!*[5]

The freedom and the fun, however, created difficulties as the text of *Marco's Millions*[6] clearly demonstrates. The dramatist's controls were tossed aside. The game of "every fancy in" led to the composition of a sprawling play whose production in prospect was daunting. Who would be brave enough to contemplate a comedy in eight acts (fourteen scenes) and an epilogue? Who could begin to afford the scenery, costumes, extensive musical score, and the tribe of extras required by the uncut script? The problem of finding a producer hung over the work from the time of its copyrighting in January 1925.

First in line came David Belasco, who optioned the work in May 1925. His enthusiasm was loudly expressed: Robert Edmond Jones was to design it and was to be sent to China to soak up the proper atmosphere. A year passed; concrete plans for production did not emerge; finally, Belasco dropped the option. Next came O'Neill's publisher, Horace Liveright, who hoped to produce the work with the backing of the financier Otto Kahn. Kahn, who perhaps had heard O'Neill's pun comparing him to the great Kaan in the play, declined the honor and Liveright dropped from the field. O'Neill thought perhaps that George M. Cohan would be interested in the role of Marco,

---

4. Ibid., p. 51.
5. Not that the comedy did not have its serious side. In the pathetic subtext of the play, concerned with the death of poetic spirit in Marco, there may be a reflection of O'Neill's sorrow at the failure of his brother Jamie to find any spiritual salvation in his life. Jamie, it may be remembered, had scored his greatest success as an actor in a play called *The Travelling Salesman.*
6. O'Neill considered "Mr. Mark Millions" as a third alternate title. In his notebooks, the play is for the most part referred to by its final title.

but nothing came either of this idea or his hope that Max Reinhardt could be induced to come to the United States to direct the play. Gilbert Miller for a time was a possibility and there was a moment when O'Neill's former mentor, George Pierce Baker, thought of offering the play as the attraction to open his new theatre at Yale University, where he had gone to teach. Attempting to get the play some form of public attention, O'Neill spent several weeks in December 1926 revising it for publication in April 1927 prior to any production.[7]

It was not until Lawrence Langner, a member of the Theatre Guild's guiding committee, came to Bermuda to attempt to bring O'Neill into the Guild's stable that *Marco Millions* finally found a stage. O'Neill's relations with the Guild had not been cordial since the organization had turned down several of his early efforts. Langner handled him with a smooth touch and in April 1927 persuaded his fellow directors to accept not only *Marco Millions* but *Strange Interlude* as well. The two were produced in the same month, January 1928.

Just when O'Neill worked over the long version to cut it to a one-evening length is uncertain. Belasco had demanded cuts, and it is inconceivable that the Theatre Guild, facing the massive length of *Strange Interlude*, would have optioned a second marathon production. The major restructuring was probably made early in 1926 with additions at the year's end when he readied the play for printing.

The cuts that pruned away the exuberance of the play's writing must surely be seen as an improvement. There seems little point in act 1, scene 2, when Marco in a Genoese prison begins to dictate his memoirs to Rusticiano. The scene throws the play into flashback, but this effect has already been achieved by the first act, when Kokachin's[8] coffin is seen on its journey from Persia to China. Similarly act 7, scene 1, is a return to the prison, whose only function is to bring Marco to the point of realization of the truth of Kokachin's love for him. He does not see the truth, however, and the scene in consequence only reworks what has happened in act 6.

The only cut that might be debated as unwise is the deletion of act 4, which provides a middle for the play that in its final version has a beginning—Marco's journey to the East—and an end—Marco's return to Venice—but no fully developed central section showing what happens to him in China. What he becomes in China is narrated, not dramatized. The closest O'Neill came to showing the development of Marco under the Kaan's tutelage lies in the original fourth act. Yet even this scene, concerned with Marco's education under the tutelage of two Chinese sages, leaves his career as the mayor of Yang-Chau to his own bragging account in act 5, scene 1.

The major loss is the development of Kokachin's love for Marco. Her presence upon his arrival in China as a child of four, and her second appearance as a love-struck eight-year-old prepare the way for her sentimental and fatal love for the Venetian. In the final version, when Kukachin is first seen in act 2, scene 1, her frustrated love is a fait accompli for which no preparation is made other than the suggestion contained in her lines spoken from her coffin in the prologue.

Other than direct cuts for length there is not much reworking. Some of the

7. O'Neill was later to consider this publication in advance of production a misadventure for the play in performance.
8. In the copyright typescript, the spelling varies. "Kukachin" does not appear until the published version.

anachronistic slang is pared. In *Marco's Millions*, Marco is given an excessive amount of twentieth-century phraseology:

> After all, when you stop to think, who was it first told them gold was money? I'll bet my last shirt it was some far-sighted, quick-thinker who'd just discovered a gold mine! . . . You're flabbergasted, I can see that. Paper money! It's as simple— and yet, whoever hit on it before me. I was knocked out too. [act 5 (p. 262)]

In the reworking, the speech is tempered to:

> After all, when you stop to think, who was it first told them gold was money? I'll bet anything it was some quick-thinker who'd just discovered a gold mine! . . . You're stunned, I can see that. It's so simple—and yet who ever thought of it before me? I was amazed myself. [act 2, scene 1]

In similar fashion, the verse in the songs and the recitatives is sometimes pruned and somewhat improved.

Comparison of the long version with the final play offers an opportunity to see O'Neill at work with his blue pencil in a process of controlling his fancies and disciplining his art. Yet this was not to be the necessary consequence of work to come. Already *Strange Interlude* had spread to similar length and ahead was the expansive *Lazarus Laughed*. *Dynamo*, which had been conceived about the same time as *Marco Millions*, was planned as part of a trilogy that would never be completed, and the trilogy, *Mourning Becomes Electra*, would shortly be his major occupation. Dimly beyond this, the first glimmerings of the eleven-play cycle, *A Tale of Possessors, Self-dispossessed*, can be sensed. *Marco's Millions* was the first indication of the perhaps foolhardy commitment to length.

Marco's Millions

CHARACTERS

CHRISTIAN [*In the order in which they appear*]

A Traveller
Marco Polo, a gentleman from Venice
Rusticiano, an author from Pisa
Nicolo Polo, Marco's father
Maffeo Polo, Marco's uncle
Donata, wife of Marco
Giovanni, a turnkey from Genoa
Tedaldo, Legate of Syria (Afterward Pope Gregory X)
A Dominican Monk
A Knight-Crusader
A Papal Courier
Paulo Loredano, Donata's father, a gentleman from Venice
Ladies and gentlemen from Venice, soldiers, people of Acre, musicians,
servants, etc.

HEATHEN [*In the order in which they appear*]

A Magian traveller
A Buddhist traveller
A Mahometan Captain of Arglum's army
The Ali Brothers, Mahometan merchants
A prostitute
A dervish
Two Buddhist Merchants
Two Tartar Merchants
A Mongol priest
Emissary from Kublai
A Tartar Captain
Kublai, the Great Kaan over all the Tartar Empire
Princess Kokachin, his granddaughter
Chu-Yin, a Cathayan sage
A Nurse to the Princess

A Staff Officer

A professor of Science
A professor of Classics }—tutors to Marco

General Bayan, of the Tartar armies

A messenger from Persia

Ghazan, Khan of Persia

A Buddhist Priest

A Taoist Priest

A Confucian Priest

A Moslem Priest

A Tartar Chronicler

Villagers, people of Persia, India, Mongolia, Cathay, Courtiers, nobles, ladies, wives, warriors, etc. of Kublai's court, musicians, dancers, Chorus of Mourners

SCENE: *The center of a vast naked plain in Persia near the confines of India. An immense sacred tree of enormous girth of trunk, stands at the center of the stage proper. The foliage of this tree, in startling contrast to the arid waste around it, is dense and luxuriant. Votive offerings from worshippers—pieces of cloth torn from clothing or bangles, armlets, ornaments, tapers, etc.—have been nailed or pinned in great numbers to the trunk and tied to the branches. The mighty limbs of this tree spread outward to a great length from the trunk forming a pavilion-like roof under which is deep cool shade, contrasting with the blinding glare of the sun on the sandy plain in the background, shimering in the fierce heat of the noon sun.*

From below, up the path to the foreground, a merchant with a case in each hand, which curiously resemble worn modern sample cases, plods wearily and makes his way to the foot of the tree. He puts the cases down with a deep sigh of relief and takes out a handkerchief to mop his forehead. He is a white CHRISTIAN, *middle-aged, average-looking, with a mustache and beard beginning to show grey. His clothes in the style of the Italian merchant class of the thirteenth century are worn and travel-stained. He mutters, tired and hot.* Phoo! *From the left a* MAGIAN, *a Persian, dressed in the fashion of a trader, comes in. He carries a small, square bag. He also is hot, weary, and dust-covered. In age and appearance, making allowance for the difference in race, he closely resembles the Christian. He and the latter stare at each other, then bow perfunctorily. The Magian sets down his bag and wipes his brow.*

CHRISTIAN   [*Sympathetically*] Hot as hell!

MAGIAN   [*Grimly*] Much hotter! [*They both chuckle. A Buddhist, a Kashmiri travelling merchant comes in, puffing and sweating, from the right. He has a pack strapped on his back. He resembles very much the other two in the general character of his body and face. He stops on seeing them. After eyeing each other for an appraising second, all bow again, and the Buddhist comes forward to set his pack beside the bags of the others.*]

BUDDHIST   [*With relief*] Phoo. [*Then breaking the ice*] The sun would cook you today.

MAGIAN   It is hot, certainly.

CHRISTIAN   I shouldn't wonder if it set a record for this date. [*They all sit down simultaneously to rest. The* CHRISTIAN *looks from one to the other—jovially*] Funny! You'd think we three had an appointment here. Do you know, your faces look familiar. Haven't I seen you someplace before?

MAGIAN   In the house of the courtesans at Shiraz. You were drunk.

BUDDHIST   I happened to be there that night, too. You danced and sang lewd songs.

CHRISTIAN   [*A bit embarrassed, but grinning*] Humn—oh yes—I remember—it was my birthday and I'd taken a drop too much—a very unusual thing for me. [*Then abruptly changing the subject*] How are business conditions down your way?

BUDDHIST   [*Pursing his lips*] Slow. I come from Delhi. There is a new import tax and trade is very unsettled. We manufacture prayer beads, and people are not praying as much as they used to.

MAGIAN   [*Gloomily*] And I for my sins, am hawking a bizarre novelty—a real block-printed book—for an Arab house. I was in Aleppo without money and I had to take the first position that offered. This work contains one thousand Arabian lies, with one over for good measure, all full of lechery—as least so they instructed me to tell people to induce them to buy. I cannot read myself—and if I could, I would have no time—and even if I had the time, I dislike learning of sex. There is quite enough of it for me in real life without ———— [*Then piously*] But I like moral literature. I regularly attend readings of the Words of the Holy Son of God, Zoroaster.

CHRISTIAN   [*Staring at him rather superciliously*] Oh, so you're a Fire-Worshipper, are you?

MAGIAN   I belong to the True Faith, yes! [*Lamentingly*] And I know my present ill fortune is a punishment because I, a Magian, have polluted myself by working for Mahometan unbelievers!

CHRISTIAN   [*Perfunctorily*] Well, luck always changes sometime. Did your present trip take you down around Ispahan way?

MAGIAN   I just came from there. It is a sad city now. All the stores have been closed by an imperial edict in mourning for the Khan's favorite wife, Queen Kokachin.

CHRISTIAN   [*Bounding to his feet as if a wasp had stung him*] What? Is Queen Kokachin dead?

MAGIAN   Dead as the meanest cur a chariot crushes in the streets!

CHRISTIAN   [*Stunned*] Well—talk about luck! [*Then excitedly*] Why, I've got a personal letter of introduction to her from the president of my firm—Marco Polo of Polo Brothers and Son, Venice. He acted as her official escort by request of the Great Kaan, Kublai, and took her from Cathay to Persia to be married! And now she's dead? Why I was counting on selling her and her husband a whole fleet load of goods! God, won't Mr. Mark be put out! And the poor man is in jail now, too! He was captured prisoner fighting with our fleet against the dirty Genoese!

MAGIAN [*Suddenly*] What makes that cloud of dust I see yonder? [*They all stare and begin to grow worried*]

CHRISTIAN It don't look like camels, or horses—

MAGIAN It is more like a squad of foot soldiers—

CHRISTIAN What would soldiers be doing here?

BUDDHIST [*Fearfully*] Truly, it has a strange, inhuman look!

MAGIAN Like some sinister serpent!

CHRISTIAN It is coming directly this way.

BUDDHIST I have heard these plains are the abiding place of devils.

MAGIAN Yes, they say they are haunted by evil spirits.

CHRISTIAN [*Very frightened, but striving to put up a brave front*] I've heard those rumors—and I know for a fact that people are sometimes possessed by devils—but I don't believe—

BUDDHIST [*Suddenly pointing to the tree*] For my part, I am going to offer a prayer for protection to this tree which is sacred to the Buddha—

CHRISTIAN
               [*In chorus—irritably*] Sacred to Buddha?
MAGIAN

BUDDHIST Certainly. Do you not know the legend how the Holy Sakya one day picked a twig with which to cleanse his teeth, after our fashion, and then throwing it away, it took root, and sprang up into this mighty tree to testify forever to his power?

CHRISTIAN [*Resentfully*] I don't want to argue but you're absolutely wrong. This tree was the staff of our first father, Adam. It was handed down to Moses who used it for a rod to get water out of stones and finally planted it because he foresaw that the cross on which our Lord was to be crucified would be made of the wood of that tree. And so it came to pass, and ever since this tree has been sacred to Christ, the Son of God!

MAGIAN [*Cuttingly*] You have both of you been duped by sacriligeous lies. This tree is sacred to the founder of the one true religion, Zoroaster, who brought a shoot of the tree of Life down from Paradise and planted it here.

BUDDHIST [*Scornfully*] You are a pair of ignorant sheep!

CHRISTIAN You are a couple of idolatrous dogs!

MAGIAN The two of you are stupid hogs! [*They glare at each other in-*

sultingly, their hands on their daggers. Suddenly they all hear a faint noise from the left. All eyes at once are turned in that direction and, forgetting their personal animosities, they give a startled exclamation at what they see]

BUDDHIST   It's a file of men—pulling a chariot—

CHRISTIAN   They must be slaves. See how the driver lashes them! What cruelty! But what speed they're making!

MAGIAN   That driver is a captain of Ghazan Kahn's.

CHRISTIAN   And those are soldiers riding with him. [*With a sigh of relief*] So we're safe.

BUDDHIST   But what can that be on the wagon—like a coffin covered with a pall—

CHRISTIAN   It must be a treasure they're transporting—

MAGIAN   No. It is a coffin, I think. And those driven wretches look like my countrymen, not slaves! [*Trembling*] Ssst! I fear evil. They are coming! Let us abase ourselves! [*They prostrate themselves their faces to the ground. A moment later, preceded by shouts, a cracking of whips, and dull stamping of feet, a double file of thirty men of all ages, stripped to the waist, harnessed to each other waist-to-waist and to the long pole of a two-wheeled wagon, run in straining forward under the lashes of two soldiers who run beside them and the long whips of the* CAPTAIN *and two* CORPORALS *who are riding on the wagon, the* CAPTAIN *driving. As they reach the middle of the shade they stop]*

CAPTAIN   [*A brutal, determined-looking Mahometan of forty bellows*] Halt! [*The files of bleeding and sweating men collapse in their tracks forming panting, groaning human heaps. The soldiers sit down, also very tired, as do the two* CORPORALS. *The* CAPTAIN *springs off the wagon*] Phoo! I am baked! This shade is grateful. [*He looks at the tree—then in an awed tone*] This must be the Holy tree which was once the staff of Mahomet and, passing down through generations, was buried in the grave of Abu Abdallah where it struck root and grew by the will of Allah into this tree. [*He makes obeisance and prays to the tree as do the other soldiers, imitating him. He gets up and takes a gulp of water—then, looking around, notices the three merchants—with superstitious surprise, drawing his sword*] Ho! What's this? What are you? Get up and let me see you! [*They do so, frightenedly. He stares at them and laughs coarsely with relief*] By all the demons, but you startled me! One doesn't expect to meet men here—but you traders are like fleas, one finds you everywhere! [*Then with a scowl*] Three dogs of unbelievers, too, I see! [*Sharply*] Give an account of yourselves!

BUDDHIST   I was proceeding westward on a business venture, good sir.

MAGIAN   And I to the northward.

CHRISTIAN   And I to the court of Ghazan Kahn to present this letter to Queen Kokachin—but I hear she's dead. [*He hands him the letter but the* CAPTAIN *backs away superstitiously*]

CAPTAIN   Allah forbid that I touch what belongs to a corpse. [*Then with forced coarse laughter*] You needn't journey farther. She lies within—there! [*His voice has dropped, he points toward the coffin which is draped in a sweeping white pall. The others stare at it, dumbfounded and awed. The* CAPTAIN *goes on dryly*] You cannot cheat her with your goods now, Christian! [*Then lowering his voice as if afraid he will be overheard*] And yet, to look at her face even now you would think her still alive and sleeping.

CHRISTIAN   [*Astonished*] What? Can you still look at her?

CAPTAIN   Her coffin is of glass most cunningly contrived. Her body was anointed by Egyptian necromancers so that she will preserve the appearance of life for many years. This was done by our King at the express wish of Kublai, the Great Kaan over all Tartary, who foresaw his granddaughter's death. She is being taken home to him for burial—and I am commanded under penalty of the torture to transport her over the first stage of her journey by dark tonight! [*Suddenly lamenting*] But Allah afflicted me! When I reached the last village with my horses and camels foundering, I found the accursed villagers had driven off their beasts to escape requisition. But the dogs could not balk me. I hitched them to the pole instead, and, thanks to the lash, we have arrived here in due time. [*He looks at the moaning figures with a cruel appraising eye*] But will they last till night? Their failure means death to me. Hi, there! Water to revive them! [*The soldiers carry around jugs of water which the panting men reach out for avidly, then sink back. But three of the more elderly are too spent to move or drink*]

CHRISTIAN   [*Timorously—anxious to change the subject*] Was the Queen very beautiful?

CAPTAIN   Was and is. [*With bravado*] Would you care to see? You had a letter. It can do no harm—and it is a very great wonder! Besides, why should I, a true Believer, be frightened by the body of a souless one who, if the gossip is true, was never converted to Islam but remained an infidel to the end. And, being a woman, she would like her beauty to be praised by men even when dead. And, under this tree sacred to Allah, the One God, and his Prophet, what evil could come to me?

CHRISTIAN   [*Reassuringly, because he is now very curious*] Dead Queens usually lie in state and may be looked at by many people to honor their memory.

CAPTAIN   [*Hesitating*] Do you pull back the cloth then since that is your custom. [*The Christian goes to the wagon and gingerly pulls back the pall from the head of the glass coffin—then retreats with an exclamation as Kokachin's lifelike face, that of a beautiful Tartar princess of twenty-three, her calm expression seeming to glow with the intense peace of a life beyond death, the eyes shut as if asleep, is revealed inside the glass. They all stare breathlessly fascinated*]

CHRISTIAN   [*After a pause—crossing himself awedly*] What a marvel! Are you sure she is dead?

BUDDHIST   [*In a voice of awe*] She is too beautiful for a corpse.

MAGIAN   [*In a voice of dread*] That is magic, not death.

CAPTAIN   [*In an awed whisper*] In the palace I commanded the company who guarded her coffin at night. I alone was awake. I could not take my eyes from her face. It seemed as if any moment she must awake and open her eyes and she would speak. [*While they have been speaking, unnoticed by them, it grows darker and darker. An unearthly light, like a halo, lights up the face of* KOKACHIN. *From the branches of the tree comes a sound of sweet yet sad music as if the leaves had become tiny harps strummed by the wind. The face of* KO-KACHIN *becomes more and more living. Finally her lips part and her eyes open to look up at the tree*]

CAPTAIN   [*Kneeling down to pray*] Allah, be pitiful!

BUDDHIST   O Buddha! Protect thy servant!

MAGIAN   Mithra, All-Powerful One!

CHRISTIAN   Jesus, have mercy! [*A voice which is Kokachin's and yet more musical than a human voice could be comes from the coffin as her lips are seen to move*] Because I was not love, I died. Now I am love, and live. And living, have forgotten. And loving, can forgive. Love is a great peace wherein all souls dissolve into the One. [*Here her lips part in a smile of beautiful pity*] Say this for me in Venice! [*A sound of tender laughter, of an intoxicating, supernatural gaiety, comes from her lips and is taken up in chorus in the branches of the tree as if every harp-leaf were laughing in music with her. The laughter flies up heavenward and dies as the halo of light about her face fades and noonday rushes back in a blaze of lighted plain. Everyone is prostrate with faces hidden, the harnessed wretches in the exhausted attitudes of sleep, the others visibly trembling with superstitious terror*]

CHRISTIAN   [*The first to recover, bewilderedly*] Venice! It must have been a message for me to take back—

CAPTAIN   Allah defend thy faithful one! [*His terror going and rage taking its place leaps to his feet*] It was the voice of some Christian devil you must have summoned! It bewitched even me—until Allah heard me and drove it back to hell! [*He draws his sword*] Cover up that coffin, accursed sorcerer!

CHRISTIAN   [*Pulls the covering over the head of the coffin with indecent haste*] I pledge you my word, good Captain—

CAPTAIN   [*To his soldiers*] Attention! Kick them! Get them up! We must push on! [*With blows and kicks the soldiers get their human beasts to their feet. There are groans and curses and cries of pain. But in spite of all urging three cannot be gotten to their feet for they are dead. In the meantime, the* CAPTAIN *growls savagely to keep up his courage, being very apparently ill-at-ease in this spot*] Pig of an infidel! [*Then glaring at the Buddhist and Magian*] You too! You were in league with him! How do I know that you are not all three devils in human disguise come to hinder me and cause my death? [*Here he grits his teeth savagely*] We shall see! With the help of Allah I can defy a legion of fiends! [*He grips his sword and advances as if to attack them*]

ALL THREE   [*Kneeling—pitiably*] Mercy! Spare us! We are only poor traders.

A CORPORAL   [*Comes up and salutes*] We can't get three of them up, sir.

CAPTAIN   [*Raging*] Why not? Lash them! Prick them with your swords!

CORPORAL   They're dead.

CAPTAIN   [*Taken aback*] Oh. [*Then an idea comes—with cruel satisfaction*] Three, did you say? That is fortunate. Cut them out and put these in their places! [*At a sign, the soldiers fall upon the three merchants, strip off their upper clothes, untie the dead men, and hitch them in their places. All the time the three set up a miserable scream of protest, punctuated by the blows and kicks they receive. The others look on with exhausted indifference*]

CHRISTIAN   [*Making himself heard above the tumult*] My letter! It was to the Queen! When Polo Brothers hear of this outrage they'll get the Kaan to flay you alive!

CAPTAIN   [*Taken aback a bit—then craftily*] You are lying! Show me your letter again!

CHRISTIAN   [*Produces it from his trousers*] Here! Now set me free!

CAPTAIN   [*Calmly tears it up*] I cannot read but I think you were lying. At any rate, now you have no letter! [*The* CHRISTIAN *sets up a wailing cry and receives a blow. The* CAPTAIN *and* CORPORALS *spring up on the wagon*] And now forward march! [*With a great, cracking of whips and shouts of pain the human team springs forward and pulls the wagon swiftly away. On the ground under the sacred tree the three bodies lie in crumpled heaps*]

CURTAIN

SCENE: *Marco Polo's cell in the fortress of the Malapaga, Genoa. Darkness. Gradually it grows light. Figures can be made out on the forestage. The sound of men's voices are heard. The proscenium is filled by a curtain representing the interior of the fortress wall. The daylight filters dimly through a row of four small barred windows high up on the wall. In front, on the forestage, is the cell of Marco Polo, its boundaries indicated by a screen in rear, in one side of which is a barred door, in the other a barred window.*

The people in the cell are gradually revealed by a light from above that grows into an intense flood which is concentrated on them. As this light has increased their voices have risen until now their conversation is audible.

The persons discovered are MARCO POLO *and* RUSTICIANO, *the Pisan author, his fellow prisoner.* MARCO *is a man of thirty-eight with a large, bearded, good-natured, handsome face. His figure is strong and well preserved. His personality is direct, aggressive in its lack of complication. He is a conscious success, satisfied with himself, a man of shrewd ability in trade, resolute with a force of will that amounts to stubbornness, full of the gravity of material things. Yet likable—a certain sincerity, frankness, a courage of his prejudices, a naive childish vanity, and sentimentality.*

RUSTICIANO *is undersized, pale and sickly, with thin hair and beard. His simple face wears an expression of childlike credulity, his eyes are misty with sentimental, romantic dreams, his attitude toward Marco Polo is that of a humble hero-worshipper. Both have chain manacles on their legs.*

MARCO   [*His tone is that of a self-conscious oracle*] You'll have to bear one thing in mind, Rusticiano: I'm a hard-headed business man—a man of few words—and I attribute my success to my ability to concentrate on facts and figures and not waste time on side issues. [*Condescendingly*] So if I decide to go in on this travel book proposition with you it'll be your job to furnish all the literary frills. I'll dictate the facts. You take them down and fill in the writing part afterwards as stylish as you can make it.

RUSTICIANO   If you have any doubts of my proficiency, my past work will speak for me. I am on the Advisory Board of the Authors League of Pisa. I have written a romance of Lancelot and Guinevere which attracted considerable attention because of its originality. [*Casting down his eyes—embarrassedly*] Out of my concern for the honor of the great Queen and her noble knight I omitted all mention of their alleged sin together.

MARCO [*Stares at him with cynical amusement*] Humph! You evidently lack what I call the sixth selling sense. Well, don't go expurgating my book without first asking me. There's such a thing as being too good for your own good.

RUSTICIANO [*Proudly*] I shall write as becomes a gentleman.

MARCO [*Bored*] Of course. I'm one, too. [*He yawns*] Frankly, I wouldn't bother with this book if I didn't feel morally guilty of wasting so much time here in jail.

RUSTICIANO It is not your fault you are a prisoner but the fortunes of war, noble sir!

MARCO [*Stands stiffly at salute—importantly*] For my Republic and my flag! Venice over all of them!

RUSTICIANO [*With a cavalierish flourish*] Pisa forever!

BOTH IN CHORUS To hell with Genoa! [*They embrace and kiss each other on both cheeks*]

MARCO [*More familiarly now*] I know it isn't patriotic to complain but this enforced idleness just about kills me. [*Proudly*] I'm a man of action. For me the worst sin is keeping still. When I'm idle, I don't know what to do with myself. I start thinking. And I worry about nothing. For instance, I keep wondering how Polo Brothers and Son are getting along without me, whether my father and uncle are putting to account our exclusive information on Far Eastern conditions to develop the foreign trade; and yet I realize they're capable enough—

RUSTICIANO Their repute is of men singularly wise and provident.

MARCO [*Not exactly pleased*] Yes—provident all right. [*Then confidentially*] But—getting on in years. I want to introduce modern methods—nothing radical or extreme but up to date ideas for taking advantage of new conditions— but that's a long story. [*A pause. Then he sighs sentimentally*] Then again, I sit here and worry about my wife. I miss the comforts of my home. I miss my wife. I love my wife. [*He stares earnestly at Rusticiano, proud of this unmanly confession*]

RUSTICIANO [*Rolling his eyes expectantly*] A romance, was it not?

MARCO Yes, and what's more important, a fact, a slice of my life! For twenty-one long years she waited for me, never doubting my promise made to her before I started East that I'd come back rich and marry her. And I *did* come back, and I *was* rich, and I *did* marry her!

RUSTICIANO [*Eagerly*] It resembles somewhat the story of Ulysses.

MARCO   But there were no sirens in this, you can depend on that. [*Pompously*] No, only a good pure Venetian woman—Mrs. Polo! [*After a slight pause—with a grin*] Unless you'd call the Princess a Siren——[*He smiles meaningly*]

RUSTICIANO   [*His eyes melting*] A Princess?

MARCO   Kokachin. The Grand Daughter of the Great Kaan. She's the Queen of Persia at present. My father always claims she——but it may have been all his imagination——Anyway, she's married now. [*He sighs self-consciously*] Besides, there's no use raking up the past——

RUSTICIANO   [*His mouth watering*] But, sir—the mere name of a Princess—a real Queen!—in a book—!

MARCO   Well—I'll mention her—Toward the very end, you know—— [*Then virtuously*] But I'm not writing this book about myself. There's to be no romance in it. Facts, statistics, useful data in general—a book that'll do good, that's what I want to write—an educational influence—something that'll convince the old-timers in Venice that there's more opportunities for expanding our commerce than they dream about!

RUSTICIANO   [*Disconsolate but admiring*] You possess that rare modesty of the hero——

MARCO   Deeds speak louder than words is my philosophy! [*Then with sudden shrewdness*] By the way, I asked you yesterday to show me a sample of your work. Did you bring it?

RUSTICIANO   [*Takes out a sheet of script*] I did, sir. I have here out-lined in brief a few words of introduction to the book itself which I trust you will find achieves the correct style, rhythm and tone suitable to the subject.

MARCO   I'll see. Read it.

RUSTICIANO   [*Reads*] "Great Princes, Emperors, and Kings, Dukes and Marquises, Counts, Knights and Burgesses!"

MARCO   [*With heavy sagacity*] Good! You appeal immediately to the best elements.

RUSTICIANO   [*Reads*] "And people of all degrees who desire to get knowledge of the various races of mankind and of the diversities of the sundry regions of the World, take this book and cause it to be read to you."

MARCO   That's the idea—arouse their curiosity!

RUSTICIANO   "For ye shall find therein all kinds of wonderful things, according to the description of Messer Marco Polo, a wise and noble citizen of Venice."

MARCO [*Pleased but protesting modestly*] Wise and noble? That sounds like flattery. [*Then assertively*] Well, I've got a damn sight more claim to nobility than a lot of our citizens who go about with their noses in the air trying not to smell the poor people! [*Then grandly*] In the Republic of Venice, thank God, nobility is beginning to be paired with ability!

RUSTICIANO Who that reads your brave deeds could doubt your noble blood? If I may continue——? [MARCO *nods. He reads*] "For let me tell you that since our Lord God did mould with His hands our first Father Adam, even until this day, never hath there been Christian, or Pagan, or Tartar or Indian, or any man of any nation, who in his own person hath so much knowledge and experience of the diverse parts of the World and its Wonders as hath this Messer Marco!"

MARCO [*Doubtfully*] Humm! That's piling it on rather thick.

RUSTICIANO But it's no more than the truth, sir.

MARCO [*Assertively*] Yes, and by God, I can prove it! The whole book'll prove it! I'll give 'em names and dates and places and figures for every marvel I mention—that is, all I saw myself. At the end any damn fool that reads can know as much about life as I do!

RUSTICIANO [*Humbly*] You will be a public benefactor, sir! This is my conclusion to the preface: "Now, being an inmate of the Prison at Genoa, he caused Messer Rusticiano of Pisa, who was in the said prison likewise, to reduce the whole to writing."

MARCO [*With a cunning but good-natured wink*] Well, I see you managed to get yourself in at the end! You writers certainly hate yourselves. Ha—ha! Well, after all, why not? It's fair enough. You do the labor, I furnish the capital, and raw material. In a manner of speaking, we're partners—and if no millions of money are involved in our deal at least millions of facts are, and someday those facts'll be worth millions. Ha—ha! [*He claps Rusticiano on the back. The turnkey,* GIOVANNI, *appears at the door in rear rattling his huge keys. He is a lumbering oaf of a fellow with droll, malicious eyes. He peers through the bars, grinning*]

GIOVANNI Blowing about millions again, old windbag? [MARCO *immediately gets stiffly upon his dignity, and turns away with a great pretence of scorning the turnkey's existence.* GIOVANNI *unlocks the door, throws it open on its groaning hinges, and steps inside the cell. In the corridor behind him are seen a woman with a baby in arms and two old men. The turnkey makes an elaborate mocking bow and announces*] Marco Millions, I beg to respectfully introduce one Venetian sow with young, who says she is your wife, and two aged swine from the same cesspool by the sea, who claim to be your father and uncle. They have a permit to visit you—stolen, no doubt! [*The three sweep past him into the room with exaggerated disdain. He goes out chuckling and slams the door to, locking them in. Then he peers through the bars, grinning*] I've just thought of a riddle. Would you like to hear it? When is a room a sty? When it's full of Venetians! Ho—ho! [*He goes off, laughing to himself. They wait stiffly until he is out of hearing*]

MARCO [*Suddenly exploding*] Barbarian! [*Then solemnly lifting up his right hand*] May God smite Genoa!

ALL [*With the same gesture, in chorus*] May God smite Genoa!

MARCO [*Stern as a bust of Cato—to his wife*] Let these be the first words his baby lips are taught to form!

DONATA Yes, dear. [*Then reproachfully*] But, are you forgetting, Mark, she isn't a he. She's a girl.

MARCO [*Suddenly bursting into good-natured laughter at himself*] Well, that's one on me, eh? [*Then sternly again*] But she'll be a mother to Venetian heroes who'll avenge us! Teach her that as her patriotic duty! [*Then relaxing, hugs and kisses his wife affectionately*] Old girl, it's good to see you again. Seems to me you're getting prettier every day! [*His wife, DONATA, is a stoutish, pretty woman of thirty-five. Her round pretty face beams sentimentally, her soft black eyes are beautiful as a cow's. She is all curves and maternal instinct, a capable close-haggling housewife, otherwise an incorrigible ninny*]

DONATA [*Swelling with pleasure*] Do you really think so?

MARCO [*Chucking the baby under the chin*] Fast asleep. Wake up, sonny.

DONATA Not "sonny," Mark. Don't you think she looks like you?

MARCO [*Humorously*] Exactly. We've both got ears. [*Then turning to greet his father and uncle, NICOLO and MAFFEO POLO, two very old men, withered and bent, white-haired and bearded, leaning on canes, but with eyes still shrewdly alert and cunning*] Hello, Father, you look as if you could row a race with a gondolier—and here's Uncle still as spry as an antelope! [*Both old men are pleased although Maffeo snickers dryly*]

DONATA [*Who has been staring at RUSTICIANO, who is waiting embarrassedly, nudges Marco and whispers*] Who's your friend?

MARCO Well, well, pardon me, Rusticiano. I want you to meet Mrs. Polo—and my father—and my uncle. Mr. Rusticiano of Pisa, the famous author—my companion in misfortune—a gentleman and a scholar. [*All bow, muttering the usual inanities*]

DONATA [*Her eyes popping a bit*] It's the first time I've ever met a real author. It must be wonderful to write—to be able to——

RUSTICIANO [*Pleased*] Yes, it is a rare gift and I am grateful to God——

DONATA Yes, you ought to be.

MARCO [*Who has been in whispered conference with his father and uncle—indignantly*] The old grafter! It's highway robbery!

DONATA What is it, Mark?

MARCO [*Fuming*] Here we offer the Governor a good fair bribe to let me escape and he demands a hundred soldi more! No! I won't be cheated by a rascally Genoese! It's a matter of patriotic principle. I'd rather stay here and rot——!

DONATA [*Imploringly*] But, dear, surely your freedom is worth an extra hundred soldi——

MARCO You women never learn the value of money. If you had to earn it by the sweat of your brows you'd soon—— [*As* DONATA *is about to protest*] No more talk! I've decided. I rot right here! [*Changing his tone*] And he won't hold out long. I happen to know he needs cash badly. [*Changing tone again*] Besides, I've launched a new enterprise right here in jail with Mr. Rusticiano as partner and what I start, I make it a practice to finish. I'm going to write the book of my travels!

DONATA [*Admiringly*] Why, Mark Polo! What next!

NICOLO [*Suspiciously*] A book? What nonsense!

MAFFEO What sort of a deal is it, Mark? There's not much to be made from a book, is there?

RUSTICIANO [*Huffily*] I am writing it for Art, not for money!

MARCO [*Pushing him aside*] Here. You let me do the explaining. It's to be the story of our travels. You two'll be in it.

NICOLO Humm! Not such a bad idea, at that, when you stop to think.

MAFFEO [*Matter-of-factly*] Yes. We've lived through more than most. But just what return do you see in this, Mark? You can't convince me you're undertaking it for love.

MARCO [*Grandly*] For the honor of the house of Polo—to give our firm international standing—and to help Venice in her trade with the East! [*Then he adds as an afterthought*] And for the general instruction of men of all nations.

MAFFEO [*With a chuckle*] Never mind the last. I begin to see the idea.

Good boy! I always said you had a head on you. There'll be a million's worth of advertising in it.

NICOLO [*Nodding appreciatively*] Everybody'll hear of us. [*Suddenly*] Are you going to tell about the time I killed the lion?

DONATA And about how you led the attack at Curzola fighting alone with your one galley against the whole Genoese fleet?

MARCO [*Regretfully*] No. I'm keeping myself out of it. I don't believe in blowing your own horn. Besides if I mentioned the battle I'd have to tell what I thought of our fool Admiral, and now he's dead I wouldn't feel justified in criticizing—— [*Then indignantly*] But just think, if that old ass had only used common sense I'd have escaped with the rest back to Venice and I'd be out in the open now, hawk in hand, having a good tight game of falconry instead of sweating here in prison!

DONATA You were a hero!

MARCO [*Shaking his head*] You're the only one who remembers it—and you wouldn't if you weren't in the family.

NICOLO [*Suddenly pointing to Rusticiano*] Is he going to do the writing part?

MARCO Yes.

NICOLO How much are you paying him?

RUSTICIANO [*Flushing—proudly*] I am an artist, sir. I am not hired like a cook!

MARCO A gentleman's agreement. We haven't gone into the details yet. [*Giving his father a crafty wink*] I'm going to let him in on a percentage of the profits basis.

NICOLO [*Suddenly grinning*] I see! I see! [*He chuckles and whispers to* MAFFEO, *who joins in the laughter.* MARCO *motions them to stop*]

DONATA [*Archly*] You've simply got to put me in the book, Mark!

MARCO Of course. [*A bit confusedly*] Your woman's influence—the hand that rocks the cradle—that'll all be understood——

DONATA [*Hurt*] Then I won't be in it?

MARCO [*Lamely*] Well—not personally.

DONATA [*Indignantly*] I don't see why——

MARCO Because—because—well—[*Then decisively*] For business reasons!

DONATA [*Squelched*] Oh.

MARCO [*Putting his arms around her*] It's only going to be a plain statement of our travels while you were waiting faithfully for me. I was telling
Rusticiano there *was* a sure fire romance out of real life—for some other book
he can write sometime maybe. How you waited faithfully because I promised
you I'd come back sometime and marry you; and how after twenty-one years I
did come back just as I said I would when I kissed you goodbye that last night
before I left. [*As he is speaking the light slowly fades out and the figures in the
cell disappear*]

CURTAIN

ACT TWO   SCENE ONE

SCENE: *The light slowly comes up. A fresh boy's voice, with an indescribable
something in its quality recalling Marco Polo's, is heard singing a love song in
a subdued tone. The light reveals the exterior of Donata's home on the canal,
Venice. It is a moonlit night almost twenty-five years before Part One.* MARCO
*is a boy of fifteen, youthfully handsome and well made. He is standing in a
gondola beneath a barred window of the house, a guitar over his shoulder. The
song finished, he waits anxiously. A white hand is thrust out to him through
the bars. He kisses it passionately. It is hurriedly withdrawn. Donata's face
appears pressed against the bars. She is a girl of twelve, her face pale and pretty
in the moonlight.*

DONATA [*Coyly and tenderly*] You mustn't, Mark.

MARCO [*Intensely*] Give me back your hand! Please, Donata, won't you?
There's no harm in that, is there—just letting me hold your hand?

DONATA But you didn't just hold it.

MARCO Well, there's no harm, either—in what I did do.

DONATA [*Demurely*] It was a sin, I'm sure of it. I'll have to confess it and
Father Peter will give me an awful penance.

MARCO [*Manfully*] I'm willing to take the blame. [*Then pleadingly*]
Please, Donata, let me have it again.

DONATA It's a sin.

MARCO [*With a quick movement of his own hand captures hers through
the bars*] Then I'll have to steal it—and that's a worse sin. [*He pulls her willing
hand down toward his lips.*]

DONATA You're hurting my fingers.

MARCO [*Boldly now*] Then I know how to cure them. [*He kisses them
one by one.*] There!

DONATA [*Tenderly*] You silly boy! Why do you want—to do that?

MARCO Because—I like to.

DONATA But why do you like to?

MARCO [*Very seriously*] You know, Donata.

DONATA No, I don't.

MARCO Yes, you do.

DONATA How should I know, Mark? Did you ever tell me?

MARCO No—but you could see.

DONATA See what? [*Softly*] Go on and tell me, Mark.

MARCO [*Blurts out gruffly*] Well—I love you! That's what! I've loved you ever since I can remember. And you've known it right along, too, so there's no good in you pretending——

DONATA [*Softly*] I wasn't sure.

MARCO You are now, aren't you?

DONATA Are you?

MARCO [*Vehemently*] Damn sure!

DONATA Sssh! You'll wake up Father!

MARCO [*Defiantly*] I don't care. [*Recklessly*] And how about you? Do you love me? You've got to answer me that.

DONATA You know—without my saying it.

MARCO Please say it!

DONATA [*In a whisper*] I love you. There, silly.

MARCO And you'll promise to marry me when I come back?

DONATA Yes—but you'll have to ask my parents——

MARCO [*Easily*] Don't worry about them. They'll be glad—and my folks, too. It'll bring the two firms into closer relationship.

DONATA [*Frantically*] Yes, I think so, too. [*A pause. Songs and music come from near and far-off in the night about them. Marco has gained possession of her two hands now and his face is close to the bars of her window*]

MARCO [*With a sigh*] It's beautiful tonight. I wish I didn't have to leave you.

DONATA I wish, too! Do you really have to go?

MARCO Yes. And I want to, too—all but leaving you. I don't want to just stick here in Venice and work in an office. I want to travel, see the whole world and all the different people, learn a little of their languages, know their habits and needs from a sympathetic first-hand knowledge. You've got to do that if you want to become a real figure—really big and important—in the world. That's what Father says—and Uncle—and they ought to know.

DONATA   [*Proudly*] I know you'll become—big.

MARCO   I'll try hard, Donata, you can trust me for that—for both our sakes. I want to come back rich, too, so we can get married right away and we can have everything, in reason, we want. I want to be able to give you everything I can, Donata.

DONATA   I know you do, Mark—and I want to do everything I can for you. [*He kisses her hands. She goes on a bit uneasily*] But won't this trip so very far away be full of danger?

MARCO   [*Boastfully*] I can take care of myself. I'm no chicken-liver, Donata. Uncle says taking chances—absolutely *necessary* chances of course—is the best schooling for a real merchant; and Father has a saying that where there's nothing risked, there's nothing gained. And they ought to know, oughtn't they—after spending nine years at the court of the Great Kaan and traveling there and back?

DONATA   Is that where you're going?

MARCO   Yes. He's the richest king in the world and Uncle and Father are personal friends of his. They did a lot of work for him. I'll be on the right side of him from the start—and Father and Uncle both say there's millions and millions to be made in his service if you're not afraid of work and keep awake to opportunity.

DONATA   I'm sure you'll succeed. You're so bright. But I wish you weren't going—for so long.

MARCO   It won't seem long passing—

DONATA   You'll be traveling. I'll be only—waiting.

MARCO   I'll miss you as much as you miss me. [*Huskily*] I hate to leave you, Donata—but I've got to make my own way—so we can marry—and the sooner I start, the sooner——

DONATA   [*Hurriedly*] Yes—of course—only come back as soon as you can——

MARCO   But you'll wait, won't you, no matter how long? You'll swear to do that, won't you?

DONATA   [*Solemnly*] Yes, I swear to, Mark.

MARCO   And I swear by God I'll come back and marry you, and I'll always be true and never forget or do anything—

DONATA   [*Startled by a noise from within*] Ssshh! There's someone moving inside. You'll have to go. Here. [*She hands him a medallion locket*] It's a medallion of me painted by an artist who owed Father for groceries and couldn't pay with money. Will you keep looking at this all the time you're away and never forget me?

MARCO   [*Kissing it passionately*] Every day!

DONATA   And you'll write me?

MARCO   I promise. Every chance I get.

DONATA   [*Hesitatingly*] Will you write me—a poem? I won't care how short it is if it's only a poem—about you loving me.

MARCO   I'll try, Donata. I'll do my best.

DONATA   I'll just love it to death, Mark! [*Startledly*] Ssshh! I hear it again. It must be Father—I've got to sneak back——

MARCO   [*Desperately*] Won't you kiss me once—let me really kiss you on the lips—just once—for good'bye? Please!

DONATA   I'm afraid——

MARCO   Just once?—When I'm going so far away? [*Desperately*] I—I—I'll die if you don't——

DONATA   Well—just once—— [*Their lips meet as their faces are pressed toward each other against the bars. The moonlight fades into darkness as their lips cling together. Then from the darkness are heard their hushed, trembling voices.*]

DONATA   Goodbye, Mark.

MARCO   Goodbye, Donata.

THE CURTAIN FALLS

ACT TWO   SCENE TWO

SCENE: *Six months later. Interior of the Papal Legate's palace at Acre—a combination of church and government building. (Occupying the forestage and extreme front of stage proper.) The legate* TEDALDO, *a man of sixty with a strong, intelligent face, a weary, cynical distinction, is seated on a sort of throne placed against the rear wall. On his right, stands a warrior noble, a* KNIGHT CRUSADER, *in full armour, leaning on his sword. On his left, a* DOMINICAN MONK, *his adviser.*

On the left of the room is an altar with candles burning. On the right, an open portal with a SENTRY *pacing up and down, spear in hand.*

The two elder Polos, NICOLO *and* MAFFEO, *stand in attitudes of patient servility before the throne.* MARCO *is sitting on a stool at center of forestage, his body all screwed up into an awkward intensity, striving with all his might to compose a poem to Donata, but constantly distracted in spite of himself.*

TEDALDO [*Bored but tolerantly*] I can only repeat that I'm sorry, gentlemen, but what can I do except advise you to be patient. I'm sure the Conclave of Cardinals will break its deadlock soon and elect a Pope—if only out of each one's desire to get home after such a long absence.

NICOLO Two years in session! [*Then suddenly—consolingly*] Well, it's a new world's record, anyway.

MAFFEO [*Shaking his head*] This uncertainty is bad for business. The big interests have drawn into their shells waiting to see which way the cat'll jump.

TEDALDO [*With a bored yawn*] No doubt. [*Then rather impatiently*] Then, when business so evidently calls you back to the East, why delay longer? Why not simply explain to your Great Kaan that there was no Pope to whom you could deliver his message?

NICOLO He mightn't understand our elective system—being an unbeliever.

MAFFEO Yes, and although he's kind—he can be very severe——

NICOLO His instructions to us were pretty emphatic——

MAFFEO To request the Pope to send him a hundred wise men of the West——

MONK [*Breaking in rudely*] Yes, yes—we've heard all that presumptuous nonsense before. Send him a hundred wise men of the West, indeed!

TEDALDO Your Kaan is an optimist.

NICOLO He wanted them to argue with his Buddhists and Taoists and Confucianists which religion in the world was best, and he'd promise to join the winner.

MONK [*Outraged*] Impudent ignoramus! Does he imagine the church would stoop to such bickering?

TEDALDO [*With a weary smile*] I begin to think he's a humorist.

MAFFEO [*Craftily*] It'd pay to convert him. He's the richest king in the world. He rules over millions of subjects, his empire covers millions of square miles of great undeveloped natural resources, his wealth in personal cash and jewels and goods alone easily runs into millions of millions—!

MARCO [*Stares at his uncle—then mutters fascinatedly*] Millions! [*Then, shaking away this interruption, bends to his writing again*]

MONK [*Sneeringly*] It ill becomes one of my cloth to call anyone a liar—but—haven't you let your trader's instinct for tall tales——?

KNIGHT [*Suddenly—gruffly*] Of course, he lies. If it was true, we'd have sacked the country long ago.

MAFFEO [*Resentment under his humility*] But, sir, the Kaan has the greatest army in the world.

KNIGHT [*Angrily*] What? Do you dare defame God's Own Army?

MAFFEO I meant—in numbers. He has millions of soldiers.

KNIGHT [*Complacently*] One white soldier of the Cross can slay a hundred yellow heathen!

TEDALDO [*Dryly*] Thus explaining your complete success in the Crusades. [*Then wearily*] The truth is all lies are equally stupid. I'm bored with your millions, Messers Polo. My imagination balks at such figures. Even if they're true, it's too much effort to conceive them. They're only puzzling beads on the rosaries of accountants—and, hereafter, if you please, tell yours in silence. [*They bow humbly and retire backward. His eyes following them listlessly,* TEDALDO *sees* MARCO, *who at this moment is scratching himself, twisting and turning his legs and feet, tearing his hair in a perfect frenzy of balked inspiration.* TEDALDO *smiles and addresses him in an affectionate, humorous tone.*] God's mercy on you, Master Marco! Are you suddenly possessed by a devil—or is it only those infernal Mahometan fleas the Almighty sends us for our sins?

MARCO [*Coming out of his fit—sheepishly*] I'm only writing something.

TEDALDO [*Sympathetically*] An invoice for Polo Brothers, I'll wager, judging from your torment. Mathematics are the spawn of the Father of Lies.

MAFFEO [*Respectful but pointedly*] But a necessary evil for a future merchant. Mark is surprisingly quick at figures.

NICOLO But still heedless—a dreamer—[*To* MARCO *with a condescending paternal air of property*] What are you writing, son? [*He and* MAFFEO *draw near* MARCO]

MARCO [*More confused*] Nothing, sir—just—something—[*He tries to hide it*]

MAFFEO Why are you so mysterious? Come, let's see.

MARCO   No—if you please, Uncle——

MAFFEO   [*With a sudden cunning motion snatches it from beneath Marco's hand—looks and gives a sudden burst of laughter*] Look, Nicolo, look!

MARCO   [*Rebelliously*] Give that back! You have no right——It isn't fair to——

NICOLO   [*Sternly*] You forget yourself! [*To* MAFFEO] What is it?

MAFFEO   See for yourself. [*He hands it to him*] Did you know you'd hatched a nightingale? [*He laughs coarsely.* NICOLO *reads, a scornful grin coming to his lips*]

TEDALDO   Surely, it can't be a song he has written? Show me it.

NICOLO   [*Going to him—laughing*] A rhyme! A love poem, no less! So that's what you were sweating over, simpleton, when I supposed you were occupied in useful figures——

TEDALDO   [*Severely, as he takes the poem*] Don't mock at him! Rather be grateful if a thistle can bring forth figs. Don't be downhearted, Master Marco. If you are a true poet——[MARCO *remains sullenly apart, shamefaced and angry, his fists clenched.* TEDALDO *reads—frowns—laughs—then smiling, to* NICOLO] You fear that this as a poem is—humm—exaggerated! [*He reads amusedly as* MARCO *squirms*]

> You are lovely as the gold in the sun
> Your skin is like silver in the moon
> Your eyes are real black pearls I have worn
> I kiss your genuine ruby lips and you swoon
> Smiling your thanks as I promise you
> A fortune in cash if you will be true
> While I am away earning millions in gold
> And silver currency so when we're old
> We'll have a nest egg million in the bank
> And in the meantime can easily afford
> To pay for a big wedding of high rank
> And start having children, bless the Lord!

[*There is a roar of laughter in which* TEDALDO *joins.* MARCO *looks about for a hole in which to crawl.* TEDALDO *addresses him amusedly but with kindliness*] Come, Marco. Here is your poem; I must own your lady is a bit too mineral—your heaven of love a trifle monetary—but, never mind, you'll be happier as a Polo than as a poet. Here! [*He gives it to* MARCO. *The latter fiercely crumples it up and throws it on the floor and stamps on it*]

NICOLO   [*Approvingly*] Sensibly done, my boy. This is no time for fooling.

TEDALDO   [*Looking searchingly at Marco's face—gently*] Perhaps I was too critical. Your poem had virtues of its own. I'm sure it would touch the lady's heart.

MARCO   [*With a great bluster of manliness*] Oh, I don't mind your making fun. I can take a joke. It *was* silly. Poetry's all stupid, anyway. What's the use in making words rhyme? It's easy. I was only trying it for fun—as a sort of stunt, to see if I could. You won't catch me ever being such a fool again!

MAFFEO   [*Clapping him on the back*] Spoken like a real man!

KNIGHT   [*Approvingly*] You ought to let us make a soldier of him! He has the right stuff!

MONK   [*As a noise of shouting comes toward them*] Ssstt! What's that clamor? Can it be an attack? [*The* KNIGHT *goes to the portal*]

KNIGHT   Someone is running here—and a crowd behind—I hear them shouting "Pope."

MONK   Then the Conclave has chosen——!

POLOS   [*Joyfully*] At last! We can go soon! [*The cries of many voices. The* SENTINEL *and* KNIGHT *admit the* MESSENGER *but press back the others*]

MESSENGER   [*Exhausted—falls on his knees before* TEDALDO, *holding out a sealed paper*] I came—at full haste—over seas and land—stopping for naught to bring you the greatest tidings—from the Conclave—you were chosen—Your Holiness—[*He falls fainting. The crowds cheer and sweep in*]

TEDALDO   [*Rising—pale and trembling*] What—does he say? There must be a mistake——

MONK   [*Has picked up the document and broken the seals—joyfully*] Ho! See! The official seal! You are the Pope! [*He kneels humbly*] Your Holiness, let me be the first——[*He kisses Tedaldo's hand. All are kneeling now, their heads bowed low. The bells of the city's churches begin to ring*]

TEDALDO   [*Raising his hands to heaven—dazedly*] Lord, I am not worthy! I am not worthy! [*Then to those about him—tremblingly*] Leave me—for a time—I would pray to God, alone—for strength—for guidance—

CROWD   [*In a clamor*] Your blessing! [TEDALDO, *full of a simple dignity and power, blesses them. They file out slowly, the* MONK *and* KNIGHT *last. The* POLOS *group together down at the apex of the triangle forestage, holding a whispered conference.* TEDALDO *goes and kneels before the altar and prays intensely*]

MAFFEO   Now that he's the Pope—if we could get some answer from him—we could start right away——

NICOLO   Yes. We couldn't hope for better weather.

MAFFEO   Do we dare interrupt him? He's already getting stuck-up, I think.

NICOLO   He seemed to take a fancy to Mark. You speak to him, Mark. He won't be severe with you.

MARCO   [*Unwillingly*] He's praying.

MAFFEO   He'll have time enough for that—but with us time is money. [*Giving the unwilling* MARCO *a push*] This will test your nerve, Mark! Don't shirk! Prove to your father and me you've got the makings of a success!

MARCO   [*Gritting his teeth*] All right. I'll show you I'm not scared—[*He advances boldly toward the altar, stands there for a moment awkwardly as Tedaldo is oblivious—then he falls on knees, humbly but insistently*] Your Holiness. Forgive me, Your Holiness, if I ask a favor——

TEDALDO   [*Turns to him and springs to his feet—imperiously*] Didn't you hear me? I wish to be alone! [*Then as* MARCO *is shrinking back—more kindly*] Well, what is it? I owe you a recompense, perhaps—for an injury.

MARCO   [*Stammeringly*] Your Holiness—if you could give us some answer to deliver to the Great Kaan—we could start now—with such favorable weather——

TEDALDO   [*Amused in spite of himself*] On the last day some one of your seed will undoubtedly interrupt Gabriel to try and sell him an improved trumpet! [*Then tensely and sarcastically*] I have no hundred wise men—nor one. Tell the Great Kaan he must have been imposed upon by your patriotic lies about God's Country—or he could never seriously make such a request.

POLOS   [*Terrified*] But—Your Holiness—we dare not repeat—he'd have us killed.

TEDALDO   I'll send him a monk or two. That's quite sufficient to teach the first principles of religion to a Tartar barbarian!

MAFFEO   But—Your Holiness—I swear to you he's not a barbarian. Why, every plate on his table is solid gold!

TEDALDO   No more lies! [*Then with a sudden whimsical smile*] And if the monks fail, let Master Marco be our missionary from the West. Let him set an example of virtuous Western manhood—amid all the levities of paganism—be oblivious and level-headed—shun the frailty of poetry—have a nest-egg million in the bank, as he so beautifully phrased it—and I'll wager a million of something or other myself that the Kaan will soon be driven to seek spiritual salvation! Mark my words, Marco is worth a million wise men—in the cause of wisdom! [*He laughs gaily, raising his hand over Marco's head*] Go with my benison! But what need have you for a blessing? You were born with success in your pocket.

And, now, addio—[*With a last gesture he turns, going quickly out of door in rear.*]

MAFFEO [*As he goes—approvingly*] Mark is making good already!

NICOLO Well, he's got a head on him!

MARCO [*Beginning to swell out a bit—matter-of-factly*] Well, never mind about me—when do we start?

POLOS [*Hurriedly*] At once. Let's go and pack. [*They go out left*] Come, Marco! Hurry!

MARCO I'm coming. [*He waits, looks after them, stops and picks up the crumpled poem, starts to hide it in his doublet, stops, mutters with brave self-contempt*] Aw! You damn fool! [*He throws poem down again, starts to go, hesitates, suddenly turns back, picks it up, crams it into his doublet and runs wildly out of the door. The scene fades into darkness*]

CURTAIN

ACT THREE   SCENE ONE   PART ONE

Light comes, gradually revealing the scene. In the rear, is the front of a Mahometan mosque. Before the mosque, is a throne on which sits a Mahometan ruler. On his right, the inevitable warrior—on his left, the inevitable priest—the two pillars of the State. At the ruler's feet his wives crouch like slaves. Everything is jewelled, high-colored, gorgeous in this background. Squatted against the side walls, forming a sort of semicircle with the throne at the center, counting from left to right consecutively are a nurse rocking a baby, two children playing a game, a young girl and young man in loving embrace, a middle aged couple, an aged couple, a coffin. All these Mahometan figures remain motionless. Only their eyes move, staring fixedly but indifferently at the Polos. The POLOS, *standing at the proscenium line, center, walk away into this land.* MARCO *follows them. He is carrying in each hand bags which curiously resemble modern sample cases. He sets these down and gazes around with a bewildered awe at the gorgeousness of Islam.*

NICOLO [*Turning on him—genially*] Well, son, here we are in Islam.

MARCO [*Round-eyed*] On the way a man told me that the Ark of Noah is still somewhere around here on top of a mountain.

MAFFEO [*With a sophisticated, skeptical air*] There may be an Ark—but is it Noah's?

NICOLO [*Reprovingly*] Ssshh! Do you doubt the Bible?

MARCO   [*Eagerly*] He proved it to me. Look! [*He shows them a piece of wood*] He broke this off of the Ark. See, it's got Noah's initials on it.

MAFFEO   [*Grimly*] How much did you pay him for it?

MARCO   Ten soldi in silver.

NICOLO   [*Dashing it out of Marco's hand—bitterly*] Muttonhead! You're a disgrace to the Polos! Do you suppose Almighty God would allow infidels to cut up Noah's Ark into souvenirs? Have you no more sense than a tourist?

MAFFEO   [*Placatingly*] He's only a boy. He'll learn. And before we go farther, Nicolo, we better read him from the notes we made on our last trip, all there is to remember about this corner of the earth.

NICOLO   [*They take out notebooks closely resembling a modern business-man's date book and read*] We're now passing through Kingdoms where they worship Mahomet. These Saracens are always beaten and slain in battle by Christians and their lands so wasted it's something wonderful! And in sooth, it's well done and serves them right!

MAFFEO   And there's a kingdom called Musul and in it a district of Baku where there's a great fountain of oil. It isn't good to eat but to burn.

NICOLO   Also to anoint mangey camels.

MAFFEO   People come from great distances to fetch it. There's a growing demand for it. Make a mental note of that.

MARCO   Yes, sir.

NICOLO   In some provinces silk is produced in great abundance. They weave the finest carpets, and cloth of gold. And there's another province producing an immense quantity of cotton. There's great sport to be had hunting and hawking and merchants have plenty of diversion.

MAFFEO   In Tabriz there's a big market for precious stones. It's a city where merchants make great profits. The people there are simple creatures. And in the mountains there are turquoises—but it's very cold in winter. The women are beautiful and wear cotton drawers, and into the making of these same will put one hundred ells of stuff. This they do to make themselves look large in the hips, for the men in these parts think that to be a great beauty in women.

NICOLO   In Hormuz the heat of the sun is frightful but it's a great sea port because of the trade with India. There are natural baths there which have excellent medicinal virtues.

MAFFEO   [*With a snicker*] They cure the itch—and other diseases you're too young to know about. [*The two Mahometan merchants enter from the left.* MAFFEO *recognizes them immediately—in a swift aside to his brother*] There's those damned Ali brothers. *They'll try to cut under our prices with their cheap junk as usual. [The Ali brothers have seen the* POLOS *and a whispered aside, evidently of the same nature, passes between them. Then simultaneously the two firms advance to meet each other putting on expressions of the utmost cordiality]*

MAFFEO   Well, well, greetings! You folks are a sight for sore eyes!

ONE ALI   My dear, dear friends! Praise be to Allah for the blessing of this meeting with you! *[They shake hands, embrace, kiss, rub noses, etc.]*

NICOLO   Well, well, who'd have thought it?

THE OTHER ALI   The world's a small place, after all!

MAFFEO   And that's a fact! *[Then with a cunning smirk]* Selling a big bill of goods hereabouts, I'll wager, you old rascals!

ALI   *[Airily]* My dear friend, don't speak of business. We're merely obeying the doctor's orders to take a vacation trip.

NICOLO   *[Meaning "you're a liar"]* Ah, is that so? What's the trouble?

ALI   My brother. His liver. Quite serious. *[The brother groans and places one hand over his kidney by way of evidence]*

NICOLO   I never saw him looking better. You'd never imagine——

ALI   But you, my friends. You are on a great exclusive venture to the court of the Great Kaan, we hear?

NICOLO   *[Looking at his brother in amazement]* What? Maffeo, did you hear that?

MAFFEO   Well, it just goes to show you what crazy lies get around! Nothing in it—absolutely nothing! We've been there once and that's enough.

ALI   A very rich country, we have heard.

MAFFEO   Rich? We almost starved to death there. Trade is dead, the people have no money, the Kaan himself had to pawn the crown to pay his debts, they were expecting a financial panic, there'd been a universal crop failure and famine. No sir, I wouldn't advise any merchant to go there.

ALI   The reports are evidently contradictory. We had heard—

NICOLO   For heaven's sake, let's not talk shop! Let's sit down and have a nice friendly chat. *[The four squat together in a circle]*

MAFFEO   *[With a wink]* I'll tell you a good one an Armenian doily-dealer told me down in Bagdad—only be sure and stop me if you've heard it before. *[They all bend their heads toward him with expectant grins. He looks around— then begins in a cautious lowered tone]* Well, there was an old Jew named Ikey and he married a young girl named Rebecca but he drank too much wine at the wedding dinner and later when he went upstairs it was all dark——[*He tells the rest of the story with much vaudeville-Jewish pantomime but in a voice too low to be heard. At the end there is a roar of laughter*]

ALI   Here's one they were telling in the club at Damascus you may not have heard. It seems once upon a time there was a Princess—— [*In the meantime, taking advantage of the Alis' appearance,* MARCO *has slipped off, full of curiosity and wonder, to look at this strange life. He goes first to the left, stops before the mother and baby, smiles down at it uncertainly, bends down to take hold of its hand*]

MARCO   Hello! [*Then to the mother*] He's fat as butter! [*Both remain silent and motionless, staring at him from a great distance with indifferent calm, noting his existence only as a phenomenon. Marco is rebuffed, grows embarrassed, cannot bear their stare, turns away and looks at the children who, frozen in the midst of their game of jackstraws, are looking at him. Marco adopts a lofty condescending air*] Humh! Do you still play that game here? I remember it— when I was a kid. How old are you kids? [*They stare silently. He mutters disgustedly*] Thickheads! [*And turns to the lovers who with their arms about each other, cheek to cheek, stare at him. He looks back at them, fascinated and stirred, and murmurs enviously*] Pretty nice for him! She's cute all right. They don't care who sees—I suppose they're engaged—like Donata and me. [*He fumbles and pulls out the miniature locket which is hung around his neck on a ribbon— stares at it*] Donata's prettier. [*Then embarrassedly, he holds it out for them to see*] Don't you think she's pretty? She and I are going to be married someday. [*They don't look except into his eyes. He turns away, hurt and angry*] Go to the devil, you infidel dogs! [*He stuffs the locket back—stops before the throne—tries to stare insolently at the king but is awed in spite of himself, makes a grudging bow and passes on, stops before the family group, sneers and passes on, stops before the old couple and cannot restrain his curiosity*] Would you mind telling me how old you are? [*He passes on, rebuffed again, stops fascinatedly before the coffin, leans out and touches it with defiant daring, shudders superstitiously and shrinks hurriedly away, going to the merchant group who are laughing again at same story*]

MAFFEO   [*With a smirk*] Keep away, Mark. You're too young. If you ever heard your father——!

ALI   [*To* NICOLO] Your son?

NICOLO   Yes—and a chip off the old block. Mark, meet the Ali brothers, our old time competitors and friends. [MARCO *salutes them absentmindedly, his mind still on the coffin*]

ALI A fine boy! Handsome! You should be proud! Will he follow in your footsteps?

NICOLO [*Jocosely*] Yes, and you better look out then, boys. He's as keen as they make 'em already.

ALI [*With a trace of a biting smile*] He greatly resembles a youth I saw back on the road buying a piece of Noah's Ark from a wayside sharper.

MAFFEO [*Hastily coming to the rescue as* NICOLO *cannot hide his chagrin—boastfully*] It wasn't Mark. Mark could sell any of your crooks the lions of St. Mark's as good mousers.

MARCO [*Suddenly, to his father pointing to the coffin*] Is there a dead person in there?

NICOLO Yes, my boy. [*Then in a low tone—vindictively?*] And damned in hell as all these infidel dogs eventually will be, thank God! [*The* PROSTITUTE *enters from the right. She is painted, half-naked, very alluring in a brazen, sensual way. She smiles at Marco enticingly*]

MARCO [*With a gasp*] Look! Who's that? [*They all turn, and, recognizing her, laugh with coarse familiarity*]

MAFFEO [*Jokingly*] So here you are again. You're like a bad lire—always turning up.

PROSTITUTE [*Smiling*] Shut up. You can bet it isn't old fools like you that turn me.

NICOLO [*With a lecherous grin at her*] No? But it's the old who have the money.

PROSTITUTE Money isn't everything—not always, anyway. One takes a vacation of love—once in a while. Now I wouldn't ask for money from him— [*She points to* MARCO]

NICOLO [*Crossly and jealously*] Leave him alone, you filth!

MAFFEO [*Broad-mindedly*] Come, come, Nicolo. Let the boy have his fling. We were no saints, remember, and it's time Mark learned something of life.

PROSTITUTE [*Her eyes on* MARCO] Hello, Handsome.

MARCO [*Bewilderedly*] You've learned—our language?

PROSTITUTE I attend strictly to business. I had to learn to sell to all nations.

MARCO What goods do you sell?

PROSTITUTE [*Mockingly*] A precious jewel. Myself. [*Then desirously*] But for you I'm a gift. [*Putting her hands on his shoulders and lifting her lips*] Why don't you kiss me?

MARCO   [*Terribly confused—strugglingly*] I—I don't know—I mean, I'm sorry but—you see I promised someone I'd never—[*Suddenly freeing himself—half-hysterically*] Leave go! I don't want your kind of kisses. [*A roar of coarse taunting laughter from the men.* MARCO *runs away off left*]

NICOLO   [*Between his teeth*] What a dolt!

MAFFEO   [*Slapping the* PROSTITUTE *on the bare shoulder*] He's too bashful. Better luck next time. He'll learn!

PROSTITUTE   [*Trying to hide her pique—forcing a cynical smile*] Oh yes, next time he'll fall—but I won't be a gift then. I'll make him pay—just to show him! [*She laughs harshly and goes out left. A pause. All four squat again in silence*]

ALI   [*Suddenly*] Many wonders have come to pass in these regions. They relate that in old times three kings from this country went away to worship a Prophet that was born and they carried with them three manner of offerings—Gold and Frankincense and Myrrh—and when they had come to the place where the Child was born, they marvelled and knelt before him——

NICOLO   That's written in the Bible. They were led there by a star.

ALI   There was no star in my tale, but if there was one it makes it even more wonderful——

NICOLO   The child was Jesus Christ, our Lord. [*He blesses himself,* MAFFEO *likewise*]

ALI   Your Jesus was a great prophet.

NICOLO   [*Defiantly*] He was the Son of God!

ALI   [*Stubbornly*] There is no God but Allah!

MAFFEO   [*With forced friendliness*] Let's keep off of religion. It's a subject where you're always stepping on somebody's corn. [*A strained pause. A* DERVISH *of the desert runs in shrieking madly and begins to whirl in a circle. No one is surprised except the two* POLOS, *who get up to gape at him with the thrilled appreciation inspired by a freak in a side show.* MARCO *comes back and joins them in staring*]

MAFFEO   [*With sudden appreciation*] If we had him in Venice we could make a mint of money exhibiting him. [NICOLO *nods.*]

MARCO   I'll have to write Donata about all this. [*Wonderingly*] Is he crazy?

MAFFEO   [*In a low aside to him*] My boy, all Mahometans are crazy. That's the only charitable way to look at it. They simply aren't responsible.

NICOLO   [*Grumblingly*] But they'll all be damned just the same. [*Suddenly the call to prayer sounds from* MUEZZINS *in the minarets of the mosque. The dervish falls on his face. Everyone sinks into the attitude of prayer except the Polos who stand embarrassedly, not knowing what to do*]

MARCO   Are they praying?

NICOLO   Yes, they call it that. Much good it does them!

MAFFEO   Ssshh! Come! This is a good time to set out again. Marco! Wake up! Attend to business! [*They go quickly out right,* MARCO *following with the sample cases. The scene fades quickly into darkness*]

ACT THREE   SCENE ONE   PART TWO

The slowly rising light reveals a scene which in the placing of its people and the characters and types represented is the exact duplicate of the last except that here the scene is India. The background for the ruler's throne is now a Buddhist temple instead of a mosque. The motionless staring figures are all East Indians. Looming directly above and in back of the ruler's throne is an immense Buddha. The POLOS *stand at center as before,* MARCO *still lugging the sample cases. He is seventeen now. Some of the freshness of youth has worn off.*

MARCO   [*Sits on one of the cases and stares about with a forced contempt—in a smart-aleck tone*] So this is India!

NICOLO   [*Begins to read from his notebook*] These people have a peculiar language and are idolators. They are great adepts in sorcery and diabolic arts. They are pestilent and crafty. It is their practice that everyone wash the whole body every day. They adore the ox and hold it holy. They paint their gods black and their devils white. They sit on the ground to honor the earth. They eat sulphur and quicksilver and that gives them long life. They burn the dead because they breed worms and when the corpse is consumed the worms starve to death and thus the soul of that body is guilty of the sin of murdering worms. It is so unendurably hot here that 'tis something wonderful. [*He mops his brow*] In fact, if you put an egg in their rivers it will be boiled.

MAFFEO   [*Taking up the reading from his book in the same tone*] There is great business to be done here. The merchants make great profits by export and import. Ginger, pepper, and indigo grow in abundance. They have the largest sheep in the world. Diamonds of great size are to be got and many fine and great pearls. The Kings possess vast treasures. They wear rubies, sapphires, emeralds, pearls around their necks and arms and ankles, worth more than a city's ransom, and 'tis no wonder, for they have great store of such gear. They have five hundred or more wives apiece, and whenever a King hears of a beautiful damsel, he takes her to wife—for the man who has most wives is the most respected.

MARCO   [*Stares at the ruler and his wives—appreciatively*] He ought to be. The girls are good lookers, though.

NICOLO   [*Sharply*] Wait till you're worth your salt before you think of girls. [*Then in his instructive tone*] There are fierce beasts—lions as black all over as devils.

MAFFEO   They make wine from the palm tree—a capital drink to very speedily make a man drunk. [*He smacks his lips*]

MARCO   [*Disgustedly*] This is a devilish land—hotter than hell.

MAFFEO   [*Warningly*] Sshhh! Don't let the natives hear you. Remember a good business man finds any climate healthy where trade is brisk.

MARCO   [*Smartly*] Even hell's?

MAFFEO   [*Offended—huffily*] Shut up! Don't play the dunce when I give you good advice. Remember you're still only a half-hatched young squirt! [*He turns his back on* MARCO, *who walks sullenly off to left. At the same moment, the two* MERCHANTS, *this time, Indians, come in. The same interplay as in the previous scene goes on with them and the* POLOS *only this time it is all done in pantomime right up to the time they are seated when* MAFFEO *again begins a story*] Let me tell you a rich one a corn-doctor told me in the Vale of Kashmir—

[*As he is telling the story,* MARCO *has gone off to look over the people but this time he assumes the casual, indifferent attitude of the worldly-wise. He makes a silly gesture to attract the child's attention, then passes by the two children with only a contemptuous glance, but stops and stares impudently at the lovers— finally spits with exaggerated scorn*] Where do you think you are—home with the light out? Aw, why don't you charge admission? [*He stalks on—pauses before the middle-aged couple who have a bowl of rice between them—in astonishment as though this evidence of a humanity common with his struck him as strange*] If it isn't real food, by Gosh! [*He passes quickly by the old people with a glance of aversion and very obviously averts his head from any sight of the coffin. As he returns to the group at center,* MAFFEO *has just finished his story. There is the same roar of laughter*]

MARCO   [*Grinning eagerly*] What was it, Uncle? Tell me!

MAFFEO   [*Grinning teasingly*] You're too young.

MARCO   [*Boastfully*] Is that so? You ought to hear the one a rose-bug exterminator got a big laugh with in Samarkand——

NICOLO   [*Severely*] Mark! Behave yourself! [*The* PROSTITUTE, *the same but now in Indian garb, has entered from left and comes up behind* MARCO]

PROSTITUTE   A chip of the old block, Nicolo!

NICOLO   [*Angrily*] You again!

MARCO   [*Pleased to see her again—embarrassedly*] Why, hello.

PROSTITUTE   [*Cynically*] I know you'd want to see me again. [*She raises her lips*] Will you kiss me now? [*As he hesitates*] Forget your promise. You know you want to.

MAFFEO   [*Grinning*] There's no spirit in the youngsters nowadays. I'll wager you he won't dare——

PROSTITUTE   [*Her eyes on Marco's*] How much will you bet?

MAFFEO   Ten—[MARCO *suddenly kisses her*]

PROSTITUTE   [*Turning to* MAFFEO] Pay me, Uncle.

MARCO   [*With a grin*] No. I kissed you before he said ten what.

MAFFEO   That's right! Good boy, Mark!

PROSTITUTE   [*Turning to* MARCO—*cynically*] You're learning, aren't you? You're becoming shrewd even about kisses. You only need me now to make you into a real man—for ten pieces of gold.

MARCO   [*Genuinely overcome by a sudden shame*] No, please. I—I didn't mean it—it was only in fun.

PROSTITUTE   [*With a sure smile*] Later, then—when we meet again. [*She walks out at left.* MARCO *looks after her*]

NICOLO   Shameless bitch! Such women should be kept locked up.

MARCO   [*As she evidently turns to look back at him, waves his hand and grins—then abashed*] Well—she's pretty. It's too bad she's—what she is.

MAFFEO   Don't waste pity. Her kind are necessary evils. You'll realize that—sooner or later. All of us are human. [*A long pause*]

BUDDHIST MERCHANT   [*Suddenly*] The Buddha taught us to meditate that our loving-kindness should embrace all forms of life, that one's compassion should suffer with the suffering, that one's sympathy should understand all things as if oneself had experienced each one, and last that one's impartial judgment should regard all persons and things as of equal importance. To the selfless eye a holy man or a dog appear alike.

NICOLO   [*Harshly*] Who was this Buddha?

BUDDHIST MERCHANT   The Son of God. [*He indicates the state of Buddha*]

NICOLO   You mean Jesus?

BUDDHIST MERCHANT   [*Unheedingly*] He was immaculately conceived.

The Light passed into the womb of Maya, and she bore a son who, when he came to manhood, renounced wife and child, riches and power, and went out as a beggar on the roads to seek the supreme enlightenment which would conquer birth and death; and at last he attained the wisdom where all desire has ended and experienced the heaven of peace which we call Nirvana. And when he died he became a God. [*The temple bells begin to ring in chorus. All except the* POLOS *prostrate themselves before Buddha*]

MARCO [*To his uncle—in a whispered chuckle*] Died and became a God?—So that's what they believe about that stone statue, is it?

MAFFEO They're all crazy, too—like the Mahometans. That's the only charitable way——They simply aren't responsible.

MARCO [*Suddenly*] But I saw two of them with a bowl of rice——

MAFFEO Oh yes. They eat rice the same as we do. [*Then abruptly*] Come on! This is our chance to make a start. Don't forget our cases, Mark. [*They go out left followed by* MARCO *with the sample cases. The scene fades into darkness*]

ACT THREE   SCENE ONE   PART THREE

[*The darkness gradually lifts. In the rear is a section of the Great Wall of China with an enormous shut gate. It is late afternoon, just before sunset. Immediately before the gate is a rude throne on which sits a Mongol ruler with warrior and sorcerer to right and left of him. At the sides are Mongol circular huts. The motionless figures sit before these. In the back of the throne and above it is a small idol made of felt and cloth. The clothes of the ruler and his court are of rich silk stuffs, lined with costly furs. The squatting figures of the people are clothed in rough robes. The* POLOS *stand at center,* MARCO *still lugging the now battered sample cases. He is now nearly 18, a brash, self-confident young man, assertive and talky. All the* POLOS *are weary and their clothes shabby and travel worn.*]

MARCO [*Setting down the bags with a thump and staring about with an appraising contempt*] Welcome to that dear old Motherland, Mongolia!

MAFFEO [*Wearily takes out his guidebook and begins to read in the monotone of a boring formula*] Flocks—goats—horses—cattle. Jasper—chalcedony—jade and rhubarb. The women do all the buying and selling. Business is all in cattle and crops. In short, the people live like beasts. They eat horses, dogs, and rats and drink mare's milk.

NICOLO [*Reading from his book*] They have two Gods—a most High God of Heaven whom they only pray to for health of mind, and a God of Earth in their own image—and they also make him a wife—who watches over their cattle and corn and earthly goods. They pray to these and do many other stupid things.

MARCO [*Boredly*] I believe you. [*He walks away and makes the circuit of the figures, but now he hardly glances at them. The two* MERCHANTS, *this time,* TARTARS, *again enter and there is the same pantomime.* MARCO *joins them and squats down.* MAFFEO *tells his story, this time all in pantomime, with pantomime laughter following, but it is apparent the whole company is very weary. After the laughter, they yawn, prepare to lie down*]

MAFFEO We'll have time to steal a nap before they open the Gate in the Great Wall.

MARCO [*With an assertive importance*] Wait! Just a moment! I've got a good one an albino idol-polisher told me in Tibet. He was the funniest fellow I ever saw! And this is the funniest story you ever heard! Well, it seems that an Irishman got drunk in Tangut and wandered into a temple where he mistook one of the female statues for a real woman and—[*He goes on, laughing and chuckling to himself, with endless comic pantomime. The two* TARTAR MERCHANTS *yawn and fall asleep.* NICOLO *stares at his son bitterly,* MAFFEO *with great pity. Finally* MARCO *finishes to his own uproarious amusement and rocks with laughter*]

NICOLO [*Bitterly*] Dolt!

MAFFEO [*Mockingly sentimental*] Ah youth, youth! Youth will have its laugh! [MARCO *stops open-mouthed and glares from one to the other*]

NICOLO When he was four he fell into a gondola and hit his head. Do you think that can be it?

MARCO [*Faintly*] What's the matter? Don't you see the point?

MAFFEO [*Reminiscently*] When my great great grandfather first saw that point he laughed so hard he broke a spring in his cradle.

MARCO [*Utterly squelched*] Aw—you'd say that anyway.

NICOLO [*Pettishly*] You didn't get that sense of humor from my side of the family! Unless your jokes improve you'll never be able to sell anything that isn't worth the price!

MAFFEO Well, a sense of humor can be acquired by hard practice like anything else. I'll have to give Marco some lessons in how to tell a short story. [*Warningly*] And until I pronounce you graduated, mum's the word, understand! The people on the other side of that wall may look simple but they're not, as you'll soon find out when you bargain with them. And don't tell the

Kaan any of your funny ones unless you want us all beheaded. [*The* PROSTITUTE *enters dressed now as a Tartar. She comes and puts her hand on his head*]

PROSTITUTE   What has this bad boy been doing now?

MAFFEO   He's getting too killing for words! [*He rests his head on his arms and goes to sleep*]

PROSTITUTE   Shall I expect you again tonight?

MARCO   No. You've got me dead broke. [*Suddenly gets to his feet and faces her—disgustedly*] And I'm through with you anyway.

PROSTITUTE   [*With a scornful smile*] And I with you—now that you're a man—and broke. [*She turns away*]

MARCO   [*Angrily*] Listen here! Give me back what you stole! Don't lie! I know I had it on a ribbon around my neck last night and this morning it was gone. [*Threateningly*] Give it to me, you, or I'll make trouble——

PROSTITUTE   [*Takes a crumpled paper from her bosom*] Do you mean this?

MARCO   [*Tries to snatch it*] No!

PROSTITUTE   [*She unfolds it and reads*]
"We'll have a nest egg million in the bank
And in the meantime can easily afford
To pay for a church wedding of high rank
And start having children, Bless the Lord!"
[*She laughs*] Are you a poet, too?

MARCO   [*Abashed and furious*] I didn't write that.

PROSTITUTE   You're lying. You must have. It is your soul singing its sweet epiphany! Why deny? Don't sell your soul for nothing. That's bad business. [*She laughs, waving the poem in her upraised hand, staring mockingly*] Going! Going! Gone! [*She lets it fall and grinds it under her feet into the earth. Laughing*] Your soul! Dead and buried! You strong man! [*She laughs*]

MARCO   [*Threateningly*] And now give me what was wrapped up in that, d'you hear!

PROSTITUTE   [*Scornfully—takes the miniature from her bosom*] You mean—this cheap chromo. I was bringing it to you. It isn't worth anything. It must have fallen off in bed. D'you think I want her ugly face around? Here! [*She throws it at his feet. He leans down and picks it up, polishing it on his sleeve remorsefully. The* PROSTITUTE, *walking away, calls back over her shoulder*] I kissed it—so you'd remember my kiss—whenever you kiss her. [*She laughs.* MARCO *starts as if to run after her angrily. Suddenly a shout rises from the lips of all the* TARTARS, *and with one accord they raise their arms and eyes to the sky. One of the* TARTAR MERCHANTS *prays aloud:* God of the Heaven, be in our souls! *Then they all prostrate themselves on the ground as he chants:* God of the Earth, be in our bodies! *They remain prostrate, crooning in a low monotone. The* POLOS *rise up, stretch sleepily*]

MARCO   [*Inquisitively*] Two gods. Are they in one person, like our Holy Trinity?

MAFFEO   [*Shocked*] Don't be impious! These are damned and degraded pagans—or crazy, that's a more charitable way to—[*From behind the wall comes the sound of martial Chinese music. The gate opens. The blinding glare of the setting sun floods in from beyond. A file of soldiers, accompanying a richly-dressed Court* MESSENGER, *come through. He walks directly up to the* POLOS *and bows deeply*]

MESSENGER   The Great Kaan, Lord of the World, had rumor of your approach and sent me to welcome—[*He looks around*] But where are the hundred wise men of the West?

NICOLO   [*Confused*] We had two Dominicans—but they soon deserted us——

MAFFEO   [*Warningly*] Ssst! [*Then smoothly*] A great misfortune—through none of our fault, you understand——

MESSENGER   [*Indifferently*] You will explain to the Emperor. It is naught to me, except I was ordered to arrange a welcome for them—and for you.

MAFFEO   [*Claps him on the back*] Well, here we are, large as life—and hungry as hunters! So bring on your Welcome, Brother. [*The* MESSENGER *bows, starts back, the* POLOS *following him,* MAFFEO *calling*] Get on the job, Mark. Don't forget the cases. [*They pass through the gate*]

MARCO   [*Wearily picks up the cases—then goading himself on*] Giddap! Cathay or bust! [*He struggles through the gate. For a second he is framed in it, outlined against the brilliant sky, tugging a sample case in each hand. Then the gate shuts, the light fades out. The* TARTARS *remain prostrate in prayer, their heads toward the sun*]

CURTAIN

SCENE TWO

SCENE: *The forestage of a sort of court before the great palace of Kublai Kaan at Cambalin, the exterior of which is represented by the curtain at the proscenium. A squad of Chinese soldiers stand guard by a grand entrance at center. The two elder* POLOS, *spruced up in new clothes, sit each on a sample case. They are very apparently apprehensive and nervous.* MARCO, *on the other hand, has put on a bold front and is resolutely scornful and unimpressed. He is well-dressed, good-looking, and his consciousness of his attributes gives him a cocky, confident air.*

MARCO [*Looking around*] This Cathay doesn't knock me out of my seat. Little old Venice is good enough for me!

NICOLO Sshh-h!! Those soldiers are watching you.

MARCO Well, they can. Perhaps it will do them good. [*Then scornfully*] They don't look like man-eaters to me. One of the Doge's strong arm squad could lick the whole crowd.

NICOLO Fool! Don't talk so loud!

MAFFEO And wipe that silly grin off your face! We'll be ushered into his presence any moment now so try not to look like a born numskull.

MARCO [*Teasingly*] But you said a cheerful grin can sell old sieves for new rain coats.

MAFFEO But it must be grinned with judgment. Use your brains on it! Grade the grin according as you size up the customer. [*Lowering his voice*] Now the Great Kaan's weak spot is that he's a philosopher. So you can smile but you mustn't grin. Smile as if at your hidden thoughts; don't grin because you have none to hide and are proud of it!!

NICOLO It's a serious matter. The Kaan gives millions and millions of orders yearly to merchants like us.

MAFFEO And we want to get another slice of that melon for Polo Brothers.

MARCO [*With sudden brightness*] Then your best entrance argument would have been those hundred Christian wise men. You should have brought them along as presents even if you had to dress up a hundred retired gondoliers in scholar's gowns!

MAFFEO [*Sarcastically*] The gondoliers could, of course, convince the Kaan of their wisdom.

MARCO [*Brightly*] Yes. He couldn't understand a word they said and they'd be too stupid ever to learn Tartar as I have.

MAFFEO [*Bitingly*] The Kaan's interpreters speak all languages.

MARCO Oh. [*Then, after a pause, unabashed*] Well, His Holiness told me to act as proxy for the Wise Men. He said for me to show 'em all out here in the sticks what's what.

MAFFEO [*Grimly*] Yes, that does make matters worse, doesn't it? [*To* NICOLO, *dryly*] Perhaps it would be safer to do without your son's entertaining company until our visit is over. We could say he was only our sample-keeper—

NICOLO [*Nodding*] Yes, perhaps it is better.

MARCO [*Pleading*] No. Please. I'll act right.

NICOLO Then be a man!

MAFFEO [*Sternly and patriotically*] Remember you're a Venetian—and a gentleman. You can't afford to act like a Genoese, or a Pisan, or a Florentine, or any such scum! Never forget that by the blessing of God you were born in the finest little old spot on God's green footstool!

MARCO [*The sterling stuff in him emerging—erect and manly*] I'll never forget that, I promise you, Uncle!

NICOLO [*Fire in his eye*] And bear always in your heart the slogan of our noble republic! The flag follows trade!

MARCO [*Nobly*] It is written in my blood, Dad! [*His teeth snap together as his strong jaw clamps determinedly, and his heels click as he stands at salute*] Venice Irredenta!

MAFFEO AND NICOLO [*In chorus, hands raised*] Salute! [*A great clanging of gongs comes from within the palace. The* GUARD *stands at salute. The* CAPTAIN *steps to the edge of the forestage and calls to the* POLOS] The Ruler of the World awaits you! Come!

MAFFEO AND NICOLO [*Bowing humbly*] We are his humble servants. [*The lights go out. The* GUARD *can be heard tramping off. Maffeo's voice can be heard*] Don't forget the samples, Mark. These foreigners would steal your ears right off your head if you didn't keep listening every second!!

The light slowly comes on to a pitch of blinding brightness. Music from full Chinese and Tartar bands crashes up to a tremendous blaring crescendo of drums, gongs, and the piercing shrilling of flutes. Then, as the light and sound rise to their highest point, there is a sudden dead silence. The scene is revealed as the Grand Throne room in the palace of KUBLAI, *the* GREAT KAAN *in the city of Cambaluc, Cathay, an immense octagonal room, the lofty walls adorned in gold and silver. In the far rear wall, within a deep recess like the shrine of an idol, is the throne of the* GREAT KAAN. *It rises in three tiers, three steps to a tier. On golden cushions at the top* KUBLAI *sits dressed in his heavy gold robes of state. He is a man of sixty but still seemingly in the full prime of his powers, his face proud and noble, his expression tinged with an ironic humor and bitterness yet full of sympathetic humanness. In his person are combined the conquering power and indomitable force of a descendant of Chinghiz with the humanizing culture of the conquered Chinese who have already begun to absorb their conquerors.*

On the level of the throne below KUBLAI *are: on his right a* MONGOL WARRIOR *in full armor with shield and spear; his face grim, cruel and fierce, powerful with the pride of the conqueror. On his left* CHU-YIN, *the Cathayan sage and adviser to the* KAAN, *a venerable old man with white hair, dressed in a simple black robe; immediately in front and at the feet of* KUBLAI *sits a beautiful little girl of four, the* PRINCESS KOKACHIN.

On the main floor, grouped close to the throne are: on the right, the sons of the KAAN. *Farther away, the nobles and warriors of all degrees with their wives behind them. On the left, the wives and concubines of the* KAAN, *then the courtiers, officers, poets, scholars, etc.—all the non-military officials and hangers-on of government, with their women beside them.*

MARCO *now stands, a sample case in each hand, bewildered and dazzled, gawking about him on every side. His father and uncle, bowing, walk to the foot of the throne and kneel before the* KAAN. *They make frantic signals to* MARCO *to do likewise but he is too dazed to notice. All the people in the room are staring at him. The* KAAN *is looking at the two brothers with a stern air. An* USHER *of the palace comes quietly to* MARCO *and makes violent gestures to him to kneel down.*

MARCO [*Misunderstanding him—gratefully*] Thank you, brother. [*He sits down on one of the sample cases. The* PRINCESS KOKACHIN, *a little girl of four, who has been standing at the Kaan's right hand, sees* MARCO *and comes down to look at him. A barely perceptible titter goes around the court as the people turn their heads from the throne to hide their amusement. This grows louder as* KOKACHIN, *her expression a mixture of fascinated but wary amusement, circles about* MARCO, *staring at him as at some strange animal.* MARCO *is embarrassed but grins at her. She smiles back. He holds out his hand to her*] Hello, Little Sister! How's everything with you, eh? [*She is startled by his voice but finally timidly takes his hand. He pulls her toward him, grinning*] Come on, don't be scared, I don't bite. Let's you and me get acquainted. What's your name, eh? Here, sit down and make yourself comfortable. [*He sets her on his knee to her own pleasurable amazement, but to the gasping horror of all the Court. The* KAAN *is still looking frowningly at the two* POLOS *as he listens to the report of their* MESSENGER *escort. He does not notice. An outraged* CHAMBERLAIN *rushes over to* MARCO, *orders him to set the* PRINCESS *down, threatening him while at the same time bowing to the* PRINCESS *abjectly*]

MARCO [*Bewilderedly*] What's the trouble now?

KOKACHIN [*Slips off his knee—with a regal gesture to the* CHAMBERLAIN] Begone, dirt! [*Then after another pleased glance at* MARCO *calls to* KUBLAI *in the voice of a spoiled child*] Grandfather, what is he? [*There is another suppressed gale of laughter*]

KUBLAI [*Dismissing the* MESSENGER, *having heard his report—not noticing* KOKACHIN *beyond a silencing gesture*] Sshhh! [*Then addressing the* POLOS—*coldly*] I bid you welcome, Messers Polo; but why have you failed to carry out my commissions? Where are the hundred wise men of the West who were to dispute before me with my wise men of the sacred teachings of Lao-Tzu and the Buddha and Christ?

MAFFEO [*Hurriedly*] There was no Pope elected until just before——

NICOLO And he had no wise men anyway—but he sent two monks who soon deserted us.

KOKACHIN Grandfather, he's nice, give him to me. [*Again laughter. This time the* KAAN *sees* MARCO *and a puzzled expression of interest comes over his face*]

KUBLAI [*To* KOKACHIN—*tenderly*] Ssshh, Little Parrot! [*To the* POLOS] Is he with you?

NICOLO [*Hesitantly*] My son, Marco, your Majesty—still young and graceless—

KUBLAI Come here, Marco Polo. [MARCO *comes forward, trying feebly to assume a bold, confident air. The* PRINCESS *walks beside him, looking him over in motion with a possessive satisfaction*]

MAFFEO [*In a loud, furious aside*] Kneel, you ass! [MARCO *flounders to his knees*]

KUBLAI [*With a smile*] I bid you welcome, too, Master Marco.

MARCO Thank you, sir—I mean, your Lordship—your—

KUBLAI [*Kindly*] Never mind. I have enough slaves already. [*Regarding him closely*] How old are you?

MARCO [*A good deal more at ease now*] Eighteen. [*Then boastfully*] But I've knocked around the world a lot—done most everything once and I guess I know a thing or two.

KUBLAI Indeed? [*Regards him wonderingly. To* KOKACHIN] Why do you like this man, my Princess?

KOKACHIN Because he's—so queer and funny!

MARCO [*Suddenly*] Before I forget—the Pope gave me a message for you, sir.

KUBLAI [*Smiling*] Are you his hundred wise men?

MARCO   [*Beaming*] You've guessed it! He sent me in their place. He said I'd be worth a million wise men to you—in the cause of wisdom!

KUBLAI   [*Puzzled*] What did he mean?

NICOLO   May I explain? He meant that Marco by leading an upright, honest life—not neglecting the practical side, of course—might set an example which would illustrate, better than long words, the flesh and blood product of our Christian civilization.

KUBLAI   [*With a quiet smile*] I shall study this apotheosis with unwearied interest, I promise you!

MARCO   [*Suddenly—with a confidential air*] Honestly, wasn't that all a joke, your asking for the wise men?

KUBLAI   No. I couldn't conceive a West which contained only your relatives.

MARCO   His Holiness thought you must have a sense of humor.

KUBLAI   He was mistaken. I'm credulous about the unknown.

MARCO   Or that you must be an optimist.

KUBLAI   [*With a smile of appreciation*] I'm afraid your Holy Pope is a most unholy cynic.

MARCO   [*His face gradually becoming red and sullen*] Say—maybe we better leave family and religion out of the argument.

KUBLAI   [*Trying to solve a riddle in his own mind*] Did he believe your youth might reveal that thing you call soul which the West dreams can defeat death? [*Suddenly to* MARCO] Have you an immortal soul?

MARCO   [*Angrily*] Of course! Any fool knows that.

KUBLAI   [*Humbly*] But I am not a fool. Can you prove it to me?

MARCO   Why, if you didn't have a soul, what would happen when you died?

KUBLAI   What indeed?

MARCO   Why nothing—you'd be dead—just like an animal.

KUBLAI   Your logic is irrefutable.

MARCO   Well, I'm not an animal, am I? That is certainly plain enough!

KUBLAI   Are you then a spirit?

MARCO   [*With a guffaw*] A ghost? Do I look it? [*Then arrogantly*] No sir! I'm a man, that's what, made by Almighty God in His Own Image for His greater glory!

KUBLAI [*Staring at him for a long moment with appalled appreciation—ecstatically*] So you are the Image of God! There is certainly something about you—something complete and unanswerable—but wait—a test!—[*He slaps his hands, pointing to* MARCO. *Soldiers with drawn swords leap forward and seize him, trussing up his hands behind his back*]

MAFFEO [*Grovelling*] Mercy! He is only a boy!

NICOLO [*Grovelling*] Mercy! He is only a fool!

KUBLAI [*Sternly*] Silence! [*To* MARCO, *with inhuman calm*] Since you possess eternal life, it can do you no harm to cut off your head. [*He makes a sign to a soldier, who flourishes his sword*]

MARCO [*Trying to conceal his fear under a joking tone*] Look out with that knife! You're liable to hurt someone!

KUBLAI Your voice trembles. What! Are you afraid to die, immortal youth?

MARCO [*With a ghastly grin*] I'm too young!

KUBLAI [*With implacable calm*] You are too young to live! But if you will confess that your soul is a stupid invention of your fear and that when you died you are as dead as a dead dog is dead, then I will spare——

MARCO [*With sudden fury*] I'll show you who's a dog! You're a yellow liar and you'll roast forever in hell! [*He glares defiantly. His father and uncle moan with horror*]

KUBLAI [*Laughs and claps his hands.* MARCO *is freed. The* KAAN *studies his sullen but relieved face with amusement*] Your pardon, Master Marco! I suspected a flaw but you are perfect. You cannot imagine your death. You are a born hero. I shall keep you near me. You may tell me about your soul and I shall listen as to a hundred wise men from the West! I still have my doubts. You must convert me—by your example. Is it agreed?

MARCO [*Hesitatingly*] I know it's a great honor, sir—but forgetting the soul side of it—I've got to eat, you know.

KUBLAI [*Astonished*] To eat?

MARCO I mean, I'm young and ambitious. I'm not afraid of hard work. I love action, I'm honest and sober and no fool—and—well—I've got to get to the top—and— [*Suddenly blurts out*] When do I start and what's the salary?

KUBLAI Ha! You are a mortal also! Well, you will find me a practical man, too. Here. Let this be in lieu of an option on your services. [*He hands him a splendid ring, which* MARCO *turns over in his fingers shrewdly*]

MARCO [*Perfunctorily*] Thanks. [*Then insinuatingly*] Is it possible that such a large stone can be genuine?

KUBLAI I think I shall train you for a diplomat. Yes, it is genuine. Your uncle will tell you it is worth three thousand. He once sold it to me for seven thousand.

MAFFEO Your majesty wrongs me. I would be willing right now to give you seven thousand.

KUBLAI Sell it to him, Marco. [*With a grin,* MARCO *holds it out to* MAFFEO *who refuses to take it, but* KUBLAI *is implacable*] Pay him your offer! It is just! I command it! [*Tremblingly* MAFFEO *does so. The* KAAN *smiles*] Messers Nicolo and Maffeo, you will find quarters in the merchant's village. Master Marco remains with me—for the good of his soul. [*As they seem about to protest*] It is my order. [*He claps his hands and, descending from the throne, walks off left to the strains of a hidden orchestra. A gong is struck. The courtiers and all other people disappear from the room. The two* POLOS *bow themselves back to their sample cases.* MARCO *walks with them, unmindful of their resentful glances, with a very superior air. He is followed by* KOKACHIN. *He kicks each sample case disdainfully and motions his father and uncle to take them out of his sight. They are furious but dare not protest and meekly lug the sample cases off left. The music ceases*]

MARCO [*Notices* KOKACHIN, *who has watched him with the approving eyes of a proprietor—glumly as he dusts off his coat*] Say, you're a nice, kind little girl, aren't you? Why didn't you speak up when your Grandpa almost murdered me? I suppose you'd have liked to play catch with my head, wouldn't you?

KOKACHIN I knew he was only joking. When he means it the wart on his nose wriggles.

MARCO [*Craftily*] I'll watch that wart from now on! [*Briskly*] Where's the front yard? I want to get a breath of air.

KOKACHIN [*Imperiously*] I command you to stay with me!

MARCO [*Decidedly*] No, you don't. I've got a lot of things to think over. I can't be bothered with kids. [*He stalks out. She watches him go with amazement—then suddenly bursts into a fit of rage and claps her hands and stamps her feet. Attendants hurry in from every side and prostrate themselves. Her old* NURSE *comes wobbling in hysterically*]

NURSE Daughter of the stars, what is it?

KOKACHIN Find the front yard.

ALL [*In astonishment*] The front yard?

KOKACHIN   And let a hungry tiger be loosed in it!—or I shall order you all beaten!

CHAMBERLAIN   [*Trembling*] It shall be done!

KOKACHIN   [*As he turns to go—hysterically*] Stop! No! Do nothing at all! Don't dare do anything! Get out of here! [*She begins to sob*]

NURSE   [*Taking her in her arms*] My baby! My lamb! Little precious!

KOKACHIN   [*After a pause, in a sniffling voice*] Nurse.

NURSE   Yes, Little Plum Blossom?

KOKACHIN   Can I have a piece of candy?

CURTAIN

ACT FOUR

SCENE: *The Little Throne Room in the bamboo summer palace of the* KAAN *at Xandu, the city of Peace—smaller, more intimate than the one at Cambaluc, but possessing an atmosphere of aloof dignity and simplicity fitting to the philosopher ruler who retreats here to contemplate in peace the vanity of his authority.*

About three years have elapsed. It is a beautiful sunlit morning in late June. The KAAN *reclines comfortably on his cushioned bamboo throne. His face appears to have grown softer in expression, his whole attitude is relaxed and tranquil as compared with his regal, absolute air in the last scene. A smile of amused curiosity approaching incredulity, is on his lips as he regards* MARCO, *who, seated at a desk at center where the forestage meets the stage, with his hunched back toward the* KAAN, *is assiduously writing characters with a brush into a rough copy book. The* PROFESSORS, *one a classicist and the other a scientist, the two official tutors of* MARCO, *stand stiffly on each side in back of him, peering critically over his shoulders as he writes. Both are middle-aged men, their thoughtful faces aged by professional expressions of premature omniscience.*

At the apex of the forestage, MAFFEO *and* NICOLO *are squatting face to face, a bag of money between them which* MAFFEO *is stacking into piles of various denominations while* NICOLO *notes these down in an account book.*

Below the KAAN, *on his right, the* PRINCESS KOKACHIN, *now almost eight, sits at a chess board with* CHU YIN, *who is smilingly teaching her the game, much to her intolerant impatience, for her attention is preoccupied by* MARCO POLO. *A* CHAMBERLAIN *of the palace enters and prostrates himself before the throne.*

CHAMBERLAIN   A Staff Officer with dispatches from the front, Your Majesty.

KUBLAI [*With a sigh*] Bringing war to my peace. [*With a resigned shrug*] Let him enter. [*The* CHAMBERLAIN *backs out. A moment later the* STAFF OFFICER *in rich uniform enters and kneels before the throne. For a while* KUBLAI *stares at him in silence, absent-mindedly.* KOKACHIN *twists about to survey him critically*]

CHU YIN [*Smilingly recalling her attention to the chess board*] You're in check, Princess.

KOKACHIN [*Turns back impatiently*] I'll never learn this old game. [*Then confidentially*] That officer looks pretty, doesn't he?—but not as pretty as Marco.

CHU YIN [*Good-naturedly inexorable*] Solve chess men first before you play with men.

KOKACHIN [*Impatiently shoves a piece somewhere*] There! If Marco wore that uniform he'd look like—a hero!

CHU YIN You're still in check, Princess.

KOKACHIN [*Angrily*] Oh! [*Makes another move*]

CHU YIN [*Calmly*] You're still in check.

KOKACHIN [*With a sudden angry motion scatters the chess men all over the board—regally*] I order this game suppressed. A Princess of the Blood may not lose! [*Then she suddenly sticks out her tongue at* CHU YIN] Now, who's in check?

KUBLAI [*To the* OFFICER *at last—wearily*] Well? You may speak.

OFFICER [*Beamingly*] A glorious victory, sire! Fifty thousand dead, one hundred thousand wounded! General Bayan has taken their capital Kinsay. The Sung dynasty is perished. The kingdom of Manzi is no more! The war is over!

KUBLAI [*Ironically*] Forcing me to see to it that we are soon involved in another. I can't afford to support an immense army in idleness. You must conquer for your keep!

OFFICER [*Gloriously*] We'll conquer the world!

KUBLAI [*Quizzically*] And then—what? [*Then, as the officer looks confused, he drives home his meaning*] Even now, with Manzi finished, there's no more work for you. [*Then, as the* OFFICER *still looks dull—sharply*] As the bearer of such decisive tidings, I award you the Order of the Golden Dragon, Fifth Class. You are at the same time retired on half-pay, the Empire having no further use for your services.

OFFICER [*Appalled*] But—Your Majesty—my wife—my children—we shall starve——

KUBLAI [*Gravely*] True. [*Then letting the ghost of a smile appear*] Then

I must retain you idly on active service. Well, return to General Bayan and order him to march home at the head of a handsome, well-dressed guard of honor, bearing the captured banners of Manzi, with twenty full military bands, and fifty caravan loads of loot and fireworks. I shall proclaim a national holiday and my taxpayers will be given a soothing laxative dose of glory. [*The* OFFICER *bows, turning to go*] But tell the General on no account to withdraw the army from Manzi. [*Ironically*] On behalf of the hospitable Manzians, I invite my soldiers to remain as their guests indefinitely.

OFFICER   Yes, sire! [*He goes.* KUBLAI *sinks back on the couch dejectedly.* CHU YIN *gets up and goes to him*]

CHU YIN   Is mockery wisdom?

KUBLAI   [*Shrugging his shoulders*] One must laugh at man—or die of him!

CHU YIN   Laughter is complicity unless you stand on a mountain peak and laugh downward at yourself!

KUBLAI   [*Bitterly*] But I happen to be chained to this [*He pounds the throne*] summit of a dung heap. So give me some barnyard wisdom to encourage my imperial posing as the son of Heaven! [*He smiles*]

CHU YIN   [*Shades his head in rebuke but smiles also*] Wisdom is not won by self-invasion and looting oneself but by peaceful means, by relaxing the grip of self on the soul, releasing it to sink deep and dissolve its identity into the great pure tide of the World Soul, which flows in eternal calm beneath the changing simulacra of Being.

KUBLAI   [*With an impatient sigh*] To drown in dream until you become a dream? [*Shrugging his shoulders*] I am a Mongol. Our conquering truth has been that power over others is the highest goal. It is a simple old childish mob truth but a lusty one. Your truth that power over oneself is all, is a simple old truth, too, but an individual weak one. It was easily crushed.

CHU YIN   [*With a smile*] You conquered the illusion of us—not us. That which is within—our old wisdom—is absorbing you.

KUBLAI   [*Half-mockingly*] And its outcome will be neither man nor monkey. I offer myself as an example. I have found no new faith in your Way, and I have lost the old faith in mine. I no longer believe in my significance nor in man's. That we should imagine a meaning for ourselves beyond the obvious one of gorging our greedy pride with wind is for me only a final proof of idiotic vanity. No, Man does not yet deserve a soul. He is still the least human species of ape and because he is the only house-broken one we call him civilized—but we shouldn't be cheated by our own make-believe.

CHU YIN [*Smiling*] And the Great Kaan, the Son of Heaven, the Ruler of the World—?

KUBLAI [*Gaily now*] Is an ape who is bilious from surfeit; and you, Chu Yin, the sage, are an old monkey who makes solemn faces into a mirror and believes it is the window of eternity!

CHU YIN [*Laughing himself*] I am content. I like old monkeys.

KOKACHIN [*Who has been listening solemn and wide-eyed—suddenly*] And what am I?

KUBLAI You? You are a tiny golden bird singing beside a black river. [*He bends down and pats her head. Smilingly*] Sing, while you can. When the voice fails, listen to song. When the heart fails, be sung asleep. Go, Kokachin, tell the musicians in the garden to play meditatively—and bring back two cups of wine. [KOKACHIN *goes. A few moments later the orchestra in the garden can be heard playing softly, and* KOKACHIN *returns with the two cups of wine.* KUBLAI *and* CHU YIN *sit in contemplation, listening, sipping their wine and exchanging a few words every now and then.* KOKACHIN *sits at the foot of the throne, staring at* MARCO. *At the same moment,* MARCO *dashes down his brush, hands his copybook to his tutors with a grave flourish, gets up and stretches importantly and gives an enormous yawning sigh of relief. He then walks stiffly down to where his* FATHER *and* UNCLE *are squatting, as the two* PROFESSORS *pore over Marco's notebook*]

MARCO [*To his relatives, with assumed carelessness*] Well, thank God, that's over!

NICOLO Now your education's finished, what are you going to do with it? I hope palace life hasn't made you forget what you owe to Polo Brothers.

MAFFEO No, he's a good boy. Come, Mark, tell us your plans. Your father and I haven't had a talk with you in ages.

MARCO You've always been away on the road.

NICOLO We'd have been back much sooner if it wasn't for the Kaan's orders. [*Resentfully*] I suspect he wanted to keep us away from you—for some heathen purpose.

MAFFEO He's trying to make Mark over into an Easterner. [*Eyeing his nephew critically*] Well, I'm glad to say you don't seem to have changed much—a little fatter, maybe—but a Simon-pure Venetian still, every inch.

NICOLO [*Primly*] You haven't forgotten God, I hope?

MARCO [*Soberly*] I pray morning and night, rain or shine. In the morning before I take my twelve exercises, at night after I do them.

NICOLO   Do you ever think to write home?

MARCO   What's the use? I'd never get an answer. [*Then boyishly*] But I'll admit I do get homesick every once in a while when I stop to think. . . .

MAFFEO   [*Slyly*] Of Donata?

MARCO   Yes, her, of course—and the rest of the folks, too.

NICOLO   Don't neglect Donata. That marriage is, in every respect, an attractive merger.

MARCO   Oh, she'll wait—but will we ever get back there?

NICOLO   Well, with trade here so brisk—and you with a career just starting with everything in its favor—it's no time to think of leaving.

MARCO   No. Certainly not. I've got to make my pile first. [*With a sentimental sigh*] But, after all, there's no place like home, is there?

NICOLO   [*Sentimentally*] No, my boy, home is home!

MAFFEO   I'd give ten silver lire if I could hear one of our gondoliers singing right this minute!

MARCO   Remember how I used to feed the pigeons of St. Mark's?

NICOLO   There should be a municipal ordinance against those pigeons! [*Irritably*] They dirty up the window ledges for blocks around!

MAFFEO   [*Gives a final sigh to banish the subject*] Well, let's get back to brass tacks in Cathay! [*To* MARK, *briskly*] We've heard great reports of you. People say no outsider before ever had such a pull with the Kaan.

MARCO   [*Airily*] As far as that goes, I like him, too. He's a big man who's done big things and he's white even if his skin is yellow! He'd had those tutors keep my nose to the grindstone learning Tartar dialects and Chinese and foreign history and philosophy and ethics and economics and other high-brow impractical stuff, but I don't mind hard work and I guess I've proved to him I've got the stuff. I've gotten thoroughly well-informed and I can talk to him now about anything he picks out.

MAFFEO   And they also say you're the one original household pet of the granddaughter, the apple of the old gentleman's eye. [*With a wink*] Always play for the children first, if you want to sell to the grown-ups. It's a sound policy, Mark, my boy, proven by the ages, and I'm glad to see you took to it by instinct. You'll be able to write your check for a million yet, or I'm no prophet!

MARCO   [*Proudly*] Well, I don't know—that's a pretty big ideal and I don't pretend to be a genius—but if common sense and hard work can do it—[*Then embarrassedly*] But I honestly haven't been playing any game with the little

Princess. I like her. I and she are real pals. The poor kid's been lonely. She's the only grandchild the old man'll allow in the palace. Seems she's the only kid of his favorite daughter that died when she was born. [*Enthusiastically*] Kokachin's great fun! If it weren't for her, I'd have been bored stiff here. I've taught her lots of games. She's bright as a silver yen. And she's certainly taken to me, if I do say so myself. Kids always did like me, if you remember—and dogs, too.

MAFFEO [*Showing impatience but with forced heartiness*] I can well understand that. [*Then with abrupt, matter-of-fact shrewdness*] But let's talk business. Now you know all there is in books, the Kaan'll be giving you a regular job. [*Keenly*] What have you figured is your particular line?

MARCO Well,—business, naturally—and then I'd like some government job—it gives you a certain social standing—

MAFFEO [*Appreciatively*] Business and Politics—blended in the right mixture—that's always a winning combine! [*Then with a knowing wink*] And here's your opening wedge. Ask to be appointed a Second Class government commission agent.

MARCO [*Offendedly*] No, sir! I'll be first-class or nothing!

MAFFEO Don't get on your high horse. Listen to reason. A First Class agent is all brass buttons and no opportunities. A Second Class travels around, is allowed an expense account, gets in with all the dealers, learns how to pull wires, bluffs the small town trade into letting him in on everything—and gets what's coming to him! [*Then with a crafty look and a nudge in the ribs*] And, being always in the know, you'll be able to tip us off to all the gravy!

MARCO [*A bit flustered—with bluff assertion*] I don't know. I don't intend to be a grafter, I can tell you! The Kaan's been square with me and I'm going to be with him! After all, honesty's the best policy, Uncle, and pays best in the long run.

MAFFEO [*Looking him over soothingly*] No wonder dogs like you! [*Then angrily*] You'd think I was advising you to steal—I, Maffeo Polo, whose conservatism is unquestioned in any Chamber of Commerce on the green shores of the blue Mediterranean Sea!

MARCO [*Awed*] I didn't mean—

MAFFEO [*Solemnly*] Do you imagine the Kaan is such a Nero as to expect you to live on your salary? Do you think this Great Kind Silent Man wants to deliberately murder you by the horrible process of slow starvation?

MARCO [*Bewilderedly*] No, of course not.

MAFFEO [*Laying down the law*] There always have been and always will be such things as the legitimate privileges of office. They're recognized by the rules of the game—the big give-and-take game of life, my boy, in which the players aren't theorists but practical psychologists who understand their own and other human nature. [*Then with a grin and a wink*] It may not be as pure as you sing about in hymns, but none of us poor sinners can touch high C anyway.

NICOLO [*Who has been restraining his wrath*] You overgrown booby, do you dare insinuate your own father is a thief?

MARCO [*Flustered—hastily*] No, Dad, no—never for a second! I just wanted to be sure I was right—

NICOLO [*Mollified—nodding*] And now you can go ahead. That's the spirit, son!

MARCO [*After a pause—suddenly looking at* MAFFEO *with a crafty wink*] When I do give you a tip, what's in it for me from Polo Brothers?

MAFFEO [*Between appreciation and dismay*] Ha! You learn quickly, don't you? [*Then hastily*] Why, we—your dear old doting father and your uncle who helped teach you to walk when you were a little rascal so high—we've already thought of that—trust us to look after your best interests—and decided to—to make you a junior partner in the firm—eh, Nick?—Polo Brothers and Son, doesn't that sound bully, eh!

MARCO [*Reservedly*] It's a great honor, gentlemen—a very great honor. [*Then meaningly*] But as neither of you are Neros, naturally you'll also offer me a living wage to support this honor in proper style.

MAFFEO [*Grinning in spite of himself*] Hmm! Hmm! You Judas!

MARCO And a fair commission on all deals I swing your way.

NICOLO [*Blustering—but his eyes beaming with paternal pride*] You young scamp!

MAFFEO [*Laughing*] Ha-ha! Kiss me, Mark, and kiss your Old Man! Polos will be Polos! [*They all kiss laughingly*] And now that's settled, let's sit down and forget business and have a real family chat. [*They do so*] Tell us some of the inside stuff about high life here in the palace. We've heard rumors—but you know how the folks always gossip about kings—nothing but envy I say—so we've let such stories go in one ear and out the other. [*Edging closer*] But is it straight goods about the two hundred concubines?

MARCO [*With a blasé air*] Oh, the old Guv'nor's got more than that, I guess. No one keeps count. His domestic affairs aren't run on any efficient system.

NICOLO [*His eyes popping a bit*] And do you see—those females—often?

MARCO You're bumping into 'em all the time. Some of 'em are pretty—in their way. The Kaan made me a present of one—a nice one, too!

MAFFEO [*Gloatingly*] No! What did you do with her?

MARCO [*With a suggestive smirk. Heavily sarcastic*] I gave her my blessing and told her little girls ought to go to bed early—what did you suppose? [NICOLO *and* MAFFEO *laugh uproariously*]

MAFFEO [*Elatedly*] He's learning! And who said he didn't have a sense of humor?

MARCO But Kokachin got jealous of her being around—the funny way kids do—and she disappeared and the next I heard they had her hitched in a span with a big mule, hauling ore down in the mercury mines. The work was telling on her figure, they said. [*Philosophically*] Well, I didn't wish her any harm, but I was honestly glad to be alone again. She'd gotten too familiar, hinting all the time about how marriage had been tested by time and proved to be the only workable love-relationship—and all such slop.

MAFFEO They're all alike—whether they're free women or not—all they want is to tie a man down. [*Then eagerly*] Speaking of concubines reminds me, Mark. Here's a lulu I heard up in Siberia. A man who's making a good little thing out of melting down Polar bear fat into beauty lotions told it to me. It seems there was a hot-blooded Esquimo dame whose husband made her live with him in an icehouse and—[*Their heads bend together as his voice gets lower with much dialect pantomime. At this point, the two* PROFESSORS, *having finished going over Marco's copy book, approach the throne and bow low.* KOKACHIN *gets up and comes down to edge of forestage trying to attract Marco's attention*]

CLASSICIST Our task is finished, Sire.

KUBLAI [*Makes a sign. The musicians cease playing. His interest aroused—with smiling anticipation*] You have educated his mind to knowledge?

SCIENTIST All it would hold, Sire.

CLASSICIST [*With a grim smile*] In a way, you might say he has been educating us.

KUBLAI [*Smacking his lips*] You arouse my curiosity. For three years now I have observed him off and on—and yet this young example of Western philosophy remains an enigma; but I hope you, with your more intimate observation—

CLASSICIST [*Shaking his head*] No.

SCIENTIST [*Ditto*] No.

BOTH [*Together*] Wisdom stops where he begins. [MAFFEO *finishes his joke. The three* POLOS *rock with suppressed laughter, a ha-ha breaking out in spite of them every now and again.* KOKACHIN *catches* MARCO's *eye and beckons him to come to her. He puts his hand to his lips—warningly*] Ssstt! It's the Princess. I've got to go. [*He gets up—goes to her—they sit down side by side and presently are absorbingly engaged in a game of jackstraws*]

KUBLAI Did he not learn readily?

BOTH He has learned everything and learned nothing from it.

CLASSICIST He is a shrewd numskull.

SCIENTIST He is a clever moron.

CLASSICIST He is a muddy materialist, a grubber after the facts, a belly-dreamer! He is blind to the spiritual and adores Matter as his gross God. He should make a renowned and edifying scientist. [*He bows mockingly to him*]

SCIENTIST [*Coldly*] On the contrary, he is a mystic idealist. He uses his fabricated facts as narcotics to escape from the scientific truth into infantile fantasies. He knows nothing of Matter, not even his own body of which he is piously ashamed, and he worships a grey-whiskered Ghost with a bad temper whose address is a golden street somewhere in the sky. So obviously he should make a famous philosopher or a worker in the arts. [*He bows in turn. Both glare at each other*]

KUBLAI [*Amused*] Come! No professional rivalry! But surely this youth must have some good qualities—

CLASSICIST He has what he himself calls the sterling virtues. As near as I can determine from his generalizing these seem to be compulsory honesty, compulsory chastity for women only, compulsory love of one's wife, children, country and God and compulsory heroism in their defense.

KUBLAI But, in dealing with materials, has he no imagination?

SCIENTIST [*Grimly*] He contrived a plan for a perpetual motion machine explaining that, of course, it would never do to have it really run forever as then there'd be no market for next year's models. [*He cannot help smiling at this notion*]

KUBLAI [*To the philosopher*] And does he ever discuss philosophy—or the religion of Christ?

CLASSICIST He asserts pessimism is all a fake, and that it would be a great little old world if it weren't for some people. He believes their Christ was a flesh and blood Son of a Deity and that anyone who denies it is either a dirty, malicious liar, trying to make trouble, or else not responsible. But when I quoted some of the wise sayings of Christ, hoping to correct and inspire him, he cursed and said he'd like to meet whoever the damned Anarchist was who wrote such red rot—so he could punch him in the nose. [*He smiles*]

KUBLAI [*Smiling himself*] But you are both smiling. There is even affection in your eyes. Can it be possible that you like this monstrosity?

BOTH [*Shamefacedly*] There is something about him.

CLASSICIST He reminds me of my pet chimpanzee of whom I am very fond.

SCIENTIST He displays the laughable cunning of a tame crow hoarding shells.

CLASSICIST His sayings are as naively remarkable as a parrot's!

SCIENTIST He is as amazingly adolescent as a chow puppy.

CLASSICIST When he gloats over his own shrewdness his face wears the enigmatic charm of an altered tom cat who purrs with content, ignorant of lack in his perfect world.

KUBLAI [*Amusedly*] Then, in your judgment, the only valuable talent he has is that of an amazing clown?

SCIENTIST Oh no! He will make a useful statesman for you. Or a judge.

CLASSICIST Or a merchant prince. Or a High Priest.

BOTH Or—anything else requiring merely the primitive, acquisitive instincts—

KUBLAI Then he possesses no soul of any discoverable mortal or immortal variety?

CLASSICIST [*With a smile*] Yes—on his feet!

SCIENTIST Two souls—to be scientifically exact! [*They both laugh foolishly*]

KUBLAI [*Dryly*] I can see by your humor he has been educating you. [*Then dismissing them*] Your report is comprehensive but not illuminating. You may withdraw, gentlemen. [*With offended dignity they back out right, bowing stiffly.* KUBLAI *turns to* CHU YIN *and they both smile*] So much for education! And now, my wise friend, can you make another guess at the human riddle? [*He indicates* MARCO] Did their Pope mean that a fool is a wiser study for a ruler of fools than a hundred wise men could be? [*Then, observing* MARCO *who is now much interested in his game with* KOKACHIN—*with affection*] Look, see how he plays with her. She loves him. What does she sense in him?—his soul?—the secret of his Pope?—but it must be some fundamental goodness, don't you think.

CHU YIN It is that spiritually he is the same age as she. Life is to him an earnest game of jackstraws.

KUBLAI [Nodding] He touches me—as a child might—but, at the same time, there is something warped, undernourished, deformed—a morbid possibility of evil in his retarded growth—. Tell me, what shall I do with him?

CHU YIN Let him develop according to his own wish. Give him every opportunity and incentive for true growth if he so chooses. Let us observe. At least, if he cannot learn, we shall.

KUBLAI [Thoughtfully] Yes. That is best. [Then, dismally] And now for the first step. [He calls commandingly] Marco Polo, attend me! [MARCO gets up rather frightenedly and comes toward the throne]

KOKACHIN [Encouragingly taking his hand] Don't be afraid, you goose! I won't let him hurt you!

MARCO [Gratefully] Thanks. You're all right. [They get to the throne. MARCO kneels. KOKACHIN perches by her grandfather. The two elder POLOS crane their necks, straining their ears]

MAFFEO He must ask now—strike while the iron is hot!

NICOLO He looks frightened, the big booby!

KUBLAI Rise. [MARCO does so] Your tutors' report is favorable. I can now start you upon any career you choose. Have you decided—

MARCO [Promptly] I'd like to be appointed a commission-agent of the Second Class.

KUBLAI [Somewhat taken aback—puzzledly] You are modest enough! Why this singularly humble choice?

MARCO [Manfully] I want to start at the bottom! I want hard work that'll keep me traveling and seeing all angles of the world.

KOKACHIN [Imperiously] Don't let him, Grandfather! I want him to stay here and be a soldier.

MARCO [Quickly] But I've got no natural ability in the military line, Little Princess! It may sound cowardly to say so but I can't see any fun in killing people. And besides, whoever heard of a really rich soldier? I want to be a genuine success, not a stuffed uniform. [Wheedlingly] And have lots of money so I can send you a toy back from every place I go—

KUBLAI [Smiling] This is rank bribery, Little Flower!

KOKACHIN [Her mouth beginning to fall] I've got all the toys I want. [Wheedling in her turn] Please be a soldier, Mark! If you knew what a hero you'd look—

MARCO [*Firmly—resisting temptation*] No. I said no and that settles it. I thought you were my friend.

KOKACHIN [*Huskily*] Well then, all right for you, I don't care, let him have his pig-headed way, Grandfather. [*She hides her face with her hands*]

KUBLAI [*With mocking grandeur*] Arise then, Second Class Mark. You will receive your agent's commission and start on your official duties at once. Each time you return from your travels you must report to me and state your personal observations and comments on the people of each locality, their customs, prosperity, religious views, morality and so on. Be warned and never dare fail me in this!

MARCO [*Cocksuredly*] Don't worry. I'll never fail, I'll take copious notes. [*Then meaningly*] And I can memorize any little humorous incidents or tales—

MAFFEO [*Apprehensively*] Blessed Savior, preserve us. He's going to tell a funny story. [*He gives a violent fit of coughing*]

MARCO [*Looks around at them questioningly*] Hum! [*Misinterpreting this sign*] And, may I announce to your Majesty, a signal honor has just been conferred on me. . . .

KUBLAI An honor? I would hardly—you need not thank me—

MARCO Not that—but my father and uncle have taken me into the firm— will be Polo Brothers and Son now—and any way we can serve your Majesty—

KUBLAI [*A light coming over his face*] Aha! I begin to smell all the rats in Cathay! [*The two elder* POLOS *are bowed to the ground, trembling with apprehension.* KUBLAI *suddenly laughs quietly*] Marvelous! Well—I am sure you wish to celebrate this family triumph together—and as you have given me some deep reflecting to do— [*The two elders hurry up and, after bowing frightenedly, sieze* MARK *one by each arm and try to hustle him off right.* KUBLAI *rings a gong and a* CHAMBERLAIN *enters*] Quick! As a symbol of my delighted anticipation of the future services to my State of Messers Polo Brothers and Son, let my full symphony orchestra play a triumphal march as they leave the palace! [*The* CHAMBERLAIN *darts away. The* POLOS, *reassured now, bow themselves out with smiles of astonished gratification, but* MARCO *stops for a parting climactic speech*]

MARCO [*Politely*] Thank you, your Majesty. I'm fond of music—and I will always serve your best interests, so help me God, to the height of my ability; and of hard work and the will to succeed—[*He goes grandly.* KUBLAI *laughs and turns to* CHU YIN, *who is smiling but pointing rather sadly to* KOKACHIN, *who is now shaking with sobs*]

KUBLAI [*Putting his arms around her and taking her on his lap—consol-*

ingly] There! There! You mustn't weep, Little Flower! Princesses must learn never to weep.

KOKACHIN   I want him to stay home with me! I want him to be a hero!

KUBLAI   [*With gentle cynicism*] Even a Princess must not expect too much of men. But, be comforted, I prophesy that some day he will surely lead a parade in a brighter uniform with more bands than any hero ever did! [*As he finishes speaking, the full imperial band in the garden bursts into a military march with a deafening clangor of gongs and cymbals*]

KOKACHIN   [*Dashing her tears aside and rushing to the window*] Oh, I want to see! I want to see! [*Then suddenly beginning to laugh*] What is he taking off his hat for? Oh, isn't he crazy! He's trying to shake the right hand of the leader!

CURTAIN

ACT FIVE   SCENE ONE

SCENE: *Same as Act Four. About twelve years later. The* KAAN *is seated in the same position on his bamboo throne. He has aged greatly. The expression of his face has grown mask-like, full of a philosophic calm. He has the detached air of an idol.* KOKACHIN, *now a beautiful young girl of twenty, very pale and delicate, is sitting at the foot of the throne, much as she did when a child. Her air is crushed and grief-stricken. A flute player in the garden is playing a melancholy air.* KOKACHIN *recites in a low tone:*

KOKACHIN   My thoughts in this autumn are lonely and sad.
A chill wind from the mountain blows in the garden.
The sky is grey, a snow flake falls, the last
   chrysanthemum
Withers beside the deserted summer-house.
I walk along the path in which weeds have grown.
My heart is bitter and tears blur my eyes.
I grieve for the days when we lingered together
In this same garden, along these paths between flowers.
In the spring we sang of love and laughed with youth
But now we are parted by many leagues and years.
And I weep that never again shall I see your face.

[*She finishes and relapses into her attitude of broken resignation. The flute player ceases his playing.* KUBLAI *looks down at her tenderly*]

KUBLAI   [*Chidingly*] That's a sad poem for youth, Little Flower. Are you sad because you must soon become Queen of Persia? But Arghun is a great hero, a Khan of the blood of Chinghiz. He'll make you a noble husband. You'll be blessed with strong sons who will become Khans and fulfill the destiny of our blood.

KOKACHIN [*Dully*] Your will is my law.

KUBLAI Not mine. The will of life to preserve and continue the strong. [*Forcing a consoling tone*] Come, Little Flower. You've been fading here. See how pale you've grown! Your eyes are listless, your lips droop even in smiling! But life at the Court of Persia is gay. There will be feasts, celebrations, diverting pleasures. You'll be their Queen of beauty; Poets will sing of you in strange new songs; life will be painted over with fresh color—

KOKACHIN [*With a sigh*] Queen of Persia or her lowest slave, each may be only a woman who is unhappy. [*Forcing a joking tone*] Do you want me to be cheated by appearances. I'll have to tell Chu Yin he hasn't thoroughly converted you to wisdom yet!

KUBLAI Wisdom is the youth of old age—but youth is its own wisdom. Be! Feel! Don't invite sorrow by seeking to know.

KOKACHIN My youth contains no happiness—

KUBLAI [*Teasingly*] What despair! You're like the languishing ladies in poems who have lost a lover! [KOKACHIN *gives a violent start which he does not notice and a spasm of pain comes over her face*] You, who have driven every prince in my realm to the verge of suicide with your indifference! But, never mind, Arghun of Persia is a hero no woman could fail to love—

KOKACHIN [*Starting to her feet—desperately*] No! I can be his wife, I can bear his children, but you cannot force me to—[*She breaks down, weeping*]

KUBLAI [*Astonished—gazing at her searchingly—tenderly*] Have I ever forced you to anything? [*A pause—decisively*] I shall tell his ambassadors he must select someone else.

KOKACHIN [*Recovering herself—resolutely*] No. Your refusal would insult him, and Persia would become your enemy. It might mean war with your brother's son. [*Resignedly*] And Arghun is as acceptable as any other. Forgive my weakness. You once told me a Princess must never weep. [*She forces a smile*] It make no difference whether I stay or go—except that I shall be homesick for you. [*She kisses his hand again*]

KUBLAI [*Gratefully*] Little Daughter of my Heart! [*He strokes her hair. After a pause during which he looks at her thoughtfully—tenderly*] We have never had secrets from each other, you and I. Tell me, can you really have fallen in love at last?

KOKACHIN   [*After a pause—tremblingly*] You must not ask—if you respect my pride! [*With a pitiful smile*] You see, I am not loved.

KUBLAI   [*Vehemently*] Nonsense! There can't be such a fool!

KOKACHIN   He does not know—[*Then immediately defensive*] He isn't a fool. No one can say that. He may seem strange, perhaps, to people who don't understand him, but that's only because he's so different from other men. [*Then lamely*] I don't believe even I know him well enough to explain to you his— what I can feel in him—[*She is blushing and hanging her head with confusion.* CHU YIN *enters hurriedly from the right. He is very old but still upright. He is a bit breathless from haste but his face is wreathed in smiles.* KOKACHIN *makes his entrance an excuse for hurrying out at left.* KUBLAI *stares after her frowning*]

CHU YIN   [*Making an obeisance*] Your Majesty, I intrude to warn you of approaching joy. [*He is smiling*] Listen. Do you hear that martial music? His Honor, Marco Polo, mayor of Yang Chau, is about to visit you in state! [*The strains of a distant band can be heard*]

KUBLAI   [*Still looking after* KOKACHIN—*half-preoccupied*] Impossible! [*Then to* CHU YIN] Eh? Marco? I've given no orders for him to return.

CHU YIN   [*Ironically*] A good servant anticipates his master's wish! No doubt he foresaw you'd be getting bored and he comes to refresh your humor with new copious notes on our manners and customs.

KUBLAI   [*Beguiled into smiling*] Marco has made an active mayor. Yang-Chau, according to a petition for mercy I've received from its inhabitants, is the most governed of all my cities.

CHU YIN   I talked with a poet who had fled from there in terror. Yang-Chau used to have a soul, he said. Now it has a brand new Court House. And another, a man of wide culture told me, our Christian mayor is exterminating our pleasures and our rats as if they were twin breeds of vermin. [*The voice of the band has grown louder.* KOKACHIN *enters again from the left. Her face is flushed, excited*]

KOKACHIN   Who is coming? It sounds like the band of—[*Embarrassedly*] His honor the Mayor of Yang-Chau!

CHU YIN   [*Teasingly*] You are very formal about your former playmate— and how can you recognize his band at such a distance?

KOKACHIN   [*Eagerly*] Then it is he? [*She claps her hands and cannot restrain her frank exhibitions of joy*]

KUBLAI   [*Whose eyes are searching her face—suddenly aghast*] Kokachin! [*She looks up at him, sees he has guessed her secret, at first quails and shrinks, then gradually stiffens regally and returns his gaze unflinchingly.* CHU YIN *looks from one to the other comprehendingly. Finally* KUBLAI *addresses her sternly*] I shall inform the ambassadors you will be ready to sail for Persia within ten days. You may retire. [*She bows with a proud humility and walks off left.* KUBLAI *sits in a somber study, frowning and biting his lips. The blaring of the band grows steadily nearer*]

CHU YIN   [*Gently*] Is intolerance wisdom? [*A pause. Then he goes on*] I have suspected her love for him for a long time.

KUBLAI   Why didn't you warn me?

CHU YIN   Love is to wisdom what wisdom seems to love—a folly. I reasoned, loves come like the shadow of wind on water and is gone leaving calm and reflection. I reasoned, but this is an enchanted moment and it will remain a poignant memory to recompense her when she is no longer a girl but only a Queen. And I reasoned, who knows but some day this Marco will see into her eyes and his soul may be born and that will make a very interesting study—for Kokachin, and her grandfather, the Son of Heaven and Ruler of the World. [*He bows mockingly*]—And for the old fool who is I.

KUBLAI   [*Exasperatedly*] I can't believe Kokachin can be so incredibly tasteless! What could she ever see—? Besides, since she was a little girl, she has only talked to him once or twice every two years or more!

CHU YIN   That was unwise—for thus he has remained a strange, a mysterious dream knight from the exotic West, an enigma with something about him of a likeable boy who brought her home each time a humble, foolish, touching little gift! And also remember that on each occasion he returned in triumph, having accomplished a given task, a success, a victor, more or less, acting the hero. [*The band has crashed and dinned its way into the courtyard*]

KUBLAI   [*Exasperatedly*] But, most grotesque of all, she says he doesn't know it, does not love her! But that I simply can't believe!

CHU YIN   I can. He is a monogamist in love. He remains blindly faithful to his first and only mate—himself. [*He goes to the window and looks down— with ironical but intense amusement*] Ah! He wears the regalia of an Exalted Cock of Paradise in his secretly organized fraternal order of the Mystic Knights of Confucius over his mayor's uniform! The band of the Xandu lodge is with him as well as his own! He is riding on a very fat, white horse. He dismounts, aided by the steps of your Imperial Palace! He slaps a policeman on the back and asks his name! He chucks a baby under the chin and asks the mother its name. She lies and says Marco although the baby is a girl. He smiles. He is talking loudly so the reporters can overhear. He gives the baby one yen to start a savings bank account and encourage its thrift. The mother looks savagely disappointed. The crowd cheers. He keeps his smile frozen as he notices an artist sketching him. He shakes hands with a one-legged veteran of the Manzi campaign and asks his name. The veteran is touched. Tears come to his eyes. He tells him—but the Polo forgets his name even as he turns to address the crowd. [*The band stops*] He waves one hand for silence. It is the hand on which he wears five large jade rings. The other hand alternately rests upon—and pats— the head of a bronze dragon, our ancient symbol of Yang, the celestial, male principle of the Cosmos. He clears his throat, the crowd stands petrified, he is about to draw a deep breath and open his mouth carefully in position A of the five phonetic exercises—[*Here* CHU YIN *chuckles*] *but* I am an old man full of malice and venom and it embitters me to see others unreasonably happy so— [*Here just as* MARCO *is heard starting to speak, he throws open the window and calls in a loud, commanding tone*] Messer Polo, His Imperial Majesty, the Great Kaan, commands that you stop talking, dismiss your followers, and repair to his presence at once!

MARCO'S VOICE   [*Very faint and crestfallen*] Oh—all right—I'll be right there.

KUBLAI   [*Cannot control a laugh in spite of himself—helplessly*] How can one deal seriously with such a child actor?

CHU YIN   [*Coming back from the window—ironically*] Women, including Kokachin, love children—and must take acting seriously in order to love at all. [*Just as he finishes speaking,* KOKACHIN *enters from the left. She is terribly alarmed. She throws herself at Kublai's feet*]

KOKACHIN   Why did you summon him? Why were you so stern? Surely you won't punish him? He knows nothing! It's all my fault! Punish me, if you will! But promise you won't harm him!

KUBLAI   [*Looking down at her—sadly*] Is it my custom to take vengeance—? [*Then as people are heard approaching—quickly*] Compose yourself! Remember again, Princesses may not weep! [*She springs to her feet, turns away for a moment, then turns back her face rigidly calm and emotionless.* KUBLAI *nods with appreciation of her control*] Good. You will make a Queen. [*She bows and retires backward to the left side of throne. At the same moment,* NICOLO *and* MAFFEO POLO *enter ceremoniously from the right. They wear the regalia of officers in the Mystic Knights of Confucius over their rich merchants' robes. (This costume resembles a queer jumble of the parade uniforms of our Knights Templar, of Columbus, of Pathias, Mystic Shriners, etc. etc., including the Ku Klux Klan.) They are absurdly conscious and proud of this get-up. Like two old men in a children's play.* KUBLAI *and* CHU YIN *regard them with amused astonishment. Even* KOKACHIN *cannot restrain a smile. They prostrate themselves at the foot of the throne*]

KUBLAI   You may rise, Messers Polo. I am glad to see you well and prosperous. But where is my loyal servitor, Marco?

NICOLO   He stopped to wash his hands.

MAFFEO   He wanted to comb his hair.

BOTH   [*As if reciting something they had memorized*] It is the unanimous opinion, except among certain radicals and subversive elements of the lowest class, that Marco Polo has made the best mayor Yang-Chau ever had.

NICOLO   The streets are clean.

MAFFEO   Property booms.

NICOLO   The city pays.

MAFFEO   The grafters are out.

NICOLO   The police are purged.

MAFFEO   Houses of ill fame—

NICOLO   And theatres closed.

BOTH   But sacred concerts may be licensed in barrel houses, hooker shanties, dance halls, and peep shows. Mark does not wish to restrict legitimate entertainment.

NICOLO   He has given the city a marble court house.

MAFFEO   And a granite jail.

NICOLO   Passed ten thousand laws per year.

MAFFEO   Instituted beneficent new charities.

NICOLO   A magnificent asylum for Indigent Members of the Chamber of Commerce.

MAFFEO   And a white marble Home for aged Venetian Christians.

NICOLO   Fitted out with a swimming pool, a harem, and a race track.

MAFFEO   Since our departure—to let.

BOTH   Throughout Cathay and Manzi Yang-Chau is now known as the City of Married Mothers!

NICOLO   One hundred bronze medals are pinned yearly on the poorest fathers who have begotten the most numerous offspring.

MAFFEO   This promotes a sporting rivalry in home industries.

NICOLO   And, as Mark patriotically foresaw,

MAFFEO   Will in time restore to a healthy activity,

NICOLO   Army and navy recruiting.

MAFFEO And—[*He "goes up" in his lines, looks at* NICOLO *as if for a cue*]

NICOLO   [*Embarrassedly*] And—

BOTH   [*Suddenly hitting on their finale in chorus*] And he is universally beloved by rich and poor, high and low alike. Every man in Yang-Chau respects him, every woman admires him. The young folks regard him as one of the gang, the kiddies treat him like a big brother, the dogs know him as their two-legged pal—[*They stop abruptly. In this prepared silence, just at the right moment, preceded by an important cough,* MARCO POLO *makes his entrance. Over his gorgeous uniform of Mayor, he wears his childishly fantastic regalia as chief of the Mystic Knights of Confucius. As he steps on, he takes off his gilded, laced hat with its Bird of Paradise plumes and bows with a mechanical dignity on all sides. He has the manner and appearance of a successful movie star at a masquerade ball, disguised so that no one can fail to recognize him. His regular well-groomed face is carefully arranged into the grave responsible expression of a modern Southern Senator about to propose an amendment to the Constitution restricting the migration of non-Nordic birds into Texas—or prohibiting the practice of the laws of biology within the twelve-mile limit. He moves in stately fashion to the throne and prostrates himself before the* KAAN. KOKACHIN *stares at him with boundless admiration, hoping to catch his eye. The* KAAN *looks from her to him and his face grows stern.* CHU YIN *is enjoying himself*]

KUBLAI   Rise. [MARCO *does so.* KUBLAI *continues dryly*] To what do I owe the honor of this unexpected visit?

MARCO   [*Hastily, but with full confidence*] Well, it's like this: I was sending in to your treasury the net tax profit of Yang-Chau for the fiscal year, and I know you'd be so astonished and pleased at the unprecedented amount I had sweated out of them that you'd want to know how I did it—so I just made up my mind I'd travel right along with the coin caravan, and here I am. [*An awkward pause.* MARCO *is disconcerted at the Kaan's steady impersonal stare. He glances about—sees the* PRINCESS—*welcomes this opportunity for a diverting of attention. Bowing with humble respect*] Excuse me, Princess. I didn't recognize you before, you've gotten so grown up. [*Flatteringly*] You look like a Queen.

KOKACHIN   [*Falteringly*] I bid you welcome, Your Honor.

KUBLAI   [*As a warning to* KOKACHIN *to control her emotion*] The Princess will soon be a Queen of Persia.

MARCO [*Flustered and awed, bowing to her again—flatteringly*] Then—
Your Majesty—if I may be humbly permitted [*Bowing to* KUBLAI] before I settle
down to discussing business—if her Highness—Majesty—will accept a small
token of my esteem—[*Here he stamps his foot. An African* SLAVE, *dressed in a
pink livery with green hat and shoes and stockings and carrying a golden jar
enters. He kneels, presents the jar to* MARCO, *who lifts the cover and pulls out a
small rubber plant in a gilded flower pot with a pink ribbon tied to the stem.
He steps forward and offers this to the* PRINCESS] A contribution to your conser-
vatory. I suddenly remembered that two months ago was your birthday.

KOKACHIN [*Taking it—flushing with pleasure*] Oh, isn't it dear! So
strange looking! Such an exquisite green! I've never seen anything like it before!

MARCO [*Boastfully*] It's a genuine rubber plant. I procured it at great—
hum—I mean it's exceedingly rare, a native of the mysterious feverish gloom
of tropic forests—

KOKACHIN Oh thank you, Mark—[*Stammering*]—I mean, Your Honor.

KUBLAI [*Warningly*] His Honor wishes to talk business, Princess.

KOKACHIN [*Controlling herself*] I ask pardon. [*She bows and retires to left,
rear, where she stands fondling her plant and watching* MARCO]

MARCO [*Plunging in on what he thinks is his best bet*] My tax scheme,
Your Majesty, that got such wonderful results is simplicity itself. I simply re-
versed the old system. For one thing I found they had a high tax on excess
profits. Imagine a profit being excess! Why, it isn't humanly possible! A profit
is always a fair profit, that's the basis of all economic justice. That fool tax was
embarrassing business and the best firms were talking of pulling up stakes and
moving from town. I repealed it and I also repealed the tax on luxuries. I found
out the great majority in Yang-Chau couldn't afford luxuries. The tax wasn't
democratic enough to make it a paying proposition. I crossed it off and I wrote
on the statute books a fool-proof law that taxes every necessity in life from
polished rice to rickets medicine, a law that hits every man's pocket equally, be
he beggar or banker! And I got results!

CHU YIN [*Gravely*] In beggars?

MARCO [*Undecidedly whether this is a joke, ventures a forced*] Ha! [*Then
quickly*] But speaking of beggars, I've practically done away with unemployment.
To practise unemployment in Yang-Chau now you have to have passed a Civil
Service examination, and if you're caught without a license, you're heavily
fined. You'll hardly find a beggar on the streets any more.

CHU YIN [*Genially*] I suppose they're all well provided for—in jail.

MARCO [*Coldly*] I really can't say offhand. I'm not the Superintendent of Prisons. But they don't annoy people in public, always begging for jobs, I'm confident of that. [*A pause.* KUBLAI *stares at him. He becomes flustered again—suddenly turns to* MAFFEO] Uncle, give His Majesty the figures on what we calculated would be his net profit yearly if he applied my system of taxation to every man, woman and child in his empire.

MAFFEO   [*Rolls out an account book and reads glibly*] Five hundred and twenty-one billion, nine hundred and eighty-seven million, four hundred and sixty-five thousand, three hundred and forty-two gold yen!

MARCO   [*Enthusiastically*] Grand, isn't it? Sounds too good to be true—but figures don't lie! [*He taps the book in his uncle's hand. A pause. The* POLOS *grow extremely uncomfortable, and* MARCO *hurt and offended at his cold reception*]

KUBLAI   [*After a pause—with a chilling casual air*] I have received an urgent petition from the inhabitants of Yang-Chau enumerating over three thousand cases of your gross abuse of power, and imploring me to remove you from office before all their natural liberties as human beings are completely abolished.

MARCO   [*Abashed only for a moment*] Oh, so they've sent that vile slander to you, have they? That's the work of the radicals, the immoral minority who hate a strong hand at the helm—

KUBLAI   [*Dryly*] Five hundred thousand names are signed to it.

MARCO   [*With a wink*] Yes, I've heard they've had their agents out copying down names in all the old cemeteries.

KUBLAI   [*Still more dryly*] Members of the oldest clans and noblest families are represented.

MARCO   A few boudoir reformers! Liberals! She-men! I know 'em! They think the world would be wrecked if they didn't write one editorial a week about other unskilled labor. [*Philosophically*] Well, if they weren't monkeying in politics, they'd be losing stitches in grandma's knitting—or doing something else to encourage revolution. [*Warmly*] They ought to be exiled for life to a Lecture Bureau for Women's Clubs.

KUBLAI   [*Meaningly*] Half a million citizens accuse you of endeavoring to stamp out their ancient culture!

MARCO   Why? Because their culture is old-timey and, as they have to acknowledge, ancient. I'm not opposed to culture as long as it keeps up to date and coming. I think, in some ways, it's a good moral influence. Why, I even had a law passed that anyone caught interfering with or obstructing culture, would be subject to a heavy fine. It was the last law but one I thought up. The last was a blanket statute that every citizen must be happy or go to jail. I find it's the unhappy ones who are always making trouble and getting discontented. Well, a good stiff sentence is just the right medicine to convince such folks that they've got a whole lot to be happy about when they're out of prison. You see, here's the way I figure it: If a man's good, he's happy—and if he isn't happy, it's a sure sign he's no good to himself or anyone else and he better be put where he can't do harm.

KUBLAI [A bit helplessly now] Their chief complaint is that you have entirely prohibited all free expression of opinion.

MARCO [Feelingly] Well, when they go to the extremes of circulating such treasonable opinions as that petition contains, isn't it time for me to protect your sovereignty against their lawless agitators by strong measures? [KUBLAI stares at this effrontery with amazement. MARCO watches this impression and hurries on with an injured dignity] But I decline to stoop to defend myself against their foul insinuations—except to say there exists not a scintilla of evidence to support their infamous charges. I fear, however, that your Majesty's opinion has been unduly influenced, that those vampires in human form may have alienated your former affection for my character—

KUBLAI [Conquered—suddenly overpowered by a great smile] Not so! You are a marvel of mankind—and I would be lost without you!

MARCO [Flattered but at the same time non-plussed] I thank you! I thank you! [Hesitatingly] But, to tell the truth—I want to resign anyhow. I've gotten— I mean, I've done all I could. I've appointed five hundred and two committees, each from a separate Bureau I've had established, to carry on my work and I quit, confident in the knowledge that with the system I've instituted everything will go on automatically and brains are no longer needed. [He adds as a bitter afterthought] And it's lucky they're not or Yang-Chau would be sunk.

KUBLAI [With mock seriousness] In behalf of the population of Yang-Chau I accept your resignation—with deep regret for the loss of your unique and extraordinary services. [Then suddenly in a strange voice] Do you still possess your immortal soul, Marco Polo?

MARCO [Flustered] Ha-ha! Yes, of course, at least I hope so. But I see the joke. You mean that Yang-Chau used to be a good place to lose one. Well, you wouldn't know the old town now. Sin is practically unseen. [Hurrying on to another subject—boisterously] But however much I may have accomplished there in your service, it is nothing to the big surprise I've got in reserve for you. May I demonstrate? I won't take a second of your time. [Without waiting for permission] Good. [Takes a piece of printed paper like a dollar bill from his *pocket*] What is it? Paper, you answer. Correct! But what is it worth? Practically nothing, you say. Oh, but that's where you're mistaken. It's worth ten yen. No, I'm not a liar! See ten written on it, don't you? Well, I'll tell you the secret. This is paper money—legal tender to the value of ten yen's worth of anything you wish to buy—by order of His Imperial Majesty, the Great Kaan and guaranteed by his command. Its advantages over gold and silver coin are obvious. It's handy, light, easy to carry. [*Here he gives a prodigious wink*] Wears out quickly, can be turned out in bulk at very slight expense and yields a perfectly enormous profit. Think of getting ten yen for this piece of paper. Yet it can be done. If you make the people believe it's worth it, it's so. After all, when you stop to think, who was it first told them gold was money? I'll bet my last shirt it was some far-sighted, quick-thinker who'd just discovered a gold mine! [KUBLAI *and* CHU YIN *stare at him in petrified incredulity. He mistakes it for admiration and is flattered. Bows and lays his paper money on the Kaan's knee*] You're flabbergasted, I can see that. Paper money! It's as simple—and yet, whoever hit on it before me? I was knocked out too. Think it over, Your Majesty, and let the endless possibilities dawn on you! And now I want to show another little first aid to your government that I thought out. [*He makes a sign to his uncle and father. The former takes a mechanical contrivance out of a box and sets it up on the floor. It is a working model of a clumsy cannon.* NICOLO, *meanwhile, takes children's blocks out of his box and builds them into a fortress wall. Meanwhile* MARCO *is talking. His manner and voice have become grave and portentous*] It all came to me, like an inspiration, last Easter Sunday when Dad and Uncle and I were holding a little service. Uncle read a prayer which spoke of Our Lord Jesus [*The three* POLOS *bless themselves*] as the Prince of Peace. Somehow, that took hold of me. I thought to myself, well, it's funny, there always have been wars and there always will be, I guess, because I've never read much in any history about heroes who waged peace. Still, that's the wrong idea. There's a leak in the process of progress somewhere. War is a waste of labor and material which eats into the dividends of life like thunder! Then why war, I asked myself? Why not a lasting peace with profit? But isn't war a natural resource of our human natures, poisoned at birth by the justice of God with original sin? How are you going to end it? Then the flash came and gave me the answer! There's only one workable way and that's to lick everybody else in the world so soundly that they'll never dare to fight you again! A tough proposition, you object? Not any more! This little invention you see before you makes conquering easy. Let me demonstrate with these working models. On our right, you see a fortress wall of a hostile capital of some cantankerous country that's forced you to use force. Under your present inefficient system of besieging with battering rams, to make an effective paying breach in this wall would cost you the lives of ten thousand men. Valuing each life conservatively at ten yen, this mounts up to one hundred thousand yen. This darn near makes the cost of breaching prohibitive. But all of this waste can be saved. How? Just keep your eyes peeled on your right and permit Mark Polo's exclusive invention, Little David, the Giant-Killer, to solve the problem. [*He addresses the fortress in a matter-of-fact tone*] So you won't surrender, eh? [*Then in a mock-heroic falsetto, answering himself like a ventriloquist*] We die but we never surrender! [*Then matter-of-factly*] Well, Brother, these high-flown heroic sentiments may do you a lot of credit, but this is war and not a tragedy. I warn you for your own good, you're up against modern methods this time, none of the old battering ram stuff, and you better give in and avoid wasteful bloodshed. [*Answering himself*] No! Victory or Death! [*Then again*] All right, Brother, don't blame me. Hold on to your hair if you want to keep your head on, for here we come. Give 'em hell, boys! [*His uncle releases the spring and a leaden ball is shot out which knocks a big breach in the wall of blocks.* MARCO *beams.* KOKACHIN *gives a scream of fright, then a gasp of delight and claps her hands.* MARCO *bows to her the more gratefully as* KUBLAI *and* CHU YIN *are staring at him with a queer appalled wonder that puzzles him although he cannot imagine it is not in admiration*] I see you are stunned. What made it do that, you're wondering? Where did the noise and the destructive force come from? From this! [*He takes a little package out of his pocket and pours some black powder out of it on his palm*] It's the same powder they've been using here in kid's fireworks to make 'em pop. They've had it under their noses for years without a single soul ever having creative imagination enough to spot the enormous possibilities. But you can bet I did. It was a kiddie crying with half a finger blown off where he held a fire-cracker too long that first opened my eyes. I went at once and had the mixture analyzed. I learned the formula, improved on it, experimented in secret, patented it in my name to insure my exclusive right to ownership, and here's the gratifying result! Gunpowder, that's my trade name for it, the powder of power! [*He takes the cannonball from his father, who has retrieved it*] You see? Now just picture to yourself this little ball magnified into one weighing one hundred pounds or so and then you'll really grasp my idea. The destruction of property and loss of life would be tremendous! No one could resist you! You'd conquer the world into one great peace-loving, hard-working brotherhood of Man!

KUBLAI [*After a pause—suddenly*] But I am interested in the fate of the hero of that city who preferred death to defeat. Did you conquer his immortal soul?

MARCO [*With puzzled frankness*] Oh, he was an idolator and bound to be damned anyway even if he'd died a natural death. [*Then hastily, feeling that he has put his foot in it*] I mean, you can't consider souls when you're dealing with soldiers.

KUBLAI   But perhaps his soul conquered you.

MARCO   [*With a grin*] Well, let him win a moral victory as long as he's licked. We're satisfied. [*He takes his model and places it on the Kaan's knee with the paper money*] When you have time, I wish you'd look this over. In fact—and this is the big idea I've been saving for the last—consider these two inventions of mine in combination. You conquer the world with this [*He pats the cannon-model*] and you pay for its construction and operation with this [*He pats the paper money. Rhetorically*] You become the long-awaited deliverer, a bringer of peace on earth and good will to man, and it doesn't cost you a yen hardly. Your initial outlay—my price—is as low as I can possibly make it out of my deep affection for your Majesty—only a million yen.

KUBLAI   [*Quickly*] In paper?

MARCO   [*With a grin and a wink*] No. I'll take mine in gold, if you don't mind. [*Silence.* MARCO *goes on meaningly*] Of course, I don't want to force it on you. I'm confident there's a ready market for it elsewhere—

KUBLAI   [*Grimly smiling*] Oh, I quite realize that in self-protection I've got to buy them!

MARCO   [*Briskly*] Then it's a bargain? But I've still got two provisos. The first is that you won't ever use my Little David against my home town, Venice. But you can batter Genoa to dust with it if you like—with my best wishes!

KUBLAI   [*With aversion*] I shall never touch the West!

MARCO   The other proviso is—that you give me permission to go home. [KOKACHIN *gives a little gasp.* MARCO *goes on feelingly*] We're kind of homesick, Your Majesty. We've served you faithfully, we've done our best by you, and frankly now that we've made our pile, we want to go home and enjoy it. There's no place like home, Your Majesty! I'm sure even a King in his palace appreciates that.

KUBLAI   But—who can play your part? You have no understudy in the Eastern World. And your mission—your example? What will your Pope say when you tell him I'm still unconverted?

MARCO   [*Confidently*] Oh, you will be—on your death bed, if not before—a man of your moral will power—

KUBLAI   [*Ironically*] Courtier! [*Then solemnly*] But my last objection is insurmountable. You haven't yet proven you have an immortal soul!

MARCO   It doesn't need proving. Everyone knows it.

KUBLAI   Ah, if you could bring forward one reliable witness who had seen it—

MARCO   My father and Uncle can swear I've got one.

KUBLAI   They think it's a family trait. Their evidence is prejudiced.

MARCO   [*Worried now—looks at* CHU YIN *hopefully*] Mr. Chu Yin ought to be wise enough to acknowledge—

CHU YIN   [*Smiling*] But I believe that what can be proven cannot be true. [MARCO *stands puzzled, irritated, looking stubborn, frightened and foolish. His eyes wander about the room finally resting appealingly on* KOKACHIN]

KOKACHIN   [*Suddenly steps forward—flushed but proudly*] I will bear witness he has a soul. [KUBLAI *looks at her with a sad wonderment,* CHU YIN *smilingly,* MARCO *with gratitude,* NICOLO *and* MAFFEO *exchange a glance of congratulation*]

KUBLAI   How can you know, Princess?

KOKACHIN   Because I have seen it—once, when he bound up my dog's broken leg, once when he played with a slave's baby, once when he listened to music over water and I heard him sigh, once when he looked at sunrise, another time at sunset, another at the stars, another at the moon, and each time he said that Nature was wonderful. And all the while, whenever he has been with me I have always felt—something strange and unique and different from all other men—and that something must be His Honor's soul, must it not?

KUBLAI   [*With wondering bitterness*] The eye sees only its own sight.

CHU YIN   Who knows? A woman may feel life in the unborn.

KUBLAI   [*Mockingly but sadly*] I cannot contest with the profound intuitions of virgins and mystics. Go home, Your Honor, Immortal Mark, and live forever to speak the lie and shame the God! [*With forced gaiety*] And tell your Pope your example has done much to convert me to wisdom—if I could only find the true one!

KOKACHIN   [*Boldly now*] And may I humbly request, since His Honor—and his father and uncle—are experienced masters of navigation that they be appointed, for my greater safety, to attend me and command the fleet on my voyage to Persia?

KUBLAI   [*Astonished at her boldness—rebukingly*] Princess!

KOKACHIN   [*Returning his look—simply*] It is the last favor I shall ever ask. I wish to be converted to wisdom, too—one or another—before I become a name.

KUBLAI   [*Bitterly*] I cannot deny your last wish—even though you wish your own unhappiness. [*To the* POLOS] You will accompany the Princess and, from now on, take all your orders from her.

MARCO   [*Jubilantly*] I shall be only too willing! [*Turning to the* PRINCESS] It will be a great pleasure to—[*Then briskly*] And have we your permission to carry a line of goods aboard and trade in the ports along the way?

KOKACHIN   [*To* MARCO, *embarrassedly*] As you please, Your Honor.

MARCO   [*Bowing low*] Thanks, Your Highness. I'll promise it won't disturb you. It's really more a scheme to while away the hours and keep in training. [*Familiarly*] You see, the only trouble with a ship, for a man of action, is that there's so little you can do. And I must confess I hate idleness where there's nothing to occupy your mind but thinking. I've been so used to being out, on the jump every minute, overcoming obstacles, getting things done, creating results where there weren't any before, going after the impossible and nailing it down—well—[*Here he gives a little deprecating laugh*]—all play and no work makes Jack a dull boy—I'm sure I'd make a pretty dull person to have around if there wasn't plenty to do. You might not believe it, but when I'm idle, I actually get pessimistic sometimes!

KOKACHIN   [*Eagerly*] But we shall have dancers on the ship and singers and players of all instruments and actors who will entertain us with plays—

MARCO   [*Heartily*] That'll be grand. I like dancing and music all right—although I don't play or sing or dance myself. And there's nothing better than to sit down in a good seat at a first rate show after a hard day's work in which you know how you've accomplished something, and after you've had a good dinner, and just take it easy and enjoy a good wholesome thrill or a good laugh and get your mind off serious things until it's time to go to bed.

KOKACHIN   [*Vaguely*] Yes. [*Then eager to have him pleased*] And there will be poets to recite their poems—

MARCO   [*Not exactly overjoyed*] That'll be great. I like poetry. [*Then very confidentially—in a humorous whisper*] I'll tell you a good joke on me, Your Highness. I once wrote a poem myself, would you ever believe it to look at me?

KOKACHIN   [*Smiling at him as at a boy—teasingly*] No?

MARCO   [*Smiling back like a boy*] Yes, I did too—when I was young and foolish. It wasn't bad stuff either, considering I'd had no practice. [*Frowning with concentration*] Wait! Let me see if I can remember any—oh yes—"You are lovely as the gold in the sun" [*He hesitates*]

KOKACHIN   [*Thrilled*] That is beautiful!

MARCO   That's only the first line. [*Then jokingly*] You can consider yourself lucky. I don't remember any more!

KOKACHIN   Perhaps on the voyage it may come back to you—or you may be inspired to write another!

MARCO   [*Laughing*] God forbid! I'm too young yet for second childhood, I hope.

KUBLAI   [*Who with* CHU YIN *has been staring at them with weary amusement*] Life is so stupid it's mysterious! Life is so mad it's mystic!

CURTAIN

ACT FIVE   SCENE TWO

The wharves of the Imperial fleet at the seaport of Zaiton—several weeks later. At the left, stern to, is an enormous junk, the flagship. The wharf extends out, rear, to the right of her. In the right, is a warehouse, from a door in which an endless chain of half-naked slaves, their necks, waists, and right ankles linked up by chains, form an endless chain which revolves mechanically as it were, on sprocket wheels in the interiors of the shed and the junk. As each individual link passes out of the shed it carries a bale on its head, moves with mechanical precision across the wharf, disappears into the junk, reappears a moment later having dumped its load and moves back into the shed. The whole process is a man power replica of the endless chain engines with bucket scoops that dredge, load coal, sand, etc. By the side of the shed, a foreman sits with a drum and gong with which he marks a perfect time for the slaves, a four beat rhythm, three beats of the drum, the fourth a bang on the gong as one slave at each end loads and unloads. The effect is very like the noise of a machine.

A bamboo stair leads up to the high poop of the junk from front, left. It is just getting dawn. A forest of masts, spars, sails of woven bamboo laths, shuts out all view of the harbor at the end of the wharf. At the foot of the stairs, CHU YIN *stands like a sentinel. Above, on top of the poop, the figures of* KUBLAI *and* KOKACHIN *are outlined against the lightening sky.*

KUBLAI   [*Brokenly*] You will soon put to sea. I must go. [*He takes her in his arms*] This last farewell has been sad but comforting. We have said all we can say. Little Daughter, all rare things are secrets within which cannot be revealed to anyone. That is why life must be so lonely. But I love you more dearly than anything on earth. Since the day you were born you have been my delight and my consolation. And I know you love me. So perhaps we do not need to understand. [*Rebelliously*] Yet I wish some Power would give me true insight. I need assurance that in granting your desire I am acting for your happiness, and for eventual deliverance from sorrow to acceptance and peace. Nothing else matters.—But I am sick with doubt. [*He notices she is weeping—*

in self-reproach] Old fool! I have made you weep again! Do not listen! I am death advising life how to live! Be deaf to me! Strive after what your heart desires! Who can ever know which are the mistakes we make? One should be either sad or joyful. Contentment is a warm sty where the eaters sleep and the sleepers eat! [*Impulsively*] Do not weep! Even now I could refuse your hand to Arghun. Let it mean war!

KOKACHIN   [*Looking up and controlling herself—with a sad finality*] You do not understand. I wish to take this voyage.

KUBLAI   [*Desperately*] But I could keep Polo here. [*With impotent anger*] He shall grovel and pray for his life, and implore mercy for his soul on his knees before you!

KOKACHIN   [*With calm sadness*] What do I want with a slave? [*Dreamily*] I wish for a captain of my ship on a long voyage in dangerous, enchanted seas.

KUBLAI   [*With a fierce defiance of fate*] I am the Kaan! I shall have him killed! [*A pause*]

CHU YIN   [*In a calm, soothing tone*] The noble man ignores self. The wise man ignores action. His truth acts without deeds. His knowledge venerates the unknowable. To him birth is not a beginning nor is death an end. [*Kublai's head bends in submission.* CHU YIN *continues tenderly*] There are tears in your eyes. The Great Kaan, Ruler of the World, may not weep.

KUBLAI   [*Brokenly*] A ruler? I am my own slave! [*Then controlling himself—forcing an amused teasing tone*] Marco will soon be here, wearing the self-assurance of an immortal soul and his new admiral's uniform. I must fly in retreat from what I can neither laugh away nor kill. Write to me when you reach Persia. Tell me—all you can tell.—Particularly what his immortal soul is like. [*Then tenderly*] Farewell, Little Flower, live and serve. There is no other advice possible from one human being to another.

KOKACHIN   Live and serve—and love!

KUBLAI   One's ancestors and one's children—particularly one's grandfather. Do not forget me!

KOKACHIN   Never! [*They embrace*]

KUBLAI   [*Chokingly*] Farewell. [*He hurries down the ladder—to* CHU YIN]. You remain—See him—bring me word—[*He turns his head up to* KOKACHIN) For the last time, farewell, Little Flower of my Life! May you know happiness! [*He turns quickly and goes*]

KOKACHIN   Farewell! [*She bows her head on the rail and weeps*]

CHU YIN   [*After a pause*] You are tired, Princess. Your eyes are bloodshot from weeping and your nose is red. Your face is drawn. You look old—a little homely even. The Admiral Polo will not recognize you. [KOKACHIN *dries her eyes hastily*]

KOKACHIN [*Half-smiling and half-weeping at his teasing*] I think you are a very horrid and mean old man.

CHU YIN A little sleep, Princess, and you will again be beautiful. The old dream passes. Sleep and awake in the new. Life is perhaps most wisely regarded as a bad dream between two awakenings—and every day is a life in miniature.

KOKACHIN [*Wearily and drowsily*] Your wisdom makes me sleep. [*Her head sinks back on her arms and she is soon asleep*]

CHU YIN [*After a pause—softly*] Kokachin! [*He sees she is asleep—chuckles*] I have won a convert. [*Then speculatively*] Youth needs so much sleep and old age so little. Is that not proof that from birth to death one grows steadily closer to complete life? Hum. [*He ponders on this. From the distance comes the sound of Polo's band playing the same martial air as in the previous scene.* CHU YIN *starts—then smiles. The music quickly grows louder. The* PRINCESS *awakes with a start*]

KOKACHIN [*Startledly*] Chu Yin! Is that the Admiral coming?

CHU YIN [*Dryly*] I should suspect so. It is like him to be so considerate as not to neglect a person in the city when saying goodbye.

KOKACHIN [*Flurriedly*] I must go to my cabin for a moment. [*She hurries back*]

CHU YIN [*Listens with a pleased, ironical smile as the band gets rapidly nearer. Finally it seems to turn a corner nearby, and, a moment later, to a deafening clangor,* MARCO *enters, dressed in a gorgeous Admiral's uniform. Two paces behind, side by side, walk* MAFFEO *and* NICOLO, *dressed only a trifle less gorgeously as Commodores. Behind them comes the band.* MARCO *halts as he sees* CHU YIN, *salutes condescendingly, and signals the band to be silent.* CHU YIN *bows gravely and remarks as if answering an argument in his own mind*] Still, even though they are not house-broken, I prefer monkeys because they are so much less noisy.

MARCO [*With a condescending grin*] What's that—more philosophy? Nothing can stop you, eh? [*Clapping him on the back*] Well, I like your determination, anyway. [*He wipes his brow with a handkerchief*] Phew! I'll certainly be glad to get back home where I can hear some of God's music that I can keep step to. My feet just won't give in to your tunes. [*With a grin*] And look at the Old Man and Uncle. They're spavined and knock-kneed for life. [*Confiden-*

tially] Still, I thought the band was a good idea—to sort of cheer up the Princess and let the home folks know she's leaving at the same time. [*As people begin to come in and stare at the poop of the ship*] See the crowd gather? I routed 'em out of bed, too!

CHU YIN [*Ironically*] Yes. You also woke up the Princess. You sail at sunrise?

MARCO [*Briskly—taking operations in hand*] Thank you for reminding me. I've got to hustle. [*To his father and uncle*] You two better get aboard your ships and be ready to cast off when I signal. [*They grunt rather disagreeably and go off.* MARCO *grins*] It gets under their skins to take orders from me—but, believe me, I'm getting some sport out of it when I think of all I had to stand for from them till I grew up. [*He suddenly bawls to someone in the ship*] Much more cargo to load?

A VOICE Less than a hundred bales, sir.

MARCO Good. Call all hands on deck and standby to put sail on her and cast off!

VOICE Yes, sir.

MARCO And look lively, damn your lazy souls! [*To* CHU YIN, *approvingly*] You've got to impose a rigid discipline on shipboard.

CHU YIN [*Inquisitively*] I suppose you feel your heavy responsibility as escort of the future Queen of Persia?

MARCO [*Soberly*] Yes, I do. I'll confess I do. If she were a million lire's worth of silk or spices, I wouldn't worry an instant—but a Queen, that's a different proposition. However, when you give my last word to His Majesty, you can tell him that I've always done my duty by him and I won't fail him this time. As long as I've a breath in me, I'll take care of her!

CHU YIN [*With genuine appreciation*] That is bravely spoken.

MARCO I don't know anything about brave speaking. I'm by nature a silent man, and I let my actions do the cheering. But, as I've proved to you people in Cathay time and again, when I say I'll do a thing, I do it! So you can go ahead and consider the Princess safe in Persia and don't waste time worrying.

CHU YIN [*Suddenly*] I was forgetting—His Majesty gave me his secret last instructions for you. You are, at some time every day of the voyage, to look carefully and deeply into the Princess's eyes and note what you see there.

MARCO What for? [*Then brightly*] Oh, I know. He's afraid she'll get fever in the tropics. Well, you tell him I'll carry out my orders to the letter and I'll see to it she keeps in good condition. I'll do what's right by her without considering fear or favor. [*Then practically*] Then, of course, if she or her husband think at the end of the voyage that my work deserves a bonus—why, that's up to them. [*Inquisitively*] Do you know anything about what sort this Khan of Persia is—is he generous, I mean?

CHU YIN   [*Grimly amused*] He rewards as lavishly as he punishes.

MARCO   Good enough! And I know the Princess has a big heart. [*A pause*] She's never seen him, has she?

CHU YIN   No.

MARCO   [*With an air of an independent thinker*] Well, I believe in love matches myself, even for Kings and Queens. [*With a grin*] My gosh, come to think of it, I'll be getting married myself when I get home to little old Venice by the sea—that is, if Donata's still alive and pretty.

CHU YIN   Donata?

MARCO   [*Proudly*] The best little girl in the world! She's there waiting for me all these eighteen years—unless she's dead.

CHU YIN   You haven't heard since you came here?

MARCO   How would I? But I don't need to hear. I can trust her. And I've been true to her, too. I haven't ever thought of loving anyone else. Of course, I don't mean I've been any sissy he-virgin. I've played around with concubines considerably in odd moments when my mind needed relaxation—but that's only human nature. [*His eyes glistening reminiscently*] Some of them surely were wonders, too! [*With a sigh*] Well, I've had my fun and I suppose it's about time I settled down. [*Sentimentally*] After all, there's nothing like your own fireside with a wife and kiddies beside you when you're getting on in years, is there?

CHU YIN   Poor Princess!

MARCO   What's that? Oh, I see, yes, I sympathize with her, too—going into a harem. If there's one thing more than another that proves you in the East aren't responsible it's that harem idea. Now in the West we've learned by experience that one at a time is trouble enough. [*With a grin*] Or maybe it's because one of our girls is worth any given number of yours, eh? Ha-ha! That's one on you! No, joking aside, I guess all women are more or less the same, East or West, Queen or cook, white or black. Don't you?

CHU YIN   [*Dryly*] Be sure and converse on love and marriage often with the Princess.

MARCO   Well, I guess not! I don't want to ruin her happiness. If she's contented the way things are, it's better for her to remain in ignorance.

CHU YIN   Yes. Perhaps it's all for the best. I am certain you will cure her.

MARCO   Cure her? Is she sick already? [*Injuredly*] Well, if she's ailing when I get her, it's unreasonable to expect me to accept responsibility for delivering her well.

CHU YIN   I meant, you will cure her mind of any unreasonable imaginings.

MARCO   [*Easily*] Oh, I'll guarantee she'll be contented with the way I run the fleet. She'll have no cause for complaint, if that's what you mean. [*The human chain in back finishes its labors and disappears into the shed. The crowd of people has been steadily augmented by new arrivals, until a small multitude is gathered who all stand in silence staring up at the poop.* MARCO *says with satisfaction*] Well, cargo's all aboard, before schedule, too. That's efficiency! We killed six slaves but, by God, we did it! And look at the crowd we've drawn,—thanks to my little old band!

CHU YIN   [*Disgustedly*] They would have come without noise. They love their Princess.

MARCO   [*Cynically*] Maybe—but they love their sleep, too. I know 'em! [*A cry of adoration goes up from the crowd as with one movement they prostrate themselves as the* PRINCESS *comes from the cabin dressed in a robe of silver and stands at the rail looking down*]

THE CROWD   [*In a long, ululating whisper*] Farewell—farewell—farewell—farewell—

KOKACHIN   [*Silences them with a motion of her hand*]
   I shall know the long sorrow of an exile
   As I sail over the green water and the blue water
   Alone under a strange sky amid alien flowers and faces.
   My eyes shall be ever red with weeping, my heart bleeding,
   While I long for the land of my birth and my childhood
   Remembering with love the love of my people.
[*A sound of low weeping comes from the crowd*] Farewell!

THE CROWD   Farewell—farewell—farewell—farewell—

MARCO   [*Feeling foolish, because he is moved*] Darn it! Reciting always makes me want to bawl about something. Poetry acts worse on me than wine that way. [*He calls up—very respectfully*] Princess! We will be sailing at once. Would you mind retiring to your cabin? I'm afraid you're going to catch cold standing there with your hat off in the night air.

KOKACHIN [*Tremulously—grateful for his solicitude*] I am in your charge, Admiral. I am grateful that you should think of my health—and I will obey. [*She turns and goes back into her cabin. The crowd silently filters away, leaving only the band*]

MARCO [*Proudly and fussily*] You can't have women around when you're trying to get something done quick. I can see where I'll have to be telling her what to do every second—just as I used to when she was a kid. Well, I hope she'll take it in good part and not forget I'm acting in her husband's interests, not my own. [*Very confidentially*] You know, apart from her being a Princess, I've always respected her a lot. She's not stuck-up and she's—well, human, that's what I mean. I'd do anything I could for her, Princess or not! Yes, sir!

CHU YIN [*Wonderingly*] There may be hope—after all—

MARCO What's that?

CHU YIN Nothing. Enigma!

MARCO There's always hope! Don't be a damned pessimist! [*Clapping him on the back*] Well, good'bye old scout! I've got to get busy. [*He ascends halfway up the ladder to the poop—turns to* CHU YIN *with a chuckle when he is halfway up*] Enigma, eh? Well, if that isn't like a philosopher—to start in on riddles just at the wrong moment! [*He bends down and putting his hand to his mouth, stage-whispers to* CHU YIN] Say, listen! Take a fool's advice and don't think so much or you'll be getting bald before your time! [*More oratorically*] If you look before you leap, your will gets Charley-horse. Keep on going ahead and you can't help being right because you're bound to get somewhere. Don't stop to think and maybe some day you'll have time to get to know something! [*He suddenly breaks into a grin again*] There, you old rascal, don't ever say I never gave you the right tip. If you go wrong now, don't blame me! [*He springs swiftly to the top deck and bellows*] Cast off there amidships! Where the hell are you—asleep? Look lively! Break out those stops! Set that foresail! Hop, you kidney-footed gang of thumb-fingered infidels! A little action! [*He turns with a sudden fierceness on the band, who are standing stolidly, awaiting orders*] Hey you! Didn't I tell you when I set foot on the deck to let her rip! What do you think I paid you in advance for—to kiss me goodbye? Strike up my favorite tune! [*The band plunges madly into it. A frenzied cataract of sound results.* CHU YIN *covers his ears and moves away, shaking his head, as* MARCO *leans over the rail and bawls after him*] And tell the Kaan—anything he wants—write me— just Venice, that'll get me. They all know me there—and if they don't, by God, they're going to!! [*He takes off his lacy hat, and stands with one hand on the rail, bowing to the band in grateful acknowledgement as*

THE CURTAIN FALLS

SCENE: *Poop deck of the royal junk of the* PRINCESS KOKACHIN *at anchor in the harbor of Hormuz, Persia—a moonlight night some two years later. On a silver throne at center* KOKACHIN *is sitting dressed in a gorgeous golden robe of ceremony. Her beauty has grown more intense, her face has undergone a change, it is the face of a woman who has known real sorrow and suffering. In the shadows of the highest deck in rear her women in waiting are in a group, sitting on cushions. On the highest deck in rear nine sailors lower and furl the sail of the mizzenmast, every movement being carried out with a machine-like rhythm in unison. The bulwarks of the junk are battered and splintered, the sail is frayed and full of jagged holes and patches. At the apex of the forestage (the port side of deck), the two elder* POLOS *are squatting. Each has a bag of money before him and a treasure chest in which they are carefully packing stacks of gold coin.*

MARCO   [*His voice, hoarse and domineering, comes from the left just before the curtain rises*] Let go that anchor! [*A meek "Aye-aye, sir" is heard replying and then a great splash and a long rattling of chains. The curtain then rises discovering the scene as above. Marco's voice is again heard.*] Lower that mizzensail! Look lively now!

BOATSWAIN   [*With the sailors*] Aye-aye, sir! [*They lower the sail, hauling on the ropes—then tie it up trimly with stops*]

MAFFEO   [*Looking up and straightening his cramped back—with a relieved sigh*] Here's Persia! I'll be glad to get on dry land again. Two years on this foreign tub are too much.

NICOLO   [*With a grunt, intent on the money*] Keep counting if you want to finish before you go ashore. It's nine hundred thousand now in our money, isn't it?

MAFFEO   [*Nods—counting again*] It'll reach a million. [*He begins sorting and packing again*]

BOATSWAIN   [*Chanting as his men work*]
　　　　　　　Great were the waves
　　　　　　　Mountains of water
　　　　　　　Volcanoes of foam
　　　　　　　Ridge after ridge
　　　　　　　To the edge of the world!
　　　　　　　Great were the waves!

CHORUS OF SAILORS   Great were the waves!

BOATSWAIN   Fierce were the winds!
            Their demons screamed!
            Their claws rended
            Our sails into rags,
            Our spars into splinters
            Fierce were the winds!

CHORUS   Fierce were the winds!

BOATSWAIN   Fire was the sun!
            It roasted the skin
            Boiled the blood black
            Till our veins hummed
            Like bronze tea kettles
            Fire was the sun!

CHORUS   Fire was the sun!

BOATSWAIN   Long was the voyage!
            Our hearts wept for home
            Life drifted becalmed
            Like a dead whale awash
            In the toil of tides.
            Long was the voyage!

CHORUS   Long was the voyage!

BOATSWAIN   Many of us died
            And sleep in green water
            While wan faces at home
            Stare through eastern windows
            Praying bitterly to the sea.
            Many of us died!

CHORUS   Many of us died!

KOKACHIN   [*Chants the last line after them—sadly*] Many of us died!
[*After a brooding pause she rises and chants in a low voice*]
            If I were asleep in deep, green water
            No new pang could be added to my sorrow
            All old grief would be numbed and forgotten
            I would know peace

SAILORS   There is a great peace in the deep sea
          But the surface is sorrow.

WOMEN   Kokachin will be a Queen!
A Queen may not sorrow
Save for her King!

KOKACHIN   When love is not loved it loves death,
Death who possesses and is forever faithful.
When I sank drowning, I heard Death wooing,
But the man I love saved me.
When the pirate's knife gleamed, I saw Death beckon,
But the man I love saved me.
When fever ate my flesh with teeth of ice I felt
     Death's lips
But the man I love saved me.

SAILORS   Death lives in a silent sea
Grey and cold under cold grey sky
Where there is neither sun nor wind
Nor any joy nor sorrow!

WOMEN   Kokachin will be a wife.
A wife must not sorrow
Save for her husband.

KOKACHIN   The true hero is merciful to women.
Why could not this man hear or see or feel or know?
Then he would have let me die.

SAILORS   There are harbors at every voyage-end
Where we rest from the sorrows of the sea.

WOMEN   Kokachin will be a mother
A mother may not sorrow
Save for her son.

KOKACHIN   [*With sudden sad determination*] I must practice the wisdom
I have learned. Happiness and sorrow are twin appearances of the identical
illusion. Knowing that, the wise man—or any woman—becomes free! [MARCO
POLO *enters briskly from below on the left. He is dressed in full uniform, looking
spic and span, and self-conscious. His face wears an expression of humorous
scorn. He bows ceremoniously to the* PRINCESS, *his attitude a queer mixture of
familiarity and an uncertain awe*]

MARCO   Your Highness—[*Then ingratiatingly*]—or I suppose I'd better
say Majesty now that we've reached Persia—I've got funny news for you. A boat
just came from the shore with an official notification that your intended hus-

band, Arghun Khan, is dead and that I'm to hand you over to his son Ghazan to marry. [*He hands her a sealed paper*] See.

KOKACHIN   [*Letting the paper slip from her hand without a glance—dully*] It doesn't matter.

MARCO   [*Admiringly—as he picks it up*] I must say you take it coolly. Of course, come to think of it, never having seen either, one's as good as another. [*He winds up philosophically*] And you'll be Queen of Persia just the same, that's the main thing.

KOKACHIN   [*With bitter irony*] So you think—power is the main thing?

MARCO   [*Condescendingly*] Well—power means success, doesn't it? But I'll acknowledge you women of the East ought to have more voice in your actions. [*Then complacently*] Naturally—I'm prejudiced, coming from Venice, which is a free Republic where every woman is born more or less equally entitled to—

KOKACHIN   [*Interrupting him harshly*] To be unhappy?

MARCO   [*Rebukingly*] I'd hardly say that. Everybody in Venice is happy— you never heard such a place for singing. No, what I was going to say was equally entitled to certain feminine privileges—

KOKACHIN   [*Sharply*] I don't care to hear! [*Then as* MARCO *stares at her uncertainly, she turns away and looks out over the sea with a sigh—after a pause*] There—where I see the lights—is that Hormuz?

MARCO   Yes. And I was forgetting, the messenger said Ghazan Khan would come out to take you ashore tonight.

KOKACHIN   [*With sudden fear*] So soon? Tonight? [*Then rebelliously*] Is the granddaughter of the Great Kublai no better than a slave? I will not go until it pleases me!

MARCO   Good for you! That's the spirit! [*Then alarmed at his own temerity—hastily*] But don't be rash! The Khan is a gentleman. He probably meant he'd take you when you were willing. And don't mind what I said.

KOKACHIN   [*Looks at him with a sudden dawning of hope—gently*] Why should you be afraid of what you said?

MARCO   [*Offended*] I'm not afraid of anything alive—when it comes to the point!

KOKACHIN   What point?

MARCO   [*Nonplussed*] Why—well—when I feel someone's trying to do me out of what's rightfully mine, for instance.

KOKACHIN   And now—here—you don't feel that?

MARCO   [*With a forced laugh, thinking she is joking*] Well, hardly! [*Uncertainly*] That is—I don't see your meaning—[*Then changing the subject abruptly*] But here's something I want to ask you; Your grandfather entrusted you, his greatest treasure, to my care. He trusted me to prove equal to the dangerous and difficult job of bringing you safe and sound to your husband. Now I want to ask you frankly if you yourself won't be the first to acknowledge that in spite of typhoons, shipwrecks, pirates and every other known form of bad luck, I've brought you through in good shape—and, by God, if you'll pardon my language, I managed to make a record passage from Cathay to Persia in the bargain, even though we lost six hundred lives doing it!

KOKACHIN   [*With an irony almost hysterical*] More than anyone in the world, I can appreciate your devotion to duty! You have been a prodigy of heroic accomplishment! In the typhoon when a wave swept me from the deck, was it not you who swam to me as I was drowning?

MARCO   [*Modestly*] It was easy. Venetians make the best swimmers in the world.

KOKACHIN   When the pirates attacked us, was it not your brave sword that warded off their curved knives from my breast and struck them dead at my feet?

MARCO   I was out of practice, too. I used to be one of the crack swordsmen of Venice—and they're the world's foremost, as everyone knows.

KOKACHIN   [*With a sudden change—softly*] And when the frightful fever wasted me, was it not you who tended me night and day, watching by my bedside like a gentle nurse, even brewing yourself the medicines that brought me back to life?

MARCO   My mother's recipes. Simple home remedies—from the best friend I ever had!

KOKACHIN   [*A trifle wildly*] Oh yes, you have been a model guardian, Admiral Polo!

MARCO   [*Quickly*] Thank you, Princess. If I have satisfied you—then I might ask you a favor—that you put in writing all you've just said in your first letter to the Great Kaan—and also tell your husband—?

KOKACHIN   [*Suddenly wildly bitter*] I will assuredly! I will tell them both of your heroic cruelty in saving me from death! [*Intensely*] Why could you not let me die? Will you tell me that?

MARCO   [*Confusedly*] It was my job—but you're joking—you certainly didn't want to die, did you?

KOKACHIN [*Slowly and intensely*] Yes, I did.

MARCO [*Puzzled and severe*] Hum. You shouldn't talk that way. Anyone that didn't know you would think you were pessimistic.

KOKACHIN [*Longingly*] I would be asleep in deep green water!

MARCO [*Worriedly. Suddenly reaches out and takes her hand*] Here now, young lady! Don't start getting morbid!

KOKACHIN [*With a thrill of love*] Marco!

MARCO I believe you're feverish. Let me feel your pulse!

KOKACHIN [*Violently*] No! [*She draws her hand from his as if she had been stung*]

MARCO [*Worriedly*] Please don't be unreasonable. I'm only trying to act for the best. There'd be the devil to pay if you should suffer a relapse of the fever I sweated blood to pull you through once before! The Great Kaan wouldn't think so much of my work then—and it would be a poor testimonial of my ability to your husband if he found you running a temperature. Do your limbs feel hot?

KOKACHIN [*Wildly*] No! Yes, they are on fire!

MARCO Are your feet cold?

KOKACHIN No! Yes! I don't know! [*Gravely* MARCO *kneels, removes a slipper, and feels the sole of her foot—then pats her foot playfully*]

MARCO No. They're all right. [*He gets up—professionally*] Any cramps?

KOKACHIN You fool! No! Yes! My heart feels as if it were bursting!

MARCO It burns?

KOKACHIN Like a red hot ember flaring up for the last time before it chills into grey ash forever!

MARCO Then something must have disagreed with you! Will you let me see your tongue?

KOKACHIN [*In a queer hysterical state where she delights in self-humiliation*] Yes! Yes! Anything! I am a Princess of the Imperial blood of Chinghiz and you are a dog! Anything! [*She sticks out her tongue, the tears streaming down her face as he looks at it*]

MARCO [*Shakes his head*] No sign of biliousness. Please, Princess, don't worry. There's nothing seriously wrong. Don't make yourself sick. It's only over-wrought nerves, too much excitement—if only you could take a nap—

KOKACHIN O Celestial God of the Heaven! What have I done that thou should torture me? [*Then wildly to* MARCO] I wished to sleep in the depths of the sea. Why did you awaken me?

MARCO [*Worried again*] Perhaps it's brain fever. Does your head ache?

KOKACHIN No! Does your immortal soul?

MARCO Hush! Don't blaspheme! Really, you're talking as if you were delirious! [*Then pleadingly*] For Heaven's sake, try and be calm, Princess! What if your husband, Ghazan Khan, should find you in such a state?

KOKACHIN My husband may go to the devil!

MARCO Sshhh! Remember you're in the East!

KOKACHIN [*Calming herself with difficulty after a pause, bitterly*] I suppose you are relieved to complete your task—to get me here alive and deliver me—like a cow!

MARCO [*Injuredly*] I've only carried out your own grandfather's orders!

KOKACHIN [*Forcing a smile*] Won't you miss being my guardian? [*Striving pitifully to arouse his jealousy*] When you think of Ghazan protecting and guarding and nursing me when I am sick—and—and loving me? Yes. I will compel him to love me—even though I never love him! I will make this king my slave! He shall look into my eyes and see that I am a woman and beautiful!

MARCO That is a husband's privilege.

KOKACHIN Or a man's—a man who has a soul. [*Mockingly but intensely*] And that reminds me, Admiral Polo! You are taking advantage of this being the last day to shirk your duty!

MARCO Shirk! If there's one thing that no one could ever say about me—!

KOKACHIN It was my grandfather's special command, given to you by Chu Yin, you told me, that every day you should look into my eyes!

MARCO [*Resignedly*] Well—it isn't too late yet, is it? [*He moves toward her with a sigh of half-impatience with her whims*]

KOKACHIN Wait. This is the one part of your duty in which I shall have to report you as incompetent.

MARCO [*Hurt*] I've done my best. I never could discover anything out of the way.

KOKACHIN Yet there must be something in my eyes for you to deserve! The Great Kaan is wise. So is Chu Yin. There must have been something they wished you to find, else why should they give the order? I myself feel there is something peculiar in them, something I cannot understand, something you must interpret for me! And remember this is your last chance! Look long and deeply! There is nothing in life I would not give you—nothing I would not do—even now it is not too late—see my eyes as those of a woman and not a Princess—look deeply—I will die if you do not see what is there! I will kill myself! [*She finishes hysterically and beseechingly*]

MARCO [*Worried—soothingly*] There! There! Certainly, Princess! Calm yourself! Of course, I'll look—and you will promise me that afterwards you'll do as I prescribe—

KOKACHIN Look deeply! See! [*She throws her head back, her arms outstretched. He bends over and looks into her eyes. She raises her hands slowly above his head as if she were going to pull it down to hers. Her lips part, her whole being strains out to him. He looks for a moment critically, then he grows tense, his face moves hypnotically toward hers, their lips seem about to meet in a kiss. She murmurs compellingly*] Marco!

MARCO [*His voice thrilling for this second with oblivious passion*] Kokachin!

MAFFEO [*Suddenly slapping a stack of coins into the chest with a resounding clank*] One million!

MARCO [*With a start, comes to himself and backs away from the* PRINCESS *in terror*] What, Uncle? Did you call?

MAFFEO One million in God's money! [*He and* NICOLO *lock and fasten the box jubilantly*]

KOKACHIN [*In despair*] Marco!

MARCO [*Flusteredly*] Yes, Princess. I saw something queer! It made me feel feverish too. I saw myself melting in fire! [*Recovering a bit—with a sickly smile*] Oh there's trouble there, all right—and you must be sick—you must be delirious—I advise you to go to sleep—

KOKACHIN [*With wild despair pulls out a small dagger from the bosom of her dress*] I shall obey. I shall sleep forever! [*But* MARCO, *the man of action, springs forward and wresting the dagger from her hand, flings it over the side. She confronts him defiantly, her eyes wild with grief and rage. He stares at her, dumbfounded and bewildered*]

MARCO [*His first reaction of injury*] What would your grandfather think of me if he saw you do that? Why, he'd never trust me again! [*Then bewilderedly*] I never believed people—sane people—ever seriously meant—Whatever put it in your head, anyway? You must be—insane!

KOKACHIN [*Intensely*] Because I had permitted an ox to see my soul I no longer wished to endure the shame of living!

MARCO [*Sheepishly*] You mean—it was a terrible insult when I called you—by your name?

KOKACHIN [*Blurting into hysterical laughter*] Yes! How dared you!

MARCO [*Hastily*] I ask pardon, Princess—I mean Your Majesty—please forgive me. I acknowledge you've a perfect right to get mad. My only excuse is, for a moment there I forgot myself. I was out of my head—must have been! Honestly! Something seemed to happen. I didn't know whether I was standing on my head or my feet. I guess I'll have to stop overworking or I'll suffer a nervous breakdown. This would never have occurred, you can believe me, if I was a well man. You know, in all my years of service, I've never before failed in respect to any of the Royal Family. I'm usually extremely circumspect in such matters. Honor where honor is due has always been one of my pet slogans. I simply can't figure what came over me. Maybe it was something I ate. My brain turned queer all of a sudden. I felt like one of those figures in a puppet show with someone manipulating the wires. It wasn't me, you understand. My lips spoke without me saying a word. And here's the funniest part of it all and what'll explain matters in full, if you can believe it. I admit it doesn't sound plausible but it's the God's honest truth. Well, it wasn't you I was seeing and talking to—not a Princess at all—you'd changed into someone else—someone I've got a good right to get familiar with—just a girl—

KOKACHIN [*Again clutching at hope*] A girl—a woman—you saw in me?

MARCO [*Enthusiastically, groping in his shirt front*] Yes. The best little girl in the world! Here she is! [*He jerks the miniature out of an under pocket and presents it to her proudly*] The future Mrs. Mark Polo! [*The* PRINCESS *takes it and stares at it in a stupor as* MARCO *rambles on*] You may believe it or not but like a flash, she was standing there in your place and I was talking to her, not you at all! Yes, sir!

KOKACHIN [*Dully*] But it was my name you spoke.

MARCO [*Confused*] Was it? I meant to say Donata. That's her name. We're going to be married as soon as I get home. I'm tired of wandering. It's about time I settled down and had some children I can pass on my pile to when I die. There's no good working for yourself alone, I say. [*Then as she stares at the miniature—proudly*] Pretty, isn't she? She was rated one of the best-lookers in Venice and our town is noted for its fair women. Of course, that was painted years ago. She'll be a full-blown woman now.

KOKACHIN [*Dully*] Are you so sure she has waited all these years? She may have married another.

MARCO [*Confidently*] No. Her family needs an alliance with Polo Brothers & Son.

KOKACHIN Then she may have had lovers.

MARCO [*Simply*] Oh no. She's not that kind.

KOKACHIN [*Staring at the picture*] She will be middle-aged—fat—and stupid!

MARCO [*With a grin*] Well, I don't mind a wife being a bit over-weight—and who wants a great thinker as long as you can count on sound common-sense? A home full of peace and quiet, where everything runs smoothly, that's what I'm after.

KOKACHIN [*Looks from him to the miniature*] There is no soul even in your love—which is no better than a mating of swine! And I—[*A spasm of pain covers her face—which then grows calm with a cold hatred and disdain*] Pig of a Christian! Will you return to this sow and boast that a Princess and a Queen—? [*With rage*] Shall I ask as my first wedding present from Ghazan Khan that he have you flayed alive and then cast in the street as carrion to be devoured by dogs?

MAFFEO & NICOLO [*Who have pricked up their ears at this last, rush to the* PRINCESS, *dragging their box between them and prostrate themselves at her feet*] Mercy! Mercy!

MAFFEO Whatever he did, he meant well!

NICOLO His only fault is his recklessness! [*She seems not to hear or see them but stares ahead stonily.* MARCO *beckons* MAFFEO *to one side*]

MARCO [*In a whisper*] Don't be scared. She doesn't mean a word of it. She's gone crazy, like all these Easterners, that's the only charitable way— Listen, I just noticed the royal barge coming. I'll go and meet the Khan. You keep her from doing anything rash until he gets here. Once he takes possession, we're not responsible for her any longer. Do you see?

MAFFEO Yes. [*He goes back and crouches again before the* PRINCESS, *keeping a wary eye on her, but she seems turned to stone.* MARCO *comes down and off left. Suddenly there is the blare of a trumpet from off left—the reflections of lanterns and torches, the sound of running about on deck and Marco's voice giving commands. The women come out to attend the* PRINCESS. *She remains rigid, giving no sign*]

WOMEN [*In chorus*]
The lover comes
Who becomes a husband

Who becomes a son
Who becomes a father
In this contemplation lives the woman.

KOKACHIN [*Her face now a fatalistic acceptance*]
I am not, Life is—
A cloud obscures the sun.
A life is lived,
The sun shines again.
Nothing has changed,
Centuries wither into tired dust
A new dew freshens the grass
Somewhere this dream is being dreamed.

[*From the left* MARCO *comes escorting* GHAZAN KHAN, *attended by a train of nobles and slaves with lights. He can be heard saying: "She is a little feverish—the excitement—" All are magnificently dressed, glittering with jewels.* GHAZAN *is a young man, not handsome but noble and manly looking. He comes forward and bows low before her, his attendants likewise. Then he looks into her face and stands fascinated by her beauty. She looks back at him with a calm indifference*]

GHAZAN [*After a pause—his voice thrilling with admiration*] If it were possible for a son who loved a noble father to rejoice at that father's death, then I should be that guilty son. [*As she makes no reply*] You have heard? Arghun Khan is dead. You needs must bear the humiliation of accepting his son for husband in his stead—a crow to replace an eagle! Forgive me—but with your eyes to watch I may become at least a worthy shadow of his greatness.

KOKACHIN [*Calmly*] What am I? I shall obey the eternal will which governs your destiny and mine.

GHAZAN [*Impetuously*] You are more beautiful than I had dared to dream! It shall not be I who rules, but you! I shall be your slave! All Persia shall be your conquest and everywhere songs are sung they shall be in praise of your beauty! You shall be hymned as Queen of Love—!

KOKACHIN [*Sharply with pain*] No! [*She drops the miniature on the floor and grinds it into pieces under her foot*]

MARCO [*Excitedly*] Princess! Look out! You're stepping on—[*She kicks the thing away from her.* MARCO *stoops on his knees and begins picking up the fragments in his handkerchief.* KOKACHIN *turns to* GHAZAN *and points to* MARCO] My first request of you, my Lord, is that you reward this Christian who has brought me here in safety, in good health, despite all dangers and vicissitudes. He is shrewd and capable—faithful and ambitious—loyal to his own interest—

invariably successful, possessing eyes by which one can distinguish him from a mole. I ask, as a fitting tribute to his character, that you give tonight an immense feast in his honor. Let there be food in large amounts. He is a connoisseur of quantity. Let him be urged to eat and drink until he can hold no more—until he becomes an ideal figure of stuffed self-satisfaction. Will you do this? [*She is a trifle hectic now and her manner has grown wilder*]

GHAZAN   Your wish is my will!

KOKACHIN   [*Pointing to his breast*] What is that magnificent glittering beast?

GHAZAN   It is the emblem of the Order of the Lion which only great heroes and the Kings of men may wear.

KOKACHIN   [*Gives a laugh of wild irony*] Only great heroes? [*Then eagerly*] Will you give it to me? I implore you! [GHAZAN, *fascinated, yet with a wondering glance, unpins it and hands it to her without a word. She prods* MARCO, *who is still collecting the fragments of the miniature, with her foot*] Arise! Let me give you the noble order of the Lion! [*She pins the blazing diamond figure on the breast of the stunned* MARCO, *laughing with bitter mockery*] How well it is set off on the bosom of a sheep! [*She laughs more wildly*] Kneel again! Bring me a chest of gold! [GHAZAN *makes a sign. Two slaves bring a chest of gold coins to her. She takes handfuls and throws them over the kneeling forms of the* POLOS, *laughing*] Here! Guzzle! Grunt! Wallow for our amusement! [*The two elder* POLOS *are surreptitiously snatching at the coins but* MARCO *jumps to his feet, his face flushing*]

MARCO   [*In a hurt tone*] I don't see why you're trying to insult me—just at the last moment. What have I done? [*Then suddenly forcing a smile*] But I realize you're not yourself. [*He turns to* GHAZAN] It's just as I told you, Your Majesty, she's a trifle delirious.

GHAZAN   [*Sensing something*] Has this man offended you? Shall he be killed?

KOKACHIN   [*Wearily*] No. He has amused me. Let him be fed. Stuff him and send him home. And you, My Lord, may I ask that this first night I be allowed to remain aboard alone with my women? I am weary! I need to sleep.

GHAZAN   Again your wish is my will—even though I shall not live until I see you again!

KOKACHIN   [*Exhaustedly*] I am humbly grateful. Good night, My Lord. [*She bows.* GHAZAN *and the Court bow before her. They retreat toward the left,* MARCO *talking earnestly to the oblivious* GHAZAN, *whose eyes are riveted on the*

PRINCESS, *who has turned away from them. The two elder* POLOS, *carrying their chest, their pockets stuffed, trudge along last*]

MARCO   The close confinement of a long voyage—no invigorating exercise in the open—I think probably her liver's out of kilter—[*They are gone from right. Kokachin's shoulders quiver as, her head bowed in her hands, she sobs quietly. The ship can be heard making off*]

WOMEN   Weep, Princess of the Tired Heart,
   Weeping heals the wounds of sorrow
   Till only the scars remain
   And the heart forgets.

KOKACHIN   [*Suddenly runs up to the upper deck and stands outlined against the sky, her arms outstretched—in a voice which is a final, complete renunciation, calls*] Farewell, Marco Polo!

MARCO   [*His voice comes from over the water, cheery and relieved*] Goodbye, Princess—I mean, Your Majesty—and thank you for all you've done! [*The* PRINCESS *turns back and descends*]

THE CURTAIN FALLS

ACT SEVEN

SCENE: *One year later. The Grand Throne Room in the Imperial palace at Cambaluc.* KUBLAI *squats on his throne, aged and sad, listening with an impassive face to* GENERAL BAYAN, *who, dressed in full military uniform and armor of the Commander-in-Chief, is explaining earnestly with several maps in his hand. On Kublai's left stands* CHU YIN, *who is reading a book. Behind* BAYAN *are grouped at attention all the chief's generals of his army with a multitude of young staff officers, all gorgeously uniformed and armored. From the room on the right, the ballroom, a sound of dance music and laughter comes through the closed doors.*

BAYAN   [*Impressively—pointing to the map*] Here, Your Majesty, is the line of the river Danube which marks the Western boundary to your Empire. Beyond it, lies the West. Our spies report their many petty states are always quarreling. So great is their envy of each other that we could crush each singly and the rest would rejoice. We can mobilize one million—

CHU YIN   [*Without looking up from his book—mildly*] You are like Marco Polo's God, General, who seemed to be worth at least a million of everything!

BAYAN   One must admit that Christian was good at figures. [*Going on imperturbably*] One million horsemen across the Danube within seven days.

[*Proudly*] We would ride down their armies to the sea! Your Empire would extend from ocean to ocean!

KUBLAI [*Wearily*] It is much too large already. Why do you want to conquer the West? It must be a pitiful land, poor in spirit and material wealth. We have everything to lose by contact with its greedy hypocrisy. The conqueror acquires first of all the vices of the conquered. Let the West devour itself.

BAYAN [*Helplessly*] But—everywhere in the East there is peace.

KUBLAI [*With hopeless irony*] Ah! And you are becoming restless?

BAYAN [*Wistfully*] I feel—lost. [*Proudly*] I am a Mongol—a man of action!

KUBLAI [*Looking at him with musing irony*] Hum! You have already conquered the West, I think.

BAYAN [*Puzzled*] What, Sir? [*Then persuasively*] The West may not be strong but it is crafty. Remember how that Polo invented the engine to batter down walls? It would be better to wipe out their cunning now before they make too many engines to weaken the power of men. [*Then with a sudden inspiration*] And it would be a righteous war! We would tear down their Christian idols and set up the image of the Buddha.

KUBLAI Buddha, the Prince of Peace?

BAYAN [*Bowing his head as do all his retinue*] The Gentle One, The Good, The Kind, The Pitiful, The Wise, The Eternal Contemplative One!

KUBLAI In His Name?

BAYAN [*Fiercely*] Death to those who deny Him!

ALL [*With a great fierce shout and a clanking of swords*] Death!

KUBLAI [*Looks up at the ceiling quizzically*] A thunderbolt? [*Waits*] No? Then there is no God. [*Then to* BAYAN *with a cynical bitter smile*] August Commander, if you must have war, let it be one without fine phrases—a practical war of few words, as that Polo you admire would say. Leave the West alone. Our interests do not conflict—yet. But there is a group of islands where silk industry is beginning to threaten the supremacy of our own in the export trade. Lead your gallant million there—And see to it your war leaves me in peace!

BAYAN I hear and obey! [*He turns to his staff exultantly*] His Majesty has declared war!

ALL [*With a fierce cheer*] Down with Europe!

BAYAN [*Hastily*] No. Not yet. Down with Cipangu! [*They cheer with equal enthusiasm—then he harangues with the air of a disciplined, patriotic exhorter*] His Majesty's benevolence and patience have been exhausted by the continued outrages against our silk nationals perpetuated by unscrupulous Cipangun trade—pirates who in spite of our protests, are cruelly breeding and maintaining silk worms for immoral purposes! We fight in the cause of moral justice—that our silkmakers who are universally kind to their worms, may keep their share of the eternal sunlight! [*A long cheer*]

KUBLAI [*Smiling—distractedly*] War without poetry, please! Polo has infected you with cant! The West already invades us. Throw open the doors! Music! [*The doors are thrown open. The dance music sounds loudly*] Go in and dance, everyone! You too, General! I revoke my declaration of war—unless you go! First learn to dance and be silent! [*They all go into the ballroom,* BAYAN *stalking majestically with an injured mien*] Bring the dancers in! [*Two professional* DANCERS, *slaves, come in and start to do a wild barbaric dance.* KUBLAI, *after a moment, waves them away in disgust*] Go! [*They rush out*] Dancing makes me remember Kokachin whose little dancing feet—Shut the doors! Music brings back her voice singing—[*Turning to* CHU YIN—*harshly*] Wisdom! No, don't read! What good are wise books to fight stupidity? One must have stupid books that men can understand. In order to live and fight, wisdom must learn to be stupid!

CHU YIN [*Smiling*] That, as our Marco would have said, is all damn pessimism!

A CHAMBERLAIN [*Enters hurriedly and prostrates himself*] A courier from Persia!

KUBLAI [*Excitedly*] From Kokachin! Bring him here! [*The* CHAMBERLAIN *dashes to the door and a moment later the* COURIER *enters, travel-stained and weary. He lets himself sink into a prostrate heap before the throne.* KUBLAI *shouts at him impatiently*] Have you a letter—?

CHU YIN He is exhausted. [*He goes down to him*]

KUBLAI [*Shouts to the* CHAMBERLAIN] Wine!

COURIER [*With a great effort holds out a letter*] Here! [*He collapses.* CHU YIN *hands the letter up to* KUBLAI, *who takes it eagerly from him. He begins to read at once. The* CHAMBERLAIN *comes back with a cup of wine. The* COURIER *is revived and gets to his knees, waiting humbly*]

CHU YIN [*Goes back to* KUBLAI, *who has finished reading the short note and is staring somberly before him*] And did the Little Flower save his Immortal Soul? [KUBLAI *does not look at him but mutely hands him the letter.* CHU YIN *becomes grave. He reads aloud*] Arghun had died. I am the wife of his son,

Ghazan. It does not matter. He is kind but I miss my home and you. I doubt if I shall be blessed with a son. I do not care. I have lost my love of life. My heart beats more and more wearily. Death woos me with a passionate desire. You must not grieve. You wish me to be happy, do you not? And my body may resist his wooing for a long time yet. Too long. My soul he has already possessed. I wish to commend the unremitting attention to his duty of the Admiral. He saved my life three separate times at the risk of his own. He made a record passage. He delivered me to Ghazan. Send him another million. You were right about his soul. What I had mistaken for one turned out to be a fat woman with a patient virtue. By the time you receive this they will be getting married in Venice. I do not blame him. But I cannot forgive myself—nor forget—nor believe again in any beauty in the world. I love you the best in life. And tell Chu Yin I love him too. [*He lets the letter in his hand drop to his side, his eyes filling, his voice grows husky.* KUBLAI *stares bleakly ahead of him*]

KUBLAI [*At last rouses himself—harshly to the* COURIER] Did the Queen give you this in person?

COURIER Yes, Your Majesty—with a generous gift.

KUBLAI I can be generous too. Did she appear—ill?

COURIER Pale and sad. I could scarcely hear her voice.

KUBLAI You brought no other word?

COURIER Not from the Queen. I came privately from her. But Admiral Polo suspected my departure and gave me a verbal message which he caused me to memorize. He said that only a fool wrote letters to or about women.

KUBLAI [*Harshly—his eyes beginning to gleam with anger*] Ha! Go on! Repeat!

COURIER [*Stopping for a moment to freshen his memory*] He said, tell the Great Kaan that in spite of perils too numerous to relate, I have delivered my charge safely and in good condition to Ghazan Khan and have his receipt therefore. In general, she gave but little trouble on the voyage, for although flighty in temper and of a passionate disposition, she never refused to heed my advice for her welfare and as I informed His Majesty, King Ghazan, the responsibilities of marriage and the duties of motherhood will sober her spirit and she will eventually settle down as a virtuous wife should. This much I further add, that in humble obedience to your final instructions given me by Mr. Chu Yin, I looked daily into her eyes—

KUBLAI [*Bewilderedly to* CHU YIN] What? Did you—?

CHU YIN [*Miserably*] Forgive an old fool! I meant it partly in jest as a last chance—to cure her—or to awaken him—

COURIER [*Continuing*] But I have never noted any alarming change in them. At all times, the sight seemed normal, the color remained black, the size, large, the quality constant. At the termination of our trip, particularly on the last day, I noticed a rather unseemly expression but this I took to be fever due to her Highness' liver being sluggish after the long confinement of ship board and I humbly suggested to her future husband that he ordain that she be given a mild physic.

KUBLAI [*Choking with wrath*] O God of the Somber Heaven!

COURIER And he said if there was anything he could do for you in the West not to hesitate to let him know—just Venice, he said, would reach him. And he gave me no money for delivering the message but he promised that you would reward me nobly!

KUBLAI [*With wild laughter*] Ha-ha-ha! Stop! Do you dare madden me? [*Then suddenly raging*] Out of my sight, dog, before I order you impaled! [*The terror-stricken* COURIER *scrambles out like a flash.* KUBLAI *stands up with flashing eyes—revengefully*] I have reconsidered! I will conquer the West! I shall lead the armies in person! I shall leave not one temple standing nor one Christian alive who is not enslaved! Their cities shall vanish in flame, their fields shall be wasted! Famine shall finish what I leave undone! And of the city of Venice not one vestige shall remain! And of the body of Marco Polo there shall not be a fragment of bone nor an atom of flesh which will not have shrieked through ten days torture before it died!

CHU YIN Master! [*He throw himself on his face at Kublai's feet*] Do not torture yourself! Is this Wisdom? Is this the peace of the soul?

KUBLAI [*Distractedly*] To revenge oneself—that brings a kind of peace!

CHU YIN To revenge equally the wrong of an equal perhaps—but this—? Can you confess yourself weaker than his stupidity?

KUBLAI He has murdered her!

CHU YIN She does not accuse him. What would be her wish?

KUBLAI [*His anger passing—wearily and bitterly, after a pause*] Rise, my old friend, it is I who should be at your feet, not you at mine, if life were not insane. [*He sinks dejectedly on his throne again. After a pause, sadly*] She will die—slowly fading away—an emanation of Beauty from the soul of Youth! Why is this? What purpose can it serve? My hideous intuition is that the very essence of life may be merely an infinite, crazy energy which creates and destroys without other purpose than to pass infinite time in avoiding thought. Then the stupid man becomes the perfect Incarnation of Omnipotence and the Polos are the true children of God! [*He laughs bitterly*] Ha! How long before we shall be permitted to die, my friend? I begin to resent my life as the insult of an ignoble inferior with whom it is a degradation to fight!

CHU YIN   Do not judge the bidden by what appears! The mind is a false-witness. What it thinks has no other existence beyond its thought.

KUBLAI   [*Scornfully*] And what is not, is? Bah! Mystic! [*Broodingly—after a pause*] I have had a foreboding that she would die. Lately, to while away time, I experimented with the crystal. I do not believe the magic nonsense about it but I do consider that, given a focus, the will can perhaps overcome the limit of the sense. Whatever the explanation be, I looked into the crystal and willed to see Kokachin in Persia and she appeared, sitting alone in a garden, beautiful and sad, apart from life, waiting—[*Brokenly*] My eyes filled with tears. I cried out to her—and she was gone! [*Then with sudden bitter savageness—to the* CHAMBERLAIN] Bring me the crystal! [*Then to* CHU YIN *as the* CHAMBERLAIN *goes*] Marco, the true ruler of the world, will have come to Venice by this time. My loathing grows so intense I feel he must jump into the crystal at my bidding. And—in the cause of wisdom, say—we must see what he is doing now. [*The* CHAMBERLAIN *returns with the crystal.* KUBLAI *takes it eagerly from his hand and stares fixedly into it*]

CHU YIN   [*Protestingly*] Why do you seek to wound yourself further?

KUBLAI   [*Staring fixedly*] I promise I shall only observe dispassionately. It is a test of myself I wish to make as a penalty for my weakness a moment since—[*He sees something*] Ah—it begins. [*A pause. The light grows dimmer and dimmer on the stage proper as it begins to come up on the forestage*] I see— a city whose streets are canals—it is evening—a house—I begin to see through the walls—Ah. [*The lights come up on the backstage as the forestage is fully revealed. At the center is a great banquet table with chairs garishly set with an ornate gold service. A tall majordomo in a gorgeous uniform enters and stands at respectful stiff attention as the procession begins. First come the guests, male and female, a crowd of good substantial bourgeois, who stare about with awe and envy and are greatly impressed by the gold plate*]

A MAN   They've laid out a pile of money here!

A WOMAN   What luxury! Is that gold service really gold?

A WOMAN   Absolutely. I can tell without biting it.

A MAN   They must have cash, whoever they are.

A WOMAN   Do you think they're really the Polos?

ANOTHER   They look like greasy Tartars to me.

ANOTHER   That was their queer clothes.

A MAN   And remember they've been gone twenty-odd years.

ANOTHER   In spite of that, I thought I could recognize Maffeo.

A WOMAN   Will Donata know Marco, I wonder?

A MAN   What's more to her point, will he recognize her?

A WOMAN   Imagine her waiting all this time!

ANOTHER   How romantic! He must be terribly rich—if it's really him.

A MAN   We'll soon know. That's why we were invited.

A WOMAN   Ssshh! Here comes Donata now. How old she's getting to look!

ANOTHER   And how fat in the hips!

A MAN   [*Jokingly*] That's the way I like 'em and perhaps Marco—[DONATA *enters on the arm of her father, a crafty, wizened old man. She has grown into a stout middle-age but her face is unlined and still pretty in a bovine, good-natured, brainless way. All bow and they return this salutation*]

ALL   Congratulations, Donata! [*She blushes and turns aside in an incongruous girlish confusion*]

FATHER   [*Proud but pretending querulousness*] Don't tease her now! The girl's nervous enough already—and it may not be Marco after all but only a joke someone's put up on us.

WOMAN   No one could be so cruel!

ALL   [*Suddenly with a great gasp*] Oh listen! [*An orchestra vigorously begins a flowery, sentimental Italian street song. This grows into quite a blare as the musicians enter from the right, six in number, in brilliant uniforms*] Oh look! [*The musicians form a lane, three on each side by the stairs on the right*] Oh see! [*A procession of servants begins to file one by one through the ranks of musicians, each carrying on his head or upraised hand enormous platters on which are whole pigs, fowl of all varieties, roasts, vegetables, salads, fruits, nuts, dozens of bottles of wine. The servants arrange these on the table, in symmetrical groups, with the trained eye for display of window-dressers, until the table, with the bright light flooding down on it, closely resembles the front of a pretentious delicatessen store*]

ALL   [*Meanwhile*] See! What a turkey! Such a goose! The fattest little pig I ever saw! What ducks! What vegetables! Look at the wine! A feast for the Gods! And all those servants! An army! And the orchestra! What expense! Lavish! They care nothing for money, that's evident! They must be worth millions. [*The three POLOS make their grand entrance from the stairs on right, walking with bursting self-importance between the files of musicians, who now blare out*] *a triumphal march. The two elder precede* MARCO. *All three are dressed in long robes of embroidered crimson satin reaching almost to the ground. The guests give a new united gasp of astonishment*] Is it they? Is that old Nicolo? That's Maffeo's nose! No! It isn't them at all! Well, if it's a joke, I don't see the point. But such robes! Such hand embroidery! Such material! They must be worth millions!

DONATA   [*Falteringly*] Is that him, father? I cannot tell. [*She calls*] Marco! [*But he pretends not to hear. He gives a sign at which the three take off their robes and hand them to the servants. They have even more gorgeous blue robes underneath.* MARCO *addresses the servants in concealed voice*] "My good men, you may sell these rich robes and divide the proceeds among yourselves! And here is a little something extra." [*He tosses a handful of gold to the servants and another to the musicians. A mad scramble results. The guests gasp. They seem inclined to join in the scramble.* "How generous! What prodigality! What indifference to money! They throw it like dirt. They must be worth millions!"]

MARCO   [*In the same false voice*] Our guests look thirsty. Pass around the wine! [*The servants do so. The guests gaze, smell, even taste*]

ALL   What a vintage! What flavor! What bouquet! How aged! It must have cost twenty lire a bottle! [*At another signal the three* POLOS *take off their blue robes*]

MARCO   [*Regally*] Give those to the musicians! [*They are revealed now in their old dirty, loose Tartar travelling dress and look quite shabby. The guests gape uncertainly. Then* MARCO *declares grandly*] You look astonished, good people, but this is a moral lesson to teach you not to put too much faith in appearances—for see—

DONATA   [*Calls*] Marco! [*Then uncertainly*] It is his voice and not his voice! [*Without pretending to hear her* MARCO *has slit up the wide sleeves of his own robe, as have his father and uncle, and now the three, standing beside a big empty space which has been purposely left at the very center of the table at the front, lower their opened sleeves and, as the musicians obeying this signal, start up a great blare, let pour from them a perfect stream of precious stones which form a glittering multicolored heap. This is a final blow. The guests stare pop-eyed, open-mouthed, speechless for a second. Then their pent up admiration breaks forth*]

ALL   Extraordinary! Jewels! Gems! Rubies! Emeralds! Diamonds! Pearls! Worth a king's ransom! What millions!

MARCO   [*Suddenly with his hail-fellow-well-met joviality*] Well, folks, are you all tongue-tied? Isn't one of you going to say welcome home? And Miss

Donata, don't I get a kiss? I'm still a bachelor! [*Immediately with mad shouts of "Bravo!" "Welcome home" "Hurrah for the Polos" etc., etc., the guests bear down on them in a flood. There is a confused whirl of embraces, kisses, back-slaps, handshakes and loud greetings of all sorts.* MARCO *manages to get separated and pulls* DONATA *down front to the apex of forestage*]

DONATA   [*Half swooning*] Marco! My Dream Man!

MARCO   [*Moved*] My old girl! [*They kiss, then he pushes her away*] Here! Let me get a good look at you! Why, you're still as pretty as a picture and you don't look a day older!

DONATA   [*Exaltedly*] My beloved prince!

MARCO   [*Jokingly*] No, if I was a prince I'd never have remained single all these years in the East! I'm a hero, that's what! And all the twenty-six years I kept thinking of you, and I was always intending to write—[*He pulls the pieces of the miniature wrapped in the handkerchief out of his pocket*] Here's proof for you! Look at yourself! You're a bit smashed but that was done in a hand-to-hand fight I had with a mad elephant. Now don't I deserve another kiss?

DONATA   [*Giving it*] My hero! [*Then jealously*] But I know all the heathen women must have fallen in love with you.

MARCO   Oh, maybe one or two or so—but I didn't have time to waste on females. I kept my nose to the grindstone every minute. [*Proudly*] And I got results. I don't mind telling you, Donata, I'm worth a cool two or three million. How's that for keeping my promise? Worth while your waiting, eh? [*He slaps her on the back*]

DONATA   Yes, you wonderful Man! [*Then worriedly*] You said there were one or two women—? But you were true to me in spite of them, weren't you?

MARCO   I tell you I wouldn't have married the prettiest girl in Cathay! [*This with emphasis. Then abruptly*] But never mind any other girl. [*He chucks her under the chin*] What I want to know is when this girl is going to marry me?

DONATA   [*Softly*] Any time! [*They hug. The guests group about them kittenishly, pointing and murmuring, "What a romance! What a romance!"*]

DONATA'S FATHER   [*Seizing the opportunity*] Friends, I take this opportunity to publicly announce the betrothal of my daughter, Donata, to Marco Polo, Esquire of this Queen City! [*Another wild round of congratulations, kisses, etc.*]

MARCO   [*His voice sounding above the hubbub*] Let's eat, folks! [*They swirl to their places behind the long table. When they stand their faces can be seen above the piles of food but when they sit they are out of sight*] No ceremony among friends. Just pick your chair. All ready? Let's sit then! [*With one motion they disappear*]

VOICE OF DONATA'S FATHER But first, before we regale ourselves with your cheer, won't you address a few words to your old friends and neighbors who have gathered here in this happy occasion—? [*Applause.* MARCO *is heard expostulating but finally he gives in*]

MARCO All right—if you'll promise to go ahead and eat and not wait for me—[*His head appears, his expression full of importance. Servants flit about noisily. He coughs and begins with dramatic feeling*] My friends and neighbors of old—your generous and whole-hearted welcome touches me profoundly. I would I had the gift of oratory to thank you fittingly, but I am a simple man, an ordinary man, I might almost say,—a man of affairs used to dealing in the hard facts of life—a silent man—given to deeds not words—[*Here he falters fittingly*] And so now—forgive my emotion—words fail me—[*Here he clears his throat with an important cough and bursts forth into a memorized speech in the grand Chamber of Commerce style*] But I'll be glad to let you have a few instructive facts about the silk industry as we observed it in the Far East, laying special emphasis upon the keystone of the whole silk business—I refer to the breeding of worms! [*A few hungry guests start to eat. Knives and forks and spoons rattle against plates. Soup is heard.* MARCO *strikes a good listening attitude so he'll be sure not to miss a word his voice utters and warms to his work*] Now, to begin with there are millions upon millions of capital invested in this industry, millions of contented slaves labor unremittingly millions of hours per annum to obtain the best results in the dying and weaving of the finished product, but I don't hesitate to state that all this activity is relatively unimportant beside the astounding fact that in the production of the raw material there are constantly employed millions upon millions of millions of worms!

ONE VOICE [*Rather muffled by roast pig*] Hear! [*But the rest are all absorbed in eating and a perfect clamor of knives and forks resounds.* MARCO *begins again but this time the clamor is too great, his words are lost, only the one he lays such underlying emphasis on can be distinguished*]

MARCO Millions—millions—millions—

KUBLAI [*Who from the height of his golden throne, crystal in hand, has watched all this with fascinated disgust while* CHU YIN *has sat down to read his book again now turns away with a shudder of loathing and, in spite of himself a shadow of a smile, and lets the crystal fall from his hand and shatter into bits with a loud report. Instantly there is darkness and from high up in the darkness Kublai's voice speaking with a pitying scorn*] The Word became their flesh. They shall not be saved until their flesh becomes the Word again.

THE CURTAIN FALLS

SCENE: *The same as Act One, Scene Two—Marco's cell in the prison of the Malapaga, Genoa. He has passed several months in the prison since that scene and since the homecoming of the* POLOS *about two years have elapsed.*

At first, the light is so dim the figures in the cell can be barely made out but a voice, which one recognizes as that of RUSTICIANO, *can be heard reading aloud although his words cannot be distinguished. Then it lightens and the interior is revealed.* MARCO *lolls back at ease on his stone bench, his arm around* DONATA, *who is sitting beside him nursing her baby.* RUSTICIANO *stands before them, holding a script and marking his cadences with a graceful hand.*

RUSTICIANO   And here is my termination to the work. [*Reads*] "And I believe it was God's special pleasure that I, Marco Polo, should return to my country in order that people might learn about the things the world contains. For, as I have conclusively proven in this book, there never was a man, be he Christian or heathen, who ever travelled over so much of the world as did I, the noble and illustrious citizen of the City of Venice, Mark, the son of Nicholas Polo. Thanks be to God! Amen! Amen! [*He blesses himself*]

DONATA   [*Blesses herself*] Amen.

MARCO   [*Blesses himself*] Amen. [*Then with a patronizing smile*] Well, that's a good striking twist you've wrung in for the end. It ought to catch them.

RUSTICIANO   [*Pleased*] I flatter myself it is felicitious. But what constructive criticism have you to make on my book—pardon me, our book—as a sufficing work of art?

MARCO   [*Frowning portentously*] Humm. Let me turn it over in my mind a minute. It's quite a long book to consider in toto. [*He considers*]

DONATA   [*Ecstatically*] I love it! I think it's just too nice for words! It's exactly like Mark! Why, at times I could close my eyes and imagine I heard him speaking! And that's the very highest art, isn't it? [*To her sleeping daughter*] Isn't it too wonderful, Baby? Your father is an artist, too!

RUSTICIANO   [*In a bit of a huff*] I had something to do with that, Mrs. Polo.

DONATA   [*Effusively*] Why, of course you did! I know how hard you've worked and now you have a right to be proud. Why, I don't think you've left out anything he said!

RUSTICIANO   [*A bit bitingly*] No, but I did attempt to embellish—

MARCO   [*Suddenly. And portentously*] A very neat job, that's my verdict. Satisfactory in every way. I'm pleased with it—and here's my congratulations to myself and you! [*They shake hands gravely,* RUSTICIANO *beaming*]

RUSTICIANO   [*Gratefully*] To merit the praise of a world figure like Marco Polo—!

MARCO   I give credit where credit is due—always did and always will and no favors asked! [*Suddenly sentimental*] And I want to thank you for that little touch at the end where you say I'm the son of Nicholas Polo. That'll please the old gentleman. He's getting very conceited in his second childhood and it does no harm to humor him.

DONATA   [*To her daughter*] Yes, won't Grandpa be proud, baby?

MARCO   [*Frowning judicially*] Properly handled, my book ought to have a wide educational influence. I don't mind saying that aspect of it tickles me. I like to do good. Why, this book has a little bit of everything and no matter what sort of person reads it he's sure to find something to interest and instruct him. And my story'll help Venice, wait and see. Now if the Council of Ten want to use my influence with the Great Kaan as shown to them in this book, we can arrange an exclusive trade agreement with the East that'll drive every merchant and shipowner here in Genoa into bankruptcy within a year! They'll have to put a standing room only sign on the poor house before I get through with 'em. Hit 'em in the surplus, that's the way to fight 'em!

DONATA   [*Worriedly*] You've already fought enough for Venice, my precious hero. When you get out of jail this time, you want to stay out, don't you? Your book will fight for you from now on. My Author Husband! [*She kisses him and snuggles to him—persuasively*] There's just one thing in the book—

MARCO   [*Immediately*] Now don't start to complain!

DONATA   It's where you say that that pretty pagan Princess cried when you left her.

MARCO   When *we* left her—the three of us.

DONATA   No one'll ever believe she was crying over those two old men! And you know very well what people'll say when they read—

MARCO   [*Scenting a squall and shifting the blame*] Mr. Rusticiano probably misquoted me. [*He gives the latter a vigorous wink*]

RUSTICIANO   [*Perplexed*] No—I'm sure you said. . . .

DONATA   [*Following her own thoughts—jealously*] I suppose it's regret for that heathen hussy that makes you so grouchy at times?

MARCO   Don't talk silly! Can't a man be miserable because he's in jail without your getting jealous?

DONATA   [*Scornfully*] That's a likely story, isn't it?—a fine excuse! [*But the gathering storm is interrupted by the turnkey* GIOVANNI, *who comes to the door and rattles the bars*]

GIOVANNI   [*Jeeringly*] Time is up, Mister Mark Millions! Stop your damned lying about the millions of concubines you enjoyed in the East and let your wife go home. [*He winks at her*] Don't mind him, Missus. Even if there was a million, he'd never win one for love or money!

DONATA   [*Flushing*] You're a filthy obscene rascal!

GIOVANNI   [*Grinning*] And you're what they think is a lady—in Venice! [*He turns away, chuckling at their discomfiture*]

MARCO   [*Sputtering*] Genoese gorilla! [*Then hastily*] My dear, he's a malicious liar! What I said was that there were millions of loose women in the Kaan's Empire—and there are, millions and millions of them! [*From the hallway,* GIOVANNI *lets out a great trumpeting raspberry followed by a good imitation of a dog barking.* MARCO *stamps his foot and shakes his fist*] Insolent son of a sow! [*Then with the air of a martyr*] You see! His mentality is typical of the narrow-minded stay-at-homes who will call my book a tissue of lies!

RUSTICIANO   Posterity will glorify you, sir!

MARCO   Well, I wish posterity would fire that jailer! I don't dare complain or he'll put me on water and use my rations to fatten his pigs. The corruption in this prison is a scandal!

DONATA   Perhaps I could bribe him to be more respectful.

MARCO   I doubt it. He says he gets a million lire's worth of fun—But you might try—perhaps a woman—but don't pay too great a price—

DONATA   [*Suddenly with the full dignity of virtuous womanhood*] No! Not that! Not even for you!

MARCO   [*Stares at her blankly—irritably*] I don't know what you're talking about. I was saying don't offer more than a thousand.

DONATA   [*Let down*] Oh, all right.

GIOVANNI   [*Appears at door again*] Shake a leg, lady. You can't stay all night. All lights out in a minute—and I wouldn't trust Mister Million alone with you in the dark. This is a respectable house.

DONATA   [*About to burst*] You—

MARCO   Ssshh! [*He kisses her—in a whisper*] Keep your temper. Try a thousand.

DONATA   I will. Good'bye. [*Holds up the baby*] Kiss Baby. [*He does so. The* JAILER *opens the door. She passes out. He closes door again and calls back*]

GIOVANNI   And you, Brother Rusty Piano, get ready to go to your own kennel. [*He goes off whistling.* RUSTICIANO *sighs meekly.* MARCO *broods irritably*]

MARCO   [*Suddenly*] You don't seem to have much gumption when it comes to women, Rusticiano. Why didn't you take the blame for that stuff about the Princess weeping? She couldn't take it out on you—but I can see where I'll never hear the end of it!

RUSTICIANO   [*Defensively*] But I cannot understand how anyone could object—why, it is the most delightfully romantic touch in the book.

MARCO   [*Dryly*] Yes. Donata saw that.

RUSTICIANO   [*Uncertainly*] And, honored sir, what I wrote is a verbatim rendering of your own words—

MARCO   [*Irritably*] Brother, you've got one crowning drawback. You have no sense of humor. You'd never have gotten along even as far as you have without it unless you were an author—and that reminds me that, come to think of it, my one objection to my book is you make me out to be as humorless as yourself. Why, you never even quote one of my stories! People will get the wrong idea—for although it's all right to have 'em know that I'm an intensive man of affairs with no frills—and proud of it, too!—still there's another more homey side to me and that is that I love a joke and I've always been noted for my keen sense of humor.

RUSTICIANO   [*Who has passed into a dream—vaguely*] Yes, sir. [*Then with romantic eagerness*] Was the Princess young and beautiful?

MARCO   Now don't try to change the subject! [*Aggressively*] You seem to doubt my statement about my more human side. Now listen: [*He buttonholes* RUSTICIANO *and fixes him with an aggressively grinning eye*] Here's the funniest story you ever heard! I got it from the funniest fellow you ever met—a natural born wit if there ever was one!—a general manager at the Birds Nest factory in Cambaluc—a plant which I did a good deal to organize and float, by the way, although the original inspiration was Uncle's.—Well, never mind that, here's the story: [*With a smirk which grows broader as he goes on and keeps lowering his voice*] It seems there was an old Jew somewhere named Ikey and he'd just married a young girl called Rebecca but he drank too much wine at the wedding dinner and that night when he went upstairs it was all dark and—[*He whispers the rest of the story into Rusticiano's ear with much Jewish gesture pantomime and then bursts into a guffaw*] Haw-haw! Isn't that a peach?

RUSTICIANO   [*Looking a bit green forces a sickly laugh*] Ha-ha.

MARCO [*Put out, turns away from him—scornfully*] Hope I didn't shock you!

RUSTICIANO [*Shakes his head as if to get rid of all memory of the joke—then blurts out suddenly*] You never told me much about the Princess.

MARCO [*Brusquely*] No.

RUSTICIANO [*Persistently—scenting romantic secrets*] Why, if I may be so bold as to inquire, sir?

MARCO Oh, I suppose I've forgotten. [*Then drifting into sentimental self-interest—meaningly*] That is, I mean I ought to forget. Now that I'm married—and a father—well, you understand—

RUSTICIANO [*Breathlessly*] You mean—

MARCO [*Meaningly*] I mean nothing. You writers are always snooping around for free plots.

RUSTICIANO [*Craftily*] I would promise not to put it in a book.

MARCO Hmmm!

RUSTICIANO [*After a pause*] She wept with grief when you left?

MARCO Well—yes. Frankly—and confidentially, remember!—the Princess thought a whole lot of me.

RUSTICIANO She—loved you?

MARCO [*Really embarrassed here*] Well—I wouldn't care to answer that. Ask my father. He claims—I don't know. That last day she wasn't herself. Neither was I. Everyone was upset about getting to Persia at last. Her eyes got looking pretty burning, I tell you—fever, I guess—her liver, I imagine. Even Princesses have livers.

RUSTICIANO [*Quite violently agitated*] No! Princesses have hearts!

MARCO Oh, all right. [*Then musingly*] And eyes. She certainly had wonderful eyes.

RUSTICIANO [*In his ecstatic element now*] Were they like stars?

MARCO Yes, I guess so. Shiny and blinkey.

RUSTICIANO Were her teeth like pearls?

MARCO Very much—but with a trifle more body to 'em, I imagine.

RUSTICIANO Were her lips like the petals of a crimson rose?

MARCO I think so. I've never noticed roses much.

RUSTICIANO Then she was altogether lovely?

MARCO [*Almost in spite of himself*] Lovely as the gold in the sun. [*Then with a queer laugh*] Hullo! How'd I ever happen to remember that? That's the first line of a poem I once wrote. I've forgotten the rest of it.

RUSTICIANO   [*Avidly*] A poem you wrote to the Princess?

MARCO   [*Harshly*] Not on your life! To Donata—years ago when I was foolish.

RUSTICIANO   [*Following his own obsession*] Then a royal Princess really loved you?

MARCO   [*With satisfaction*] She's a Queen now!

RUSTICIANO   [*Reproachfully*] And you never requited—!

MARCO   [*With sudden irritation*] Never mind what I did. [*A pause— meaningly*] I'd be a fine fool to trust a writer with a secret, wouldn't I? [*A pause. Then a bit sadly with a trace of self-overcoming*] But I won't make any bluff one way or the other. Nothing whatsoever happened, that's the plain fact. If she saw me now she probably wouldn't remember me from Adam. But I'd know her. She was a real beauty! [*Then squirming out of all this onto a high moral plane*] I was true to a trust that was placed in me. I had a job to do and I did it, that's all there was to it. I acted as a man of honesty and integrity ought to act, for Thank God, my moral sense of duty has always proved stronger than any temptation! [*He ends up, having earned his own complete approval*]

RUSTICIANO   [*A bit slyly ironic*] Yes. You are a good man. [*The light begins to fade out, the cell and its occupants to disappear. From a great distance a musical clamor of many temple bells is heard. This grows louder as the light disappears and reaches its climax of all the temple bells of Cambaluc ringing at once as the curtain rises on the next scene*]

ACT EIGHT   SCENE TWO

SCENE: *Same as Act Three, Scene Two. Grand Throne Room in the Imperial palace at Cambaluc, about two years later. The walls tower majestically in shadow, their elaborate detail blurred into a background of half-darkness.* KUBLAI *sits at the top of his throne, cross-legged in the posture of an idol, motionless, wrapped in contemplation. He wears a simple white robe without adornment of any sort. A brilliant light floods down upon him in one concentrated ray. His eyes are fixed on a catafalque, draped in heavy white silk, which stands in the center of the room, emphasized by another downpouring shaft of light.*

CHU YIN *stands on the level below, on Kublai's left. On the main floor are all the nobles and people of the court, grouped as in Act Three, Scene Two.*

There is a long pause clamorous with the pealing of the thousands of bells in the city, big and little, near and far. Every figure in the room is as motionless as the KAAN himself. Their eyes are kept on him with the ardent humility and respect of worship. Behind their impassive faces, one senses a tense expectancy of some sign from the throne. At last, without in any way shifting his concentrated attention from the catafalque, KUBLAI makes a slight but imperious motion of command with his right hand. Immediately the WOMEN all turn with arms outstretched toward the catafalque. Their voices rise together in a long, rhythmic wail of mourning; their arms with one motion move slowly up, up; their voices attain a prolonged note of unbearable poignancy; their heads are thrown back, their arms appeal to Heaven in an agonized gesture of despair. Here the KAAN makes the same barely perceptible sign of command again. The voices are instantly silenced, the arms fall to their sides in one significant motion of obedience, the WOMEN wait with heads bowed down in humility. The bells, except for one slow deep-toned one in the palace itself, are almost instantly hushed and still. The same signal comes again from KUBLAI. In one rhythm, the WOMEN sink prostrate on the floor. At the same instant, from outside, at first faint and distant but growing momentarily in intensity and volume, comes the sound of funeral music. A moment later the funeral procession enters. The MEN sink to the squatting position of prayer, their heads bowed low, their bodies swaying. Only the KAAN himself does not bow his head but remains immovable, his eyes on the catafalque.

First in the funeral procession, as it enters from the left, come the MUSICIANS, nine in number, men in robes of bright red. They are followed by the nine SINGERS, five men and four women, all of them aged, with bent bodies, their thin, cracked voices accompanying the music in queer, breaking waves of lamentation. All are masked, the men with the identical mask of male grief, the women with a female. All are dressed in deep black with white edging to their robes. After them comes a troop of YOUNG GIRLS AND BOYS, dressed in white with black edging, moving slowly backward in a gliding, interweaving dance motive. Their faces are not masked but are fixed in a disciplined, traditional expression of bewildered, uncomprehending grief which is like a mask. They carry silver censers which they swing in unison toward the corpse of the PRINCESS KOKACHIN, carried on its bier directly behind them on the shoulders of eight PRINCES of the blood in full armour. Accompanying the bier in positions one at each corner are four PRIESTS—the foremost two, a Confucian and a Taoist, the latter two, a Buddhist and a Moslem. Each walks with bent head reading aloud to himself from his Holy Book of God.

The PRINCES lift the bier of KOKACHIN to the top of the catafalque. Her body is wrapped in a winding sheet of deep blue, a jewelled gold head-dress is on her black hair, her face is white and clear as a statue's as she lies in the downpouring shaft of light. The YOUNG BOYS AND GIRLS place their smoking censers about the catafalque, the incense ascending in clouds about the PRINCESS as if it were bearing her soul aloft with it. The PRIESTS stand at each corner with bowed head reading silently from their Holy Books. The music and the singing cease as the DANCERS, SINGERS, and MUSICIANS form on each side, and to the rear, of the catafalque and sink into the bent attitudes of prayer.

KUBLAI emerges from contemplation. His eyes are removed from the corpse. He speaks to the PRIESTS in an imperturable voice of command in which is a tone of weariness and disbelief.

KUBLAI Peace! She does not need your prayers. She was a prayer! [*With one motion they shut their books, raise their heads and stare before them in silence.* KUBLAI *continues sadly*] Can words recall life to her beauty? [*To the* PRIEST OF TAO] Priest of Tao, will you conquer death by your mystic Way?

PRIEST OF TAO [*Bowing his head in submission—fatalistically*] Which is the greater evil, to possess or to be without? Death is.

CHORUS [*In an echo of vast sadness*] Death is.

KUBLAI [*To the* CONFUCIAN] Follower of Confucius, the Wise, have you this wisdom?

PRIEST OF CONFUCIUS [*Slowly*] Before we know life, how can we know death? [*Then as the* TAOIST, *submissively*] Death is.

CHORUS [*As before*] Death is.

KUBLAI [*To the* BUDDHIST PRIEST] Worshipper of Buddhas, can your self-overcoming overcome that greatest overcomer of self?

BUDDHIST PRIEST This is a thing which no god nor any being in the universe can bring about: that what is subject to death should not die. [*Then as the others, submissively*] Death is.

CHORUS [*As before*] Death is.

KUBLAI [*Wearily*] And your answer, priest of Islam?

PRIEST OF ISLAM It is the will of Allah! [*Submissively*] Death is.

CHORUS Death is. Death is. Death is. [*Their voices die away*]

KUBLAI [*After a pause*] What is death? [*A long pause. His eyes rest in loving contemplation on the body of* KOKACHIN. *Finally he speaks tenderly to her with a sad smile*] Girl whom we call dead, whose beauty is even in death more living than we, smile with infinite silence upon our speech, smile with infinite forbearance upon our wisdom, smile with infinite remoteness upon our sorrow, smile as a star smiles—[*His voice appears about to break. A muffled sound of sobbing comes from the prostrate* WOMEN. KUBLAI *regains control over his weakness and rises to his feet—with angry self-contempt*] No more! That is for poets! [*With over-stressed arrogance—assertively*] And I am the Great Kaan! [*Everyone in the room rises with one motion of the assertion of life*]

CHORUS [*Accompanied by a clangor of brass from the musicians—recite with discordant vigor*]
>The Greatest of the Great!
>Son of Heaven! Lord of the Earth!
>Ruler of the World!
>Sovereign over Life and Death!—

KUBLAI [*Silences them by an imperious gesture—and now even the great palace bell is stilled—half-mockingly but assertively*] The Son of Heaven? Then I should know a prayer. Sovereign of the World? Then I command the World to pray! [*With one motion all sink to the position of prayer*] In silence! Prayer is beyond words! Contemplate the eternal life of Life. Pray thus. [*He himself sinks to the position of prayer—a pause—then slowly*] In silence—for one concentrated moment—be proud of life! Know in your heart that the living of life can be noble! Know that the dying of death can be noble! Be exalted by life! Be inspired by death! Be humbly proud! Be proudly grateful! Be immortal because life is immortal. Contain the harmony of womb and grave within you! Possess life as a lover—then sleep requited in the arms of death! If you awake, love again! If you sleep on, rest in peace! Who knows which? What does it matter? It is nobler not to know! [*A pause of silence. He rises to his feet. With one motion all do likewise.* KUBLAI *sits back on his cushions again, withdrawing himself into contemplation. The* MONGOL CHRONICLER *comes forward to fulfill his function of chanting the official lament for the dead. He declaims in a high wailing voice accompanied by the musicians and by the chorus, who sway rhythmically and hum a rising and falling mourning accompaniment*]

CHRONICLER We lament the shortness of life. Life at its longest is brief enough.
Too brief for the wisdom of joy, too long for the knowledge of sorrow.
Sorrow becomes despair when death comes to the young, untimely.
Oh that her beauty could live again—that her youth could be born again.
Our Princess was young as spring, she was beautiful as a bird or flower.
Cruel when Spring is smitten by Winter; when birds are struck dead in full song; when the budding blossom is blighted!
Alas that our Princess is dead, she who was the song of all songs, the perfume of perfumes, the uniquely perfect one!

Our sobs stifle us, our tears wet the ground, our lamentations sadden the wind from the West.

[*Bows submissively—speaks*] Yet we must bow humbly before the Omnipotent.

CHORUS   We must be humble.

CHRONICLER   Against Death even Gods are powerless.

CHORUS   Gods are powerless. [*Their voices die into silence*]

KUBLAI   [*After a pause—wearily*] Leave her in peace. Go. [*The court leaves at his command in a formal, expressionless order. The four PRIESTS go first, beginning to pray again. They are followed by the NOBLES, OFFICIALS, led by the WARRIOR from the throne, etc., with their WOMEN coming after, led by the WOMAN from the foot of the throne with the child in her arms. The music has started on the same strains as on its entrance. Finally the YOUNG BOYS AND GIRLS take up their censers and dance out backward, preceded by the musicians. Only the CHORUS remain, grouped in a semi-circle behind the catafalque, motionless, and the SAGE, stays at the left hand of KUBLAI. The music fades away into distance. KUBLAI takes his eyes from the dead girl with a sigh of bitter irony*] Oh, Chu Yin, my Wise Friend, was the prayer I taught them wisdom?

CHU YIN   It was the wisdom of pride. It was thy wisdom.

CHORUS   [*Echoing with infinite sadness*] Thy wisdom.

KUBLAI   Was it not truth?

CHU YIN   It was the truth of power. It was thy truth.

CHORUS   [*As before*] Thy truth.

KUBLAI   My pride, my power? My wisdom, my truth? For me there remains only—her truth! [*Then after staring at her for a second, bitterly*] Her truth!—she died for love of a fool! [*He smiles bitterly*] Can wisdom be born of that truth?

CHU YIN   She loved love. She died for beauty.

KUBLAI   Your words are old and empty. They are hollow echoes in the brain. Do not wound me any longer with wisdom. Speak to my heart!

CHU YIN   [*Bowing with elaborate submission—meaningly*] You are the Greatest of the Great.

CHORUS   [*Again with discordant assertion*] The Greatest of the Great!

CHU YIN   The Sovereign of the World!

CHORUS   [*As before*] The Sovereign of the World!

KUBLAI   [*Sadly*] Her little feet danced away the stamp of armies. Her smile made me forget the servile grin on the face of the World. In her eyes' mirror I watched myself live secluded from life in her affection—a simple old man dying contentedly a little day after pleasant day.

CHU YIN [*Bowing with sincere respect—compassionately*] Then weep, old man. Be humble and weep for your child. The old should cherish sorrow. [*He bows again and goes out silently*]

KUBLAI [*After a pause, gets up and descending from his throne, slowly approaches the catafalque speaking to the dead girl softly as he does so—with a trembling smile*] I think you are hiding your eyes, Kokachin. You are a little girl again. You are playing hide and seek. You are pretending. Did we not once play such games together, you and I? You have made your face still, you have made your face cold, you have set your lips in a smile so remote—you are pretending even that you are dead! [*He is very near her now. His voice breaks— more and more intensely*] Let us stop playing! It is late. It is time you were asleep. Open your eyes and laugh! Laugh now that the game is over. Take the blindfold from my dim eyes. Whisper your secret in my ear. I—I am dead and you are living! Weep for me, Kokachin! Weep for the dead! [*He stretches his arms out to her beseechingly—then pauses, standing beside the body, staring down at her still face, then, after a moment, he passes his hand over her face— tremblingly—with a beautiful tenderness of grief*] So, little Kokachin—so, Little Flower—you have come back—they could not keep you—you were too home-sick—you wanted to return—to gladden my last days—[*He no longer tries to control his grief. He sobs like a simple old man, bending and kissing his grand-daughter on the forehead—with heart-breaking playfulness*] I bid you welcome home—[*He weeps, his tears falling and glistening on her calm white face*]

CURTAIN

EPILOGUE

SCENE: *The play is over. The lights come up brilliantly in the theatre. In an aisle seat in the first row a man gets up, conceals a yawn in his palm, stretches his legs as if they had become cramped by too long an evening, takes his hat from under the seat and starts to file out slowly with the others in the audience. But, although there is nothing out of the ordinary in his actions, his appearance excites general comment and surprise for he is dressed as a Venetian merchant of the later 13th century. In fact, it is none other than* MARCO POLO *himself looking a bit sleepy, a trifle puzzled and not a little irritated as his thoughts, in spite of himself, cling for a passing moment to the play just ended. He appears quite unaware of being unusual and walks in the crowd without self-consciousness, very much as one of them. Arrived at the lobby his face begins to clear of all disturbing memories of what had transpired on the stage. The noise, the lights of the streets, all recall him at once to himself. Impatiently he waits for his car, casting a glance here and there at faces in the groups around him, his eyes impersonally speculative, his bearing stolid with the dignity of one who is sure of his place in the world. His car, a luxurious Pierce-Arrow limousine, draws up at the curb. He gets in briskly, the door is slammed, the car edges away into the traffic and* POLO, *with a satisfied sigh at the comfort of it all, comes back to life.*

Fiction

Tomorrow

On March 26, 1917, from Provincetown, O'Neill sent Waldo Frank, an editor of *The Seven Arts* magazine, a typed copy of his short story "Tomorrow" "a bit battered due to its being a working copy, but I hope still presentable." The intermediary between O'Neill and Frank had been Louise Bryant, who told Frank that O'Neill was a playwright of promise. O'Neill informed Frank that he would send several plays as soon as they had been "translated" into typescript from his cramped handwriting.[1]

Frank accepted the story at once, paying O'Neill $50. On March 31, O'Neill wrote him:

> I spent all this afternoon and evening going over "Tomorrow" with a view to eliminating the imperfections you mentioned in your letter and I think I have done so in a great many cases at any rate.
>
> The postscript goes overboard. You are quite right about it. When I first wrote the story I planned it as the first of a series of Tommy the Priest's yarns in which the story-teller was to hog most of the lime light—a sort of Conrad's Marlow—and once I had that idea I couldn't let go, and it rode me into the anti-climax. I see all this now, but didn't when, under the influence of said obsession, I jammed in that postcript.
>
> I hope I have sharpened the story. At least I have shortened it about a thousand words.
>
> I must ask your pardon again for sending back the old faithful m.s.s. to you. The cuts have been made in pencil so you can see exactly what has been pruned and whether they accord with your ideas or not.
>
> Also my typewriter has not come yet; also there is no typist in this hamlet; also, if there were, I could not pay her!
>
> The last reason having it, I remain
>
> Apologetically yours
Eugene G. O'Neill[2]

In 1944, to aid a war bond campaign,[3] O'Neill contributed to the cause several scripts for auction, including the handwritten original of "Tomorrow." He wrote to Mark Van Doren that "As a short story—well, let's not go into that, but I thought it was pretty

---

1. Frank also bought *In the Zone*, but the magazine went out of business before the play could be published. Cf. Louis Sheaffer, *Eugene O'Neill, Son and Playwright*, p. 382.
2. The correspondence with Waldo Frank is in the library of the University of Pennsylvania. It should be noted that not only Conrad's Marlow but the theme of Conrad's short story and his one-act play, "One Day More" and "Tomorrow," were important sources for O'Neill's story.
3. See his 1944 appeal for support for the Fourth War Bond Drive, p. 429, below.

devastating stuff at the time, and so evidently did Van Wyck Brooks, Waldo Frank, etc., although I doubt if they were as overwhelmed by its hideous beauty as I was."[4]

By 1944, O'Neill had completed *The Iceman Cometh*, where in James Cameron he recreated the character of Jimmy Tomorrow, the protagonist of his story, and transferred Jimmy's fate to Don Parritt. The fictional Jimmy was based on a down-and-out press agent O'Neill had known in his days on skid row, a man named James Byth, who committed suicide much as O'Neill describes the death in his story.[5] No doubt in writing the play, his thoughts returned to the early story, where he first faced the theme of man's belief in an evanescent tomorrow, a hope that would prove the sole consolation of those living at the bottom of life.

The uncut manuscript, featuring a self-portrait in the narrator, "Art," is of autobiographical interest, notably in the descriptions of alcoholism. Much of Don Parritt's contempt for the residents of Harry Hope's is anticipated in Art's response to his roommate's vagaries, and the story offers clear observation of what life was like at the saloon.[6] Most of these reactions and observations were deleted, but the later, greater work makes O'Neill's record of life at the saloon that was to become Harry Hope's of more than superficial interest. The manuscript is filled with additions and deletions in O'Neill's sometimes illegible hand. The more important alterations are printed in the footnotes; the text is as it was first published.

4. The correspondence with Mark Van Doren is in the Firestone Library of Princeton University.
5. For the autobiographical elements, see Sheaffer, *Eugene O'Neill, Son and Playwright*, passim. In a destroyed one-act play, "Exorcism," produced by the Provincetown Players in 1920, O'Neill again dealt with the subject of suicide among the saloon derelicts. This time, presumably, the subject was his own attempt.
6. See Sheaffer, *Eugene O'Neill, Son and Playwright*, p. 191, for a description of the rooms at Jimmy the Priest's saloon, which were several degrees worse than those O'Neill describes in his story.

Tomorrow[1]

It was back in my sailor days, in the winter of my great down-and-outness, that all this happened. In those years of wandering, to be broke and "on the beach" in some seaport or other of the world was no new experience; but this had been an unusually long period of inaction even for me. Six months before I had landed in New York after a voyage from Buenos Aires as able seaman on a British tramp. Since that time I had loafed around the water front, eking out an existence on a small allowance from my family, too lazy of body and mind, too indifferent to things in general, to ship to sea again or do anything else. I shared a small rear room with another "gentleman-ranker," Jimmy Anderson, an old friend of mine, over an all-night dive near South Street known as Tommy the Priest's.

This is the story of Jimmy, my roommate, and it begins on a cold night in the early part of March. I had waited in Tommy the Priest's, hunched up on a chair near the stove in the back room, all the late afternoon until long after dark.[2] My nerves were on edge as a result of a two days' carouse ensuing on the receipt of my weekly allowance. Now all that money was gone—over the bar—and the next few days gloomed up as a dreary, sober and hungry ordeal which must, barring miracles, be endured patiently or otherwise. Three or four others of the crowd I knew were sitting near me, equally sick and penniless. We stared gloomily before us, in listless attitudes, spitting dejectedly at the glowing paunch of the stove. Every now and then someone would come in bringing with him a chill of the freezing wind outside. We would all look up hopefully. No, only a stranger. Nothing in the way of hospitality to be expected from him. "Close that damned door!" we would growl in chorus and huddle closer to the stove, shivering, muttering disappointed curses. In mocking contrast

1. At the head of the story, O'Neill typed: "Tommy the Priests' 2." The "2" after "Tommy the Priests'" suggests that this may be the second of several stories to be laid at the flophouse bar. O'Neill said that he had written three, of which one became *The Hairy Ape*.
2. It began a cold night in the [illegible] of early April, six months after my first introduction to ~~Johnnys~~ [sic] ["Tommy's" written over "Johnny"] "You ought to get to work and do something— with your ability. It's a shame for you to be letting yourself go to seed this way. Really, Art, I mean it." Jimmie wound up his long and tolerably boring homily on the evil of strong drink and idleness and stood looking at me with an expression of much reproach in his round, lusterless [?] eyes.
    You're a fine one to go around preaching, aren't you," I retorted, intensely irritated. I wasn't feeling in the best of humors [?] anyway. It was early in the evening, and I was broke, hungry and very thirsty [?]. My nerves were shattered to shreds. . . .

the crowd at the bar were drinking, singing, arguing in each other's ears with loud, care-free voices.[3] None of them noticed our existence.

Surely a bad night for Good Samaritans, I thought, and reflected with bitterness that I counted several in that jubilant throng who had eagerly accepted my favors of the two nights previous. Now they saw me and nodded—but that was all. Suddenly sick with human ingratitude, I got out of my chair and, grumbling a surly "good-night, all" to the others, went out the side door and up the rickety stairs to our room—Jimmy's and mine.

The thought of spending a long evening alone in the room seemed intolerable to me. I lit the lamp and glanced around angrily. A fine hole! The two beds took up nearly all the space but Jimmy had managed to cram in, in front of the window, a small table on which stood his dilapidated typewriter. The typewriter, of course, was broken and wouldn't work. Jimmy was always going to have it fixed—tomorrow. But then Jimmy lived in a dream[4] of tomorrows; and nothing he was ever associated with ever worked.

The lamp on the table threw a stream of light through the dirty window, revealing the fire-escape outside. Inside, on a shelf along the windowsill, a dyspeptic geranium plant sulked in a small red pot. This plant was Jimmy's garden and his joy. Even when he was too sick to wash his own face he never forgot to water it the first thing after getting up. It goes without saying, the silly thing never bloomed. Nothing that Jimmy loved ever bloomed; but he always hoped, in fact he was quite sure, it would eventually blossom out[5]—in the dawn of some vague tomorrow.

For me it had value only as a symbol of Jimmy's everlasting futility, of his irritating inefficiency.[6] However, at that period in my life, all flowers were yellow primroses and nothing more, and Jimmy's pet was out of place, I thought, and in the way.

Books were piled on the floor against the walls—and what books! Where Jimmy got them and what for, God only knows. He never read them, except a few pages at haphazard to put him to sleep. Yet there must have been fifty at

---

3. There was the jingle of coin cast carelessly on the bar, the call for other rounds, the gleam of reflected light on bottles and glasses. It was all indescribably munificent and beyond our reach. Someone suggested in a hopeless tone that we ask Big John, the squarehead night bartender for credit. One glance at his stodgy unsympathetic face was enough. No [illegible] hope there; neither were any of us good for a ten cent beef stew at the restaurant around the corner in ~~West~~ ["South" written above "West"] Street.

The time dragged on slowly but nothing happened to enliven us. The crowds at the bar increased in numbers and enthusiasm.

4. dope-dream

5. give birth to some wondrous crimson flower

6. Now when he and his geranium plant have passed on to, let us hope, a more fertile soil where even the most futile plants and men can blossom out in peace, I recognize it as the expression of the innate poetry in his [illegible] crushed soul.

least cluttering up the room—books about history, about journalism, about economics—books of impossible poetry and incredible prose, written by unknown authors and published by firms one had never heard of.[7] He had a craze for buying them and never failed, on the days he was paid for the odd bits of work he did as occasional stenographer for a theatrical booking firm, to stagger weakly into Tommy's, very drunk, with two or three of the unreadable volumes clutched to his breast—books with titles like: "A Commentary on the Bulls of Pope Leo XIII,"[8] or "God and the Darwinian Theory," by John Jones, or "Sunflowers and Other Verses" by Lydia Smith.[9] Think of it!

I used to grow wild with rage as I watched him showing them to Tommy, or Big John if he was on, or to anyone else who would look and listen, with all the besotted pride in the world. I would think of the drinks and the food—kippered herring and bread and good Italian cheese—he might have purchased for the price of these dull works; and I would swear to myself to thrash him good and hard if he even dared to speak to me.

And then—Jimmy would come and lay his idiotic books on my table and I would look up at him furiously; and there he would stand, wavering a bit, smiling his sweet, good-natured smile, trying to force half his remaining change into my hand, his lonely, wistful eyes watching me with the appealing look of a lost dog hungry for an affectionate pat. What could I do but laugh and love him and show him I did by a slap on the back or in some small way or another? It was worth while forgetting all the injuries in the world just to see the light of gratitude shine up in his eyes.[10]

This night I am speaking of I picked up one of the books in desperation and lay down to read with the lamp at the head of the bed;[11] but I couldn't concentrate. I was too sick in body, brain, and soul to follow even the words.

I threw the book aside and lay on my back staring gloomily at the ceiling. The inmate of the next room, a broken-down telegrapher—"the Lunger" we used to call him—had a violent attack of coughing which seemed to be tearing his chest to pieces. I shuddered. He used to spit blood in the back room below.

7. The second-hand bookshop dealers must have seen he was drunk—he was always drunk when he added to his library—and forced their unsaleable tomes on his befuddled fancy.
8. by Reverend Timothy O'Farrell,
9. I don't exaggerate either the titles or authors a bit.
10. The funniest part about the books was that Jimmie was a highly educated man, was graduated from Edinburgh University about twenty years before, and knew something of literature and the classics, even if he did think Dickens and Thackeray the greatest novelists of all time. In his rarified University he admired [illegible] the library of his inclination.
11. I had picked out a play in seven acts about the feast of Belshazzar & the Fall of Babylon. I never got past the first act but I remember it had lots of action. Eight Babalonian [sic] nobles fell on their swords in blank verse during this period. It was worse than an Artzibashef novel. I couldn't concentrate. There were too many windy invocations to all the gods & godesses [sic] of Babylonian mythology even for a robust man with an alert brain.

In fact, when drunk, he was quite proud of this achievement, but grew terrified at all allusions to consumption and wildly insisted that he only had "bloody bronchitis," and that he was getting better every day. He died soon after in that same room next to ours. Perhaps his treatment was at fault. A quart and a half of five-cent whiskey a day and only a plate of free soup at noon to eat is hardly a diet conducive to the cure of any disease—not even "bloody bronchitis."

He coughed and coughed until, in a frenzy of tortured nerves,[12] I yelled to him: "For God's sake, shut up!" Then he subsided into a series of groans and querulous, choking complaints. I thought of consumption, the danger of contagion, and remembered that the window ought to be open. But it was too cold. Besides, what was the difference? "Con" or something else, today or tomorrow, it was all the same—the end. What did I care? I[13] had failed—or rather I had never cared enough about it all to want to succeed.[14]

I must have dozed for I came to with a nervous jump to find the lamp sputtering and smoking and the light growing dimmer every minute. No oil! That fool Jimmy had promised to bring back some. I had given him my last twenty cents and he had taken the can with him. He was sober, had been for almost a week, was suffering from one of his infrequent and brief efforts of reformation. No, there was no excuse. I cursed him viciously for the greatest imbecile on earth. The lamp was going out. I would have to lie in darkness or return to the misery of the back room downstairs.

Just then I recognized his step on the stairs and a moment later he came in, bringing the oil. I glared at him. "Where've you been?" I shouted. "Look at that lamp, you idiot! I'd have been in the dark in another second."

Jimmy came forward shrinkingly, a look of deep hurt in his faded blue eyes. He murmured something about "office" and stooped down to fill the lamp.

"Office!" I taunted scornfully, "what office? What do you take me for? I've heard that bunk of yours a million times."

Jimmy finished filling the lamp and sat down on the side of his bed opposite me. He didn't answer; only stared at me with an irritating sort of compassionate pity. How prim he was sitting there in his black suit, wispy, grey hair combed over his bald spot, his jowly face scraped close and[15] chalky with too much cheap powder, the vile odor of which filled the room. I noticed for the first time his clean collar, his fresh shirt. He must have been to the China-man's and retrieved part of his laundry. This was what he usually did when he

12. and my nerves jangled like the strings of some instrument, cracked and out of tune
13. was twenty-three, I had run the gamut, and
14. I gave myself up to this fit of suicidal melancholia. I wandered in that grey country of alcohol in which all worldly hopes are as naught and the great longing one for annihilation. Ah, to fall quietly asleep and never awake again to cower before the fetish of life.
15. looking like a white-washed wall from too much powder

had a windfall of a dollar or so from some unexpected source. Never took out all his laundry. That would have been too expensive. Just called at the Chink's and changed his shirt and collar. His other articles of clothing he washed himself at the sink in the hallway.

I eyed him up and down resentfully. Here was a man who ought always to remain drunk. Sober, he was a respectable nuisance. And his shoes were shined![16]

"Why the profound meditation?" I asked. "You'd think, to look at you, you were sitting up with my corpse. Cheer up! I feel bad enough without your adding to the gloom.

"That's just it, Art," he began in slow, doleful tones. "I hate to see you in this condition. You wouldn't ever feel this way if you'd—only—only—" he hesitated as he saw my sneer.

"Only what?" I urged.

"Only stop your hard drinking," he mumbled, avoiding my eyes.

"This is almost too much, Jimmy. The water wagon is fatal to your sense of humor. After a week's ride you've accumulated more cheap moralizing than any anchorite in all his years of fasting."

"I'm your friend," he blundered on, "and you know it, Art—or I wouldn't say it."

"And it hurts you more than it does me, I'll bet!"

Jimmy had the piqued air of the rebuffed but well-intentioned. "If that's the way you want to take it—" he was staring unhappily at the floor. We were silent for a time. Then he continued with the obstinacy of the reformed turned reformer: "I'm your friend, the best friend you've got." His eyes looked up into mine and his glance was timidly questioning. "You know that, don't you, Art?"

All my peevishness vanished in a flash before his woeful sincerity. I reached over and grabbed his hand—his white, pudgy little hand so in keeping with the rest of him—warm and soft. "Of course I know it Jimmy. Don't be foolish and take what I've said seriously. I've got a full-sized grouch against everything tonight."

Jimmy brightened up and cleared his throat. He evidently thought my remarks an expression of willingness to serve as audience for his temperance lecture. Still he hesitated politely. "I know you don't want to listen—"

I laughed shortly. "Go ahead. Shoot. I'm all ears."[17]

Then he began. You know the sort of drool—introduced by a sage wag of the head and the inevitable remark: "I've been through it all myself, and I

16. I felt like telling him my thoughts, making him writhe beneath my ill-natured sarcasm. Bah! What was the use? It was like kicking a wet worm.
17. There was a pause pregnant for me with the foreboding of boredom.

know." I won't bore you with it. Coming from Jimmy it was the last word in absurdity.[18]

I tried not to listen, concentrating my mind on the man himself, my nerves soothed by the monotonous flow of his soft-voiced syllables. Yes, he'd been through it all, there was no doubt of that, from soup to nuts. What he didn't realize was that none of it had ever touched him deeply. Forgetful of the last kick his eyes had always looked up at life again with the same appealing, timid uncertainty, pleading for a caress, fearful of a blow. And life had never failed to deal him the expected kick, never a vicious one, more of a shove to get him out of the way of a spirited boot at someone who really mattered. Spurned, Jimmy had always returned, affectionate, uncomprehending, wagging his tail ingratiatingly, so to speak. The longed-for caress would come, he was sure of it, if not today, then tomorrow. Ah, tomorrow!

I looked searchingly at his face—the squat nose, the wistful eyes, the fleshy cheeks hanging down like dewlaps on either side of his weak mouth with its pale, thick lips. The usual marks of dissipation were there but none of the scars of intense suffering. The whole effect was characterless, unfinished; as if some sculptor at the last moment had suddenly lost interest in his clay model of a face and abandoned his work in disgust. I wondered what Jimmy would do if he ever saw that face in the clear, cruel mirror of Truth. Straggle on in the same lost way, no doubt, and cease to have faith in mirrors.

Although most of his lecture was being lost on me I couldn't prevent a chance word now and then from seeping into my consciousness. "Wasted youth—your education—ability—a shame—lost opportunity—drink—some nice girl"—these words my ears retained against my will, and each word had a sting to it. Gradually my feeling of kindliness toward Jimmy petered out. I began to hate him for a pestiferous little crank. What right had he to meddle with my sins? Some of the things he was saying were true; and truth—that kind of truth—should be seen and not heard.

I was becoming angry enough to shrivel him up with some contemptuous remark about his hypocrisy and the doubtful duration of time he would stay on the wagon when he suddenly digressed from my misdeeds and began holding himself up as a horrible example.

He began at the beginning, and, even though I welcomed the change of subject, I swore inwardly at the prospect of hearing the history of his life all over again. He had told me this tale at least fifty times while in all stages of

18. Why must the reformed drunkard always blindly ignore or forget the psychology of drinking and seem unable to consider anything but the superficial, sentimental surface aspects? As if alcohol were merely a poisonous liquid one drank to quench one's thirst in preference to water. Well, never mind. Perhaps I'll reform—psychologically—myself someday and write an essay about it.

maudlin drunkenness. Usually he wept—which was sometimes funny and sometimes not, all depending on my own condition. At all events it would be a novelty to hear his sober version. I might get at some facts this time.

To my surprise this story seemed to be identical with the others I had been lulled to sleep by on so many nights. Making allowances for the natural exaggeration of one in liquor, there was little difference. It started with the Anderson estate in Scotland where Jimmy had spent his boyhood. This estate of the family extended over the greater part of a Scotch county, so Jimmy claimed, and he was touchy when anyone seemed skeptical regarding its existence.[19]

He loved to dilate on the beauty of the country, the old manor house, the farms, the game park, and all the rest of it. All this was heavily mortgaged, he admitted; and he was not in good standing with most of his relatives on the other side; but he declared that there was one aunt, far gone in years and hoarded wealth, who still treasured his memory, and he promised all the gang in the back room a rare blowout should the old lady pass away in the proper frame of mind. To all of this the crowd would listen with an amiable pretence of belief. For, after all, he was Jimmy and they all swore by him, and a fairy tale like that is no great matter to hold against a man.

But here he was spinning the same yarn in all its details! I looked at him suspiciously. No, he was certainly stone sober. Could there be any truth in it then? Impossible. I finally concluded that Jimmy, after the fashion of liars, had ended by mistaking his own fabrications for fact.

He continued on through his years in Edinburgh University, his graduation with honors, his going into journalism first in Scotland, then in England, afterwards as a correspondent on the Continent, and finally his work in South Africa during the Boer War as representative of some news service.

I had never been able to verify any of this except that relating to the Boer War. An old friend of his had once told me that Jimmy did hold a responsible position in South Africa during the war and had received a large salary. Then the old friend, old-friendlike, shook his head gravely and muttered: "Too bad! Too bad! Drink!" Whether the rest of Jimmy's life, as related by him, had ever been lived or not hardly mattered, I thought. Undoubtedly he had been well educated and what is called a gentleman over there. Of course the Anderson estate was a work of fiction, or, at best, a glorified country house.

"And mind you, Art, up to that time," Jimmy's story had reached the point where he was at the front in South Africa for the news service company, "I had never touched a drop except a glass of wine with dinner now and again.

19. I nearly lost his friendship once by assuring him I knew its exact location because my castle in Spain was right next door.

That was ten years ago and I was thirty-five. Then—something happened. Ten years," he repeated sadly, "and now look where I am!" He stared despondently before him for a moment, then brightened up and squared his bent shoulders. "But that's all past and gone now, and I'm through with this kind of life for good and all."[20]

"There's always tomorrow," I ventured ironically.

"Yes, and I'm going to make the most of it." His eyes were bright with the dream of a new hope; or rather, the old hope eternally redreamed. He glanced at the table. "I'll have to have that typewriter fixed up."

"Tomorrow?"

"Yes, tomorrow, if I can spare the time." He hadn't noticed my sarcasm.

"Why, is your day all taken up?" I asked, marvelling at his imagination.

"Pretty well so." He put on an air of importance. "I saw Edwards today"— Edwards was a friend of his who had risen to be an editor on one of the big morning papers—"and he's found an opening for me—a real opening which will give me an opportunity to show them all I'm still in the race."

"And you start in tomorrow?" I was dumbfounded.

"Yes, in the afternoon." His face was alive with energy. "Oh, I'll show them all, Art, that I'm still one of the best when I want to be. They've sneered at me long enough."

"Then you really are about to become a wage slave?" I simply couldn't believe it.

"Honestly, Art. Tomorrow. Do you think I'm spoofing you about it?"

"I must admit you seem to be confessing the shameless truth. Well, at any rate, you seem to be pleased, so—" here I jumped up and pumped his hand up and down—"a million congratulations, Jimmy, old scout!" Jimmy's joy was good to see. There were tears in his eyes as he thanked me. Good old Jimmy! It took him quite a while to get over his emotion. Then, as if he had suddenly remembered something, he began hurriedly fumbling through all his pockets.

"I must have lost it," he said finally, giving up the search. "I wanted to show it to you."

"What?"

"A letter I received today from Aunt Mary." Aunt Mary was the elderly relative in whose will Jimmy hoped to be remembered. "She complains of having felt very feeble for the past half year. She appears to be entirely ignorant of my present condition, thank God. Writes that I'm to come and pay her a long visit should I decide to take a trip abroad this Spring. Fancy!"

20. What a difference a few sober days can bring! Doesn't he remember how often he had said the same thing to me before in exactly the same circumstances, I wondered.

"And you've lost the letter?" I asked, trying to hide my skepticism.

"Yes—was showing it to Edwards—must have dropped on the floor—or else he—" Jimmy stopped abruptly. I think he must have sensed my amused incredulity, for he seemed very put out at something and didn't look at me. "I do hope the poor old lady isn't seriously ill," he murmured after a pause.

"What!" I laughed. "Have you the face to tell me that, when you know you've been looking forward to her timely taking off ever since I've known you?"

Jimmy's face grew red and he stammered confusedly. He knew he'd said things which might have sounded that way when he'd been drinking. It was whiskey talking and he didn't mean it. Really he liked her a lot. He remembered she'd been very kind to him when he was a lad. Had hardly seen her since then—twenty-five years ago. No, money or no money, he wanted her to live to be a hundred.

"But you've told me she's almost ninety now! Isn't she?"

"Yes, eighty-six, I think."

"Then," I said with finality, "she's overlingered her welcome, and you're a simpleton to be wasting your crocodile tears—in advance, at that. Besides, I've never noticed her sending you any of her vast fortune. She might at least have made you a present once in a while if she cared to earn any regrets over her demise."

"I've never written her about my hard luck. I hardly ever wrote to her," Jimmy said slowly. His tones were ridiculously dismal, and he sat holding his face in his hands in the woebegone attitude of a mourner.[21]

"Well, you should have written.[22] A sudden thought made me smile. "What will the bunch in the back room say when they hear this? You may give them that long-promised blow-out—tomorrow," I added maliciously.

Jimmy stirred uneasily and turned on me a glance full of dim suspicion. "Why do you keep repeating that word tomorrow? You've said it now a dozen times."

"Because tomorrow is your day, Jimmy," I answered carelessly. "Doesn't your career as a sober, industrious citizen begin then?"

"Oh," he sighed with relief, "I thought—" he walked up and down the narrow space between the beds, his hands deep in his pockets. Finally he stopped and stood beside me. There was an exultant ring to his voice. "Ah, I tell you, Art, it's great to feel like a man again, to know you're done for good and all

21. It was preposterous. I wanted to laugh in his face.
22. What are relatives for, I'd like to know—or parents for that matter. They begat[?] you, they bore you and surely as a compensation they ought to board you." Jimmie permitted himself a [illegible] repressed smile at this [illegible] wagging. "Well, after all then, Jimmie you may be able to treat the gang to that long-promised blowout—Tomorrow" I added maliciously.

with that mess downstairs." After a pause he went on in a coaxing, motherly tone. "Don't you think you ought to go to work and do something? I hate to see you—like this. You know what a pal I am, Art. You can listen to me. It's a shame for you to let yourself go to seed this way. Really, Art, I mean it."

"Now Jimmy," I got up and put my hands on his shoulders. "I say it without any hard feeling, but I've had about enough of your reform movement for one night.[23] It'll be more truly charitable of you to offer me the price of a drink—if you have it. Your day of reformation is none so remote you can't realize from experience how rotten I feel. I can hear polar bears baying at the Northern Lights."

Jimmy sighed disconsolately and dug some small change out of his pocket. "I borrowed a dollar from Edwards," he explained. "I'll pay him back out of my first salary." The self-sufficient pride he put into that word salary!

But his financial aid proved to be unnecessary. As I was about to take half of his change, there was a great trampling from the stairs outside. Our door was kicked open with a bang and Lyons, the stoker, and Paddy Mehan, the old deep-water sailor, came crowding into the room. Lyons was in the first jovial frenzy of drink but poor Paddy was already awash and rapidly sinking. They had been paid off that afternoon after a trip across on the American liner St. Paul.

"Hello, Lyons! Hello, Paddy!" Jimmy and I hailed them in pleased chorus.

"Hello, yourself!" Lyons crushed Jimmy's hand in one huge paw and patted me affectionately on the back with the other. The jar of it nearly knocked me off my feet but I managed to smile. Lyons and I were old pals. I had once made a trip as a sailor on the Philadelphia when he was in her stokehold, and we had become great friends through a chance adventure together ashore in Southampton—which is another story. He stood grinning, swaying a bit in the lamplight, a great, hard bulk of a man, dwarfing the proportions of our little room. Paddy lurched over to one of the beds and fell on it. "Thick weather! Thick weather!" he groaned to himself, and started to sing an old chanty in a thin, quavering, nasal whine:

> "A-roving, a-roving
> Since roving's been my ru-i-in,
> No more I'll go a-ro-o-ving with you, fair maid."

"Shut up!" roared Lyons and turned again to me. "Art,[24] how are ye?" I dodged an attempt at another love-tap and replied that I was well but thirsty.

"Thirsty, is ut? D'ye hear that Paddy, ye slimy Corkonian? Here's a mate

23. Soar into virtuous ether yourself if you must, but let me wallow in the nice warm mire. My soul is sick and old. Doc Life advises mud baths. They either kill or cure.
24. God blarst you for a stinkin' swine.

complainin' av thirst and we wid a full pay day in our pockets." He pulled out a roll of bills and flaunted them before me with a splendid, spendthrift gesture.

"Oh, whiskey killed my poor old dad! Whiskey! O Johnny!" carolled Paddy dolorously.

"Listen to 'im![25]" Lyons reached over and shook him vigorously. "That's the trouble with all thim lazy, deck-scrubbers the loike av 'im. They can't stand up to their dhrink loike men. Wake up, Paddy! We'll be goin' below." He hauled Paddy to his feet and held him there. Come on, Art. There's some av the boys ye know below waitin'. Ye'll have all the dhrink ye can pour down your throat, and welcome; and anything more you're wishful for ye've but to name. Come on, Jimmy, you're wan av us."

"I've got something to do before I go down. I'll join you in a few minutes," Jimmy replied, wisely evading a direct refusal.

"See that ye do, me sonny boy," warned Lyons, pushing Paddy to the door. I turned to Jimmy as I was going out. "Well good luck till tomorrow, Jimmy, if I don't see you before then."

"Thank you, Art," he murmured huskily and shook my hand. I started down. From the bottom of the flight below I heard Lyons' rough curses and Paddy wailing lugubriously:

> "Old Joe is dead, and gone to hell,
> Poor old Joe!"

"Ye'll be in hell yourself[26] if ye fall in this black hole," Lyons cautioned, steering him to the top of the second flight as I caught up with them.

The fiesta which began with our arrival in the bar didn't break up until long after daylight the next morning. It was one of the old, lusty debauches of my sailor days—songs of the sea and yarns about ships punctuated by rounds of drinks.[27]

The last I remember was Lyons bawling out for someone to come down to the docks and strip to him and see which was the better man. "Have a bit av fun wid 'im" was the way he put it.[28] I believe I was Dutch-courageous enough to accept his challenge but he pushed me back in my chair with a

25. He's dhrunk, the skut!
26. ye dhrunken sow
27. None of your pink tea café seances, but a swearing, fighting primitive outburst of virile, red-blooded men with the simple hearts of children. Crude and raw, if you will, tough and vulgar, too perhaps; but never for an instant tainted with meanness.
28. Lyons' idea of a bit of fun was to plant his number ten brogues in the pit of his oponents [sic] stomach. This was perfectly fair fighting along the Liverpool water front where he hailed from, and afterward to shake hands and buy him a drink if the said oponent [sic] had retained any interest in drinking after he regained consciousness.

warning to be "a good bye" or I'd get a spanking. So the party had no fatal ending.

As you can well imagine I slept like a corpse all the next day and didn't witness Jimmy's departure for his long hard climb back to respectability and the man who was. When he came home that night he appeared very elated, full of the dignity of labor, tremendously conscious of his position in life, provokingly solicitous concerning my welfare. It would have been insufferable in anyone else; but Jimmy—well, Jimmy was Jimmy, and the most lovable chap on earth. You couldn't stay mad at him more than a minute, if you had the slightest sense of humor.

Had he toiled and spun much on his first day, I asked him. No, he admitted after a moment's hesitation, he had spent the time mostly in feeling about, getting the hang of his work. Now tomorrow he'd get the typewriter fixed so he could do Sunday special stuff in his spare moments—stories of what he'd seen in South Africa and things of that kind. Wasn't that a bully idea? I agreed that it was, and retreated to the gang below who were still celebrating, leaving Jimmy with pencil poised over a blank sheet of paper determined to map out one of his stories then and there.

I didn't see him the next day or the day after. I was touring the water front with Lyons and Paddy and never returned to the room. The fourth day of his job I ran into him for a second in the hallway. He said hello in a hurried tone and brushed past me. For my part I was glad he didn't stop. I felt he'd immediately start on a heart-to-heart talk which I was in no mood to hear. Later on I remembered his manner had been strange and that he looked drawn and fagged out.

The fifth day Paddy and Lyons were both broke, but I collected my puny allowance and we sat at a table in the back room squandering it lingeringly on enormous scoops of lager and porter which were filling and lasted a long time. We were still sitting there talking when Jimmy came back from work. He looked in from the hallway, saw us and nodded, but went on upstairs without speaking.

"What's the matther wid Jimmy?" grumbled Lyons. "Can't he speak to a man?"

"He looks like he was sick," said Paddy. "Go up, Art, that's a good lad, and ask him if he won't take a bit of a drink, maybe."

"I'll go," I said, getting up, "but he won't drink anything. Jimmy's strictly temperance these days. He's more likely to give us all a sermon on our sins."

"Divil take him, then," growled Lyons, "but run and get him all the same. He looks loike he'd been drawn through a crack in the wall."

I ran quickly up the stairs and opened the door of our room. Jimmy was sitting on the side of his bed, his head in his hands. I glanced at the typewriter.

The keys were still grey with a layer of long-accumulated dust. Then he hadn't had it fixed. The same old tomorrow, I thought to myself.

"Jimmy," I called to him. He jumped to his feet with a frightened start. When he saw who it was a flush of anger came over his face.

"Why don't you scare the life out of a man!" he said irritably. I was astonished. I'd never known him to flare up like this over a trifle.[29]

"Come down and join us for a while. You don't have to drink, you know. You look done-up. What's the trouble—been working too hard?"

He winced at this last remark as if I'd shaken my fist in his face. Then he made a frantic gesture with his arms as though he were pushing me out of the room. "Go! Go back!" His voice was unnaturally shrill. "Leave me alone. I want to be alone."

"Jimmy!" I went to him in genuine alarm. "What's the matter? Anything wrong?"

He pressed my hand and tried a feeble attempt at a smile. There were dark rings under his eyes, and, somehow, in some indefinable manner, he seemed years older, a broken old man.

"No, Art, I'm all right. Don't mind me. I've a splitting headache—"

"Don't be a fool and let them work you to death." He raised his hands as if he were going to clap them over his ears to shut out my words.

"Leave me alone, Art, will you? I'm going to bed," he stammered.

"Right-o, that's the stuff. Get a good sleep and you'll be O.K." I went downstairs slowly, vaguely worried about him, wondering what the trouble could be. In the end I laid his peculiar actions to a struggle he was having with his craving for drink. Paddy and Lyons agreed with this opinion and called him a "game little swine" for sticking to his guns. And as such we toasted him in our lager and our porter.

When I went up to the room to turn in he was asleep, or pretending to be, and I was careful not to disturb him. The next morning I heard him moving about, but as soon as he saw I was awake, he appeared in a nervous flurry to get away, and we didn't speak more than a few words to each other. That night he never came home at all. I went to bed early—everyone was broke and there was nothing else to do—and when I was roused out of my slumber by the sun shining on my face through the dirty window, I saw that his bed hadn't been touched. A somber presentment of evil seemed to hover around that bed. The white spread, threadbare and full of holes, which he had tucked in with such precise neatness, had the suggestion of a shroud about it—a shroud symbolically woven for one whose life had been threadbare and full of holes.

29. Nerves from overwork, I concluded, when he isn't used to it.

I tried to laugh at such grim imaginings.[30] Jimmy had stayed with Edwards or someone else from his paper. What was strange in that? This wasn't the first time he'd remained away all night, was it? If I was to give way to such worries I might as well put on skirts and be done with it.

But my phantoms, however foolish, refused to be laid. I got dressed in a hurry, anxious to escape from this room, bright with sunlight, dark with uncanny threat. Before I went down, struck by a sentimental mood, I got some water from the sink in the hallway and poured it on his ridiculous geranium plant.

After a breakfast of free soup, I walked with Paddy and Lyons down to the Battery. We spent the afternoon there, lounging on one of the benches. It was as warm as a day in Spring and we sat blinking in the sunshine drowsily listening to each other's yarns about the sea and lazily watching the passing ships.

When the sun went down we returned to Tommy the Priest's. On the way back I remembered this was Jimmy's pay day and wondered if he would show up. He owed me some money which I hoped would be forthcoming. Otherwise the night was liable to prove an uneventful one. And a farewell bust-up was imperative because Paddy and Lyons would have to go on board ship the following day if they wanted to make the next trip.

The evening didn't pass off as dully as we had feared. Old McDonald, the printer, was in a festive mood and invited us to join him. Two of the telegraph operators, out of a job at that time, had borrowed some money somewhere and were anxious to return the many treats they had received from us in the past. So the time whiled away very pleasantly.[31]

It was shortly after midnight when Jimmy came in. As soon as I saw his face I knew that something had happened to him, something very serious. He was incredibly haggard and pale, and there were deep lines of suffering about his mouth and eyes. His eyes—I can't describe them. There was nothing behind them. He nodded and took his place at the bar beside us. Then he spoke, asked us what we'd have, in a strained, forced voice as though it cost him a tremendous effort to talk. He took whiskey himself, poured out a glass brim full, and downed it straight. Big John changed a bill for him, and without looking at me, he held out the couple of dollars he owed me. I put them in my pocket. Jimmy motioned to Big John and called for another round. A spell of silence was on the whole barroom. Everyone there knew him well. They had all joked with him during the week about his being on the wagon, but they had secretly admired his firmness of will. Now they stared at him with genuine regret that he should

30. What ghosts on a fine morning like this! I must be contracting the jimjams at last.
31. Nothing riotous about it for we were all in a calm lager and ale mood.

have fallen. Their faces grew sad. They had done the same thing themselves so many times. They understood.[32]

"Jimmy!" He caught the reproach in my voice and turned to me with a twisted smile. "It doesn't matter," he said. "Nothing matters." His voice became harsh. "Don't forget what you said about my lectures and start in yourself." He immediately felt sorry for having said this. "No, Art, I don't mean that. Never mind what I say. I'm upset—about something."

"Tell me what it is, Jimmy. Maybe I can help."

"Help?" He laughed hysterically. "No, no help please. After all, why shouldn't I tell you now? You're bound to find out sooner or later. They'll all know it." He indicated the others who, feeling that Jimmy wanted to be alone with me, had taken their drinks to a table in the rear and were sitting around talking in low, constrained voices. Jimmy blurted out: "My job, Art, is gone to hell!"

"What!" I pretended more astonishment than I felt. I had guessed what the trouble was.

"Yes, they asked me to quit—politely requested. Edwards was very nice about it—very kind—very charitable." He put all the bitterness of his heart into these last words.

"The rotten swine!"

"Oh, no, Art, it wasn't his fault. If they hadn't—fired me—I'd have had to resign anyway. I—I couldn't do the work."

"That's all nonsense, Jimmy. Well, cheer up. All said and done, it's only a job the less. You can always get another for the asking."

He looked at me with a sort of wild scorn in his eyes. "Can't you understand any better than that? What do I care for the job itself? It isn't that. I tell you I couldn't do the work! I tried and tried. What I wrote was rot. I couldn't get any news. No initiative—no imagination—no character—no courage! All gone. Nothing left—not even cleverness. No memory even!" He stopped, breathing hard, the perspiration glistening on his forehead. "It came to me gradually—the realization. I couldn't believe it. I had been so sure of myself all these years. All I needed was a chance. It had been so easy for me in the past—long ago. These last few days I've guessed the truth. I've been going crazy. Last night I walked—walked and walked—thinking—and finally—I knew!" He paused, choking back a sob, his face twitching convulsively with the effort he made to control himself. Then he uttered a cracked sound intended for a laugh. "I'm done—burnt out—wasted! It's time to dump the garbage. Nothing here."

32. In none of their eyes did I read that triumphant malice which delights in other's failure. They were silent and sympathetic.

He tapped his head with a silly gesture and laughed again. I began to be afraid he really was going mad. "No, Art, it isn't the job that's lost. I'm lost!"

"Now you're talking like a fool!" I spoke roughly, trying to shake him out of this mood.

"I won't talk any more," he said quite calmly. "Don't worry. I'm all shot to pieces—no sleep." He broke down suddenly and turned away from me. "But it's hell, Art, to realize all at once—you're dead!"

I put my arm around his shoulders. "Have a drink, Jimmy. Hey you, John, a little service!" What else was there to do? Life had jammed the clear, cruel mirror in front of his eyes and he had recognized himself—in that pitiful thing he saw. "Have a drink, Jimmy, and forget it. Take a real drink!" I urged. What else was there to do?

After we had had a couple at the bar, Jimmy filling his glass to the brim each time, I led him in back and we sat down at the table with the crowd. More drinks were immediately forthcoming, and it wasn't long before Jimmy became very drunk. He didn't say anything but his eyes glazed, his lips drooped loosely, his head wagged uncertainly from side to side. I saw he'd had enough and I hoped his tired brain had been numbed to a forgetful[33] oblivion.

"Come on to bed, Jimmy," I shook him by the arm.

He stared at me vacantly. "Bed—yes—sleep! sleep!" he mumbled, and came with me willingly enough. I helped him up the stairs to the room and lit the lamp. He sat on the side of the bed, swaying, unlacing his shoes with difficulty. Presently he began to weep softly to himself. "It's you, Alice—cause of all this—damn you—no—didn't mean that—beg pardon," he muttered. He lifted his head and saw me sitting on the other bed. "one word advice, Art— never get married—all rotten, all of 'em—"[34]

This was something new. "What do you know about marriage?" I asked curiously. "Nothing from experience, surely."

He winked at me with drunken cunning. "Don't I though! Not half! Never told you that, what? Never told you what happened—Cape Town?"

"No, you never did. What was it?"

"Might s'well tell Art—best friend—tell you everything tonight—all over. Yes—married in England—English girl, pretty's picture—big blue eyes—just before war—took her South Africa with me, 'n left her in Cape Town when I went to front. I was called back to Cape Town s'denly—found her with staff officer—dirty swine! No chance for doubt—didn't expect me to turn up—saw them with my own eyes—*flagrante delictu*, you know—dirty swine of a staff

33. blissful
34. body and soul, rotten.

officer! Good bye, Jimmy Anderson! All over! Drink! Drink! Forget!" He blubbered to himself, his face a grotesque mask of tragedy.

In a flash it came back to me how he'd always stopped in the stories of his life at the point where he'd commenced drinking. Even at his drunkest he'd always ended the history there by saying abruptly: "and then—something happened." I'd never attached much importance to it—thought he merely wanted to suggest a mysterious reason as an excuse for his tobogganing. Now, I knew. Who could doubt the truth of his statements, knowing all he had been through that day? He was in a mood for truth. So this was the something which happened! Here was real tragedy.

Real tragedy! And there he was sobbing, hiccuping, rolling his eyes stupidly, scratching with limp fingers at the tears which ran down and tickled the sides of his nose.[35] I felt a mad desire to laugh.[36]

"I suppose you and she were divorced?" I asked after a pause.

"No—I couldn't—no proof—no money. Besides, what'd I care about divorce? Never want to marry again—never love anyone else." He wept more violently than ever.

"But didn't she get a divorce?"

"No, she's too cute for that—thinks Aunt Mary'll leave me money—and I'll drink myself to death. No," he interrupted himself hastily, "can't be that—not s'bad s' that—not Alice—no, no, mustn't say that—not right for me to say that—don't know her reason—never can tell—about women. Damn shoes!" He gave up the attempt to get his shoes off and flung himself on the bed, fully dressed. In a minute he was dead to the world and snoring. I left him and went downstairs.

Most of the people in the back room were asleep, but Paddy and Lyons and the operators were still drinking at one table, and I sat down with them. I talked at random on every subject that came up, seeking to forget Jimmy and his woes, for a time at least. His two confessions that night had got on my nerves.

Later on I must have dozed, for I was jolted out of a half dream by a sharp cracking smash in the back yard. Everyone was awake and cursing in an instant. Big John appeared from behind the curtain, grumbling: "Dot's right! Leave bottle on the fire escape, you fellers! Dot's right! Und I have to sweep up."

We heard someone racing down the stairs and Jimmy burst into the room. His face was livid, his eyes popping out of his head. He rushed to the chair

35. —as screaming a caricature of grief as the most mocking artist could possibly conceive
36. to scream at the top of my lungs, to dance wildly around the room

beside me and sat down, shaking, his teeth chattering as if he had a chill. I told Big John to bring him a drink.

What's the trouble now, Jimmy?" I asked him when he'd calmed down a little. He appeared to be quite sober after his sleep.

The geranium—" he began, his lips trembling, his eyes filling up.

"So that's what fell down just now, is it?"

"Yes, I woke up, and I remembered I'd forgotten to water it. I got up and went to get the water. The window was open. I must have stumbled over something. I put out my hand to steady myself. It was so dark I couldn't see. I knocked it out on the fire escape. Then I heard it crash in the yard." He put his hands over his face and cried heart-brokenly like a sick child whose only remaining toy has been smashed. Not drunken tears this time, but real tears which made all of us at the table blink our eyes and swear fiercely at nothing.

After a while he grew quiet again, attempted a smile, asked our pardons for having created a foolish scene. He stared at his drink standing untouched on the table in front of him; but never made any motion to take it, didn't seem to realize what it was. For fully fifteen minutes he sat and stared, as still as stone, never moving his eyes, never even seeming to breathe. Then he got up from his chair and walked slowly to the door like a man in a trance. As he was going out he turned to me and said: "I'm tired, Art. I think I'll go to sleep," and something like a wan smile trembled on his pale lips. He left the door open behind him and I heard him climbing the stairs, and the slam of our door as he closed it behind him.

A buzz of conversation broke out as if his going had lifted a weight of silence off the room. Then it happened—a swish, a sickish thud as of a heavy rock dropping into thick mud. We looked wildly at one another. We knew. We rushed into the hall and out to the yard. There it was—a motionless, dark huddle of clothes, a splintered, protruding bone or two, a widening pool of blood black against the grey flags—Jimmy!

The sky was pale with the light of dawn. Tomorrow had come.[37]

---

37. "There isn't much more to tell," Art said with a sad ironic smile, "only a little incident. I don't expect you to believe it. It's really too good to be true. You know that I write plays and you'll lay it to my sense of the dramatic. But it is true—as true as I'm sitting here—boring you with my yarns."

Late in the afternoon of the next day, I went up to the theatrical booking office where Jimmie had done lots of work now and then as [a] stenographer. I knew he had had his mail sent to him there and I thought I might find some clue to the whereabouts of his relatives if he really had any.

I saw the manager—a fat little Jew. When I mentioned Jimmie's name he handed me a letter for him which I opened and took over to the window to read. It was from a firm of solicitors in Edinburgh. They hadn't cabled, not being sure of his address. They announced in the decorous phraseology of legal grief the death of his Aunt Mary. She had left the bulk of her estate, estimated at twenty thousand pounds, to him. Would he come over at his earliest possible convenience, so that a settlement could be made—and so forth.

I stood at the window with the letter in my hand thinking of that huddled heap of clothes in the yard downtown and of the wife who wouldn't get a divorce. It was all so finished, so complete. The artistry of it was perfect. Then I looked up at the sky.

"You ironic, cruel demon!" I cried—but couldn't help smiling.

S.O.S.

In 1913, as O'Neill took his first steps toward a playwriting career, he conceived a two-act melodrama, *Warnings*.[1] The play tells of James Knapp, a former ship's radio operator who loses his hearing. Unable to provide for his family, he hides his deafness and continues at his job. Inevitably, his deafness causes the ship to founder and, as the play ends, Knapp drowns.

The play owes something to Joseph Conrad's story *The End of the Tether*, in which a blind sea captain hides his infirmity and, like Knapp, continues at his job. He too goes to his death as the ship sinks. Conrad's story rests on an ethical base that O'Neill as a beginner could not approximate, in 1913 or later, when in 1918 he recast the material as a short story with a wartime setting as "S.O.S."

In 1918, O'Neill lived for a time in a creative doldrum. Important plays he had completed, including *Beyond the Horizon* and *Chris Christophersen*, were unproduced, and for a time the energy of his imagination flagged. His wife, Agnes Boulton, has described him drinking and sitting long hours reading *The Saturday Evening Post* and going through the motions of writing.[2] Much of the work of this period was destroyed. "S.O.S." is a surviving product of this withdrawal. It appears to have been written with the *Post* market in mind. His desire to write magazine fiction may have had the same motivation that drove his protagonist to sea—the need of money. He had sold "Tomorrow" to *The Seven Arts* in 1917, and shortly thereafter, George Jean Nathan bought *The Long Voyage Home*, *Ile*, and *The Moon of the Caribbees* for *The Smart Set*. "S.O.S.," however, despite the mild irony of its ending, shows none of the style that would attract editors of the more literate periodicals. Its quality, far below that of "Tomorrow," seems calculated to appeal to the *Post* reader.

The *Post* of the period was fond of sea stories retailing the adventures of heroic sailors who turned the trick on the enemy—often, as here, a submarine raider. That O'Neill, for all his seagoing experience, would ever have achieved the "touch" of a *Post* regular like Norman Reilly Raine or Peter B. Kyne is doubtful. Under any circumstances, by 1918 his story was out of date. The editors of the *Post* were no longer fond of war settings or of such melodramatic derring-do in the Allied cause as O'Neill's hero exhibits.

There is no record that he submitted the story to the *Post* or any other publication. "S.O.S." was his final attempt at prose fiction. Thereafter, he stuck to his last.

---

1. *Warnings* is published in *Ten "Lost" Plays* (New York: Random House, 1964).
2. Agnes Boulton, *Part of a Long Story*, chap. 5.

S.O.S.

They used to wonder in the little town of Acropolis how John Lathrop ever kept his job. His drinking was common knowledge, as it could not help but be in a town the size of Acropolis where everyone's habits good and bad were carefully noted and marked down for discussion over the supper table. The Telegraph Company relented on account of his many years of service, the more kindly surmised; but there were those of the village wiseacres, playing Kelly pool in the room behind the hotel bar on Saturday nights when Lathrop with difficulty managed to keep his sagging figure propped against the rail, who shrugged their shoulders when the question came up, and hinted vaguely at some mysterious "pull"—which was ridiculous on the face of it.

All of this conjecture was without malice, for Lathrop was in appearance and character one of those colorless individuals who never excite any of the more positive emotions. They even liked him in a neutral sort of way; yet there was something inexplicable about him, they felt, and had been feeling ever since the first night twenty years before—he must be getting on to forty-six now—when Lathrop, dropping in from nowhere to take over the position of telegrapher left vacant by his predecessor's death, had stayed up drinking in the hotel until the bar closed and taken leave for his boarding house in a very apparent, though silent, state of intoxication. Since then his weekly lapses had been continual and marked by the same taciturnity. He drank alone most of the time and never alluded to his past in any way. Where he came from and why, the town could never pry out of him. His name was John Lathrop, he said, and that was all.

If anyone had told him that the men of the town resented his silence as a suspicious lack of frankness, and that the more romantic sex attributed his drinking to some secret sorrow, Lathrop would have been astounded. He was silent because there was nothing to tell. Left to look after himself as a boy he had become a messenger in the big city in which he was born. Later, raised to the rank of telegrapher, he had led the roving, though hum-drum, life of his species. Nothing had ever happened to him which he judged interesting enough to narrate. As for his drinking, he never thought about it at all. All the telegraphers he had known drank. It was simply a commonplace episode of his uneventful existence. A more serious viewpoint had never occurred to him.

Outside of his one irregularity the town could find nothing about him to warrant criticism; and always, as a prop for his status as stable citizen in their eyes, he had the wholesome fact of having lived for twenty years in the same boarding house. Mrs. Perkins, who ran that respectable establishment, did not hesitate to tell all who were curious enough to be concerned that Mr. Lathrop was always a gentleman, quiet, and easy to please, but—"somehow, a little mite queer". Wherein she summed up the consensus of Acropolis' opinion.

*   *   *

Coming at the end of twenty years of day-after-day routine existence familiar to all, the news, breathlessly circulated one spring evening over innumerable supper tables, that John Lathrop had married Susannah Darrow in the neighboring village of Linden the day previous, threw the town into a furor. The tidings of this sudden—and to Acropolis—inexplicable wedding were received with a vast gasp of appalled incredulity, followed immediately by a general titter of ridicule. The idea of Lathrop playing at Romeo was funny; Susan in the role of a forty year old Juliet was even funnier.

The most stunning feature of the whole affair was its unexpectedness. The names of the spinster Miss Darrow and the erring telegrapher had never for a moment been connected even in the idlest gossip. The town was aware that they knew each other, as everyone knew everyone else in Acropolis, but further than that it had not dreamed. A tangible mystery was added to the elusive personality of John Lathrop.

The first shock of the news once over and the fact accepted, the town settled down with a smirk of anticipated amusement to await developments. If Lathrop had been watched closely before it was as nothing to the keen-eyed surveyance which scrutinized his every movement after his marriage. But all this amateur detective work failed to unearth anything abnormal. It seemed that John had gone courting in the prescribed manner, calling at the lady's home on Sunday evenings. The gossips had failed to notice this because Susan lived far down along the shore out of the beaten track of observers. Her father, a retired whaling captain, had insisted on building his home where, as he expressed it, he could feel the bite of the sea. The narrow confines of the town did not appeal to the old sea-rover accustomed to limitless horizons. When he died, some two years previous to her marriage, he had left Susan the house and a small income. She had not the heart to leave the old place and had resigned herself to a life of comparative isolation, broken only by an occasional trip to the town.

It was on one of these occasions that she first met John Lathrop at the home of a married acquaintance of hers. From the first few perfunctory phrases spoken they had felt drawn together by some obscure bond of common sympathy, by a sense of the sameness of their own separate lonely lives. When the time came for her to start for home, John offered to accompany her. Susan accepted gladly. When she said good night to him at her front door, she invited him to call the following Sunday. He had done so, and thus their romance had its beginning.

Clearly, Acropolis concluded, it was a case of love, and tittered at the very notion; but there was no other explanation possible. Prone as the town was to form uncharitable judgments they never suspected John of mercenary motives. They realized that such an idea was preposterous. Besides, he had a small bank account of his own and that was sufficient to disarm suspicion.

The reason, had Acropolis been wise enough to see it, why John and Susan had fallen so precipitately in love was plain on the face of it: They were both desperately lonely. To John, Susan represented every charm of an intimate personal relationship he had never known. With her he found sympathetic understanding and a home after a lifetime spent in boarding houses. Until he met her he had never loved anything nor anyone. He neither liked nor disliked. He had no eye for any color but grey. The realization of his love for Susan awakened his slumbering soul to the glory of a revelation.

As for Susan, John came into her life just as she was resigning herself to old maidhood. Her father had always discouraged the idea of suitors. With true parental selfishness he was resolved to keep her by his side attentive to his wants, and his alone. By dint of continual bullying when she was a young girl he crushed her meek spirit into subjection. Later on in her life he had no cause for complaint. She sighed her last over any dream of romance she might have had and devoted all her energies to becoming a good housekeeper. Captain Darrow viewed this change in his daughter with unmixed satisfaction. He had converted her into a refuge for his old age.

When he died she never connected his removal from her life with any sense of liberation. As if his bullying spirit still haunted their little cottage by the sea she became as much a slave to it as she had been to him. She dared not obey her secret impulse to sell the house and run away—far away—somewhere. She was afraid.

Then Lathrop came. Everything was changed in that moment. She used to listen to his matter-of-fact accounts of his wanderings before he settled in Acropolis—John found he could talk to her, and, after all, he had been around in a bit in a small way, he decided to himself—and in her eyes which had longed to see the great world beyond the town limits, he became a sort of glorious vagabond thrilled by the romance of the wanderlust, lured by the far-off lands of her dreams.

Their lives fitted together perfectly. Each found in the other the personification of a desire which had been suppressed because it seemed impossible of fulfillment. They had both reached that middle point in life when there seemed nothing for them to look back on and less to look forward to. Then they found each other, and to each of them their love came as a miracle which raised them from the dead.

The day after his marriage Lathrop packed up his things and took leave of Mrs. Perkins and her home cooking forever. That worthy lady felt aggrieved at his departure. She had grown to look upon him as a fixture, as much a part of the house as the grandfather's clock which ticked dolorously in the dimly lighted hallway, and she nourished a feeling of resentment against Susan who had come "like a thief in the night," as she morosely phrased it to herself, and robbed her of her star boarder.

John walked down Main street and stopped in at the hotel for his customary rye and plain water. Then he went home. Susan was in the kitchen preparing dinner. She laughed happily when he came in and kissed him. John noticed a sudden change come over her face. She drew away with a movement which had in it something of repulsion.

"Why, what's the matter, Sue?" he asked wonderingly.

She flushed slightly and turned to the stove. "Nothing" she evaded; then went on after a pause: "Only father used to drink and—" she hesitated.

"And you don't like it, is that what you mean?" She nodded. John put his arm around her tenderly. "Then I guess it's up to me to stop, eh, Sue? Well, I will, if that's the case. I guess it don't do me no good, anyway."

And he did stop. Acropolis viewed his reform with outspoken approbation but inwardly it felt disappointed. He had been the only town sinner respectable enough to be discussed in the family circle, a reputable horrible example. His advent as a sober citizen left an irritating gap in the conversation. There was nothing scarlet about him any more. Only the back room Kelly fiends were skeptical. "Just you wait" they remarked cynically, "and hear the crash when he tumbles." They waited one month, three months, six months, but much to their chagrin he didn't "tumble."

Those six months were to Susan and John days of attainment of undreamed blessedness. They had never known what it was to be really happy, and their love for each other, transforming the daily banalities of life into living wonder, made their marriage a holy thing in their eyes, a true sacrament filling them with awe and humility. They had an air of conserving their moments together, as if they were afraid they would suddenly awaken and it would all end as a dream ends, leaving only a fugitive memory mocked by the old eternal bleakness.

Also, toward the close of those days, a real apprehensible fear disturbed

John's peace of mind—the fear of losing his job. Before his marriage he would have laughed at such a notion. He had lost jobs before and there were always plenty of others. It was nothing to bother one's head about. But now it was different. His position had come to mean more to him than so many dollars a week. It was the proof of his ability, his manhood, in Susan's eyes, he thought, and became more punctilious in his work than ever before, hoping to make himself indispensable. He realized that he was getting old, and he fervently prayed that the Telegraph Company would not notice it.

This thought grew on him and he worried secretly. In the endeavor to be over exact he became nervous and made some stupid blunders. Some one of those who had suffered through these sent in a complaint. The Telegraph Company awoke to his age and apparent inefficiency. The axe fell. John was notified of his discharge and a younger man sent to take his place.

That night he could hardly muster up enough courage to go home. The thought of facing Susan with the news of his dismissal seemed intolerable to him. Passing the hotel, he hesitated. For the first time in his life he was conscious of a definite desire for drink. No, that would only make matters worse, he reflected, and walked on down the street. All the way home he was a prey to the most gloomy forebodings. What would she think of him? How could she continue to love such a failure as he had proved himself to be?

Much to his suprise Susan accepted the catastrophe quite calmly, even cheerily. As a matter of fact, she could hardly conceal her satisfaction. She had always hated his job, especially as there was no financial necessity involved, because it took so much of him away from her. Now she could have him all to herself. Then, too, his loss opened up an avenue for an escape from Acropolis which she had long been planning in secret. She was heartily sick of the town, and of the old house with its memories of her father. In her mind, John was never connected with any of this environment. He was a creature of the wide world, and she dreamed of adventuring forth with him into his proper element— the far-off, wonderful cities of men which called to her.

The next morning she laid her plan before him. They would rent the house—old Simpson had always wanted it and offered a good price—and leave Acropolis for all time; go to New York, she suggested. John agreed immediately. He thought she wished to run away from the sneers and contempt of the townspeople which she felt would be directed at her on his account. This suspicion caused him the keenest anguish, but, for her sake, he made a pretense of falling in eagerly with her idea. As for himself, though he would not admit it to her, the outside world had no charms. He was perfectly contented in Acropolis, had taken root there, and the prospect of starting life anew in the swirl of the metropolis filled him with alarm. However, he ought to be able to get a job immediately in New York, and rehabilitate himself in Susan's eyes. This thought encouraged him and brought a little peace to his troubled soul.

In less than two weeks all their arrangements had been made, the house was rented, and they boarded the train for New York. Acropolis watched them go with that complacent feeling of moral superiority inspired by the misfortunes of others. It was the general opinion that the loss of John Lathrop's job was due to his secret drinking.

*   *   *

During the period of home-hunting following their arrival in New York, they stayed at a hotel downtown. Susan wisely selected the suburbs as the most likely place to find what they wanted, and for a week they toured the outskirts of the city in search of a furnished house. At the end of that time they were lucky enough to find one which, if it did not fulfill all their expectations, was at least sufficiently comfortable and moderate in price. It was on the other side of the Hudson, near a great amusement park. There they settled.

The fact of his being without a position was still lying heavily on John's conscience. The morning after they moved into their new home he told Susan he was going to the city to look for employment. But she would have none of it. They had not had any real honeymoon; now was their chance, she said. He had worked in New York before and must show her the sights. She wished to cheer him up, to make him forget his fretting about work. She herself anticipated no pleasure from this sight-seeing tour. She had had enough of running about already. The crowds of people, the never ceasing clamor, the glittering lights bewildered and frightened her. She found the big city of her dreams too over-powering, too brutal. She would have liked to have remained at home where it was quiet and busied herself with the familiar routine of housework. But John was of the city and to him it meant life, she believed; besides, his mind must be distracted or he would insist on working and she would lose him again. So she determined they must enjoy themselves.

To John this hurrying from one point of interest to another was anything but enjoyable. He felt humiliated by his position of non-producer, degraded in Susan's eyes. His one longing was to get in harness again, to prove to her he was still the man she had married. However, he found it only natural she should want to go around a bit after being cooped up in Acropolis all her life. So he put a brave face on it and did his best to appear pleased.

Through the long days of a two weeks which appeared to both of them interminable they dragged each other from place to place. They went to theatres, to "movies," to the Hippodrome, the aquarium, the museums of Art and Natural History, the Bronx Zoo—everywhere that was mentioned in the guide book

Susan had purchased. At the end of that time they were worn-out and dispirited. John could no longer hide his depression. The money he had drawn from the Acropolis bank was getting low. He had steadily refused to let Susan pay for anything and the thought that the time was coming when he would no longer be able to do this brought a flush of shame to his cheek. What would she think of him then?

Susan saw that her plan of distracting his mind had been a failure. He was plainly not himself. His mind was evidently disturbed about something. She guessed what the something was and, with a sigh of renunciation, abandoned her idea of keeping him all to herself. If work was necessary for his well-being she was willing to make the sacrifice.

The next morning when he ventured to say with an attempt at a laugh that it was high time he quit loafing and got busy, Susan did not protest as usual. She merely mentioned that she had a lot of housework to do and asked him what time he expected to be home. Delighted at her tacit consent, he could hardly wait to get his hat and start for the ferry. Susan looked after him sorrowfully and there were tears in her eyes as she turned from the window to clear the breakfast table.

On the ferry a feeling of dismay crept over John. He suddenly remembered that Susan hadn't tried to prevent his going. By her manner she had even seemed to approve it. Then she was beginning to realize—. He felt a stabbing pain at his heart. For a moment he did not dare to think. Then he commenced to defend her to himself. After all, he argued doggedly, she was right. She hadn't married him to support him. But this argument failed to relieve his sense of hurt.

He looked for a position that day and many days following. Everywhere he was dismissed with a curt: "Nothing doing" or "We don't need anyone." In some few offices they told him to call again but the careless way in which they flung him this crumb of comfort was enough to convince him of its hopelessness. At the end of two weeks he had visited every place which he thought had ever used or would every be likely to use a telegrapher. The answer was always the same. There were no vacancies.

At home he grew afraid to look at Susan. He never alluded to the failure of his day's pilgrimage and she never questioned him. Supper once over, he could not get to bed quickly enough. He made excuses for his silence, his hurried departures to hide his disgrace in the darkness, his eagerness to get away in the mornings. He lamely pleaded a headache, a backache, an urgent engagement—what not. He fancied he could detect a scorn in Susan's eyes. It was horrible for him to be near her.

And Susan was hurt by all these things and wept in secret. She imagined he was tiring of her, that the great city to which he belonged and to which she was alien was claiming its own and drawing him away from her. She hated it now. Why had she ever brought him there?

Their feeling of estrangement grew daily. At the end of his two weeks' fruitless search, although neither of them were conscious of it, they were hardly speaking to each other. At night they lay side by side—as far apart as the poles.

*   *   *

In the long sleepless nights John tried to gather his shattered wits together and discover some way out of the blind alley in which he found himself. There was nothing to hope for in the line of telegraphing, that was plain. He must find something else. But what? That was all he knew and he was not hardy enough to undertake manual labor. Yet the present situation could not continue. He must get a job of some kind before Susan grew to hate him. This fixed idea of his had become an obsession.

One morning after he had fled from the breakfast table mumbling some excuse about seeing a friend, he picked up a paper on a bench in Riverside Park—he spent most of his days there now—and glanced down the front page. There was a big story about the wreck of an ocean liner and the heroism of the wireless operator. An idea came into his head with the flash of an inspiration. Why, he knew how to operate a wireless—knew it well. One of his few friends in Acropolis had been the operator for the big wrecking company there. Often at night he had sat in the wireless room at the end of the pier. This friend had explained everything to him and, being a telegrapher, he was quick to learn. Several times he had sent and received messages. It was easy to do. With a little study—he could read the matter up. He jumped to his feet and hurried off, bound for the public library.

The next few days he spent at the library reading and taking notes. At home he never mentioned this new hope. He was afraid it might all come to nothing and he did not want to encourage a faith in which might be doomed to disappointment. But she could tell by his actions that something had happened to relieve the tension, and she was happier than she had been at any time since their arrival in New York.

Once sure of his fitness for the position, John did not hesitate but commenced the weary round of steamship offices. He spent days along the waterfront, wandering from dock to dock. Wherever he saw a mast with a wireless rigged to it, there he went. He lied brazenly, saying he had been operator for the wrecking company in Acropolis for years and had only left on account of sickness. But he had no reference to prove it; and he was too old. They wanted younger men. The story was always the same.

It was in a hopeless mood that he entered the dingy office of what he thought must be the only pier he had not yet visited in all the miles of docks. It was over on the Brooklyn waterfront and he read the name East Coast Steamship Company on the front of the shed. To his overwhelming surprise the squat man behind the desk answered his faltering question with a brisk: "Yes, we can use an operator. What's your experience?" John told the old lie about the wrecking company. "Reference?" No, he had never thought to ask for one. He had been too sick. "Hmm. Well, we'll take you on for one trip on trial. There's nothing to do to speak of. It's an old outfit. We can't pay much," and he mentioned a sum five dollars less than the previous operator had been getting. John accepted with breathless eagerness. He could hardly believe his luck. The money was nothing to him. It was a job, a job, his job! He could look Susan in the eyes again. He needn't any longer be a burden on her hands. He felt like shouting with joy.

The squat man took down his name and address. "Sign on at three o'clock prompt day after tomorrow," he said. "Ship sails next morning at ten. Better take a look aboard now that you're here, and see if that drunken sot that had the job last trip left everything in shape. Good day."

John walked down the long dock to the ship. She was a small steamer named the *Rio Grande,* carrying accommodations for a few passengers. Aft of them was the wireless room. He looked over the outfit with a proud air of proprietorship, fixed the receivers over his ears to find out how they felt, examined and tinkered with the mechanism in a fascinated manner. Unfamiliar as the apparatus was to him, he could tell it was antiquated and showed the effects of long service. Its sending radius must be very restricted. That was why the man had told him there was so little to do, he concluded.

From the second mate, who happened to be on board, he found out their destination—Buenos Aires. They would stop at Rio on the way down and, coming back, they picked up a miscellaneous cargo at Santos, Bahia, and other ports. The *Rio Grande* was a slow boat, and the voyage usually took in the neighborhood of four months. Four months! John was terribly upset by this information. In his mind all ocean trips were connected with the seven day passages of transatlantic liners. To be away from Susan four months at a time! His feeling of happiness left him. He had half a mind to go back and tell the man he wouldn't take the job after all. No, he decided grimly, he must make one trip at least to prove he was a man. Besides, something might turn up. He might find a shore position as telegrapher in one of the ports they stopped at. Then Susan could join him there. It was sure to turn out right, one way or another.

By the time he reached home he was completely reassured. He could scarcely wait to tell Susan the good news. "I've got a job!" he shouted to her from the hall, and came in a kissed her triumphantly, his sallow face beaming. She was conscious of a great feeling of relief and gratitude at seeing him himself once more. Her joy was of short duration.

"A wireless operator—on a ship!" she exclaimed in alarm when he had explained to her the nature of his good news. The war was young then, and she had just been reading an account of the outbreak of the German submarine warfare against England. The thought of John on a ship was terrifying.

"Yes, a ship called the *Rio Grande*. She carries passengers, too—a very nice boat" he replied, too happy with himself to notice her dismay.

"But" she faltered, "you can't, John. Think of the submarines."

"Oh" he answered carelessly, "they won't touch us. This is an American ship. Besides, we don't go near Europe. She runs to South America."

To Susan South America sounded like the end of the world. "And how long does this boat stay away?" she asked with her lips trembling, hardly able to restrain her tears.

"Why—er—" He half turned away in confusion. He foresaw trouble on this point. "Only about four months, the second officer told me."

"Only!" For once in her meek life Susan was really angry. Did he think she would stay alone all that time—alone in a strange city with no friends to talk to even? Was he as cruel and inconsiderate as all that?

John was dumbfounded. He tried to justify himself, to explain to her the glorious possibilities the trip opened up. His mania prevented him from seeing anything but the miracle of that job, and he was deeply hurt because she did not feel proud of him. As her indignant protests continued, he, too, grew angry. They had their first real quarrel. At the end of it he stalked off to bed with an injured air leaving Susan, white-faced and silent, alone in the sitting room. He did not say good-night, and she heard him pass by their bedroom and enter the spare room, locking the door behind him. This was the last straw. She hid her face in her hands and sobbed bitterly.

After she had cried her fill and reached a state of comparative composure, she settled down to think. Eventually she became reconciled to this wild plan of his. She could not find it in her heart to blame him. It all fitted in so perfectly with her illusion. John was the eternal wanderer. Small wonder that this ship, with its promise of unknown lands, strange and far away, should have fascinated him so. He could not help it. It was in his blood. But one thing she resolved upon—he should not go alone. He had said the ship carried passengers. She had money. She would go with him.

She went upstairs and knocked boldly on the door of the spare room. "John! Open the door. I've been thinking and I've something to tell you."

The key turned in the lock, and she entered. The John she saw, his eyes still red from weeping, was so tragic a picture of remorseful grief that Susan was overcome with pity. Their reconciliation was tender and immediate.

"I've decided it's best for you to go since you're so set on it," she told him after a while, "but I'm determined you shan't go alone. I'm going with you."

John looked at her in bewilderment. "But, Sue, they don't hire women on board a ship, not a small ship like this."

"Hire, bosh!" she retorted scornfully. "Haven't I got more money than I know what to do with? I'm going as a passenger. I'd like to travel and see the world a little myself." John protested feebly but she cut him short. "Just never mind arguing because it ain't any use. There's only two things to figure: Either you go or you don't go; and if you go I'm going with you." And John was entirely willing to let it go at that.

The next morning she telephoned and reserved her passage; and two days later the East Coast Steamship Company's steamer *Rio Grande* nosed her way through the Narrows to the open sea with one woman passenger registered on her list—a Mrs. John Lathrop.

*   *   *

That first trip marked an epoch in their lives. After the inevitable spell of seasickness was overcome, they found their life on shipboard a never-ending succession of new marvels. Once assured of his ability to operate successfully John regained all of his old confidence in himself. He was once more in his own eyes a man among men; and there was a glamor of romance about this new job which had never accrued to the dreary routine of telegraphing. He was rated as an officer on the ship and had fallen heir to a faded blue uniform with tarnished buttons which he wore with conscious importance. Late at night when all on board with the exception of the watch on deck were sleep, he would sit in the wireless room with the receivers over his ears catching the faint whispers of distant Atlantic liners, the meaningless code signals of patrolling cruisers, the conversations of powerful shore stations thousands of miles apart, far to the north and south of him. The small sending radius of his own outfit was a constant source of annoyance. Those were fortunate nights indeed on which he could pick up a ship near enough to receive his answers, and exchange greetings with her operator. He wanted to be able to have his own voice mingle in all those mysterious currents which made the darkness of space audible with their silent words.

In those quiet hours he seemed to himself quite alone, the only intelligence alive on the sleeping ship; and a sense of power thrilled him at the thought that he, in great measure, was guiding the steamer through the night, was responsible for her safety. He grew to love his work with an intense passion, second only to his love for Susan.

On many nights she used to sit up with him—she had received permission to do so from the captain when he learned she was Lathrop's wife. Seated on a stool in a the corner she would busy herself sewing, or simply watch her John as he bent over his instrument, his brow furrowed with concentration, his rapt expression that of a medium in a trance listening to the occult warnings of spirit voices. Presently he would turn to her and whisper triumphantly: "I just caught Colon—something about a landslide in the canal yesterday—they suspect the Japanese." Susan would raise hands of wonder and admiration. "Think of it, and them so far away! It's miraculous!" she would say, or: "Land sakes!" To her it was not the powerful government station at Colon, nor the mechanism she saw before her which had accomplished this miracle. It was John, her John who had done it all, who had at last found scope for his latent powers and come into his own.

The sea fascinated her. She would sit in her deckchair for hours noting its changing moods, watching the play of the wind in the wave tops or the gradual rise and fall of the long ground swell on days of calm. Her longest trip on the water previous to this had been across the Hudson, yet the sea did not frighten her. Sometimes she was awed by the thought that the *Rio Grande*, which seemed to her a very large ship, was only a speck floating on immensity, but the idea never inspired her with terror. Even on their passage down when they ran into a howling *pampero* off the lower coast of South America and the *Rio Grande* could scarcely maintain steerage way through the tremendous seas, she was not afraid. The officers were surprised at her calmness. She had acquired a confidence, which nothing short of a wreck could shake, in the ship, its officers and crew, and above all in her John who directed and guided the destinies of all of them.

The days passed before she knew it. There were so many things to be done. There were the seagulls—"pigeons," she called them—to be regularly fed with bread filched from the table. She had very little to do with her fellow passengers, Latin-Americans returning home, for the most part; but there were the officers to be bedevilled with shy questions, incredible in their ignorance, concerning the ships of the sea and the men who went down in them. At first the officers were inclined to be annoyed by her presence on board. They were scornfully amused by what they believed to be Lathrop's domestic slavery, and called him "Henpeck" behind his back. But as they grew to know her better they all fell captive to her gentle charm. By the end of the voyage captain, mates, and engineers alike swore by her, and she was mending their clothes, sewing on buttons, and listening with a sympathetic ear to secret confidences about wives and sweethearts.

The ports the *Rio Grande* touched at played no great part in the lives of either Susan or John. Usually they preferred remaining on the ship to going ashore. The crowds of dark-skinned people speaking an alien tongue, the strange architecture of the buildings, the whole unfamiliar, foreign aspect of things made them feel ill at ease. New York had cured them of any desire for big cities. Montevideo, Buenos Aires, Rio de Janeiro belonged in that category and did not attract them. They liked to sit on deck in the shade and take an intimate interest in the loading of cargo, safely removed from the dust and bustle of it all. Thus their most vivid recollections of the ports they had visited were of the bags of coffee or coconuts, the bundles of hides, the logs of wood which were lowered into the holds.

The ship became to them their first real home—what the house in Acropolis had never been, connected as it was in John's mind with Susan's money, and made grim for her by the memory of her father. When they docked at New York again and the time came for them to go ashore, they felt lost. The house they had rented across the Hudson was no longer to be thought of. Susan sent a notice to the agent announcing their intention of giving it up. They hired a room in a quiet little family hotel in Brooklyn recommended by the Captain. It was within reaching distance of the wharf and they could visit the ship daily. Their first night on shore they held consultation and Susan figured out her expenses for the past trip. She found she could afford to make the ship her home in future, taking the voyage down and back regularly as a passenger, and this was decided on.

✳ ✳ ✳

For over two years they led this strange, wandering existence. As time went on they became more and more attached to the ship. They no longer went ashore at the different ports except in cases of absolute necessity. The officers, even the men forward who remained on board for more than one trip, regarded Susan as a favored person, not a passenger but one of themselves, and she was able to make arrangements whereby she lived on the ship during the *Rio Grande's* stay in Buenos Aires preceding the voyage home. She and John were like a thoroughly domesticated couple hugging the comfortable family hearth, indifferent to the world which roared outside.

It was during the latter party of their eighth trip southward that Germany announced to the world her intention of pursuing an unrestricted submarine warfare. Those on board the *Rio Grande* did not hear of it until their arrival in

Buenos Aires. John thought this peculiar. It was queer he hadn't caught the news from some steamer, or from one of the powerful land stations down the coast. They must have sent out warnings to passing vessels. He had noticed how few messages he had caught on the way down, and even those had sounded faint and blurred, and he had difficulty understanding them. He blamed it on the worn-out condition of his outfit, and while they remained in Buenos Aires he diligently set to work trying to tune it up.

During the return voyage north all on board waited nervously for some news of the world crisis. The last they had heard in Argentina, relations between the United States and Germany had reached an acute stage. The *Rio Grande* was an American vessel, most of those on board were American citizens, and, in view of the general tense expectancy, John was ordered to communicate with the Captain the minute he received anything decisive.

Up to the time they left Port of Spain, Trinidad, their last port of call, nothing had happened to change the situation. If it had they would not have known it until they touched at that town. The wireless was behaving very badly. John had intercepted hardly a score of messages during the six weeks they were out from Buenos Aires, and these were unimportant, from coast-wise steamers sailing approximately the same course as they did, so near that they were scarcely out of sight of the lookout. He grumbled about his hard luck—a thing unusual in him—and complained of the uselessness of his apparatus to the Captain. All the officers were indignant and cursed the owners for their short-sighted economy in sending a ship to sea improperly equipped in those critical times.

Steaming north from Trinidad to New York the *Rio Grande* moved in darkness as far as any news from the outside world was concerned. What feeble ticking did come to John's ear was indistinguishable. On the night before they were due to sight Sandy Hook, after listening for hours without a single call coming in, he gave up in disgust. Susan came into the wireless room and sat down in her accustomed place just as he jerked the receivers off his ears impatiently and flung them on the table.

"It's no use, Sue," he muttered in exasperation, "this darn machine is only fit for the scrap heap. They'll have to get a new one." He stared in front of him disconsolately. He felt injured, as if it were a personal reflection on himself, this failure of his mechanism at such a critical moment.

He looked over at Susan, expecting her sympathy. Her eyes were fixed on the sewing in her lap but her lips were moving as if she were speaking. "Talking to herself," he thought to himself with a smile. Her eyes were lifted from her work and fixed on his. Again her lips moved but he could hear no sound. Her expression turned to one of puzzled astonishment. Then she laughed loudly. He could hear that and the words which followed: "Well, if you don't take the prize, John, for being wrapped up in your thoughts! Here I been asking you something three times and you've not answered a word.

John felt vaguely terrified. So she had been talking to him! Why hadn't he heard her? "You talk so low at times, Sue, nobody'd hear you," he remarked with a trace of irritation.

She laughed. "Getting deaf in your old age, that's the trouble," she retorted smilingly; then seeing his serious face she hastened to add conciliatingly, and in a voice unconsciously louder: "I except I do talk uncommon quiet now and again."

John made no reply to this. He sat rigidly upright on his chair, spellbound with the horror of her joking suggestion. "Getting deaf." Supposing she was right—supposing he was—. He found himself trembling all over, cold, as if he had a chill. Perspiration poured out on his forehead. He suffered from a sensation of physical illness. Certainly she had been speaking and he had not heard her—not a word she had said. He tried to brush the thought aside, to laugh at it. Why, this was all nonsense! He was worn out, preoccupied with his own thoughts. That was why he hadn't heard. It was only natural he shouldn't. But the feeling of having suffered a sudden calamity persisted in spite of him. He felt his anguish must be visible in his face. He dared not look at Susan except out of the corner of his eyes. Thank God, she wasn't watching him! She was busy with her work, unconcernedly sewing. She must never know, he thought, never—even if it were true. But it couldn't be! He was just tired; he had strained himself some way. He kept his eyes on her lips with a dreadful fixity, fearing she would speak again and he wouldn't hear—and she would find out. Find out what? There was nothing to find out. Was he going crazy to worry about nothing in this silly fashion? See! Her lips were moving again. He tore his eyes away from them, straining his ears to catch the sound. He heard something like a mumble, something coming from a distance, incoherent. What was it she had said? Was it a question? He blurted out a brusque: "No" in answer. Was she looking at him queerly? Did she guess? He was afraid to turn his head to find out. He clapped on the receivers hurriedly. That would be an excuse. He couldn't be expected to hear her with those over his ears. He pretended to be intent on his work. He knew he would go mad if she didn't leave him alone in a moment. But it was nothing, nothing at all, his imagination—. He'd be all right in a minute. He wanted to scream.

Susan tried to chat with him but received no answer. She looked up and saw he was hard at work again, and gave up the attempt. He looked so tired, poor man. He worked too hard and worried too much. Bother his stupid machine for getting out of order! She gathered up her work and touched him on the shoulder. "You're a glum sort of body tonight, John. Stop worrying! The

Company'll buy you a new engine." She bent down and kissed him. "I'm going to turn in, as the sailors say. Good-night."

"Good-night," he muttered, turning his face away from her. He had not understood a word of what she had said. She disappeared in the darkness of the deck outside. At last he was alone. Now he could find out the truth. He removed the receivers and snatched a pencil from the table. Holding it at one end he tapped the other gently against the edge of the chair. No sound! He tapped more briskly, his heart seeming to cease its beat, his whole being concentrated in one frantic effort to hear. Nothing! The blood rushed to his head in a throbbing flood. His eyes glared insanely. Ah, now he could hear it—a faint tap, tap, tap. At the same moment he realized that he was pounding the pencil against the chair with the whole strength of his arm. He hurled it away from him with a choking cry and collapsed over the table, his face hidden on his outstretched arms, sobbing with terror and weakness.

*   *   *

At dawn the next morning they sighted Sandy Hook. Soon after they were stopped by a patrol boat which put a government pilot on board to guide them through the maze of submarine nets in the Narrows. This was the first news they had of the declaration of war by the United States, and passengers and crew of the *Rio Grande* united in denouncing the East Coast Company for its inefficient wireless service.

John did not venture out of his stateroom until long after the ship had docked. He was afraid to see anyone, afraid someone would speak to him, afraid they would guess. To Susan he pleaded illness, which she could well believe, for he looked incredibly pale and haggard. He discovered he could hear everything she said that morning, not distinctly, but still he could hear. This tended to confirm him in the belief that the attack of the night previous had been due to worry and overwork and was only temporary. Still, once ashore and settled at the little hotel, he lost no time in going to the nearest doctor. Susan, ignorant of his true complaint, had urged him to do this. "You'd best get a tonic. You look all tuckered out," she said.

The doctor examined him in a perfunctory way and acknowledged that he could do nothing. He advised him to see an ear specialist and gave him the address of one in New York. On his return home, John did not mention his visit to Susan, and when she saw how upset he seemed she resolved to postpone all questioning until the next day.

He passed a sleepless night. Early in the morning he set out for New York and went to the address given him. He was kept in the waiting room for over two hours, a prey to all the agonies of suspense. His tortured imagination would not leave him at peace. There was an old man sitting next to him, decrepit and bald, with a gruesome-looking ear trumpet. John shuddered every time he glanced at him. Was this to be his finish?

Finally he was admitted. The specialist, an elderly man with keen dark eyes which probed into John from behind his gold-rimmed glasses, put him through a searching examination. At first he was inclined to treat John as just another of the many who flocked to his office every day, but the examination had not progressed far before he was interested. He scented the unusual. Later he became absorbed in his work. John was distinctly worth while—a case which presented many novelties.

When he was through he sat staring down at the table for a moment or so as if he were undecided. He looked up and scrutinized John's face for a second with his probing eyes. Something he saw there must have reassured him for he spoke with a trace of subdued kindliness sounding through the professional impersonality of his tones: "Do you wish to know the exact truth about your case—no matter what it is?"

"Yes, sir." John was terrified by this ominous question but he managed to keep his voice steady.

"You're different from most of them," the specialist remarked dryly. "I'm sorry to have to tell you there isn't much hope for your hearing. In fact, to be quite candid, there's no hope at all. Your hearing machinery, if I may use the term, is worn out, is rapidly becoming atrophied. It will soon, very soon in my opinion, be too dead, too insensitive is a better way of putting it, to register the vibration of sound waves. When that happens, you will be deaf. For a very short time you will have, as your present symptoms indicate, days when you will hear quite well, though faintly. On the other days you will hardly hear at all. I must warn you that this condition of affairs cannot continue very long, and when the final break comes it will be sudden. You must be prepared to face it tomorrow, in a week, in a month or two at the latest. I cannot be more definite than that.

"Isn't there"—John formed the words with difficulty. His lips seemed to have forgotten their function. "Isn't there something I can do for it?"

The specialist shook his head. "Nothing—. Yet I don't want to send you away utterly hopeless. You must remember we are all of us, the best of us, fallible." His tone showed he did not put much faith in this statement, or in those which followed. "We are all mistaken once in a while. I can only judged by the symptoms revealed to me. It is possible I may be wrong. For your sake I sincerely hope so." He stroked his mustache thoughtfully: "A sudden stroke— something cataclysmal—who knows? But I wouldn't count on it. No hope is preferable to one which is doomed to disappointment."

"Yes." John stumbled to his feet. He couldn't utter another word, but fumbled awkwardly in his pocket for his money. The specialist mentioned the amount of his fee. As John turned to the door after paying him, he shook him by the hand. "Again I repeat, I hope I'm wrong," he said with genuine sympathy. "Good luck to you."

John passed through the waiting room. He saw a few blurred faces with big eyes which stared at him cruelly—then he was in the street. He stood there for a moment blinking dazedly. Snowflakes fluttered down from the leaden sky and settled on the grey flags at his feet. He watched them melt with a stupid interest. Mechanically he turned up the collar of his overcoat. "It's getting cold," he said aloud to himself, dully. Then he turned and walked down the street with the rapid, jerky steps of a marionette.

*   *   *

How he got home that day John never knew. He remembered being jostled and pushed, and a long ride in a crowded elevated train. He stood in front of the hotel entrance looking at it with bewildered eyes, unable to account for his being there.

Upstairs more bad news awaited him. Susan had received a letter from the man who had charge of her affairs in Acropolis. The Fishermen's Cold Storage Plant, in which her father had invested and to which she owed her small income, had gone into bankruptcy. Her income was wiped out. This report had robbed her of all faith in the agent. One could never tell about such people when one was so far away, she said. She would have to go back to Acropolis immediately and personally attend to the sale of the house. This was imperative. It might take quite a long time. Real estate was not active in the sleepy little town. She would be unable to make the next trip on the *Rio Grande*. That was the terrible tragedy. She wept, and John tried to comfort her in a dazed way.

The next trip! He hardly dared think of it. What could he do? He knew he ought to go to the office at once and tell them and hand in his resignation. But now, how could he? On what would he live? On Susan? Now, when she had lost everything? The thought was impossible. There was less chance than ever of his getting a position ashore. In his present condition he was worthless to everyone. Even if he got a job he couldn't hold it. Besides, the thought of giving up his place on the *Rio Grande* was intolerable to him. His pride in his work, his importance in his own and Susan's eyes, his love for the ship which was a home for both of them—all this must be lost to him. And why? All because of what a stupid doctor had said. Well, even the doctor had confessed he might be wrong, that there was still hope. His hearing was all right now—

never better. He'd heard about these doctors. They were always making matters worse to keep you coming to them. The worst wouldn't happen for months, anyway. The doctor had told him that. He could make at least one more voyage. That would give Susan a chance to get her affairs straightened out. Then he would see. There was surely some cure for his trouble, somewhere. Doctors always lied about that. If they couldn't help you themselves, they thought no one else could. And there was so little to do on the *Rio Grande*. None of the messages he took down ever amounted to anything, really. He could almost make them up out of his head, if need be. He knew the officers would never find him out. He would keep to himself, tell them he was sick. That would explain his silence. And their voices were loud. He could hear them easily. There was nothing to fear, and he could lay the blame for any omission on the old wireless. Yes, he must make one more trip at least. There was no way out of it. He simply had to. But supposing the worst did happen and something important was flashed and he couldn't—.

His thoughts whirled around and around in the same old circle. That night when he at last fell asleep there was one thing which remained steadfast in his mind—he must make the next trip, cost what it might.

The concept of the war as applying to him personally, his plain duty as a patriot never occurred to him. He had hardly ever read the reports of the struggle in Europe, or taken the smallest interest in its outcome. He was neither pro one nor the other. It was all happening on another planet as far as he was concerned. If a lot of people wanted to kill each other, why let them. He had once joined a Socialist local, not because he shared the convictions of that party or even had a clear idea of what they were, but simply because most of his friends belonged. It was like a club. Still, enough of their propaganda had remained in his mind to fill him with a vague contempt for war and the people who made it. That the United States was taking an active part in the conflict would have seemed impossible to him if he had ever thought of it. There was nothing to impress the fact on his consciousness. Outwardly everything went on the same—and, to him, was the same.

The days previous to Susan's departure for Acropolis were long and sad ordeals for both of them. The knowledge that they were soon to be parted for the first time since their marriage oppressed them with gloomy presentiments. Added to this John had his own secret trouble to brood over, and was despondent and silent. Susan attributed his manner to sorrow over her departure, and asked him no questions about his two trips to the doctor. When she spoke and he did not seem to hear her, she was too downcast herself to rally him on his preoccupation.

The dreaded day came at last. In the car on their way to the station they did not speak to each other. They were afraid of breaking down if they attempted to express what was in their hearts. At the station John was not permitted to go to the train and they said good-bye at the gate.

"Good-bye, John," Susan said, here eyes filling with tears. "Take good care of yourself. You ain't been looking well and it worries me."

He bent down and kissed her. "I'm all right. Don't worry. Good-bye, Sue." He stood and watched her until she was lost to view in the throng of hurrying passengers. Then he turned away and walked wearily to the street. He was conscious of a sickening feeling of weakness, of a sensation of vital loss, as if his backbone had just been painlessly removed.

*   *   *

Two days after Susan's departure the *Rio Grande* put to sea again with John at his usual post in the wireless room. During these two days, the longest and loneliest he had ever passed in his life, John had studiously avoided the ship. He had walked from place to place aimlessly, in a vain attempt to vanish his gnawing anxiety. Several times he had made up his mind to hand in his resignation, to tell them all about his affliction; but halfway to the dock he would be seized by that grim terror of the future and turn back to the hotel.

Once in his accustomed place, out at sea, surrounded by friendly faces, he grew calmer. The wireless had been thoroughly overhauled during their stay in port, the Captain told him, cautioning him to be alert for warnings of German raiders. John was relieved to find that, in the first week out, the messages came to him quite distinctly, if a trifle faintly. He became elated and confident once more. He was sure the doctor had been wrong, that his loss of hearing had been only a passing ailment.

Then nearly a month went by without his receiving hardly a thing. He knew he was to blame. He could sense the wireless waves converging on the ship from all sides. Besides, he no longer heard a single word that was said to him. Even the Captain's rough voice was reduced to a thin blur of sound. He told them all he was sick, and avoided speaking to anyone as far as he could, waiting for his meals until the last moment when the others were through or nearly so. And he made up messages, unimportant bits of sea news such as he might have received from passing ships. His familiarity with the vessels in the coast trade, their routes and times of sailing, enabled him to do this without fear of detection. A blind panic was upon his soul. He fought to hold his job as another man might have fought to preserve his life—even though he knew now that the struggle was hopeless, that the end was in sight.

The officers noticed his shrinking manner, his evident desire to keep to himself, and thought they understood the reason; he was all broken up on account of Susan's not being with him. They sympathized with him because they, also, missed her. The ship was not the same anymore. It had lost that atmosphere of home which had owed its charm to Susan's homely personality. As the young Fourth Mate phrased it: "The *Rio Grande's* just a rotten old tub again like the rest of them."

While they were docked at Buenos Aires John remained on shore most of the time, spending long dreary days seated on benches along the Paseo Colon; eating frugally—when he did eat—at dingy *almacens* on the calle Mexico or Bolivar where the peons gathered at noon for their *puchero* and *vino Mendoza*. He lived and moved in a profound stupor, hardly conscious of the passing of time, his brain utterly exhausted, incapable of sustaining the effort of a further thought. The strange faces, the many-gestured peons, the unfamiliar food which he ate without hunger—they were all a part of a dream he was dreaming, unsubstantial, without reality; and deep in his soul there lurked the fear of his awakening.

Her return cargo safely stowed in the holds, the *Rio Grande* steamed slowly down the muddy-colored Rio de la Plata bound for home. John had received a letter from Susan the day before. The arrangements for the sale of the house in Acropolis were nearly completed. Contrary to her expectations, there had been no trouble finding a purchaser at her own price. Real estate was booming. The rest of the letter was full of expressions of love and hope for their future. She would have enough money to continue her trips on the *Rio Grande* for a long time. Before that was gone something would turn up.

John looked up at her photograph on the wall over his table in the wireless room and the tears ran down his sallow cheeks. What would she say when she knew? He would have to tell her when he got back. It was all over, their wonderful life together on the ship. His hearing was very bad now. If could only make this return trip without accident, without being found out!

They stopped at Montevideo to take on a little additional cargo and one or two passengers. There was a strong report going the rounds there of the presence of a German raider, a converted tramp, in the South Atlantic. Those on board the *Rio Grande* paid little attention to this talk. Rumors of that kind had become daily occurrences and never turned out to amount to anything. Still the Captain doubled the lookout and advised John to keep a sharp ear for anything suspicious. John nodded mechanically; he had not heard a word.

They reached Santos in safety without having encountered a single ship. There the rumor of the raider persisted. The *Rio Grande* took on some coffee and resumed her voyage northward with one additional passenger, a young American named Stevens, a wireless operator from the interior who was travelling back to the States to escape the ravages of a fever which he had contracted.

The first night out he came to pay John a visit. He expected to be welcomed as a brother in the calling but his reception was far from cordial. John did not know who or what Stevens was and so could not appreciate his real danger; but Stevens persisted in remaining in the wireless room and John was uneasy and anxious to get rid of him. Moreover, he talked continually, telling John of his experiences in what he termed "that damn spiggity country." John answered "yes" and "no" at random, plainly showing his resentment at the other's intrusion. At length Stevens gave it up and went to the smoking room. He concluded the operator must be recovering from a spree ashore the night previous, and was nourishing a grouch. He confided his opinion to the Second Mate, who remarked feelingly: "He's homesick for his wife, poor devil, that's the trouble—and I don't blame him."

Just after dawn the next morning the lookout in the crow's nest sighted the smoke of a steamer, hull-down on the horizon to the northwest. The First Officer, who was on the bridge, shouted to him to keep his eye peeled and sing out when her hull showed. At the end of an hour the lookout hailed the bridge again: "A tramp by the trim of her sir. Seems to be heading sou'east." Southeast? Then she was coming right toward them. Remembering the reported raider, the Mate ordered the quartermaster to lay a course more to the eastward. Then he hurried below to get his glasses and awaken the Captain. Coming up on deck again he climbed to the crow's nest to have a look at the approaching ship through the binoculars. What he saw startled him. He shouted back to the Captain, who had rushed to the bridge only partly dressed. "It looks damn bad, sir. She's changed her course to the eastward, too. Bearing right down on us now, sir.

"Does she show any colors?" the Captain roared back.

"No, sir—not that I can make out." He took another look and then scrambled down the ratlines. "There's a glint on her for'ard, sir—might be a gun," he exclaimed breathlessly when he regained the bridge. The Captain lost no time making up his mind. "Head her about," he bellowed to the man at the wheel, "and we'll put back toward Santos. Can't afford to take any chances, Mr. Stone," he muttered gravely, watching the quartermaster obey his order.

While the *Rio Grande* was turning slowly back on her tracks the other vessel gained upon them appreciably. Dense black clouds of smoke were seen pouring from her funnel.

"She speeding up, sir. They've seen us swing about."

"Looks as if we're in for it, dammit," the Captain growled out a string of curses. "Well, we'll give 'em a run for it. Go below to the engine room. Tell 'em to pack on all she'll stand." The Mate hastened away. As if to dispel all doubts as to her identity, a puff of feathery smoke shot out from the bow of the raider and a few seconds later a dull boom echoed over the calm sea. The shell struck far astern of the *Rio Grande*, raising a white column of foam.

"We're out of range, I guess," the Captain said to the Mate, who had rejoined him. "If we can only hold her there. A fine business to send a ship like this to sea defenseless!" he exclaimed indignantly. "Now if we only had a gun." The yellow funnel of the *Rio Grande* began to belch forth inky clouds. The men below decks were driving her for all she was worth. The old vessel shook from stem to stern, shouldering her blunt bow through the long swells, her propeller churning up a boiling wake which stretched like a white tail on the sea behind her.

"You'd better see the passengers are woke up, Mr. Stone. Tell them to put on their life belts—as a precaution. I'm going aft and have Lathrop send out a call for help. There may be a cruiser about somewheres." The Captain walked quickly back to the wireless room. John was sitting at his instrument, staring sadly at Susan's photograph.

"Wake up, Lathrop!" the Captain said to him brusquely; "there's a raider after us. See if you can reach some warship. Give 'em our position—about two hundred miles out of Santos to the nor'west."

"Yes, sir." John put his finger on the key. The Captain went back to the bridge.

What was it the Old Man had ordered? He had not the slightest idea, but he knew something unusual had happened from the alarmed expression on the Captain's face. He sent out some meaningless call and then went cautiously to his door and looked out. His gaze fell astern and he saw the other ship following them. In a flash he understood and jumped back to his sending key. A moment later one call for help after another went whining shrilly into the air. But how could he tell if they were received by anyone? He couldn't hear a sound. He had realized for some time now that the final stroke had fallen and he was absolutely deaf. He sat at the table trembling, moaning to himself in helpless weakness, sending out frenzied appeals for rescue as fast as he could work his key.

The passengers began to come on deck and gathered in a huddled group astern, watching the pursuing steamer with frightened eyes. They talked English and Spanish in low, excited voices and helped each other to adjust the life belts. A child raised a thin, quavering whine of terror. "Hush, hush!" they all cried to it angrily as if they were afraid its sobbing would betray them.

The Captain kept his binoculars on the raider. "She's gaining on us hand over fist," he muttered, "They'll be able to shoot us full of holes damn soon if they keep up that gait. She's showing her colors now, German, of course, and flying signals for us to surrender." He cursed with impotent rage. "Not another thing in sight, either. Where are all the damned cruisers anyway? I wonder if Lathrop's found one. Find out, will you, Stone?"

"Yes, sir." The Mate walked aft and entered the wireless room. "Got anyone yet, Lathrop?" he asked anxiously.

John tried to read the movement of his lips. "Yes, sir." He finally ventured hopelessly.

"Good for you!" the Mate exulted. "Who was it?"

"No, sir" John mumbled, pretending to be preoccupied with his sending.

The Mate looked at him irritably. "Listen to what I'm asking you," he said in exasperation. "What ship did you get in touch with? Was it a warship?"

"Yes, sir," John's eyes fixed themselves on his instrument.

"Was it one of our cruisers or a Britisher? What did they say? Are they coming? How far away was she?" John kept working his key but made no reply. The Mate grabbed him roughly by the shoulder. "Lathrop! Are you sure it was a warship?"

John looked at him stupidly. "No, sir."

"You damn fool! What the hell's the matter with you?" Something he saw in John's face checked his anger. The man was evidently drunk or doped or frightened out of his wits. It was a case for the skipper, he decided, and hurried to the bridge. "There's something wrong with Lathrop, sir," he told the Captain. "I can't get a thing out of him. First he says he got in touch with a warship, then he says he didn't. Seems to be doped or drunk or something, sir."

"I'll damn soon find out." The Captain strode aft angrily, followed by the Mate, who was curious to see the outcome. They found John sprawled over his table with his face in his hands, sobbing. He realized the end had come. "What's all this nonsense, Lathrop?" the Captain demanded, touching his arm to attract his attention.

John glanced up at him and stammered confusedly: "I don't know—I don't know—"

"He's scared to death, the coward!" the Old Man was wild. "Where are your guts. Brace up and act like a man! There's no danger, you idiot! Answer my questions. What ship did you get? Is she coming? How far away is she? Answer me!" he roared, shaking John back and forth on his chair, enraged by the latter's stubborn silence.

"I don't know—I don't—" John burst into hysterical tears. "I can't—I can't hear a word you're saying. I shouldn't have made this trip. The doctor told me—I'd go deaf soon. I should have told you. It's all—my fault, I know. I should have resigned—but I couldn't bear it. I haven't taken a real message hardly, this trip. I couldn't hear a thing. The doctor said—it would be like that. I thought he was only trying to frighten me. I only wanted to make one more trip. I couldn't give up the job—then—when Susan had lost everything." He stared up into their amazed, incredulous faces and cried frenziedly: "I can't hear a thing, don't you understand. Not a word! I'm deaf! Stone deaf!" He hid his face on his arms and sobbed convulsively.

The Captain and Mate exchanged horrified glances. The former leaned over John and shouted at the top of his deep voice. "Can you hear me now? Look up at me!" The operator never moved. It was plain he hadn't heard. The Captain wiped the perspiration off his streaming forehead. "Poor devil, it's true, I guess."

"No doubt of it, sir." The Mate's tones were full of awe.

"And now what'll we do? We're in a fine, rotten mess—our last hope cut off." Suddenly his face brightened; "I've got it. Run and fetch the young chap that came on board at Santos. He's an operator, he said."

The Mate went out on deck and hailed the group of passengers: "Is Mr. Stevens there?"

"Here you are." Stevens came to the door of the wireless room. The Mate rapidly explained to him what the trouble was. "Poor chap! I noticed he acted funny last night." Stevens cast a glance of pity at John's bowed shoulders. The Captain motioned the deaf man to sit on the stool in the corner—Susan's place. He did so mechanically. Stevens sat down and adjusted the receivers. The two officers stood just inside the door and watched him nervously.

"Ah, I've got someone," he cried excitedly after a pause; then his face fell. "Only the land station at Santos." He listened intently for a few minutes; at last he gave a whistle of surprise and turned to them resentfully. "Here's a sweet stunt for you! Our deaf friend here is to blame for the whole mess we're in. Santos says they sent out a hurry call for us to come back last night. They're not supposed to, of course. They'd received authentic news last night of a British tramp that was sunk around where we are now by a raider. They tried to warn us. They thought it was funny there was no answer when we were so near. There's no cruiser in this vicinity as far as they know."

The eyes of the three men were fixed on John. He read the condemnation in their glances and shrank farther back into his corner. The Captain's face grew slowly red with suppressed rage. "So this yellow cur has lost me my ship," he blurted out and took a menacing step forward raising his closed fist. By a visible effort he controlled himself and looked at the others sheepishly, as if he were half ashamed of his anger. "He's been punished enough, I suppose," he growled, and strode out to the deck, feeling he could not endure the sight of John a moment longer without resorting to physical violence.

"I'll keep sending," Stevens told the Mate, "but there isn't much use after what Santos said. Our only chance is to beat them to it."

"Which is no chance at all—in this tub," grunted the Mate. "They're gaining every second."

To give point to this statement there was a chorus of terrified cries from the group of passengers, and a hollow boom resounded over the water. They crowded to the door in time to see the fountain of spray thrown up by a shell about two hundred yards to port of them.

"We're in range now. That's the finish." The Mate cursed and ran forward to the bridge. The Captain was searching the horizon with his binoculars. "They're going to fire again, Mr. Stone. We might as well give up. If it wasn't for the women and children I'd see them damned—." The report of the raider's gun interrupted him. This time the shell fell uncomfortably close astern. The passengers ran forward with panic-stricken faces. The Captain sighed and signaled to the engine room. The engines ceased their throbbing. The *Rio Grande* lost headway and presently lay motionless except for the slow rise and fall of the swell. "Signal 'em we give up, Stone. It's the only thing we can do under the circumstances. And get the boats ready." Then he added vindictively: "Damn Lathrop!"

The raider rapidly approached and finally drew up to port of them within hailing distance. An officer on the bridge lifted a megaphone to his lips. "Lower your boats," he ordered in good English, "and bring your people over. Be quick about it. We've no time to lose."

The Captain roared back: "As soon as we can" and went to take personal charge of the disposal of the passengers.

Stevens had left the wireless room when he felt the engines stop. He tried in a perfunctory way to get John out on deck but the latter only stared at him uncomprehendingly, and refused to leave his stool. Stevens had given it up with a shrug of his shoulders, and in the excitement outside had forgotten all about him.

The boats were slung out from the davits, each with its complement of crew and passengers, and lowered safely to the water. The calm sea made this an easy proceeding. The men seized the oars and started to row slowly toward the raider. Unconscious of all this and forgotten by everyone, John sat battling with the weight of guilt which oppressed his soul. Was he to blame directly? Had there been a warning of this raider which he hadn't heard? He couldn't tell and he was afraid to ask. He felt conscious of his responsibility and clung desperately to that last little straw of uncertainty.

As the boats approached the raider, she, in turn, lowered one. It was manned by six sailors and an officer in a naval uniform sat in the stern. They pulled quickly to the *Rio Grande* and boarded her while the captured men and women were clambering to the deck of the German vessel.

John was awakened from his brooding by a rough hand on his shoulder. He saw, with a shock of surprise, a strange man in a uniform bending over him. The man was talking to him, giving him some order, evidently.

John pointed to his ears. "I can't hear you," he muttered, "I'm deaf."

"So?" The German officer looked at him suspiciously, suspecting some trick. Then he called two of his men. They took John out on deck and forced him to slide down a rope to their boat. A moment later the officer and his men followed. Not wishing to waste ammunition sinking the *Rio Grande* they had taken advantage of the calm sea to come on board and open her seacocks.

They pushed off and rowed swiftly back to their own vessel. John stared at the *Rio Grande* as another man might have looked at a home to which he was paying an eternal farewell. Slowly the full consciousness of what he had done was penetrating his dazed brain. But had he done it? Had he? He wished he could weep but his eyes burned with a grief too great for tears. As he reached the raider a sudden remembrance stabbed him with its anguish. He had forgotten Susan's picture. It was still hanging on the wall in the wireless room. He tried to climb down into the boat again. The officer came up over the side at this moment and John appealed to him. "I've got to go back! I forgot a picture— Susan's picture. It'll only take a moment. Let me go back, please, won't you? It's only a picture," he pleaded miserably.

The officer smiled contemptuously and turned to the Captain of the *Rio Grande*, who was waiting to ask him what was to be done with the *Rio Grande's* people. "Who is this fool?" he questioned.

"He was our wireless operator" the Captain answered. "You've got him to thank for catching us. He went deaf and never told us—afraid of losing his job. We never got the warnings they sent us about you."

"I see. A stroke of good luck for us." He smiled sardonically. "And yet you claim God is not on our side." His smile broadened into a grin. "I'll see to it he has all the privileges of an ally." The idea tickled him and he laughed loudly, then as suddenly grew serious. "He's a little out of his mind, isn't he? John was still stammering out: "Please, sir—my wife's picture—just a few minutes."

"I shouldn't wonder," the Captain growled.

"I'll tell my men to be kind to him, then. He deserves the Iron Cross." The German turned on his heel, motioning the Captain to follow him, and walked away laughing to himself.

John stood at the rail and looked across the sea at the *Rio Grande*. She was sinking lower and lower, rolling sluggishly like a water soaked log. Memories of all the happy days he had lived on board of her with Susan raced through his mind. And Susan's picture—he felt he must jump into the sea and swim back. He put one leg over the rail and hesitated, terrified by the green depths below him. A German sailor grabbed him by the arm and forced him back to a sitting position on the deck. John struggled frantically. For the first time in his life he knew hatred. How he hated them all, these foreign people who were sinking his ship, his home, Susan's and his. Finally he lay back exhausted and the sailor sat on him to hold him down. How long he remained in that ignominious position he could not tell. His whole being was convulsed with its newfound passion. He pictured to himself all varieties of punishments, the most fiendish tortures to pay them back with. This offered an outlet for the boiling turmoil in his brain which had already driven him to the verge of insanity.

When he was allowed to stand up again, the *Rio Grande* was taking her last plunge. She sagged toward the bow, trembling, her stern raised high in the air. There was a metallic roar as her engines wrenched loose and crashed forward. Then she dove beneath a swell, and where she had been was only a foaming whirlpool of tossing waves. In a moment this too was gone.

John sobbed aloud—a great, dry, racking sob wrung from the heart of his anguish. The sailor who had held him on the deck glanced at him with a contemptuous sneer, then turned and said something to one of his mates. They looked at the place where the *Rio Grande* had disappeared, and then at John, and both laughed. Ah, how he hated them!

*   *   *

For two weeks the German raider, warily eluding the pursuing cruisers, continued to prowl in the lane of coastwise shipping. The commander was aware his good fortune could not last forever, and so he hugged the South American coast, ready at the first sign of a hostile craft to run his ship into a neutral port to be interned rather than surrender her as a prize to the enemy. His quest for further prey, however, proved unproductive. The warning of the German's presence, completely verified at last by the loss of the *Rio Grande*, had been communicated to all vessels in the East Coast trade, and their owners held them in port, eagerly awaiting news of the foe's destruction.

The garrulous Stevens had quickly spread the story of John's responsibility for their capture to the passengers and crew of the *Rio Grande*. These in turn passed the information to the other prisoners, the crews of five cargo ships which had met the same fate. The deaf man, pitiful in his weakness and affliction, was crushed beneath a general flood of detestation. All the spite engendered by the bitter humiliation they suffered, they vented against him. Their captors were ignored as objects for their hatred. Here was a victim ready to their hands; and the stinging taunts of "Coward! Traitor!" were hurled at John from all sides by those he had hoped to be his friends. He could not hear the words but could sense them, read them in every glowering eye which seared his soul with its message of contemptuous loathing. He felt—and was—an outcast, a pariah rejected by his kind, an unclear thing; and of the real reason for it all, the patriotic sentiment he had desecrated, the race-passion of war which made them despise him so deeply, he had no conception. He bore their scorn dumbly without protest. He even acknowledged its justice, for he guessed from their attitude that the loss of the ship must have been due directly to some failure of his. But this perception of guilt was centered in his immediate self. He had no recognition of his dereliction as a sin against an ideal beyond himself, a national ideal. His transgression was against himself and Susan. He had lost *his* job and *his* ship which had been their home by virtue of *his* position. Therein lay the crime. Nothing else existed.

All day he would sit on the Number Three hatch, shunned by everyone, steeped in an apathy profound and blind. The life of the ship passed by him unnoticed. Shut off from the world of sounds he was flung back, recoiling upon himself. Surrounded by hatred, he nourished his own particular hate with a brooding intensity, a vindictive thirst for revenge which was astounding, ridiculous in this gentle man who, even in his drinking days, had shrinkingly avoided arousing any ill feeling which might lead to a brawl. But now there was ever before his eyes the vivid picture of the *Rio Grande*, quivering in a death agony to him human, before she plunged to the bottom. He felt as a peasant feels who is forced to stand by impotently and see his home burnt by the invader; and he hated as that peasant would hate. Then there was the photograph he had lost, Susan's photograph which was the only thing of hers he had and which they had refused him. He seized upon this incident savagely; his mind tortured itself with a continual visioning of Susan's face which had smiled down at him from the wall above his table, now lost forever in the evil depths below him, slimed over by the unknown horrors of the abyss. This became for him what the sinking of the *Lusitania* had been for so many others—a concrete instance of a ruthlessness, an abuse of power, a horrid disregard for the sentiments of a humanity which still feels the vital, herd-necessity for loving one another. The cry of his wounded egotism swelled the chorus: It is not to be endured!

So he hated them, the men he held responsible for the blight which had fallen upon his life, his simple dreams. By dint of constant brooding he came in time to connect them in some fantastic way with the loss of his hearing; he blamed them for his affliction. But during all this period the fact that they were men of another nation at war with his own had no influence on his thoughts. He hated them only as strangers who, unprovoked, had done him an irreparable injury; and he hated with the ungovernable force of one whom an overwhelming, hitherto unknown passion surprises in the declining years of life.

He was perilously close to insanity and yet outwardly he appeared the same, a little thinner, paler, more nervous perhaps. Only his eyes revealed the havoc done to his soul. They were windows beyond which stretched great waste places, stark desolation. Even when the German sailors passed near to him, he gave no sign. His eyes grew bleaker, more blank; while his mind rioted in wild schemes of vengeance, each more horrible and extravagantly impossible than the last.

When night came he still sat alone on the hatch, a queer and sinister figure on the silent deck, in the tropic darkness luminous with stars. He waited until he was sure the last member of the *Rio Grande's* crew must be asleep in the quarters assigned to them aft under the poop. He had grown afraid of their eyes. Then he would sneak back past the two German sailors stationed as sentries and crawl noiselessly under his blanket. At the first faint flush of dawn in the sky he would awake and slink out on deck again.

*   *   *

The German commander observed this lone figure, and remembered the Captain's story. He felt a sort of pity for Lathrop. Also the thought of rewarding John for his unwitting services to the Fatherland appealed to his sense of humor and forced an ironic smile from his thin lips. He gave orders that the deaf man, whom he regarded as simple-minded and so, harmless, should be given the freedom of the ship and allowed to wander where he pleased. This apparent liberty of action would be noted by the others, he reflected with satisfaction, and fill them with fury. He laughed and scrawled a note in English which he gave to a sailor to take to John.

John read the note three times before he comprehended its meaning. That sailor standing close to him, within reach of his hands, filled his mind with blood. He felt impelled by an insane craving, like an animal's, to sink his teeth in that sunburned throat, to rend, to tear. But his eyes were expressionless as he looked up. The note had stated that a bunk in the room of the ship's carpenter, forward, was henceforth at his disposal. For the rest, he might go where he chose; he would be unmolested.

The sailor smilingly beckoned him forward. He followed slowly without turning his head. The prisoners watched him go with scorn in their hearts, convinced that he had sold himself neck and crop to the enemy.

He found it much pleasanter on the forward deck where there was no one but the members of the raider's crew. His sense of guilt was left behind in the accusing eyes which he need fear no longer. His tottering brain could concentrate on its mad purpose without being distracted; rather, the nearness of his enemies served to keep it fixed definitively on its one object.

He did not avail himself of the luxury of the bunk in the carpenter's room, much to that Bavarian's relief, but spread his blanket on the Number Two hatch, and slept, when he did sleep, in the open under the stars. His favorite place during the day was on the forecastle head at the very tip end of the bow. There he would lie, flat on his stomach, the muzzle of the four inch gun directly above him, and peer over the side, staring blankly at the swirling foam bubbles. But he never saw the sea or thought of it. His mind was on the forecastle full of men below him. If he could only blow them up, burn them, do something to make them suffer! The idea of suicide never occurred to him. He was dead already. Susan, the *Rio Grande*, the wireless, even the photograph grew dim. The reasons for his hatred were swallowed up in the abysmal depths of the hate itself. He knew he hated—nothing more.

The raider's crew regarded him with joking compassion. They had heard his story. It tickled them into coarse guffaws which John could not hear but which penetrated to his sensitiveness in some sub-conscious manner. He did not mind. It was only a drop more added to the cup of his bitterness, already overflowing. He dreamed of the reckoning.

Late in the afternoon of the fifteenth day the lookout sighted a sail. The raider put on full steam and rapidly drew up to her. She was a three-masted, full-rigged sailing ship flying the American flag. She lay almost becalmed in the light wind which scarcely ruffled the long swells. While still some two miles distant the German flew signals ordering her to come to. Either those on board the American did not see these or they had decided to ignore them. They kept on their course.

The commander swore. He did not care to waste his scanty supply of ammunition, but he had to convince the American he meant business. He gave an order and the gun crew hastened to man the piece on the forecastle head. They loaded it, received the range, adjusted the sighting apparatus, and stood ready to fire when the command was given from the bridge. Then they noticed John in his accustomed position, prone on the deck under the gun muzzle, his head over the side, his eyes fixed on the water. He had heard nothing, he did not lift his eyes, he was unaware of the other ship. The gun crew looked at each other and grinned. Here was a joke appealing to them. "We'll see if he hears this," grunted the gunner's mate in German, and they all laughed.

An order was shouted from the bridge: "Feuer!" There was a stunning crash. The raider trembled with the impact of the recoil. John leaped to his feet as if he had been shot upward by some invisible spring. He was choked with the acrid stench of gunpowder, the walls of his brain seemed shattered and cracking, the world was a roaring, flaming volcano. He stared at the sailors with the wild eyes of a madman. He made a ridiculous figure. They grew weak with laughter. They were laughing at him—they were laughing—*he heard them!* He crumpled up in a heap on deck and lay there in a swoon like death.

The American vessel was loaded with lumber. It was found necessary to dynamite her, and this was done. Only a mass of splintered planks remained floating on the waves. Another crew joined the captives aft. The raider resumed her stealthy prowling. The commander smiled amiably. Another ship the less!

*   *   *

John came to his senses shivering, drenched with the water the jovial sailors had doused on him. He sat up, blinking stupidly. The crew offered him dry clothes which he refused with an angry gesture which only made them laugh the louder. He got up and walked back to the Number Two hatch. He wanted to be alone.

He felt oppressed by a terrible weariness, his bones were water, everything swam before his eyes. The sun dropped behind the horizon's rim with tropic abruptness. Immediately a few stars winked wanly from the dim sky. He lay on his back on the hatch. Sleep weighed on his eyelids like a burden. Bursts of recurrent laughter sounded from the direction of the forecastle. He bit his lips in a sudden flurry of awakened fury. They were laughing at him. He heard them and was scarcely conscious of the act of hearing. Their laughter receded farther and farther off into space, into the mockery of a dream. He closed his eyes. Some words sprang into being in his torpid brain: "a sudden stroke—something cataclysmal." Who had said them? Ah, he remembered—the doctor; but he was too tired to think now. He slept.

He awakened in a darkness soft as velvet. The sky was strewn with stars. Sound flooded his ears with melody, the soft swishing of waves, the monotonous crooning throb of the engines. He lay in an ecstasy, unthinking, staring blindly into infinity—but hearing, hearing! The ship's bell tolled mournfully six times. Eleven o'clock! He sprang to his feet on the deserted deck. An evil hand clutched at his brain. He sensed evil all around him—in the dark ship, in the sleeping sea, in the pitiless eyes of the silent worlds. He burned with hate. He felt vigorous, strong, driven to action by some implacable force. What must he do? Something, but what? He sat down to think.

He did not have long to wait. His mind worked clearly and quickly with the vivid cunning of madness. He felt in his pockets for his big jack-knife. He opened it and crept aft, keeping in the shadow. Cautiously he ascended the stairs to the deck above and slunk along the rail on the port side until he came to the open door of the wireless room. The operator was sitting with his back toward the door, the receivers over his ears, reading a book. Holding his breath John tiptoed into the room. His arm was upraised. For a second his gloating eyes remained fixed on the German's back. Then with all his strength he plunged the long blade into the other's shoulder at the base of the neck. The operator whirled to his feet with a choking, stifled moan, his round eyes wide with horror. John drove the knife into his breast. They fell to the floor together. John clutched the other's throat and struck again and again in an insane frenzy of blood-lust.

The German lay still. John staggered to his feet drunkenly and let the knife fall from his hands. It was finished—no, not finished. There was something else he must do. What was it? Ah, the call.

He sat down and put his finger on the key. His hands were covered with blood, he noticed, but steady, steady as a rock. He sent out the call, a whining plea for help, smothered in the vast silence. The officer on the bridge turned his head carelessly at the sound, then stared out to sea again. It was nothing unusual. There was a shore station secretly maintained by his countrymen on the Brazilian coast with which they used to communicate at night, exchanging warnings and greetings. The raider reported the vessels sunk and gave her approximate position so that she might be warned of any cruisers known to be in the vicinity.

John sent out another call. On a pad he saw written the raider's position at noon and her course since then. A faint ticking came to his ears. At last! As he had hoped, it was a cruiser, an American, the *New Orleans*. He made haste to explain. He was a prisoner who had killed the German operator. He gave their position and the course, northeast, half east, and learned that the *New Orleans* was quite near them. Would she hurry to their rescue? The operator on the warship assured him that she ought to catch them soon after daybreak. He added as a personal compliment to John, "Fine work you did!"

John put the receivers down on the table and sat for a moment regarding them stolidly. The weariness of the tropic night afflicted him. His bobbing head sank lower in a series of jerks until his chin was resting on his chest. Then he fell asleep.

He awoke and yawned, stretching his arms. He saw the stain of the blood dried on his hands. Why? Getting up, he tripped over the body lying on the floor. He looked down at it perplexedly. Again why? A vague memory of something he had done came back to him, but he was glad, glad! He felt faint. There was fresh air out on deck. He stumbled through the doorway and leaned against the rail, looking up into a sky grown pale with the prescience of another dawn. The sea was as troubled grey as the sky. He laughed shrilly but abruptly checked himself. He had never laughed like that before—he was a mild man—and only an operator—he must remember that, but there was something he had done which justified—something. He laughed again, only this time with a ferocious satisfaction. And the German quartermaster at the wheel, grinning over his shoulder, replied to his officer's smiling question: "Only that deaf idiot—talking to the flying fish, I suppose, sir."

∗   ∗   ∗

About four bells the steward, coming to the wireless room with a cup of coffee for the operator, discovered the body of the murdered man. The cup dropped from his hand and with a terrified yell he ran to the bridge. The officer on watch listened to his chattering words, a grim frown settling on his forehead. He then went aft to verify the story. One glance into the room was enough. This was a case which would justify awakening the Commander. He hastened to the cabin to do so.

In the meantime John had left his position at the rail and gone back to the prisoners' quarters under the poop. The sentries on guard glanced at him strangely but allowed him to pass. One clear idea lighted up his whirling brain. He must set matters straight with his friends from the *Rio Grande* who despised him so unjustly. What he had done—that would make them forgive him everything. They ought to feel proud of him now.

His Captain was lying near the door. John shook him gently by the shoulder. "Captain! Captain!" he called softly. The Captain awoke, and seeing those mad eyes glaring down into his, sprang to his feet defensively. "What do you want?" he demanded sternly.

John began to blubber hysterically. "Forgive me, Captain! Forgive me! I couldn't help it—going deaf."

The Captain cursed at him: "You damn cur! Get the hell out of here!"

The insane man gave a maniacal laugh which shattered the dreams of all the sleepers. They sat up on their beds of sacking and looked at him in alarm. In a corner a child whimpered with fright. John started to speak, his words rushing forth in an incoherent jumble. "I must tell you—you must forgive me. I've made up for it, being deaf. I can hear now. They shot off the gun—" He stretched out his blood-stained hands. "Look! I killed him—with my knife—he was sitting with his back to me—I stabbed him—like this—" He made a motion downward with his upraised hand.

"You killed—who did you kill?" The Captain was horror-struck."

"The operator—their operator! He was sitting—but don't you believe me? I tell you this is his blood—here, on my hands. Don't you see? I killed him with my knife, I tell you! I hate them—all of them—I'd like to kill them all. They made me deaf—and they stole—Susan's photograph!"

He stopped, moaning to himself like an animal. At this moment the German commander entered from the main deck accompanied by four armed sailors. As he did so John began to speak again with fierce exultation. "I stabbed him in the throat." The commander made a sign to the sailors to be silent and stood motionless himself, listening. "I stabbed him—and then I sent out a call. You will all be saved. I got a cruiser, an American cruiser, the *New Orleans*— and she was quite near us and I told her where we were. She's coming! She'll be here soon—her operator said soon after daybreak. You'll all be saved, and remember—don't you forget," he added with mad pride, "I saved you! I did it!"

The commander cursed furiously in German and gave an order to his men. They flung themselves on John and, pinning his hands behind his back, handcuffed his wrists. He offered no resistance. He seemed suddenly to grow limp, the wild glare left his eyes, the tense expression of his face changed to one of sluggish indifference. He allowed himself to be led out by the sailors without saying a word. They threw him into the wireless room, from which the corpse had been removed, and locked the door.

The commander followed them. What John had said about sending the call to the *New Orleans* filled his mind with misgiving. If there was truth in that story—. As if to realize his fears his second officer met him with the information that the lookout had sighted smoke to the eastward. The commander took his binoculars and hurriedly climbed to the crow's nest. One look was sufficient for his practised eye. He recognized at a glance the fighting top of a skeleton mast such as is used only by the American navy. He sighed resignedly, and came slowly down the ratlines.

"That's an American warship," he remarked unemotionally to his officer. "Probably the *New Orleans.* She's a fast cruiser, heavily armored. The game is up," he finished with a grim smile.

"But we can still fight, sir," exploded the officer.

The commander shrugged his shoulders. "What use? It would be a waste of time, and of lives which may still be of service to the Fatherland." For a moment he gazed out over the sea at the blotch of smoke on the horizon; then he turned to the officer with an air of briskness. "And now there is nothing to do but to finish with the murderer of Karl. Whether he was a fool or whether he was fooling us, I do not even now know. At least he was brave for he knew he would have to die. Let us see if he will die bravely. Do you form a firing squad and take him out there against the port bulkward." The commander again glanced toward the horizon. "Hurry. There is not much time."

A few minutes later John was led out on the forward section of the main deck. They stood him against the port bulwark, his hands still handcuffed behind him. They did not take the trouble to bind a handkerchief over his eyes. Six sailors with rifles lined up in front of him.

Urged by a sudden curiosity the commander leaned over the rail of the bridge. "You, prisoner," he called, "can you hear what I am saying?"

John looked up at him with an expressionless face. "Yes, I can hear you." he replied dully.

The commander smiled to himself, a smile which had in it something of a grudging admiration. Then he *was* fooling us, he thought; then made a slight movement of his hand, a gesture of dismissal, and turned away carelessly.

The officer with the squad barked out some orders. There was a cracking report. John's knees sagged under him. He pitched forward on the deck, trembled a second, was still. A sailor brought a piece of canvas and the body was rapidly sewn up in this rough shroud with a heavy iron weight at the feet. When this was done the commander again leaned from the bridge. "Take him aft and bury him in the presence of his own people," he said, "They might wish to say a prayer over him."

But none of them did. They crowded around the canvas-wrapped figure, but not one of them had the courage to find a word. Each one remembered the scorn and hate with which he had treated the dead man. A sense of shame filled all their hearts. They felt guilty, responsible for what the man had done, for his madness, his death. They imagined it was their cruel treatment which had goaded him on.

So the exasperated officer read the burial service hurriedly in German. At his word of command the sailors tipped the plank on which the corpse had been laid and the body slid softly into the sea. The Captain of the *Rio Grande* cleared his throat noisily and spat over the side. "Poor devil," he murmured huskily.

*   *   *

The gloom cast over the prisoners by this somber funeral was soon forgotten in the joy of their anticipated deliverance. They had been quick to remark the uneasiness of their captors, whose anxious eyes kept peering seaward to what was now a distinct speck on the horizon. They crowded to the port bulwark to get a better view, communicating the news to each other in half-whispered asides: "It's a cruiser." A thrill of suppressed excitement passed through the throng and there were many quick glances of thinly veiled triumph in the direction of the scowling German sailors.

When still a long distance away the American fired with one of her heavy guns. The shell struck the water a hundred yards in front of the raider's bow, throwing up a geyser of foam. Immediately a string of signal flags were raised to the German's foremast. It was their message of surrender. As the commander had said, the game was up. He could not even sink his ship. There were not half enough boats to remove the people.

The cruiser approaches slowly, gingerly, fearing some trick. As if in evidence of his good faith the German commander had his gig lowered and, seating himself in the stern sheets, ordered his men to pull him to the *New Orleans*. He had not been aboard the American long before several of her boats took the water and were rowed to the raider. Unable to restrain their excitement further, the captives greeted their approach with cheers and shouts, waving their hats frantically. They clambered over the side, tumbling down in their eagerness into the waiting arms of American Jackies. In a short time all of them had been transferred to the deck of the warship. A volunteer crew from the *New Orleans* took charge of the raider, and the two vessels steamed slowly northward toward the North American coast.

The first words which had greeted the captured crews from the raider when they came on board the *New Orleans* had been excited inquiries concerning the wireless man who had sent them the message the night before. In some way every man on the warship seemed familiar with the nature of John's call for help. When they heard of his fate they were wild with rage. They recorded his execution as another fiendish atrocity.

On the voyage north John's deed became the sole topic of conversation among officers and men. As if by some strange conspiracy of silence it appeared tacitly agreed among those who had known him that his abuse of confidence which had led to the loss of the *Rio Grande*, his apparent madness, even his deafness should be forgotten. All the things for which they had hated and scorned him were ignored as if they had never been. There remained only John, their brave deliverer. Even the German commander, speaking to the Captain of the *New Orleans*, felt obliged to confess, "He was a brave man—and a cunning one. We thought he was deaf. He fooled all of us."

The story did not lose by repetition. By the time the ships reached New York, John had become a sort of Overman, super-bold and super-crafty. His deafness had been only a temporary affliction, but he had gone on pretending he was deaf in order to save them—thus they argued who had been on the *Rio Grande*. The others took an even wider view point: He had never been deaf at all, really. The whole adventure was a plot of his own to capture the German! There was nothing of the heroic their unleashed imaginations did not attribute to the man.

In New York the newspapers eagerly pounced upon the story of so romantic a figure as a wireless operator. In their accounts, flung broadcast for all who cared to read, what little remained of the truth became lost in a gush of flamboyant phrases. In a week John Lathrop was hailed as a national hero, the tale of his death a symbol to all men of that patriotism which nobly accepts the ultimate sacrifice.

After the sale of the house in Acropolis, Susan had come to New York about the time the *Rio Grande* was due to reach port. At the steamship office they had informed her of the ship's destruction by the German raider. Although they had assured her of the probable safety of all on board, she had lived in a constant state of terrified apprehension. She had remained in her room in the little hotel in Brooklyn, never going out except for a daily trip to the wharf for news. Finally they had told her of the capture of the German. All of the *Rio Grande's* people were safe, they had said, for the first wireless reports contained no mention of John's death. So she had returned to her small room to await his homecoming, dreaming eagerly of the marvelous adventures he must have been through. The manager of the East Coast Company had promised to let her know the moment he had definite information of the time the cruiser would arrive.

When he learned of John's death the manager had not the heart to tell her. So it was the Captain of the *Rio Grande* who called on her the day after he landed, and in his rough, kindly fashion broke the news. Susan was petrified by the shock. At first she would not understand, could not believe; then the whole light of the world seemed to blot out before her eyes. She sank into a very coma of despair. The old Captain stood appalled before her white-lipped torment, her dry-eyed anguish too agonizing for tears. He stayed with her an hour, repeating over and over again in a futile sort of way his exaggerated description of John's heroism. In spite of her misery Susan listened to him unconsciously. In the end, in desperation, the old man had pointed out to her the big head-lined romances in the papers he had brought with him. Then he took his leave, perspiring with embarrassment, cursing furiously as he stumbled down the three flights of stairs.

When he had gone Susan summoned up courage to look at the nearest paper. There was John's name in big letters—and she read the wonderful things they said about him. The paper slipped from her hands. Tears came in an overwhelming flood. The crisis was past; her despair was gone; she had something to cling to. Sorrow, indeed, was left, deep and abiding; but it was a sorrow which took pride in itself and gave her a reason, a reason for life.

The next day an enterprising reporter, having pried her whereabouts out of the Steamship Company, came for an interview. Susan was too frightened by this new experience even to answer his question coherently; but he was not without imagination and the following morning his paper contained a sentimental word picture of a newspaper widow fit to stand beside the newspaper John Lathrop. The result of this notoriety was immediate. Susan was besieged by reporters, each on the trail of some new detail on which to base a story. And, to her great bewilderment, a few days later she received an official notice from Washington announcing that she had been granted a pension for life.

She felt crushed by this attention and resolved to escape back to Acropolis where there was quiet, and familiar faces, and old friends to whom she could confide her pride and her sorrow. She packed up her few things hurriedly and took the train. On the way she debated with herself where she should make her home. The old house was sold. She could not live with friends forever. She must decide on some place. Suddenly she thought of Mrs. Perkins! John had stayed there for twenty years; it would be like being in his home to live there. Mrs. Perkins had been kind to him, had liked him, she knew that; and she thought of the many long talks they would have about him. With a thrill of pride she realized that Mrs. Perkins, yes, the whole town, would welcome her with open arms and would respect and look up to her now that she was John Lathrop's widow.

She leaned back in her seat in the day coach and closed her eyes; and a vision of all the peaceful years before her, haloed by a serene and gentle sorrow, arose in her dreaming thoughts. Growing ever farther away from the present she would live in her tranquil world of memories, and watch in a spirit of detached kindliness the lives, the deaths, the marriages of those around her; and deep in her heart of hearts, she would feel she had been blessed beyond all of them—for she knew that none could ever marry another like John; that no other man would ever live so glorious a life, or die a death as noble.

Poetry

To a Stolen Moment

O'Neill met Jane Caldwell shortly after he settled in Tao House, his Danville, California home. She was the daughter of Myrtle Caldwell, an old friend of Carlotta O'Neill's. The two older women renewed a friendship of long standing and Jane with her mother became frequent visitors to Tao House. In 1944, after Tao House was sold and the O'Neills had moved to San Francisco, Carlotta, too ill to type her husband's work, suggested that Jane be hired for the task. The result was that the young woman became an almost daily visitor to the O'Neill apartment.

Jane, who was about the age of O'Neill's daughter Oona, was a quiet, pretty girl, refreshingly free from adolescent pretensions. In the course of their acquaintance, O'Neill had given her presents—autographed books, a jade mirror—and had clearly taken pleasure in her youthful company. As his health deteriorated and as his disappointment and embarrassment at Oona's marriage came to rankle, he appears to have turned to Jane in search of some leavening in his life. According to Louis Sheaffer,[1] the two used to dance to phonograph records and engage in small, intimate joking encounters. Their relationship developed a flirtatious edge that alienated Carlotta and caused outbursts of temperamental jealousy.

For Jane, the relationship was flattering; for O'Neill, a sick man contemplating the youth he could never again touch, it was nostalgic and bittersweet. Theirs was never a full-blown romance, and it was short-lived. The O'Neills left San Francisco in October 1944 and did not see Jane Caldwell again. The tangible evidence of what lay between O'Neill and the girl is a poem he wrote to her after a walk along the Pacific Ocean on the San Francisco beach as Carlotta waited in the car on the highway. It recalls two earlier poems, "Upon Our Beach," which he wrote in 1917 to his New London beloved, Beatrice Ashe, and "To Alice," written to a young woman in Bermuda, about 1925.[2]

1. Louis Sheaffer, *Eugene O'Neill, Son and Artist* (Boston: Little Brown, 1973), p. 555.
2. The poems are published in Eugene O'Neill, *Poems, 1912–1944*, ed. Donald Gallup (New Haven: Ticknor and Fields, 1980).

To a Stolen Moment

We walked down the steps to the beach.

(Sands unlovely, mixed with the remains of joyless picnic lunches, long ago or yesterday, in shallow graves uncovered by the sea wind; beach littered with sprawled grotesque specimens of our semi-human race, like dead crabs spewed from the sea by a fastidious tide)

We walked to the sea's edge,
You and I,
Driven in hopeless pilgrimage
To beseech the sea
For a moment's dream
Of life's forgotten mystery.

Then suddenly
As if in answer to this prayer
Realism vanished
There was no one there.
The windswept sand
Was clean and bare
There was nothing there
Not even memory
Nor despair
Nothing but sea and sky
And the wind and sun
And I
And you
So beautiful there
With the sea and sky in your eyes,
And the sun and wind in your hair.

There was you and magic there
And years and sickness and fears
Were spray tossed in the foam
And thrown seaward any where.
I with you

The magic of love was there
For me
And you
Standing there.

Blue coat, buttoned up to your chin,
So beautiful there,
With the sea and sky in your eyes,
And the sun and wind in your hair.

Gene
June 29, 1945

Criticism

Foreword to *Anathema! Litanies of Negation* by Benjamin De Casseres

In April 1928, while O'Neill was living in Guethary in France, Benjamin de Casseres sent him a copy of his as yet unpublished book, *Anathema*, asking O'Neill to write an introduction. O'Neill had been friendly with De Casseres and his wife for several years, and the book appealed to him. Therefore, despite the problems of the moment, which included an embittering divorce negotiation with Agnes O'Neill and a creative struggle to complete *Dynamo*, O'Neill broke a long-standing custom and agreed to lend his name to another man's work. He told De Casseres that he was "an awful bum at such writing" and added that when he had tried it in the past, "the mountain groaned and volcanoed and . . . produced a very cretinish, semi-still-born, albino mouse!"[1] In the same letter, he refused to allow De Casseres to dedicate the work to him.

O'Neill's attraction to De Casseres and to his wife, Bio, was an odd commitment. De Casseres praised O'Neill extravagantly in print and sent him copies of his works. O'Neill was apparently not put off by the man who called himself "The Beethoven of Negation" and found something to admire in the rhapsodic aphorisms written in a messianic, pseudo-Nietzschean style:

> I reverse all axioms. Out of nothing comes something, as a god is born of the air, out of something comes nothing, as all things return to me,[2]

In a prose that was compounded not only of Nietzsche but of Baudelaire ("My dreams are black flowers that hang from the pale-green stems of my passion"), De Casseres indulged in the iconoclastic philosophizing that seemed daring and sometimes shocking to some in the 1920s.

The appeal of *Anathema* to the playwright may have had another source, however, for by the time he wrote the book, De Casseres had read *Lazarus Laughed*, O'Neill's own venture into the world of Nietzschean rhapsody. Some of the interest for O'Neill may have lain in the echoes De Casseres sounded of the rhetoric of the religious play.[3] At least for a time, O'Neill found De Casseres a kindred spirit, although, as the 1920s

---

1. Eugene O'Neill to Benjamin De Casseres, April 29, 1921. The correspondence is in the Dartmouth College Library, Hanover, N.H. A few years earlier, O'Neill had attempted to write an introduction to Hart Crane's *White Buildings* but was unable to finish it.
2. Benjamin De Casseres, *Anathema! Litanies of Negation* (New York: Gotham Book Mart, 1928).
3. Note O'Neill's phrase about De Casseres intoning "a chorus, part Dionysian, part biblical, and the rest elegiac."

ended, the relationship weakened and ended abruptly when De Casseres parodied *Days Without End* under the title "Drivel Without End."[4] The preface to *Anathema* is perhaps of greater interest as the testimony to a passing friendship than as a work of acute literary perception.

4. Sheaffer, *O'Neill, Son and Artist*, p. 433.

Foreword to Anathema! Litanies of Negation

For too many years Benjamin DeCasseres has spilled his glittering fancies on a deaf American ear. He has had the fabulous adventures of a philosopher who could not abandon nor deny his poetic gift. He could not turn professional and expound a system in the thick verbiage which might awe his colleagues. Nor could he descend to the level of a daily message in juicy platitudes for the tabloid mind. In such a plight, he has had little welcome in the academy and none in the crowd. All his soaring has been lonely.

To be a true philosopher in America is almost to invite oblivion. It is only fake philosophers who thrive here. Their formula is thoroughly standardized, and only requires a persistent, brainless application. One need only have a message plain or vague enough to mean nothing and announce it with a solemn countenance and an oracular bray.

DeCasseres has always been on the loose, chasing the tail of the ultimate word. It does not matter particularly to him whether he belongs as philosopher or poet or mystic. His is a capricious mind and a vagrant one. He can be goatish or severe, ricocheting or pyrotechnical. He insists in and out of season upon recording the ascending line on the graph of his soul.

An inebriate of sonorities, he chants disillusion and raises his panegyrics to the sky. He is swift, orgiastic and inexhaustible. He cries out his negations with a huge and resonant YES! He is that phenomenal ironist who does not want to be gentle, who must be supremely contemptuous and fiercely assertive.

There is nothing native about DeCasseres in the sense that he picks up the philosophical mantle where it was dropped by his immediate predecessors. The whole Concord School and the pragmatists could have spared themselves a single furrow on the brow so far as any influence on him is concerned. Nor have any of the laborious inductive thinkers left a scar upon his mind. Hair-splitting has never been in his line. He never troubles with the question of the essential validity of ideas as such. Nor does he argue the fine points of thinking as a theory. Neither classification of causes nor explanations of them on the basis of accumulated data gleaned from the observation of the workings of so-called natural laws appear anywhere in his writings. By such definitions he is no philosopher at all.

His sources must be sought elsewhere. The scientists and metaphysicians would be quick to disown him. The mystics and poets might claim him as one of their own, but would look suspiciously upon his passion for doubt and his relentless questioning. Among them he would be a heretic too. If such genealogy counts for anything, he can be traced, among the philosophers, to Schopenhauer and Nietzsche, a hybrid product mixing despair and rhapsody.

Among the poets, he stems from the ecstatic writers of the Psalms, and infiltrates his blood with the rough-house of the tavern. He can stand with one foot on a brass rail, raise his glass high in the air and intone a chorus, part Dionysian, part biblical, and the rest elegiac.

DeCasseres has undertaken the herculean job of carving his own niche as a writer in America. It is hardly likely that he will ever achieve wide public acceptance. Nor docs it appear that he will be made the object of careful critical scrutiny by some small group of pedants who might get a thesis out of him as an American phenomenon. He is too abstract for the one and too extravagant for the other. Ignored by both, his work gets only occasional publication. In truth, he is crushed between the upper and nether millstones. He is looked upon, when he is discussed at all, as a freak who is exploding with metaphors and a dazzling, colossal vocabulary. To the general reading public he is practically unknown. The schools have probably never heard his name, and would give it very scant consideration if it were forced upon them.

With whom or with what system, then, can his name be linked? What studies has he made of space and time and transcendental reasoning? To what established category can he be assigned and by what respected right has he come to the title of philosopher? None whatsoever. By any such reckoning, he is an outsider. He will have to get along under the designation of an unphilosophical philosopher.

When DeCasseres is mentioned in the prevailing literary chat, it is usually as the chronicler of an almost forgotten, bibulous New York. He is thought of as a post-mortem bard of the pre-Volsteadian era. In the minds of those who have only read his odes to Gambrinus, he stands for a quaint old bibber who is now reminiscing regretfully on the good old days.

Anathema! should dispel such fantastically idiotic notions. The essence of DeCasseres' driving imagination is to be found in these Litanies of Negation. To me *Anathema!* is a unique and inspiring poem. It plagues and provokes the mind. Its vigorous figures and its exalted invective give it immense power. Racing upward, it heaps crescendo upon crescendo. It is chaotic, extravagant, brilliant, derisive with a Satanic grin and drenched with rich imagery.

Anathema! is far more than a hymn of renunciation. It is the torment and ecstasy of a mystic's questioning of life. The answer comes up alternately as *yes* and *no*. And because the emphasis has been placed on the *no*, DeCasseres has convinced himself that he has said the final negative. It is not so. He is the "scorner of Gods and humans" and promises "salvation in a sneer." He carouses in his "inextinguishable laughter" and goes dizzy-sick on a "vintage headier than Hope." Trying to shout down the clamor in his brain with a crashing NO, his ecstasy overpowers him and sings in its own affirmation. Benjamin De-Casseres is the poet who affirms the chaos in the soul of a man. His *no* is a *yes*!!

Strindberg and Our Theatre

"Strindberg and Our Theatre" was O'Neill's program note for the opening production at the Experimental Theatre, which he, Robert Edmond Jones, the designer, and Kenneth Macgowan, the critic, had formed on the foundations of the former Provincetown Players in 1924. At O'Neill's urging, the new theatre, dedicated to productions that were to represent the highest and the newest theatrical artistry, opened with Strindberg's *The Spook Sonata*.[1]

The short essay is perhaps O'Neill's most personal critical statement, except for the comments he made on various occasions about his plays for the daily newspapers. It manifests in its fumbling with the definitions of *realism* and *naturalism* a certain classroom orthodoxy, garnered from his association with Macgowan, who adhered to conventional academic concerns in his criticism. Yet the sense conveyed here of Strindberg's importance, of what his plays meant and of the means by which they achieved their intention, was not a ready perception in the 1920s. In the essay O'Neill is speaking from his own knowledge, based not only on his reading but on his imitation of Strindberg—a process that was to continue the length of his writing career, from *Before Breakfast* to *Long Day's Journey into Night*.

O'Neill owed Strindberg more than a passing obligation. The Swedish dramatist and Nietzsche were the two major influences on O'Neill's life and work. His personal debt to Strindberg he acknowledged more forcefully in his letter to the Swedish Academy when he won the Nobel prize.[2] The program note and the Experimental Theatre production formed an early partial repayment.

1. For details, see Helen Deutsch and Stella Hanau, *The Provincetown, A Story of the Theatre* (New York: Farrar and Rinehart, 1931), and *"The Theatre We Worked For," The Letters of Eugene O'Neill and Kenneth Macgowan*, ed. Jackson Bryer.
2. See below, "The Nobel Prize Acceptance Letter."

Strindberg and Our Theatre

In creating a modern theatre which we hope will liberate for significant expression a fresh elation and joy in experimental production, it is the most apt symbol of our good intentions that we start with a play by August Strindberg; for Strindberg was the precursor of all modernity in our present theatre, just as Ibsen, a lesser man as he himself surmised, was the father of the modernity of twenty years or so ago when it was believed that A *Doll's House* wasn't—just that.

Strindberg will remain among the most modern of moderns, the greatest interpreter in the theatre of the characteristic spiritual conflicts which constitute the drama—the blood—of our lives today. He carried Naturalism to a logical attainment of such poignant intensity that, if the work of any other playwright is to be called "naturalism," we must classify a play like *The Dance of Death* as "super-naturalism," and place it in a class by itself, exclusively Strindberg's since no one before or after him has had the genius to qualify.

Yet it is only by means of some form of "super-naturalism" that we may express in the theatre what we comprehend intuitively of that self-defeating, self-obsession which is the discount we moderns have to pay for the loan of life. The old "naturalism"—or "realism" if you prefer (would to God some genius were gigantic enough to define clearly the separateness of these terms once and for all!) no longer applies. It represents our Fathers' daring aspirations toward self-recognition by holding the family kodak up to ill-nature. But to us their old audacity is blague; we have taken too many snap-shots of each other in every graceless position; we have endured too much from the banality of surfaces. We are ashamed of having peeked through so many keyholes, squinting always at heavy, uninspired bodies—the fat facts—with not a nude spirit among them; we have been sick with appearances and are convalescing; we "wipe out and pass on" to some as yet unrealized region where our souls, maddened by loneliness and the ignoble inarticulateness of flesh, are slowly evolving their new language of kinship.

Strindberg knew and suffered with our struggle years before many of us were born. He expressed it by intensifying the method of his time and by foreshadowing both in content and form the methods to come. All this is enduring in what we loosely call "Expressionism"—all that is artistically valid and sound theatre—can be clearly traced back through Wedekind to Strindberg's *The Dream Play, There Are Crimes and Crimes, The Spook Sonata*, etc.

Hence, *The Spook Sonata* at our Playhouse. One of the most difficult of Strindberg's "behind-life" (if I may coin the term) plays to interpret with insight and distinction—but the difficult is properly our special task, or we have no good reason for existing. Truth, in the theatre as in life, is eternally difficult, just as the easy is the everlasting lie.

So pray with us—and (although we don't need it, of course, but it may do some good) for us.

Are the Actors to Blame?

The essay served as a program note to *Adam Solitaire*, a three-act play by Em Jo Basshe, produced at the Provincetown Playhouse in its third organization under the direction of James Light and Elinor Fitzgerald, two of the most stalwart "Provincetowners." O'Neill, Kenneth Macgowan, and Robert Edmond Jones had left the Playhouse, confining their productions to the Greenwich Village Theatre. O'Neill, however, as a testament of loyalty to the theatre that gave him his start, remained on the board of the Provincetown directors.

Elinor Fitzgerald requested that he write a program note for their opening production. He replied that such an effort was beyond him because at the present he had fallen out of love with the theatre and had no idea when his antitheatrical melancholia would leave him. In the second paragraph, as he began to explain why this was so, he wrote the opening lines of the short essay: "I believe there is no possibility of real progress in the creative interpretation of plays . . ." and continued to tell her of the need for actors who have been trained in repertory, a constantly sought-for-panacea for the theatre in the first part of the century. The letter, with the opening and closing paragraphs deleted, was printed in the program, dated November 6, 1925. Whether O'Neill or Miss Fitzgerald made the final revisions is not known.

Are the Actors to Blame?

I believe that there is no possibility of real progress in the creative interpretation of plays of arresting imagination and insight until we develop a new quality of depth of feeling and comprehensive scope of technique in actors and actresses. For only when a play is self-expressed through sensitive, truthful, trickless acting is "the play the thing."

In the acting lies the acted play. Great acting has frequently made bad plays seem good, but a good play cannot penetrate bad acting without emerging distorted—an uneven, bumpy, ugly duckling of an offspring at whom any play-wright father must gaze with a shudder. And this in spite of the finest and most intelligent and inspiring direction. Directors can only direct. They cannot give the actors the right developing experience unless they can plan over a long period of years with the same people. This plainly isn't possible under any present system. For actors are conceived by and born of the parts they have been permitted to play.

Are the actors to blame for the present conditions in *all* theatres which urge them toward the easy goals of type casting, rather than the long, painstaking self-training in the acquiring of an art? Well, if actors are partly to blame, then we others of the theatre, including the audience who accept them are equally at fault. Do we give them parts other than the apparent one God cast them in as persons? Do we take a chance on them? Not often. We cannot afford to in an era when the theatre is primarily a realtor's medium for expression. One mistake and then comes the landlord with notice of eviction. He is usually not an artist in the theatre, this landlord! He could see Shakespeare boiled alive in Socony gasoline and have qualms only as to our diminishing national Standard Oil reserves. The answer? Repertoire. Genuine repertoire. We all know it—it's as simple as truth—and perhaps that is why we make no attempt to live and work accordingly.

What is the Provincetown going to do about acting? Does it plan to lay emphasis on building up a medium for achievement in acting that will make young actors want to grow up with it as part of a whole, giving their acting a new clear fakeless group excellence and group eloquence that will be our unique acting, our own thing, born in our American theatre as not so long ago Irish acting was born in the Irish Players, modern Russian acting in the Moscow Art Theatre, or modern German acting in the Reinhardt group? All these had humble beginnings as we have had. If we do intend to work with the future of our acting at least equally in view with the artistic production of good plays and great plays, then I am high with hope.

The immediate future of the theatre is in the actor. Until he gets his real opportunity we others—I speak as a playwright—this applies equally to all artists in the theatre—but wait for ours, or try to be contented with what we know must be an unrealizable dream.

Working Notes and Extracts from a
Fragmentary Work Diary

Throughout most of his mature creative life, O'Neill kept a diary in which he monitored the progress of his creative work. The diaries are brief, but meticulous. They scrupulously enter a profile of his life, measuring the progress of the work in hand, recording ideas for new plays, charting his health, and at the end of each month summing up the number of CWD's (Creative Working Days) he had put in.[1] Like his minuscule handwriting, they reflect the intensity of the concentration on his work—the inner turn away from the world that he was forced to make in order to create his plays. One senses that when he returned to the outer world of mundane affairs, the diaries' log helped him to chart where he had been in the sealed-off journeys through his imagination.

The diaries concerning *Mourning Becomes Electra* record more fully than most others the extraordinary labor involved in the composition of his major works. The entries do not constitute a piece of formal criticism, but they do show O'Neill in the painful act of self-criticism as he wrote and rewrote the fourteen acts of the trilogy. They provide one of the best testaments of the devotion O'Neill held for his art.

With few exceptions, O'Neill's later plays were written under creative pressure similar to that reflected in the "Electra" diary. Often the pressure did not stop with the play's production. *Dynamo*, for example, underwent major rewriting for publication, and the galleys of *Strange Interlude* had to be reset, so extensive was his rewriting. O'Neill's capacity for creative labor was inexhaustible. Such phrases as "Rewrite trilogy along these lines" are almost throwaway lines. The objective was perfection; his creed as an artist, if the phrase is not too pretentious, permitted nothing less.

In 1926, when he recorded the idea of modernizing an ancient Greek drama in the light of contemporary psychological theory, he had already written *Desire Under the Elms*, in which the legends of Oedipus and Phaedra were intermingled in a tragedy of New England farm life. He had experimented with masks and choruses in *The Hairy Ape*, *The Ancient Mariner*, *The Great God Brown*, and *Lazarus Laughed*. At least since his early association with George Cram Cook, the first director of the Provincetown Players, he had been acquainted with the art of Greek literature. Throughout the United States in the twentieth century Greek drama was being presented in new translations, and in Europe modern adaptations of Greek materials had been made. The work of Freud and Nietzsche made Greek terminology for modern psychological and philosophical concerns commonplace. Thus to write a "modern psychological drama using one

1. Eugene O'Neill, *Work Diary, 1924–1943*, 2 vols., ed. Donald Gallup (New Haven: Yale University Library, 1981).

of the old legend plots of Greek tragedy" was almost an inevitable step for O'Neill to take.

The notes trace the arduous process from the first scenario through the "scrawny" first draft to the final paring away of all theatrical excesses such as masks and thought-asides in the manner of *Strange Interlude*. This final step was an important one, for O'Neill's devotion to unusual stagecraft had up to this time been a hallmark of his style. The writing of *Mourning Becomes Electra*, however, was in a measure purgative. Setting art theatre doctrine behind him, he began to write in the realistic manner of his last, greatest plays. This was the style that had been native to him from his first one-act sea plays; it was perhaps this instinctive commitment to the realistic depiction of men in action that gave human truth to the more experimental plays.[2]

The return to a less mannered style, to one that would permit him no alternative but to penetrate the full humanity of his subjects, brought with it far-reaching and unexpected consequences. The trilogic form of the work gave him opportunity for such exploration. The popular success of *Strange Interlude* with its nine acts and of *Mourning Becomes Electra* assured him that he was following a profitable direction. Thus, the idea of a multiplay unit, in which each play complete in itself also formed part of a larger whole, became of the deepest interest. The concept had been an element in the planning of *Dynamo*, which he had thought of as the first of a three-play cycle to be called "Myths for the God-forsaken." The second play became *Days Without End* and required five drafts before it came into its final form in 1933. The third play, called in draft "The Life of Bessie Bowen," did not evolve satisfactorily, and after the failure of *Dynamo* and the struggle to complete *Days Without End*, he gave up the idea of the second trilogy. The idea, however, did not die. "The Life of Bessie Bowen" turned unexpectedly into a grandiose new project—a cycle of eleven plays tracing the lives of the members of two families from pre-Revolutionary War days to the 1930s. Compared to the work he dedicated to the long cycle, the writing of *Mourning Becomes Electra* was a five-finger exercise. Nevertheless, the diary anticipates the obsessive effort he found necessary to so massive a task. To write with such concentrated effort became in essence his entire life. The pattern of labor described in the diary continued so long as his strength lasted.

The working notes were first published in the *New York Herald Tribune* on November 3, 1931, at the time of the trilogy's opening. They were reprinted the same year in a special edition of the play by Horace Liveright.

---

2. *Days Without End* (1933) succumbed to the experimental stagecraft dear to art theatre enthusiasts by requiring the central character to be played by two actors. This, however, was the last bow he made in a completed work in the direction of self-conscious theatrical artistry.

Working Notes and Extracts from a Fragmentary Work Diary

(Spring—1926)
Modern psychological drama using one of the old legend plots of Greek tragedy for its basic theme—the Electra story?—the Medea? Is it possible to get modern psychological approximation of the Greek sense of fate into such a play, which an intelligent audience of today, possessed of no belief in gods or supernatural retribution, could accept and be moved by?—

(October, 1928—Arabian Sea en route for China)
Greek tragedy plot idea—story of Electra and family psychologically most interesting—most comprehensive—intense basic human interrelationships—can be easily widened in scope to include still others.

(November, 1928—China Sea)
Greek plot idea—Give modern Electra figure in play a tragic ending worthy of character. In Greek story she peters out into an undramatic married banality. Such a character contained too much tragic fate within her soul to permit this— why should Furies have let Electra escape unpunished? Why did the chain of fated crime and retribution ignore her mother's murderess?—a weakness in what remains to us of Greek tragedy that there is no play about Electra's life after the murder of Clytemnestra. Surely it possesses as imaginative tragic possibilities as any of their plots!

(Cap d'Ail, France—April, 1929)
Greek tragedy plot idea.—no matter in what period of American history play is laid, must remain a modern psychological drama—nothing to do with period except to use it as mask—What war?—Revolution too far off and too clogged in people's minds with romantic grammar-school-history associations. World War too near and recognizable in its obstructing (for my purpose) minor aspects and superficial character identifications (audience would not see fated wood because too busy recalling trees)—needs distance and perspective—period not too distant for audience to associate itself with, yet possessing costume, etc.— possessing sufficient mask of time and space, so that audiences will unconsciously grasp at once, it is primarily drama of hidden life forces—fate—behind the lives of characters. Civil War is only possibility—fits into picture—Civil War as background for drama of murderous family love and hate!—

(Cap d'Ail, France—April, 1929)
(Greek plot idea)—lay in New England small seaport, shipbuilding town—town's best family—shipbuilders and owners—wealthy for period—Agamemnon character town's leading citizen, mayor before war, Now Brigadier General Grant's Army—opening act of play day of Lee's surrender—house Greek temple front type that was rage in 1st half 19th century—(this fits in well and absolutely justifiable, not forced Greek similarity)—This home of New England House of Atreus was built in 1830, say, by Atreus character, Agamemnon's father—grotesque perversion of everything Greek temple expressed of meaning of life—(New England background best possible dramatically for Greek plot of crime and retribution, chain of fate—Puritan conviction of man born to sin and punishment—Orestes' furies within him, his conscience, etc.)

Departures from Greek story—Electra loves Aegisthus—always fated to be mother's rival in love, always defeated, first for father's love, then for brother's, finally for Aegisthus'—reason for Clytemnestra's hatred for Agamemnon sexual frustration by his Puritan sense of guilt turning love to lust (she had romantic love for him before marriage)—omit Iphigenia and Chrysothemis from children—only Orestes and Electra—no Cassandra—keep exact family relationship of Aegisthus (first cousin Agamemnon)—keep general outline of rivalry, hatred, love, lust, revenge in past between Agamemnon's father, Atreus, and Aegisthus' father, Thyestes (in legend Thyestes seduces Aerope, wife of Atreus)—hatred of Atreus for brother—revenge—banishment—(keep general spirit of this but pay no attention to details of legend) Clytemnestra persuades Aegisthus against his will to help her murder Agamemnon (my Aegisthus character weaker, more human and less evil character, has conscience of sort)—method of murder, poison (woman's weapon)—Aegisthus bears strong facial resemblance to Agamemnon and Orestes—his resemblance to Orestes attracts Clytemnestra—his resemblance to her father attracts Electra—Electra adores father, devoted to brother (who resembles father), hates mother—Orestes adores mother, devoted to sister (whose face resembles mother's) hates his father—Agamemnon, frustrated in love for Clytemnestra, adores daughter, Electra, who resembles her, hates and is jealous of his son, Orestes—etc.—work out this symbol of family resemblances and identification (as visible sign of the family fate) still further—use masks (?)

(Cap d'Ail, France—May, 1929)
(Greek plot idea)—Names of characters—use characteristic names with some similarity to Greek ones—for main characters, at least—but don't strain after this and make it a stunt—no real importance, only convenience in picking—right names always a tough job.

Agamemnon—(Asa), (Ezra) Mannon
Clytemnestra—Christine (?)
Orestes—Orin
{ Electra—Eleanor (?) Ellen (?) Elsa (?)
  Laodicea—Lavinia (this sounds more like it) Vinnie
  (Called in family)
Aegisthus—Augustus (?), Alan (?) Adam (?)
Pylades—Paul (?) Peter (?)
Hermione—Hazel—Hesther

(Cap d'Ail, France—May, 1929)
(Greek plot idea)—Title—"Mourning Becomes Electra"—that is, in old sense of the word—it befits—it becomes Electra to mourn—it is her fate,—also, in usual sense (made ironical here), mourning (black) is becoming to her—it is the only color that becomes her destiny—

(Cap d'Ail, France—May, 1929)
"Mourning Becomes Electra"—No chance getting full value material into one play or even two—must follow Greek practice and make it trilogy—first play Agamemnon's homecoming and murder—second, Electra's revenge on mother and lover, using Orestes to help her do this—third play, retribution Orestes and Electra. Give each play a separate title—"Mourning Becomes Electra" title for trilogy as whole—first play, "Home-coming"—second,   (?)—third, "The Haunted."

(Cap d'Ail, France—May, 1929)
"Mourning Becomes Electra"—Technique—for first draft use comparatively straight realism—this first draft only for purpose of getting plot material into definite form—then lay aside for period and later decide how to go on to final version—what departures necessary—whether to use masks, soliloquies, asides, etc.—

(Le Plessis, St. Antoine-du-Rocher, France—June 20, 1929)
"Mourning Becomes Electra"—Finished scenario first play, "Homecoming."

(Le Plessis, St. Antoine-du-Rocher, France—July 11, 1929)
"Mourning Becomes Electra"—Finished scenario second play, "The Hunted"—what an advantage it was (from plotter's standpoint, at least) for authors in other times who wrote about kings—could commit murder without having to dodge detection, arrest, trial scenes for their characters—I have to waste a lot of ingenuity to enable my plotters to get away with it without suspicion!—still, even history of comparatively recent crimes (where they happen

among people supposedly respectable) shows that rural authorities easily hood-winked—the poisoning of Mannon in "Homecoming" would probably never be suspected (under the same circumstances) even in New England town of today, let alone in 1865.

(*Le Plessis, St. Antoine-du-Rocher, France—August, 1929*)
"Mourning Becomes Electra"—Finished scenario third play, "The Haunted"—have given my Yankee Electra tragic end worthy of her—and Orestes, too.

(*Le Plessis, St. Antoine-du-Rocher, France—Sept. 29, 1929*)
Started writing 1st draft—"Mourning Becomes Electra."

(*Le Plessis, St. Antoine-du-Rocher, France—Oct., 1929*)
After several false starts, all rotten, think I have hit right line for first draft now.

(*Le Plessis, St. Antoine-du-Rocher, France—Feb. 21, 1930*)
Finished 1st draft "M.B.E."—lay aside now for at least a month—

(*Le Plessis, St. Antoine-du-Rocher, France—March 27, 1930*)
Read over first draft "M.B.E."—scrawny stuff but serves purpose as first draft—parts damned thrilling but lots more lousy—not enough meat—don't like Aegisthus character—hackneyed and thin—must find new one—not enough of sense of fate hovering over characters, fate of family—living in the house built by Atreus' hatred (Abe Mannon)—a psychological fate—reading this first draft I get feeling that more of my idea was left out of play than there is in it!—In next version I must correct this at all costs—run the risk of going to other cluttered up extreme—use every means to gain added depth and scope—can always cut what is unnecessary afterwards—will write second draft using half masks and an "Interlude" technique (combination "Lazarus" and "Interlude") and see what can be gotten out of that—think these will aid me to get just the right effect—must get more distance and perspective—more sense of fate—more sense of the unreal behind what we call reality which is the real reality!—The unrealistic truth wearing the mask of lying reality, that is the right feeling for this trilogy, if I can only catch it! Stick to modern tempo of dialogue without attempt at pretense of Civil War-time lingo. That part of 1st draft is right. Obtain more fixed formal structure for first play which succeeding plays will reiterate—pattern of exterior and interior scenes, beginning and ending with exterior in each play—with the one ship scene at the center of the second play (this, center of whole work) emphasizing sea background of family and symbolic motive of sea as means of escape and release—use townsfolk at beginning of each play, outside the house, as fixed chorus pattern—representing prying, commenting, curious town as an ever-present background for the drama of the

Mannon family. Develop South Sea Island motive—its appeal for them all (in various aspects)—release, peace, security, beauty, freedom of conscience, sinlessness, etc.—longing for the primitive—and mother symbol—yearning for prenatal non-competitive freedom from fear—make this Island theme recurrent motive—Characterization—Exclude as far as possible and consistent with living people, the easy superficial characterization of individual mannerisms—unless these mannerisms are inevitable fingerprints of inner nature—essential revelations. This applies to main people of trilogy. Townsfolk, on the other hand, should be confined to exterior characterization—main characters too interior—Peter and Hazel should be almost characterless, judged from either of these angles—they are the untroubled, contented "good," a sweet, constant unselfconscious, untempted virtue amid which evil passion works, unrecognized by them—until end—but emphasized by their contrast. Resemblance of characters by use of masks intensify Mannon family resemblance between Ezra and Orin and Adam (and family portraits), and between Christine and Lavinia—peculiar gold-brown hair exactly alike in Lavinia and her mother—same as hair of the dead woman, Adam's mother, whom Ezra's father and uncle had loved—who started the chain of recurrent love and hatred and revenge—emphasize this motivating fate out of past—hair of women another recurrent motive—strange, hidden psychic identity of Christine with the dead woman and of Lavinia (in spite of her father—Mannon imitative mannerisms) with her mother—and of Adam with the Mannons he hates, as well as of Orin with his father—The chanty "Shenandoah"—use this more—as a sort of theme song—its simple sad rhythm of hopeless sea longing peculiarly significant—even the stupid words have striking meaning when considered in relation to tragic events in play—In my scrawny first draft bare melodrama of plot runs away with my intent—this must be corrected in second draft—the unavoidable entire melodramatic action must be felt as working out of psychic fate from past—thereby attain tragic significance—or else!—a hell of a problem, a modern tragic interpretation of classic fate without benefit of gods—for it must, before everything, remain modern psychological play—fate springing out of the family—

(*Le Plessis*—*March* 31, 1930)
Start writing 2nd draft.

(*Le Plessis*—*July* 11, 1930)
Finish 2nd draft—feel drained out—have been working morning, afternoon and night everyday, without a single let-up—never worked so intensively over such a long period as I have on this damn trilogy—wish now I'd never attempted the damn thing—bitten off more than can chew!—Too close to it to see anything but blur of words—discouraged reaction natural now—after all, do know I was

deeply moved by each play as I wrote it—that test has always proved valid heretofore—lay it aside now—we are off to Paris tomorrow—nice little vacation in dentist's chair scheduled! Best anodyne for pernicious brooding over one's inadequacies, that!—anything else seems like the best of all possible when your nerves are prancing to sweet and low down of dentist's drill!—

(*Le Plessis—July 18, 1930*)
Read the trilogy—much better than I feared—but needs a lot more work before it will be anything like right—chief thing, thought asides now seem entirely unnecessary—don't reveal anything about the characters I can't bring out quite naturally in their talk or their soliloquies when alone—simply get in the way of the play's drive, make the line waver, cause action to halt and limp—must be deleted in toto—Warning!—always hereafter regard with suspicion hangover inclination to use "Interlude" technique regardless—that was what principally hurt "Dynamo," being forced into thought-asides method which was quite alien to essential psychological form of its characters—did not ring true—only clogged up play arbitrarily with obvious author's mannerisms—saw this when I re-read it after return from East—too late! "Interlude" aside technique is special expression for special type of modern neurotic, disintegrated soul—when dealing with simple direct folk or characters of strong will and intense passions, it is superfluous show-shop "business."

(*Le Plessis—July 19, 1930*)
Read trilogy again—don't like the soliloquies in their present disjointed thought-prose formula—and my use of half masks on the main protagonists seems to obscure meaning of resemblance between characters instead of dramatically intensifying this meaning—masks introduce other connotations not wanted these plays—have strong feeling there should be much more definite interrelationship between characters' masks and soliloquies, that soliloquies should be arbitrarily set in a stylized form that will be the exact expression of stylized mask symbol—Rewrite all soliloquies in plays along this line—introduce new ones so that soliloquies will recur in a fixed pattern throughout, fitting into structural pattern repeated in each play—try for prose with simple forceful repeating accent and rhythm which will express driving insistent compulsion of passions engendered in family past, which constitute family fate (always remembering fate from within the family is modern psychological approximation of the Greek conception of fate from without, from the supernatural).

(*Le Plessis—July 20, 1930*)
Start rewriting, cutting out all asides, stylizing soliloquies as per new conception—think I have hit on right rhythm of prose—monotonous, simple words driving insistence—tom-tom from "Jones" in thought repetition—

(Le Plessis—Sept. 16, 1930)
Finished rewriting—lay aside for a while—one thing am certain of right now, omitting asides has helped plays enormously—

(Paris—Sept. 20, 1930)
Read and carefully reread this last stylized-soliloquies version—absolutely convinced they don't do!—feel as I felt about asides in version before this, that they hold up plays, break rhythm, clog flow of dramatic development, reveal nothing of characters' motives, secret desires or dreams, that can't be shown directly or clearly suggested in their pantomime or talk—some of these soliloquies are gratifying as pieces of writing in themselves (most of them are not!) but even then they don't belong—have no inherent place in structure—they must come out—and with them the half-masks of the Mannons must go too—obtrude themselves too much into the foreground—introduce an obvious duality-of-character symbolism quite outside my intent in these plays—and if I leave out soliloquies, there is no excuse for these half-masks anyway—save for some future play.

(Paris—Sept. 21, 1930)
Scheme for revision and final version—in spite of labor on this stylized conception am glad I did it—not wasted time—learned a lot—stylized solil. uncovered new insights into characters and recurrent themes—job now is to get all this in naturally in straight dialogue—as simple and direct and dynamic as possible—with as few words—stop doing things to these characters—let them reveal themselves—in spite of (or because of!) their long locked-up passions, I feel them burning to do just this!

Keep mask conception—but as Mannon *background*, not foreground!—what I want from this mask concept is a dramatic arresting visual symbol of the separateness, the fated isolation of this family, the mark of their fate which makes them dramatically distinct from rest of world—I see now how to retain this effect without the use of built-in masks—by make-up—*in repose* (that is, *background*) the Mannon faces are like life-like death masks—(death-in-life motive, return to death-with-peace yearning that runs through the plays)—this can be gotten very effectively by make-up, as can also the family resemblance—(make-up isn't a lost art in European theatre, why should it be in ours?—only our shiftless inefficiency)—I can visualize the death-mask-like expression of characters' faces in repose suddenly being torn open by passion as extraordinarily effective—moreover, its exact visual representation of what I want expressed—Rewrite trilogy along these lines—and get more architectural fixed form into outer structure—and more composition (in musical sense) into inner structure—more definite recurrence of themes ("Island," death fear and death wish, the family past, etc.)—always bearing in mind—Mannon drama takes place on a plane where outer reality is mask of true fated reality—unreal realism—

Make into even more definite fixed pattern the superficial characteristic type realism of the chorus of the town (the world outside which always sees without really seeing or understanding) and the simple healthy normality—goodness—of Hazel and Peter.

Repetition of the same scene—in its essential spirit, sometimes even in its exact words, but between different characters—following plays as development of fate—theme demands this repetition—Mannon & Christine (about Brant) in 1st play, Christine & Orin (about Brant) in second play—Mannon & Christine in 4th act, 1st play, Lavinia & Orin in 2nd act, 3rd play—etc.

(*Le Plessis—Sept. 23, 1930*)
Start rewriting.

(*Le Plessis—Oct. 15, 1930*)
Finish rewriting—off for trip to Spain and Morocco.

(*Le Plessis—Nov. 19, 1930*)
Read last version—fairly well satisfied—got right line to it, at least—and quality I want—but needs considerable work yet—several new ideas I want to try out—may bring added value—not sure—only way try and see—start on this at once.

(*Paris—Jan. 10, 1931*)
Have finished most of new stuff—getting plays typed as I work—

(*Paris—Feb. 2, 1931*)
Typing finished with all new stuff in—let it rest now—

(*Le Plessis—Feb. 7, 1931*)
Read over—don't like most of new stuff—all right but introduces too many added complications—trying to get added values has blurred those I had—too much of muchness—would need another play added to do it right—and would be wrong even then!—can't crowd intuitions all hidden aspects of life form into one work!—I better throw most of this new stuff out—some valuable and can be condensed and retained—but in general revert entirely to former version.

(*Le Plessis—Feb. 20, 1931*)
Revision finished—off to Canary Islands for a sun and sea vacation—

(*Las Palmas—Canary Islands—March 8, 1931*)
Read typed script—looks damned good to me—funny how typed pages bring out clearly values that too-long familiarity with longhand had rendered vague and undynamic—but plenty of work to do—no vacation here—script much too

long, of course—needs cutting and condensing throughout—must rewrite end of "The Hunted"—weak now—Christine's talk to Lavinia toward end bad stuff—first scene of Act One "The Haunted" also needs rewriting and pointing up—flabby and faltering as now written—ends of Scenes One & Two "The Hunted" also need work—

(Las Palmas—March 26, 1931)
Finished work—return to France (Marseilles) via Casablanca and Tangier tomorrow—script retyped—

(Paris—April 4, 1931)
Decide change Scenes One & Two, Act One, "The Hunted" to Acts One & Two—they are properly acts, not scenes—but Scene One, Act One of "The Haunted" is properly a scene—question of feeling, this!—no rules about it—

(Paris—April 9, 1931)
New script retyped—copies off to Guild—

(Northport—August, 1931)
Read over galley proofs from Liveright—after nearly four months of not looking at this trilogy, get fairly fresh impact—moved by it—has power and drive and the strange quality of unreal reality I wanted—main purpose seems to me soundly achieved—there is a feeling of fate in it, or I am a fool—a psychological modern approximation of the fate in the Greek tragedies on this theme—attained without benefit of supernatural—

And technically (although this is of minor importance, naturally) I flatter myself it is unique thing in dramaturgy—each play complete episode completely realized but at same time, which is the important point, not complete in that its end begins following play and demands that play as an inevitable sequel—few trilogies in existence in drama of all time and none of them has this quality which, in any time under any conditions, could not have failed to prove an asset—if gained without harm to the separate play, of course, as I believe I have done.

("Interlude" never got credit for this technical virtue—without which its successful production would have been impossible—that the first part rounded out a complete section of Nina's life with a definite beginning and end and yet contained the suspense at its end which called for Part Two—otherwise dinner interval would have wrecked it—no other two-part play, as far as I know, has accomplished this synthesis of end and beginning—)

(Northport—August, 1931)
Work on galley proofs—cutting is needed, especially in first and third plays—

(Northport—Sept., 1931)

Work on second galleys—several points strike me—work I did at Canary Islands was of great value in most results—but feel now a few things eliminated there should be restored—Lavinia's last appeal to Peter near very end—some things in Act Two which help to clear it up—this Act Two of "The Haunted" is weak spot still—needs rearranging—but will postpone final decision on this until I hear cast read plays—then it will hit my ear.

Memoranda on Masks

In the early 1930s, O'Neill accepted George Jean Nathan's invitation to become an associate editor of The *American Spectator*. "Memoranda on Masks," with its sequent essays, "Second Thoughts" and "A Dramatist's Notebook," were published in three issues, November and December 1932 and January 1933. The essays were O'Neill's only contribution to the publication.

Since O'Neill was the chief user of the mask in the modern theatre, his speculation on their possibilities should take on special authority. Yet an irony presents itself. When he wrote the three-part essay, he had given up their use. The face of Loving in *Days Without End* was his last use of mask. His decision to eliminate masks from *Mourning Becomes Electra* was sound. The half masks with which he had experimented in the second draft of the trilogy obscured, rather than intensified, the effect he wanted. He discarded them as being unhelpful author's mannerisms. So far as is known he had no other mask dramas in serious plan. His move away from the art theatre, first announced in *Mourning Becomes Electra* and in *Ah, Wilderness!*, was to lead him to the simplicity and freedom of style of the late plays, where, as with Edmond Tyrone, "faithful realism" was to become his finest way of speaking.

Ironic too was the satisfaction he expressed in the "Memoranda" with masks in *The Great God Brown*. In the throes of production and afterward, he was anything but satisfied. In August 1926, he wrote to Kenneth Macgowan a long complaint against the conduct of the Experimental Theatre, citing the masks as an example of the group's production failures:

> Do the masks in "Brown" do what the script required of them? They do not. They only get across personal resemblance of a blurry meaninglessness. Whose fault? No one's! Not enough time to see them. Perhaps the result the script calls for is impossible to attain by the method by combination masks the script describes. I think I see this now. With more time on masks in their proper lighting, I—we— would have seen it then.[1]

He had become enthused with masks as he became enthused about many aspects of the new European ideas about theatre. The expressionism of Strindberg, Max Reinhardt's extravagances, Gordon Craig's designs, the capabilities of Robert Edmond Jones all led him toward the concept of "theatre art" as a way of redeeming the American drama from such commercialism as his father's *Monte Cristo* had represented.

He had learned something of African Negro masks from a book of photographs, *African Negro Sculpture*, upon which he based his concept of the masked witch doctor

1. *"The Theatre We Worked For*, ed. Jackson Bryer, pp. 131–32.

in *The Emperor Jones* (1920).[2] A study by Macgowan and Herman Rosse, *Masks and Demons*, led him further into the subject. He moved from theory to practice when Blanch Hays, the Provincetown Players' costumer, suggested putting masks on the Fifth Avenue strollers in *The Hairy Ape*. With this as his start, he began a series of mask dramas that the "Memoranda" reconsiders.

O'Neill put the mask to three general uses. *Masks and Demons* describes the service of the mask for symbolic purposes in ritual,[3] and in *All God's Chillun Got Wings* he calls for an African mask to symbolize the black inheritance that the play's protagonist, Jim Harris, denies. During the course of the play, the mask is ritually slaughtered, stabbed by Harris's insane wife.

A second use of the mask might be called the Freudian. It was put to such service in *The Great God Brown*, where masks dramatize the inner and outer personalities of the principal characters. The results were somewhat confusing, and he did not again use masks for this purpose. His comments on their success reflects the fascination the masks have always had for audiences in many successful revivals of the play. Confusing or not, the masks are riveting and exciting.

The third use O'Neill found for masks is perhaps best called "aesthetic." In the use to which he put them in *The Ancient Mariner* and *Lazarus Laughed* they seem to have a more important function as part of a design concept than they do in relation to character or theme. The failure of both plays to find audiences suggests that this use is essentially without true theatrical interest.

In the end, however, only the aesthetic use of the mask remained to attest to a former enthusiasm—not in O'Neill's theatre but in his home. The staircase wall at Tao House was hung with masks from various countries and times where they formed, as do the "Memoranda," an artifact of reminiscent interest.

2. Charles Sheeler, *African Negro Sculpture* (Privately printed, n.d.).
3. Kenneth Macgowan and Herman Rosse, *Masks and Demons* (New York: Harcourt, Brace, 1923).

Memoranda on Masks

Not masks for all plays, naturally. Obviously not for plays conceived in purely realistic terms. But masks for certain types of plays, especially for the new modern play, as yet only dimly foreshadowed in a few groping specimens, but which must inevitably be written in the future. For I hold more and more surely to the conviction that the use of masks will be discovered eventually to be the freest solution of the modern dramatist's problem as to how—with the greatest possible dramatic clarity and economy of means—he can express those profound hidden conflicts of the mind which the probings of psychology continue to disclose to us. He must find some method to present this inner drama in his work, or confess himself incapable of portraying one of the most characteristic preoccupations and uniquely significant, spiritual impulses of his time. With his old—and more than a bit senile!—standby of realistic technique, he can do no more than, at best, obscurely hint at it through a realistically disguised surface symbolism, superficial and misleading. But that, while sufficiently beguiling to the sentimentally mystical, is hardly enough. A comprehensive expression is demanded here, a chance for eloquent presentation, a new form of drama projected from a fresh insight into the inner forces motivating the actions and reactions of men and women (a new and truer characterization, in other words), a drama of souls, and the adventures of "free wills," with the masks that govern them and constitute their fates.

For what, at bottom, is the new psychological insight into human cause and effect but a study in masks, an exercise in unmasking? Whether we think the attempted unmasking has been successful, or has only created for itself new masks, is of no importance here. What is valid, what is unquestionable, is that this insight has uncovered the mask, has impressed the idea of mask as a symbol of inner reality upon all intelligent people of today; and I know they would welcome the use of masks in the theatre as a necessary, dramatically revealing, new convention, and not regard them as any "stunty" resurrection of archaic props.

This was strikingly demonstrated for me in practical experience by *The Great God Brown*, which ran in New York for eight months, nearly all of that time in Broadway theatres—a play in which the use of masks was an integral part of the theme. There was some misunderstanding, of course. But so is there always misunderstanding in the case of every realistic play that attempts to express anything beyond what is contained in a human-interest newspaper story. In the main, however, *The Great God Brown* was accepted and appreciated by both critics and public—a fairly extensive public, as its run gives evidence.

I emphasize this play's success because the fact that a mask drama, the main values of which are psychological, mystical, and abstract, could be played in New York for eight months, has always seemed to me a more significant proof of the deeply responsive possibilities in our public than anything that has happened in our modern theatre before or since.

2

Looked at from even the most practical standpoint of the practicing playwright, the mask *is* dramatic in itself, *has always* been dramatic in itself, *is* a proven weapon of attack. At its best, it is more subtly, imaginatively, suggestively dramatic than any actor's face can ever be. Let anyone who doubts this study the Japanese Noh masks, or Chinese theatre masks, or African primitive masks— or right here in America the faces of the big marionettes Robert Edmond Jones made for the production of Stravinsky's *Oedipus*, or Benda's famous masks, or even photographs of them.

3

Dogma for the new masked drama. One's outer life passes in a solitude haunted by the masks of others; one's inner life passes in a solitude hounded by the masks of oneself.

4

With masked mob a new type of play may be written in which the Mob as King, Hero, Villain, or Fool will be the main character—The Great Democratic Play!

5

Why not give all future Classical revivals entirely in masks? *Hamlet*, for example. Masks would liberate this play from its present confining status as exclusively a "star vehicle." We would be able to see the great drama we are now only privileged to read, to identify ourselves with the figure of Hamlet as a symbolic projection of a fate that is in each of us, instead of merely watching a star giving us his version of a great acting role. We would even be able to hear the sublime poetry as the innate expression of the spirit of the drama itself, instead of listening to it as realistic recitation—or ranting—by familiar actors.

6

Consider Goethe's *Faust*, which, psychologically speaking, should be the closest to us of all the Classics. In producing this play, I would have Mephistopheles wearing the Mephistophelean mask of the face of Faust. For is not the whole of Goethe's truth *for our time* just that Mephistopheles and Faust are one and the same—*are* Faust?

SECOND THOUGHTS

What would I change in past productions of my plays if I could live through them again? Many things. In some plays, considerable revision of the writing of some of the scenes would strike me as imperative. Other plays—*The First Man, Gold, Welded, The Fountain*, I would dismiss as being too painfully bungled in their present form to be worth producing at all.

But one thing I most certainly would not change: the use of masks in *The Hairy Ape*, in my arrangement of Coleridge's "Ancient Mariner," in *All God's Chillun Got Wings* (the symbol of the African primitive mask in the last part of the play, which, in the production in Russian by the Moscow Kamerny Theatre I saw in Paris, is dramatically intensified and emphasized), in *The Great God Brown* and, finally, in *Lazarus Laughed*, in which all the characters except Lazarus remain masked throughout the play. I regard this use of masks as having been uniformly successful.

The change I would make would be to call for more masks in some of these productions and to use them in other productions where they were not used before. In *The Emperor Jones*, for example. All the figures in Jones's flight through the forest should be masked. Masks would dramatically stress their phantasmal quality, as contrasted with the unmasked Jones, intensify the supernatural menace of the tom-tom, give the play a more complete and vivid expression. In *The Hairy Ape* a much more extensive use of masks would be of the greatest value in emphasizing the theme of the play. From the opening of the fourth scene, where Yank begins to think, he enters into a masked world; even the familiar faces of his mates in the forecastle have become strange and alien. They should be masked, and the faces of everyone he encounters thereafter, including the symbolic gorilla's.

In *All God's Chillun Got Wings*, all save the seven leading characters should be masked; for all the secondary figures are part and parcel of the Expressionistic background of the play, a world at first indifferent, then cruelly hostile, against which the tragedy of Jim Harris is outlined. In *The Great God Brown*, I would now make the masks symbolize more definitely the abstract theme of the play instead of, as in the old production, stressing the more superficial meaning that people wear masks before other people and are mistaken by them for their masks.

In *Marco Millions* all the people of the East should be masked—Kublai, the Princess Kukachin, all of them! For anyone who has been in the East, or who has read Eastern philosophy, the reason for this is obvious. It is an exact dramatic expression of West confronted by East. Moreover, it is the only possible way to project this contrast truthfully in the theatre, for Western actors cannot convey Eastern character realistically, and their only chance to suggest it convincingly is with the help of masks.

As for *Strange Interlude*, that is an attempt at the new masked psychological drama which I have discussed before, without masks—a successful attempt, perhaps, in so far as it concerns only surfaces and their immediate subsurfaces, but not where, occasionally, it tries to probe deeper.

With *Mourning Becomes Electra*, masks were called for in one draft of the three plays. But the Classical connotation was too insistent. Masks in that connection demand great language to speak—which let me out of it with a sickening bump! There was a realistic New England resistance in my mind, too, which would have barred great language even in a dramatist capable of writing it, an insistence on the dotted and dogged and inarticulate. So it evolved ultimately into the "masklike faces," which expressed my intention tempered by the circumstances. However, I should like to see *Mourning Becomes Electra* done entirely with masks, now that I can view it solely as a psychological play, quite removed from the confusing preoccupations the Classical derivation of its plot once caused me. Masks would emphasize the drama of the life and death impulses that drive the characters on to their fates and put more in its proper secondary place, as a frame, the story of the New England family.

A DRAMATIST'S NOTEBOOK

I advocate masks for stage crowds, mobs—wherever a sense of impersonal, collective mob psychology is wanted. This was one reason for such an extensive use of them in *Lazarus Laughed*. In masking the crowds in that play, I was visualizing an effect that, intensified by dramatic lighting, would give an audience visually the sense of the Crowd, not as a random collection of individuals, but as a collective whole, an entity. When the Crowd speaks, I wanted an audience to hear the voice of Crowd mind, Crowd emotion, as one voice of a body composed of, but quite distinct from, its parts.

And, for more practical reasons, I wanted to preserve the different crowds of another time and country from the blighting illusion-shattering recognitions by an audience of the supers on the stage. Have you ever seen a production of *Julius Caesar*? Did the Roman mob ever suggest to you anything more Roman than a gum-chewing Coney Island Mardi Gras or, in the case of a special all-star revival, a gathering of familiar-faced modern actors masquerading uncomfortably in togas? But with masks—and the proper intensive lighting—you would have been freed from these recognitions; you would have been able to imagine a Roman mob; you would not even have recognized the Third Avenue and Brooklyn accents among the supers, so effectively does a mask change the quality of a voice.

It was interesting to watch, in the final rehearsal of *The Great God Brown*, how after using their masks for a time the actors and actresses reacted to the demand made by the masks that their bodies become alive and expressive and participate in the drama. Usually it is only the actors' faces that participate. Their bodies remain bored spectators that have been dragged off to the theatre when they would have much preferred a quiet evening in the upholstered chair at home.

Meaning no carping disrespect to our actors. I have been exceedingly lucky in having had some exceptionally fine acting in the principal roles in my plays, for which I am exceedingly grateful. Also some damned poor acting. But let that pass. Most of the poor acting occurred in the poor plays, and there I hold only myself responsible. In the main, wherever a part challenged the actors' or actresses' greatest possibilities, they have reacted to the challenge with a splendid creative energy and skill. Especially, and this is the point I want to make now, where the play took them away from the strictly realistic parts they were accustomed to playing. They always welcomed any opportunity that gave them new scope for their talents. So when I argue here for a non-realistic imaginative theatre I am hoping, not only for added scope for playwright and director and scenic designer, but also for a chance for the actor to develop his art beyond the narrow range to which our present theatre condemns it. Most important of all, from the standpoint of future American culture, I am hoping for added imaginative scope for the audience, a chance for a public I know is growing yearly more numerous and more hungry in its spiritual need to participate in imaginative interpretations of life rather than merely identify itself with faithful surface resemblances of living.

I harp on the word "imaginative"—and with intention! But what do I mean by an "imaginative" theatre—(where I hope for it, for example, in the subtitle of *Lazarus Laughed: A Play for an Imaginative Theatre*)? I mean the one true theatre, the age-old theatre, the theatre of the Greeks and Elizabethans, a theatre that could dare to boast—without committing a farcical sacrilege— that it is a legitimate descendant of the first theatre that sprang, by virtue of man's imaginative interpretation of life, out of his worship of Dionysus. I mean a theatre returned to its highest and sole significant function as a Temple where the religion of a poetical interpretation and symbolical celebration of life is communicated to human beings, starved in spirit by their soul-stifling daily struggle to exist as masks among the masks of living!

But I anticipate the actor's objection to masks: that they would extinguish their personalities and deprive them of their greatest asset in conveying emotion by facial expression. I claim, however, that masks would give them the opportunity for a totally new kind of acting, that they would learn many undeveloped possibilities of their art if they appeared, even if only for a season or two, in masked roles. After all, masks did not extinguish the Greek actor, nor have they kept the acting of the East from being an art.

Tributes

Tributes

Many persons developed an enduring affection for O'Neill. He returned their friendships with fidelity and apparent warmth. Nevertheless, he lived most intensely in the solitariness of his creative work. Throughout his life, he resisted public displays of his affection and admiration for others. He was, as he once wrote in a poem, "a very private man."

As his fame grew, he was repeatedly asked to write introductions or publicity blurbs for others and to support causes for which he had no particular feeling. He became adept at denying such requests. Occasionally, however, he could not courteously refuse. Sometimes, indeed, he did not wish to. Then, he would commit to print—usually in a letter for publication in a newspaper—some of his enthusiasm or his affections. He did not, however, make such public statements frequently, a fact that gives these testaments their interest.

To the Kamerny Theatre

Living at Le Plessis, near Paris, O'Neill went to the city to see Alexander Tairov and his wife, Alice Koonen produce *All God's Chillun Got Wings* and *Desire Under the Elms*. Tairov's Kamerny Theatre had been founded in Moscow in 1914 in reaction against the sentimental realism of the Moscow Art Theatre. It was an intellectual's theatre, which anticipated modern resistance to stage illusion and insisted on the theatricality of what was on the stage. Tairov toured three O'Neill plays throughout Europe—*The Hairy Ape* was the third—with great success. The company welcomed O'Neill backstage with avowals of admiration and friendship, and the production so impressed him that he wrote them the letter of tribute that was published in the *New York Herald Tribune* on June 30, 1930.

To the Kamerny Theatre

Having witnessed your productions of "Desire Under the Elms" and "All God's Chillun Got Wings," my feeling is one of amazement—and most profound gratitude! Let me humbly confess I came to the theatre with secret misgivings. Not that I doubted that your presentation would be a splendid thing in itself, artistically conceived and executed. I knew the reputation of the Kamerny as one of the finest theatres of Europe too well for that. But I did have an author's fear that in the difficult process of translation and transformation into another language and milieu the inner spirit—that indefinable essential quality so dear to the creator as being for him the soul of his work!—might be excusably, considering the obstacles, distorted or lost.

Hence my amazement and gratitude when I saw your productions which in every way delighted me because they rang so true to the spirit of my work! And they were not only that! They were also productions conceived by your director, Alexander Tairov, with that rarest of all gifts in a director—creative imagination! They were interpreted by Mme. Koonen and the other extraordinary artists of your company with that rarest of all gifts in actors and actresses— creative imagination!

A theatre of creative imagination has always been my ideal! To see my plays given by such a theatre has always been my dream! The Kamerny Theatre realized this dream for me! I will never forget that experience nor cease to be grateful for it and for the privilege of meeting all of you and the warm friendships [sic] of your reception of me. Most gratifying of all to me was my feeling that, despite the barrier of language, you all felt a kinship with me as I immediately did with you, that we had known one another a long time and were united in old and tried friendship—comradeship!—by the love of the true theatre.

To the Kamerny Theatre, my gratitude, my admiration, and my friendship! May all your dreams be realized!

Your friend,
Eugene O'Neill

An Open Letter on the Death
of George Pierce Baker

George Pierce Baker was born in Rhode Island in 1866; he died in 1935. As a professor in the Department of English at Harvard University, he began to teach playwriting in his course English 47. The course, which became known as the 47 Workshop, was a haven for young men and women who had dreams of finding a career as a playwright. From the workshop several graduates achieved professional recognition.

In conflict with the Harvard authorities who felt the course to be too specifically "vocational," he transferred in 1925 to Yale University, where he was instrumental in founding the Yale School of the Drama. At his death he was the subject of grateful memorial tributes from many former students. O'Neill's praise of him as one who encouraged the tyros and gave them hope reflects with some accuracy the benefit O'Neill received from Baker's work. Baker did not enter the world of the new theatre that O'Neill, with the help of such men as Kenneth Macgowan and Robert Edmond Jones, came to envision. The technique he taught his students was old-fashioned, and the conception of a drama of ideas or of a drama whose form was other than conventional did not surface in his comments on his students' work. Nevertheless, he gave them time, flattering attention to things good and bad about their work, and, either in class or in small performance situations, a hearing.

Brunswick, Ga.

Only those of us who had the privilege of membership in the drama class of George Pierce Baker back in the dark age when the American theatre was still, for playwrights, the closed-shop, star-system, amusement racket, can know what a profound influence Professor Baker, who died last Sunday, exerted toward the encouragement and birth of modern American drama.

It is difficult in these days, when the native playwright can function in comparative freedom, to realize that in that benighted period a play of any imagination, originality or integrity by an American was almost automatically barred from a hearing in our theatre. To write plays of life as one saw and felt it, instead of concocting the conventional theatrical drivel of the time, seemed utterly hopeless.

In the face of this blank wall, the bitterest need of the young playwright was for intelligent encouragement, to be helped to believe in the dawn of a new era in our theatre where he would have a chance, at least, to be heard. And of the rare few who had the unselfish faith and vision and love of theatre to devote their life to this encouragement, Professor Baker's work stands pre-eminent. It is that encouragement which I—and I am sure all of the playwrights who knew and studied under him—will always remember with the deepest appreciation.

Not that the technical points, the analysis of the practice of playmaking taught in his class, were not of inestimable value to us in learning our trade. But the most vital thing for us, as possible future artists and creators, to learn at that time (Good God! For any one to learn anywhere at any time!) was to believe in our work and to keep on believing. And to hope. He helped us to hope—and for that we owe him all the finest we have in memory of gratitude and friendship.

[Written January 7, 1935. Published in the *New York Times*, January 13, 1935. Copyright © 1935 by The New York Times Company. Reprinted by permission]

A Letter to Brooks Atkinson
concerning the Critics' Circle

In 1935, the Pulitzer Prize, which was to be granted yearly to "an original American play," was given to Zoe Akins for her adaptation of Edith Wharton's novel, *The Old Maid*. In the same season, more "original" work was offered in *The Children's Hour*, *The Petrified Forest*, and *Awake and Sing*, to name but three. Similar debatable awards had marked the work of the Pulitzer committee in earlier years, and on more than a single occasion the Pulitzer Advisory Committee had overruled its own jury's recommendation, as in 1932, when Sidney Kingsley's *Men in White* was given the award that the jury wished to present to Maxwell Anderson's *Mary of Scotland*.

The 1935 award served to unite opposition to what the New York drama critics felt to be the capriciousness of the Pulitzer Prizes for drama. Late in the year, seventeen of the leading drama critics organized as the New York Drama Critics' Circle. In 1936 they made their first award, praising Maxwell Anderson's *Winterset* as the season's best play. O'Neill in Bermuda did not attend the awards dinner but wrote a letter of salutation to the Circle and to Anderson. It was published in the *New York Post* on April 6, 1936, the morning following the meeting.

Dear Mr. Atkinson,

You have asked me, in behalf of the Critics' Circle, to speak at the presentation of the award to Maxwell Anderson for his play, "Winterset." I would like nothing better: it would be an honor to take part in anything that does honor to the splendid contribution Mr. Anderson's work has made to what is finest in the American Theatre. But, unfortunately for me, it is a case where the weakness of the flesh has the spirit beaten before it starts. Speaking is one of those things which are emphatically not my onion. If the Circle were giving an award for the worst speech that could possibly be made in five minutes I might be tempted to accept your invitation, for I know my superlative talent in this respect, and would feel confident of winning hands down. But as it is, no thank you. You don't want me to speak, not really. You only think you do. You have never heard me try it.

Fortunately for ourselves, you have been kind enough to offer me an out on this, the alternative that if I decline to stammer a speech, I may write something to be read instead. But don't expect eloquence here either, for what I would like to say is brief and to the point. There is only one comment anyone with a love for fine plays could make on your choice for the prize this year, and that is that in honoring Mr. Anderson's work you do honor to yourselves and the American theatre and start the Critics' Circle Award with genuine distinction. May all your future awards have a like distinction, and may your future be a long one! If that isn't wishing you the best of good wishes, then I don't know what is!

And it seems to me that the Critics' Circle Award deserves the very best in the way of good wishes from all those who have the future of our drama at heart. I confess I admit this with considerable reluctance. It is a terrible, harrowing experience for a playwright to be forced by his conscience to praise critics for anything. It isn't done. It never has been done. There is something morbid and abnormal about it, something destructive to the noble tradition of what is correct conduct for dramatists period. In short it gripes. Nevertheless, conscience drives me to reiterate that I think the Critics' Circle is a damned fine idea. Prizes in themselves are neither good nor bad. They have no meaning except that which derives from the recognized authority to judge true merit of the awarders of the prize. The Critics's Circle possesses that recognized authority, and so I am sure that its awards will deservedly have a significant and growing effect in helping to shape public opinion and in directing the future course of our drama. It is my hope that these yearly awards will direct the attention of the public to the fact that our theatre is now fully adult and fully capable of standing adult comparison with that of any country in the world today, that it is no longer purely a show-shop and an amusement racket, but has grown to be a place where art may exist.

What is more important to me—I believe that when this truth has been pounded home to intelligent Americans (and it will be pounded home most effectively by examples such as your award this year) I believe then that real art theatres will at least [sic] be born in this country, theatres such as Europe has had and has, repertoire theatres, where the plays continue to live in revival and not die the sudden, complete and ignominious death that now follows so dishearteningly for authors at the close of the commercial run, theatres which will not be run primarily as just another business venture, for profit, any more than the dramatist who is an artist writes his plays primarily as trade goods, theatres where the true profit will be reckoned as that gain which accrues from the cultural value in a people of keeping alive the continuity of its past and present creative art.

But that's a long subject and I already begin to feel like a soap-boxer for the ideal, getting set to dodge the tomatoes! To wind up, and who said thank God?—there is a great big "if" attached to all this unseemly, playwrightly commendation of you critics. *If* you continue to make intelligent choices of true distinction. And, on the other hand, *if* we dramatists can go on giving you true distinction to choose. But certainly no one can deny that you, and we, in the work of Mr. Anderson, have made a damned auspicious beginning.

Eugene O'Neill

A Public Statement on the Death of Maxim Gorki

As *The Iceman Cometh* eloquently testifies, *The Lower Depths* was deeply ingrained into O'Neill's artistic sensibilities. The play was perhaps his fullest tribute to the Russian writer, but his admiration for the work of Maxim Gorky was life-long. While he was studying with Baker at Harvard, he wrote to Beatrice Ashe, recommending that she read Gorky. In 1926, writing a critique of a play by Mike Gold whose concluding scenes he felt to be too overtly propagandistic, he commented:

> Don't get me wrong. My quarrel with propaganda in the theatre is that it's such damned unconvincing propaganda—whereas, if you will restrain the propaganda purpose to the selection of life to be portrayed and then let that life live without comment, it does your trick. But this is platitude. Gorky's *Lower Depths* is a good example of what I mean.

Shortly after Gorky's death, he wrote to Sinclair Lewis, in a letter thanking him for Lewis's congratulations when he won the Nobel Prize, that it was too bad a Nobel award had not gone to Gorky, who had been "the top of all living writers." He added that he had written a short memorial tribute to Gorky for publication in "The Soviet Magazine in New York."[1]

1. The letter to Beatrice Ashe is dated November 2, 1914, and is in the American Literature Collection of the Beinecke Rare Book and Manuscript Collection, Yale University; the letter to Mike Gold is dated November 25, 1926, and is in the Dartmouth College Library, Hanover, N.H.; the letter to Sinclair Lewis is dated November 25, 1936, and is in the Beinecke Rare Book and Manuscript Library, Yale University.

By the death of Maxim Gorki world literature has lost the author who on all counts deserved the preeminent place among all the writers of our time. The one heir to the great Russian literary tradition of Dostoevsky, Turgenieff and Tolstoi, his work both as a novelist and a playwright, belongs beside that of his illustrious predecessors. Gorki is not dead. His genius and the spirit of tragic understanding and pity for humanity which characterized his work will live as long as true literature is read.

[June 1936]

The Nobel Prize Acceptance Letter

O'Neill learned that he had received the Nobel Prize for Literature on November 12, 1936, while he was visiting in Seattle. Already feeling the onset of the illness that by the end of the year would place him in an Oakland, California, hospital, he felt unable to make the journey to Sweden to address the Swedish Academy in person. Instead, on November 17 and 18 he wrote a letter to be read to the academy at their meeting on December 10.

The short letter acknowledges gracefully his debt to Strindberg, reflecting the attitude expressed years earlier in the Provincetown Playhouse program note to Strindberg's *The Spook Sonata*. To the acknowledgment, however, he adds a note of pride in the achievements of the American theatre, for which he has been in no small measure responsible. His implied self-assessment does not seem overweening.

The Nobel Prize Acceptance Letter

First, I wish to express again to you my deep regret that circumstances have made it impossible for me to visit Sweden in time for the festival, and to be present at this banquet to tell you in person of my grateful appreciation.

It is difficult to put into anything like adequate words the profound gratitude I feel for the greatest honor that my work could ever hope to attain, the award of the Nobel prize. This highest of distinctions is all the more grateful to me because I feel so deeply that it is not only my work which is being honored, but the work of all my colleagues in America—that this Nobel prize is a symbol of the recognition by Europe of the coming-of-age of the American theatre. For my plays are merely, through luck of time and circumstance, the most widely known examples of the work done by American playwrights in the years since the World War—work that has finally made modern American drama in its finest aspects an achievement of which Americans can be justly proud, worthy at last to claim kinship with the modern drama of Europe, from which our original inspiration so surely derives.

This thought of original inspiration brings me to what is, for me, the greatest happiness this occasion affords, and that is the opportunity it gives me to acknowledge, with gratitude and pride, to you and to the people of Sweden, the debt my work owes to that greatest genius of all modern dramatists, your August Strindberg.

It was reading his plays when I first started to write back in the winter of 1913–1914 that, above all else, first gave me the vision of what modern drama could be, and first inspired me with the urge to write for the theatre myself. If there is anything of lasting worth in my work, it is due to that original impulse from him, which has continued as my inspiration down all the years since then—to the ambition I received then to follow in the footsteps of his genius as worthily as my talent might permit, and with the same integrity of purpose.

Of course, it will be no news to you in Sweden that my work owes much to the influence of Strindberg. That influence runs clearly through more than a few of my plays and is plain for everyone to see. Neither will it be news for anyone who has ever known me, for I have always stressed it myself. I have never been one of those who are so timidly uncertain of their own contribution that they feel they cannot afford to admit ever having been influenced, lest they be discovered as lacking all originality.

No, I am only too proud of my debt to Strindberg, only too happy to have this opportunity of proclaiming it to his people. For me, he remains, as Nietzsche remains in his sphere, the Master, still to this day more modern than any of us, still our leader. And it is my pride to imagine that perhaps his spirit, musing over this year's Nobel award for literature, may smile with a little satisfaction, and find the follower not too unworthy of his Master.

The Fourth War Loan

The outbreak of the Second World War depressed O'Neill to such an extent that it became uncertain whether he would be able to complete the play on which he was working, A *Moon for the Misbegotten*. Like many civilians, he posted a map of Europe and charted the battle lines with pins and ribbons and cursed his sickness and his inability to be of greater service. The social life of his daughter, Oona, embarrassed him and he wrote her suggesting that a factory job would be more suitable in wartime than the Stork Club or Hollywood. His was a not untypical malaise.

When he could help, he did. He contributed the typescript of *Tomorrow* to a war bond auction and wrote, when requested to do so, an appeal in support of a War Bond drive. The Fourth War Loan Bond Drive was conducted between January 18 and February 15, 1944.

The Fourth War Loan has a new and particular importance because it is a much more significant and crucial test of the Home Front than those that have preceded it. We have now reached a point in the war when *ultimate* victory seems assured, and there is apparent among us a growing tendency to take the victory for granted, to talk and act as is if it had already been won, forgetting the long bitter bloody road of sacrifice which lies ahead of the men who must do the fighting—and the dying—for that victory. They, we may be sure, do not grow complacent, nor indulge in dangerous wasteful anticipations. Above all, they foresee the cost and do not shrink from it nor seek to evade it, though the cost to them may be their lives. The cost to us is merely money. And not even a gift of money. Just a loan, with interest. Just a good way of saving our money. Just the soundest possible investment for that peaceful future which our fighting men are giving their lives to give us. Let us remember this. Let us prove we remember it. Let us loan to our utmost, and if our utmost hurts, let us remember it does not hurt as much as a shell fragment, or a machine gun bullet.

December the 6th, 1943

The Last Will and Testament of Silverdene Emblem O'Neill

As Eugene O'Neill and Carlotta Monterey waited in France for the divorce from Agnes O'Neill to become final so that they might marry, they endeavored to adjust their lives to a proper domesticity. One of the signs of their attempt was the purchase of a suitable dog. In 1928, only a month after they had established a "permanent" residence in a chateau at Le Plessis, near Tours, they went to Paris and bought a wirehaired terrier named "Billy," whom Carlotta described in her diary as "not much of a dog."[1] Carlotta noted that she never saw an animal who could resist her husband, and Billy took to O'Neill. He was, however, restless. He howled at night, tore up the curtains, stole croissants and brioches from the table, and leaped from windows if he was shut up.

Since Billy lacked a suitable canine grace, they looked again, and on September 25, Carlotta recorded that she was in Tours collecting a new dog, a Dalmatian called "Pete." Almost at once, Billy came down with a rash and was placed with a veterinarian. Pete in his turn developed a cough that grew steadily worse. Distemper turned to double pneumonia, and epilepsy followed. Pete died in late October. Billy, on the other hand, recovered and returned to Le Plessis in mid-November. But something was wrong. Where once he had been a charming companion for nocturnal walks in the *parc*, now he seemed to Carlotta "mentally gone." On November 24, he was given to the postman's son, along with his bed, blankets, cushion, soap, and dog biscuits.

Immediately, the O'Neills sent for photographs of Dalmatians from England, and for £75 they purchased a dog who was to become the third member of their household, "Silverdene Emblem," a name quickly shortened to "Blemie."

When Blemie arrived on December 11, he made an instant hit with Carlotta. She wrote: "He is *sweet*! and beautifully bred—& looks healthy—English bred dogs are best—! Gene likes him! I love him! He weeps a little the first morning—he is lonely & things are strange! *I* know!"

He remained firm in Carlotta's favor ("such wonderful manners—a real English thoroughbred!"), but it is not clear how taken O'Neill was with the new arrival at their first meeting. Two days after he came, O'Neill asked Carlotta to write to England for a Gordon setter. Carlotta continued to dote on Blemie. Although the dog chewed everything in sight and stole food as Billy had done, Carlotta found excuses for him: "I'm sure he did it in a slow, deliberate gentlemanly fashion."

1. The details about the dogs are taken from the diaries of Carlotta Monterey O'Neill for the years 1928–1930. The diaries are in the American Literature Collection of the Beinecke Rare Book and Manuscript Library, Yale University. They are quoted with the permission of Gerald Stram.

With the new arrival, Blemie was no gentleman. When the setter, who would become "Ben," was delivered on New Year's Day, 1930, Blemie nipped him as he came out of his traveling box. Carlotta wrote, "Not a gentleman's idea of a welcome! Hence—sworn enemies!" Some sort of truce was patched between them and the animal kingdom grew peaceable. In September, Blemie became attracted to a neighboring bitch, "Mlle. Rosa Brown." Carlotta described the affair: "He was so modest & charming about it all—their honeymoon was spent in the densest part of the parc."

Ben could not compete with modest, charming Blemie. The last mention of Ben in Carlotta's diary is on December 14; thereafter he disappeared from view. As the O'Neills returned to America in May, it was Blemie who received the new coat from Hermès in Paris, who traveled with them in Carlotta's stateroom, and who cost them $45 in customs duty.

Thereafter, Blemie rested unchallenged in the household. He lived off the fat of the land with acres to run in and within Tao House at night found prepared for his comfort a small four-poster bed with sheets and blankets. He also commanded for his exclusive use a bathtub that, according to the contractor, was the most expensive single item in the house since it was installed in the basement below grade and required its own septic system.

Blemie's death on December 17, 1940, was agony for both O'Neills. O'Neill was to say later that since Blemie died, "Everything has gone wrong." They buried him on a hillside west of Tao House and set two trees to frame the grave. As a final gesture, they erected a headstone inscribed with his dates, kennel name, and the inscription "Sleep in peace, faithful friend."

O'Neill wrote *The Last Will and Testament of Silverdene Emblem O'Neill* on December 26, 1940, in an effort to assuage Carlotta's grief.

The Last Will and Testament of Silverdene Emblem O'Neill

I, SILVERDENE EMBLEM O'NEILL (familiarly known to family, friends and acquaintances as Blemie), because the burden of my years and infirmities is heavy upon me, and I realize the end of my life is near, do hereby bury my last will and testament in the mind of my Master. He will not know it is there until after I am dead. Then, remembering me in his loneliness, he will suddenly know of this testament, and I ask him then to inscribe it as a memorial to me.

I have little in the way of material things to leave. Dogs are wiser than men. They do not set great store upon things. They do not waste their days hoarding property. They do not ruin their sleep worrying about how to keep the objects they have, and to obtain the objects they have not. There is nothing of value I have to bequeath except my love and my faith. These I leave to all those who have loved me, to my Master and Mistress, who I know will mourn me most, to Freeman who has been so good to me, to Cyn and Roy and Willie and Naomi[1] and—But if I should list all those who have loved me it would force my Master to write a book. Perhaps it is vain of me to boast when I am so near death, which returns all beasts and vanities to dust, but I have always been an extremely lovable dog.

I ask my Master and Mistress to remember me always, but not to grieve for me too long. In my life I have tried to be a comfort to them in time of sorrow, and a reason for added joy in their happiness. It is painful for me to think that even in death I should cause them pain. Let them remember that while no dog has ever had a happier life (and this I owe to their love and care for me), now that I have grown blind and deaf and lame, and even my sense of smell fails me so that a rabbit could be right under my nose and I might not know, my pride has sunk to a sick, bewildering humiliation. I feel life is taunting me with having over-lingered my welcome. It is time I said goodbye, before I become too sick a burden on myself and on those who love me. It will be sorrow to leave them, but not a sorrow to die. Dogs do not fear death as men do. We accept it as part of life, not as something alien and terrible which destroys life. What may come after death, who knows? I would like to believe with those of my fellow Dalmatians who are devout Mohammedans, that there is a Paradise

1. Herbert Freeman, O'Neill's chauffeur and man of all work; Cynthia and Roy Stram, Carlotta O'Neill's daughter by her first marriage and her son-in-law; Willie and Naomi Tompkins, the O'Neills' butler and cook.

where one is always young and full-bladdered; where all the day one dillies and dallies with an amorous multitude of houris, beautifully spotted; where jack rabbits that run fast but not too fast (like the houris) are as the sands of the desert; where each blissful hour is mealtime; where in long evenings there are a million fireplaces with logs forever burning, and one curls oneself up and blinks into the flames and nods and dreams, remembering the old brave days on earth, and the love of one's Master and Mistress.

I am afraid this is too much for even such a dog as I am to expect. But peace, at least, is certain. Peace and long rest for weary old heart and head and limbs, and eternal sleep in the earth I have loved so well. Perhaps, after all, this is best.

One last request I earnestly make. I have heard my Mistress say, "When Blemie dies we must never have another dog. I love him so much I could never love another one." Now I would ask her, for love of me, to have another. It would be a poor tribute to my memory never to have a dog again. What I would like to feel is that, having once had me in the family, now she cannot live without a dog! I have never had a narrow jealous spirit. I have always held that most dogs are good (and one cat, the black one I have permitted to share the living room rug during the evenings, whose affection I have tolerated in a kindly spirit, and in rare sentimental moods, even reciprocated a trifle). Some dogs, of course, are better than others. Dalmatians, naturally, as everyone knows, are best. So I suggest a Dalmatian as my successor. He can hardly be as well bred or as well mannered or as distinguished and handsome as I was in my prime. My Master and Mistress must not ask the impossible. But he will do his best, I am sure, and even his inevitable defects will help by comparison to keep my memory green. To him I bequeath my collar and leash and my overcoat and raincoat, made to order in 1929 at Hermès in Paris. He can never wear them with the distinction I did, walking around the Place Vendôme, or later along Park Avenue, all eyes fixed on me in admiration; but again I am sure he will do his utmost not to appear a mere gauche provincial dog. Here on the ranch, he may prove himself quite worthy of comparison, in some respects. He will, I presume, come closer to jack rabbits than I have been able to in recent years. And, for all his faults, I hereby wish him the happiness I know will be his in my old home.

One last word of farewell, dear Master and Mistress. Whenever you visit my grave, say to yourselves with regret but also with happiness in your hearts at the remembrance of my long happy life with you: "Here lies one who loved us and whom we loved." No matter how deep my sleep I shall hear you, and not all the power of death can keep my spirit from wagging a grateful tail.

Tao House, December 17th, 1940